RELIGION AS ART

Religion as Art

Guadalupe, Orishas, and Sufi

Edited by **STEVEN LOZA**

University of New Mexico Press   ☙   Albuquerque

14   13   12   11   10   09   1   2   3   4   5   6

LIBRARY OF CONGRESS CATALOGING-IN-PUBLICATION DATA

Religion as art : Guadalupe, Orishas, and Sufi / edited by Steven Loza.
    p. cm.
Based on proceedings from the Inter-disciplinary Conference at the
National Hispanic Cultural Center.
Includes bibliographical references.
ISBN 978-0-8263-4570-7 (pbk. : alk. paper)
1. Arts and religion—Congresses.
2. Guadalupe, Our Lady of—Congresses.
I. Loza, Steven Joseph.
II. National Hispanic Cultural Center of New Mexico. Inter-disciplinary Conference.
NX180.R4R46 2009
701'.08—dc22

2009009206

Book design and type composition by Melissa Tandysh
Composed in 10.25/14 ScalaOT
Display type is Bernhard Modern Std

To Michael Keleher and Tobias Durán
for their unfailing commitment to this project

Contents

Acknowledgments

xi

Introduction

1

PART I.

Guadalupe and the Historical Interpretation of Religion as Art

Guadalupe and Los Remedios:
How Each Gained Its Characteristic Identity

BY FRANCISCO MIRANDA GODÍNEZ

11

Municipal Art in Early Guadalupan Processions

BY MARTINUS CAWLEY

24

Virgin Mary, Guadalupe, and Migration:
Images from the Mid-Sixteenth and Late-Twentieth Centuries

BY LINDA B. HALL

40

Our Lady of Guadalupe in Historical Perspective

BY STAFFORD POOLE, C.M.

58

PART II.

Visual and Poetic Art: History, Aesthetics, and Religion

From Merriam to Guadalupe:
Toward a Theory for Religion as Art

BY STEVEN LOZA

73

"Maravilla Americana":
The Virgin of Guadalupe and the Ideal Spectator

BY RAY HERNÁNDEZ-DURÁN

87

Editing the Anthology *Renaming Ecstasy*:
Latino Writings on the Sacred

BY ORLANDO RICARDO MENES

107

PART III.

Musical Relationships of Faith and Art in Celebrating the Guadalupe Tradition

The Presence of Miguel Bernal Jiménez in the Fiftieth
Anniversary of the Coronation of the Virgin of Guadalupe

BY LORENA DÍAZ NÚÑEZ

117

Musical Witness to the Beautiful *Mestiza*:
Art as Experience of the Sacred

BY SYLVIA TAN

128

PART IV.

Guadalupe and the Native American Experience

Indigenous Mysticism

BY MARIA WILLIAMS

137

Guadalupe:
An Indigenous Mythic Education Perspective

BY GREGORY A. CAJETE

143

The Pueblo Indian Experience

BY JOE SANDO

159

PART V.
Comparative Concepts in the Praxis of Religion as Art

The Virgins of Guadalupe (Tonantzin)
and La Caridad del Cobre (Ochún):
Two Marian Devotions as Fluid Symbols
of Collective and Individual Cultural Identities

BY FRANCISCO J. CRESPO

167

Guadalupe, Yemanjá, and the Orixás of Candomblé:
An Embodiment of Religion, Art, and Music

BY CLARENCE BERNARD HENRY

179

Afro-Cuban Danced Religious Practices as Everyday Art:
Confluence in Motion

BY TERESA MARRERO

189

Observing the Unobservable

BY CHARLES E. MOORE

203

Path to the Divine:
Music in the Sufi Experience

BY ALI JIHAD RACY

214

Yoruba Religious Arts, Secularization,
and Modern Music Theater

BY AKIN EUBA

219

PART VI.
The Spirit of Guadalupe:
Immigration, Human Rights, and Spiritual Conflict

Tlecuauhtlazupeuth:
Belief and Resonance: El contradecir de Guadalupe-Tonantzin

BY JUAN GÓMEZ-QUIÑONES

231

Can Hispanic Immigration Change Fundamental Attitudes
in United States Foreign Policy?

BY LUIS ANTONIO PAYAN

258

Religion and Art:
The Santa Fe Art Controversy About the Imprint
of Our Lady of Guadalupe

BY JANICE SCHUETZ

275

Unbraiding Stories About Law, Sexuality, and Morality

BY MARGARET MONTOYA

296

Conclusion:
The Mystical Roots of American Political Democracy:
Social Justice and Religious Belief in a Newer World

BY TIMOTHY A. CANOVA

301

The Contributors

347

Acknowledgments

This volume is the fruit of ardent, dedicated work. There are a number of agencies and individuals to be thanked for their invaluable contributions to the project.

To the staff of the Arts of the Americas Institute at the University of New Mexico during my directorship there, I wish to express my most personal and special gratitude, specifically to Dr. Maria Williams, associate director; Beverly Ortiz, program coordinator; and Angela Torres, administrative assistant. Without these three dedicated and loving people, the conference represented by the contributions in this volume would not have happened.

There are many individuals and administrative units within the University of New Mexico that gave immensely of both their time and fiscal support, including Provost Brian Foster; James McIver, associate provost for research; Steven Block, chair, Department of Music; Jorge Pérez Gómez, professor of music and director of the University Symphony Orchestra; Dorothy Baca, professor of theater arts; Greg Cajete, director of Native American studies; Shiame Okunor, director of African American studies; Enrique Lamadrid, director of Chicano studies; Richard L. Wood, director of religious studies; and Steven Feld, professor of anthropology and music.

For their very important role in facilitating the conference location and performances, I extend our appreciation to Thomas Chávez, former director, National Hispanic Cultural Center; Reeve Love, director of performing arts; and Joseph Wasson, program production manager.

In addition to the Arts of the Americas Institute, the National Hispanic Cultural Center, and the City of Albuquerque's Department of Cultural Services, sponsors include the University of New Mexico's Center for

Regional Studies; Office of the Provost; Latin American and Iberian Institute; programs in Native American, African American, Chicano, and Religious Studies; Department of Music; Office of Student Affairs; Office of Academic Affairs; and the Jonson Gallery. Off-campus sponsors include the Instituto Cervantes, the Guadalupe Institute, and the New Mexico Endowment for the Humanities.

Thanks go also to the artists who performed in the May 13, 2004, KiMo Theater conference production *Three Cultures, One Language: The Music of Mexico, Africa, and the Arabic World.* They include: Brian De La Fe, Tomas White, and Ramón Calderón (Afro-Cuban *batá* ensemble); A. J. Racy and Souhail Kaspar (Sufi medley); Kapulli Ehekatl (Aztec drum circle); Paz (narration of excerpts from the *Nican Mopohua*); Black Eagle from Jemez Pueblo (Malcom Yepa, director); Latif Bolat (Sufi devotional songs); Araceli Chapa and Orlando Ricardo Menes (poetic narrations); Bonnie Dils (flute), Donese Mayfield (harp), and the University of New Mexico Symphony Orchestra (compositions by Akin Auba, A. J. Racy, Arturo Márquez, and Steven Loza).

I also want to extend my most heartfelt thanks to the following individuals for helping in so many ways, both in institutional and personal roles: Dr. Tobias Durán, director, Center for Regional Studies; Michael Keleher, director, Guadalupe Institute; Dr. Francisco Miranda Godínez, Colegio de Michoacán; the production and administrative staff of the KiMo Theater; and Roy Betancourt, who assisted in the logistics for the Self-Help Graphics exhibit of the Guadalupe Suite at the Jonson Gallery.

As to publication production, I thank Director Luther Wilson, Managing Editor Maya Allen-Gallegos, Acquiring Editor Lisa Pacheco, the staff of the University of New Mexico Press, and my copyeditor Rosemary Carstens.

I extend my gratitude to the Latino Museum of History, Art, and Culture in Los Angeles for a grant for editing done by Nina Moss, whom I also thank for her dedication to the project.

Especially deserving of praise is David Holtby, who edited the volume during his tenure as resident scholar at the Center for Regional Studies, University of New Mexico. I thank him for his insightful and creative input in the editing, formatting, and organizational structure of the text, and I thank the Center for Regional Studies for lending us his time.

It is the hope of every person involved in the project that this collection of essays on religion as art will serve as a source of information, perspective, and philosophical insight in the years to come, and that it will inspire young and old, in heart and in wisdom, and that it can in some way encourage those younger and emerging scholars and artists to persist in this mode of hope, faith, and love.

A Dios Inantzin, Aché, As-salaam Alaykum,
Steven Loza
Los Angeles

Introduction

STEVEN LOZA

☞ THIS COLLECTION OF ESSAYS IS TESTIMONY TO THE BEAUTY NOT
only of art, but of religion, and its inherent relationship to the making
of art. Since humankind's earliest expressions of the abstract and unex-
plainable, themselves among the progenitors of religion, art, in its various manifestations, has emerged as the one constant and persistent
cross-cultural, global, universal ideal, and the common denominator of
the most divergent cultures. I have for many years agreed with Italian philosopher Benedetto Croce and so many others, both academic and artist,
that art is the most direct and purest bridge to the metaphysical, or what
may more fluidly be called the spiritual. I have agreed with the cosmological awareness of many indigenous cultures, especially that of the Native
American, of the oneness of spirit, mind, body, and the infinite universe.

This anthology probes the concept of the arts and their relationship
to religious belief in three cultural areas of the world, expressed through
the religious cultures and practices of the Mexican mestizo belief in the
Virgen de Guadalupe, the West African Yoruba religion based on *Orishas'*
divination system, and the Sufi sect of Islam and its musical/textual practices of devotional ecstasy to God. As Croce (1952) defined art as "intuition" and as the supreme form of knowledge, how do the "artistic" aspects
of religion transcend mere symbol?

The especially significant feature of this volume is based on the interdisciplinary design and dialogue that occurred at the convocation that

produced it. The essays were originally presented on May 12–14, 2004, at the international conference *Towards a Theory for Religion as Art: Guadalupe, Orishas, and Sufi*, organized by the Arts of the Americas Institute at the University of New Mexico, where I served as director from 2002–2005. In these essays, scholars from history, art history, Spanish, ethnomusicology, political science, religious studies, communications, photography, law, literature, and other disciplines exchange views on the topic of religion as art in the three specific areas of Guadalupe, Sufism, and the Orishas of the Yoruba tradition. The intellectual exchange is stimulating and productive, especially in those cases where similar practices of art and religion are discussed cross-culturally. It is also of great significance that a diversity of the arts is conceptualized cross-culturally, ranging from visual art and poetry to music and dance, with analysis of their relationships to society, politics, and culture in general. A good number of the essays are comparative studies of two of the three cultural areas focused on at the conference.

Enhancing the academic proceedings was a concert produced at the historic KiMo Theatre in the heart of downtown Albuquerque, featuring an intercultural diversity of music and dance related to the three religion/arts matrices represented at the conference. Three symphonic pieces were performed by the University of New Mexico Symphony Orchestra, directed by Jorge Pérez Gómez: *Music of the Arab World: A Sea of Memories*, composed and performed by A. J. Racy; "Ritual Dance" from *Orunmila's Voices*, composed by Akin Euba; and *Sueño Guadalupano*, composed by Arturo Márquez.

This last piece was especially commissioned for the conference by the Arts of the Americas Institute, and its performance was its world premiere (followed a week later by its California premiere at the University of California Los Angeles by the UCLA Philharmonic under the direction of Jon Robertson). The first half of the concert was equally diverse and exciting, featuring performances of an Afro-Cuban *batá* ensemble interpreting *Lucumí* (Yoruba) *toques* and *cantos* of the orishas; a Sufi medley interpreted by A. J. Racy and Souhail Kaspar; the Aztec drum circle and dancers *Kapulli Ehekatl*, which performed various pieces and recited an original Náhuatl excerpt from the *Nican mopohua*, the Aztec description of the Guadalupe apparition; Black Eagle, the Grammy Award–winning drum and vocal ensemble from Jemez Pueblo; Latif Bolat, a Turkish artist of Sufi devotional songs and poetry; and finally, three poems recited by

Araceli Chapa and Orlando Ricardo Menes from the latter's anthology of Latino writings on the sacred accompanied by harp, flute, and symphony orchestra with music by Mario Ruiz Armengol and Steven Loza.

Yet another installation of art related to the conference was a one-week exhibit at the Jonson Gallery on the University of New Mexico campus of the *Guadalupe Suite* of prints, secured for the conference from Self-Help Graphics in East Los Angeles. The suite features about twenty-five prints based on the Virgin of Guadalupe by various East Los Angeles Chicano artists.

The Essays

Twenty-five of the thirty-two papers presented at the conference are included herein. I have reorganized the eight original panels into six parts. The essays form a vast, interdisciplinary diversity of both subject areas and viewpoints, in terms of historical perspective, method, theory, and style, as some of the work is heavily research-based while some is purely philosophical or even, in specific cases, polemic. This cross-section and mixture of methodological and ideological approaches is one I have invested much thought and belief in through the years, and I continue to follow this basic philosophy of employing a diverse as possible integration of both content and form.

In Part I, Guadalupe and the Historical Interpretation of History as Art, various historical underpinnings of the Guadalupe cult, images, and social and cultural contexts are analyzed and contemplated in essays by Francisco Miranda Godínez, Martinus Crawley, Linda B. Hall, and Stafford Poole. Each of these scholars has dedicated a major portion of his/her academic life to the study of La Virgen de Guadalupe, and the four essays respond to an abundance of questions regarding origins of the cult, the use of art, the meaning of Guadalupe on both sides of the border, and the materialist validity of the apparitions.

Part II, Visual and Poetic Art: History, Aesthetics, and Religion, also focuses on a plurality of perspectives and subjects, but with a common thread of artistic expression and its conceptualization, both as art and intellectual inquiry. In my essay exploring the idea of developing a theory for religion as art, from which the conference itself germinated, I first question, relying heavily on the theories of Croce, the materialist, positivist school of reasoning art, and then present a critique of the problem of assessing the religious intersections and oneness with art, using Guadalupe as my case in point. Ray Hernández-Durán examines related issues in his essay in addition to probing the questions of how we understand works of art, especially those predating our contemporary era and contexts. In his assessment of various historical texts, Hernández-Durán detects both diversity of thought and interpretation, but also the powerfully enduring empathy and identity that Our Lady and her image evoke. In his précis on configuring an anthology of "Latino Writings on the Sacred," Orlando Ricardo Menes offers a meditation on how and why he developed the project and interprets some of the meanings and forms of two specific poems, one by Pat Mora representing what Menes terms a "Mexican identity at the level of the mythic," and another by him, a meditation in which Menes aims "to fashion a language of sacredness through images, or figures, of hybridity, in addition to surrealism and the Afro-Cuban religion of Santería."

Part III, Musical Relationships of Faith and Art in Celebrating the Guadalupe Tradition, focuses on musical expression in its relationship to religious faith, and contains essays related to the religious cultures examined in the conference. Lorena Díaz Núñez surveys the more recent role of Mexican composer Miguel Bernal Jiménez in a specific celebration of Guadalupe in Mexico City in 1945. Sylvia Tan probes the question of why La Virgen retains significance for the masses across cultures and looks at art as that which mediates sacred experience through the work of symbol.

Part IV, Guadalupe and the Native American Experience, is dedicated to the panel that contemplated the issue of Native American cultures in their solidarity of demanding not only an understanding and empathy concerning their religious/expressive beliefs, but a respectful and mutual implementation of and adherence to such beliefs and practice. Maria Williams's essay stresses the importance of comprehending indigenous mysticism, contrasting western modes of religion, which she concepts as "isolates," with the indigenous, that is, Native American worldview, which is "holistic and examines the physical world as an interconnected whole with the spiritual world." Furthermore, Williams, an Alaskan Native, emphasizes the rejection of viewing the world in a compartmentalized manner in favor of viewing what she refers to as "the meta-matrix," that which includes the spiritual and mystical, or "the ephemeral," and of incorporating this viewpoint and philosophy into one's work, especially in the areas of teaching and research. Gregory A. Cajete, Tewa and member of Santa Clara Pueblo in New Mexico and director of Native American Studies at the University of New Mexico, explores the concept of "indigenous education" from the perspective of the mythic complex of Guadalupe as an "Earth Mother" symbol. From this indigenous educational context, he presents Guadalupe as part of a continuing process of *coming to know*, combining "history, myth, legend, tradition, emotion, religion, and artistic expression to metaphorically teach about relationship to spirit and the creative, feminine, fertile, nurturing, and care-taking qualities of Earth Mother mythologies." The section's final essay is one by Joe Sando, an elder and cherished member of Jemez Pueblo in New Mexico. He offers a historical reading of the Pueblo Indian experience since its colonial invasion by the Spaniards, commenting on the issues of religious beliefs, political struggle, land rights, and traditional life.

Part V, Comparative Concepts in the Praxis of Religion as Art, presents an interplay of topics conceptualized on both Guadalupe and the Yoruba diaspora of the Orishas. Two of the papers are comparative, those of Francisco Crespo and Clarence Henry. Crespo considers the dynamic yet sensitive similarities between the virgins of Guadalupe (*Tonantzin*) of Mexico and La Caridad del Cobre and their equation with the *santería* Orisha *Ochún* of Cuba, while Henry compares Guadalupe with *Yemanjá* and the other Orishas of the Afro-Brazilian, Yoruba-derived religion *candomblé*. Teresa Marrero's essay on Afro-Cuban danced religious practices as everyday art provides us with the opportunity to focus on the art of dance and its importance "as an integral psycho-physical, cultural, and religious expression within Cuban tradition of danced religions, which include Santería, Palo Monte, and Abakuá." In this highly interesting study, Marrero observes the ritual differences between Catholic and the African-based, danced religions, and then proceeds to examine the difference between devotional dance as ritual and its folkloric interpretation as theater. Charles Moore presents a synopsis of his intellectual challenges to the understanding of religion as art, focusing on the African Yoruba Orisha within the philosophical principles of the African *First Order* lived context. A. J. Racy concepts his essay on the mysticism represented by the Sufi movement, and defines mysticism as "an approach to knowing the Divine through direct experience, through intuition rather than mere doctrine." Like Racy, Akin Euba is also both composer and musicologist, and in his essay theorizes the secularization of religious arts by examining historical and modern processes in the secularization of the religious arts of the Yoruba. He poses the question, "Is secularization a process of creating art for art's sake, or another way of celebrating the divinities?"

Part VI, The Spirit of Guadalupe: Immigration, Human Rights, and Spiritual Conflict, takes us into the realm of some of the political and social issues that emerge out of the contextual intersections of religion and art. Taking on the historically rich and complex dissemination of La Virgen de Guadalupe and her embrace of society and society's embrace of her, Juan Gómez-Quiñones critiques the historical contours of *indigenismo*, the independence movement, politicians, journalists, and symbols, all of which have characterized Mexico's national state and ideological soul. In his exposé of contemporary, discriminatory views of Mexican immigrants and their impact on U.S. culture, such as those espoused by Harvard professor Samuel P. Huntington, Luis A. Payan takes a more humanistic, optimistic, and certainly more theologically disciplined approach to the Mexican population north of the Río Bravo and its many praiseworthy values and life standards in U.S. culture. Janice Schuetz and Margaret Montoya offer some contrasting perspectives on a contemporary controversy regarding artistic interpretations of La Virgen de Guadalupe, a highly polemic issue that merits and bears debate on both sides of the body politic, and in between. As an appropriate conclusion to the volume, Timothy A. Canova submits a powerfully intense essay critiquing a number of the contradictions of current political ideologies concerning morality and foresees the great importance of social justice and its relationship to the reality of the diversity of religious beliefs in a contemporary world society.

An Experiment

The essays comprising this anthology represent an experiment. It is hoped that this experiment will proceed to grow and be further developed and disseminated; it signifies a topic that merits much more attention in our rapidly changing and problematic contemporary world. For centuries, countless seamless relationships have developed in a myriad of styles to not only express, but to *experience* and to be one with the metaphysical. One of the problems with even this rhetoric (i.e., the "metaphysical") is that the *infinite*, perhaps a good definition of God or the spiritual world or the so-called metaphysical, is a practical concept that we can actually perceive as existing. Teilhard de Chardin, a religious censured at one point for ideas that were considered too radical, pursued a concept similar to many other world religions and perceived infinity as the actual purpose and form, and so he did not separate the physical and the metaphysical. I believe we should do likewise in our thoughts and configurations of religion and its persistent oneness with the arts.

PART I

Guadalupe and the Historical Interpretation of Religion as Art

Guadalupe and Los Remedios

How Each Gained Its Characteristic Identity

FRANCISCO MIRANDA GODÍNEZ[*]

Symbolism at Guadalupe and at Los Remedios

☞ ALL ARTISTRY ORIGINATES IN KEEN USE OF THE HUMAN SENSES, which also gives each religious devotion its shape, its strength, and its assurance. Such devotions spring from the depths of the human heart as expressions of its innermost vitality, and as each changes over time and space, so do its expressions in art.

Such is my perspective in reflecting on two of Mexico City's outstanding Marian devotions, Guadalupe and Los Remedios. I call these foundational cults, for I see them not only as firm supports throughout the colonial period but also as factors in the making of Mexican nationhood.[1] My theme in this essay is the initial interlacing and mingling of these two devotions and their subsequent entrenchment in contrasting directions.

Art is central to the cult of Guadalupe, whose "Miracle of the Roses" has never ceased to inspire prolific poetry and painting, not only in Mexico but ever farther afield. Already in the 1600s the cult had spread throughout the Spanish Empire and the whole of Europe, and by the end of that century it boasted an extensive bibliography.[2] More recently it has spread to the United States and become a key bond between Catholics of differing ethnic or cultural background here.

---

[*]English translation by Martinus Cawley

Guadalupe is widespread throughout Latin America. Guadalupe has long enjoyed patronage throughout the Americas as well as in the Philippine Islands. In terms of the universal Church, Pope John Paul II made repeated pilgrimages to Tepeyac.

Guadalupe in Poetry

Although I do not intend to deal with the vast corpus of poetry on Guadalupe, I want to at least mention the studies made of it by Jesús García Gutiérrez and Joaquín Antonio Peñalosa, among others.[3] I also want to acknowledge the existence of an extensive corpus in Latin, as well as in Mexico's native tongues. In Náhuatl, the tongue of Tepeyac itself, there is the famous *Nican Mopohua*,[4] whose highly poetic content I will discuss in a moment, but first let me mention two outstanding early poems in Spanish.

One of these was written early in the 1600s by a Captain Ángel Betancur.[5] Its primary focus is on Los Remedios, but it includes extensive references to Guadalupe. The other early poem dates from the great flood of 1629–34, during which the Guadalupan image was brought into the city to be a more accessible focus for prayer. This poem celebrates its return to Tepeyac in 1634.[6]

The *Nican Mopohua* deserves a whole essay of its own, but suffice it here to mention the important link it provides between the poetry of the Christian Church and that of the prehispanic songs of the Náhua people, as highlighted by Miguel León Portilla. In it we have the story of the Guadalupan apparitions narrated in turns of phrase typical of the traditional native poetry. Any talk of the Virgin of Guadalupe has to take Náhuatl culture into account, since this is what supplies the deep symbolism linking the shrine to the "flower and song" of the mythical paradise found in native cosmogony. That paradise is seen precisely as a place of flowers and food stuffs and as a "heavenly land" (*Tlalocan*).

The *Nican Mopohua* takes up this mythic language and its authors, though themselves thoroughly Christianized, present a narrative that is syncretic in content and prehispanic in poetic character. Thus they transfer the old Tlalocan to the barren hillock of Tepeyac, which becomes a place full of marvelous vegetation, where the thorns of mesquites turn into gems and the very stones gleam with the surrealism of a dream:

Even the boulder,
　　the crag,
　　　　on which She takes Her stand
　　　　　sparkles in Resplendence,
　　　　　　　like fine Emerald Jade on a Bangle when it shines,
　　　　　　　　　like the swarming Glow of a Rainbow in the Gloom.
Even the soil,
　　the brambles and prickles
　　　　and the rest of the varied weeds that struggle to survive there
　　　　　are shining like Emerald,
　　　　　　like Divine Turquoise,
　　　　　　　to the tip of every leaf;
　　are glittering like the Golden Scourings of the Gods
　　　up every stalk and twig and thorn.[7]

It is the same when they describe the song of the birds, suggesting once more that same paradisiacal setting:

Distinctly he hears from the top of the hillock a singing, like that of varied rare birds of song.
Time and again subside those voices, as if for the hill itself to answer.
How utterly soothing to the heart,
how cheering to the soul,
　　is their song,
　　　surpassing that of the Shrill bird,
　　　　that of the Bellbird,
　　　　　that of every other kind of Lovely Songbird![8]

Hence, we should not be surprised that the Seer immediately associates this experience with his ancestral beliefs:

"Could it be that I be worthy?
　Could it be that I deserve
　　what I am hearing?
Is it that I am dreaming?
Is it that I am sleep-walking?
　　Where am I?
　　Where indeed do I seem to be?
　　　Could it be even yonder,

In the place they used to tell us of,
those Ancient Men,
those Great Great Grandfathers of ours
—there in the Land of the Flowers' Bloom,
there in the Land of our Flesh's Corn?
Could it be even yonder,
there in the Land of the Heavenly Ones?"[9]

Guadalupe and the Princedom of Tlatelolco

At the time of the conquest, the island-city of México consisted of two princedoms, or lordly domains, namely México-Tenochtitlan and México-Tlatelolco. Tepeyac, linked by a causeway directly to México-Tlatelolco, naturally had a special bond with the native leaders of that princedom. I find that this particular bond was later reflected in the cult of Guadalupe, but during the conquest itself a peculiar situation obtained in which one and the same leader had hereditary rights in both princedoms.

This leader was Cuauhtémoc, the great hero in the final defense of the whole island against Cortés. Cuauhtémoc's rights in México-Tenochtitlan stemmed from his father, Ahuízotl; and those in México-Tlatelolco from his mother, a daughter to the last great lord of that domain. On the other hand, for five decades prior to the conquest, México-Tenochtitlan had been gradually reducing México-Tlatelolco to a subordinate role. I suggest that, to resist this trend, its humiliated citizens sought to borrow prestige from the nascent Guadalupe.

Tlatelolco's original claim to fame lay in its prestigious market, a vivid description of which is to be found in Bernal Díaz del Castillo.[10] Perhaps it was the commercial success of this market that lay behind the envy and hatred directed against Tlatelolco by Tenochtitlan. The legendary founder of Tlatelolco's market was named Cuauhtlatoa (He who speaks like an eagle), and I suggest that this hero was meant to be recalled when, later on, a diminutive form of his name, Cuauhtlatoa-tzin, was proposed as the pre-Christian name of Tepeyac's beloved Seer.

In any case, Guadalupan historians need to examine to what extent Guadalupe's apparition and miracle figure in any last-ditch efforts of Tlatelolco to stave off its eclipse by Tenochtitlan. Certainly, on the level of nomenclature, the term *México* would soon cease to be a prefix applicable to both princedoms and would begin to designate Tenochtitlan alone, leaving Tlatelolco no evidence of being its twin.

Differing Symbolisms at Guadalupe and at Los Remedios

While the twin shrines of Guadalupe and Los Remedios have much in common in the details of their respective stories, each has symbolic elements connected with the particular culture of its locale. In the Guadalupe story, the barren Tepeyac undergoes a miraculous flowering reminiscent of the paradise of the local Náhua culture. In contrast, the story of Los Remedios centers on the maguey cactus, which in the local Otomí tradition was seen as given by the gods to provide the gifts of drink in its juice, food in its pulp, and clothing in its fibers.

As time went on, the two shrines took on complementary overtones. Guadalupe gradually became associated with the patriotism of the earliest Mexican-born Spaniards, the criollos. These are the ones who would pioneer the yearly galleon trips to the Philippines and who would boast that a compatriot of theirs, Felipe de Jésus, had been martyred in Japan and canonized. As for Los Remedios, devotion there was initially as eager as at Guadalupe, or even more so. This was partly due to the municipal authorities of Mexico City, who maintained it financially. In later centuries, however, the devotion would shrink in popularity to just the surrounding area. Los Remedios was to become linked to the Otomí culture in ways typical of a subjugated people who nobly resisted annihilation. In this process of cultural preservation, the maguey would play a symbolic role. Let me retell the story of Los Remedios.

A Brief History of Los Remedios

The shrine of Los Remedios is centered upon a tiny wooden statue, itself barely one foot high and carrying a thumb-sized infant in its arms. It was carved in Europe, possibly in Flanders, and was brought to New Spain by one of the original conquistadors, supposedly Captain Rodríguez de Villafuerte, who would have considered it a talisman for good luck.

From earliest times there have been suggestions that this was the image alluded to in the early Spanish chronicles, the one that Cortés's soldiers installed in the main Aztec temple and that the idolatrous priests were unable to dislocate. It was likewise thought to be the image involved when a miraculous rainfall saved the Indians' crops shortly before the famous Noche Triste, the night on which the Spaniards made their perilous retreat from Tenochtitlan. It was also linked with the lady who appeared and threw dust in the Indians' eyes as they pursued the Spaniards.

Historically, the Spaniards did make that nocturnal retreat and were mystified when, on the verge of being wiped out, they saw their pursuers suddenly abandon the chase. The Spaniards had, in fact, unwittingly stepped over the border into the territory of the Otomís, traditional enemies of the Aztecs. So they saw their escape as a miracle and attributed it to the Virgin's intercession. By morning the local Indians had relieved the Spaniards' hunger with ample food, and, once their wounds and bruises had been sufficiently soothed, they made a dash to the territory of their allies in Tlaxcala. And so Cortés resolved that, as soon as he could recapture the capital, he would erect on that hill a chapel to commemorate the Virgin's help.

Tradition also has it that the Spanish owner of the tiny statue became afraid of losing it, and so he hid it in a maguey, where, years later, it was found by a local native. This native was identified with one who had earlier experienced another personal miracle: during construction of a church at nearby Tacaba, a pillar had fallen and crushed him, but he had been promptly cured. Having once found the image, he took it home, but of its own accord it repeatedly returned to the hilltop, even though he offered it food and drink to entice it to stay. Later, an illness prompted him to make a pilgrimage to Guadalupe, and there the Virgin appeared to him and bade him go home and build a chapel for the tiny statue, there on the hilltop where it belonged.

So much for the folk traditions. A more scholarly reconstruction might run as follows. When Cortés's retreating army entered Otomí territory and their pursuers abandoned the chase, those Otomís of Otomcaupulco would indeed have come to their aid, given them food, and helped them escape to their allies in Tlaxcala, who were already in rebellion against the hated tyranny of Tenochtitlan. There the Spaniards would recuperate, enlist their allies, and plan a counterattack on the capital. In fact, as soon as Cortés finished retaking the capital, he gave orders to a man named Rodríguez de Villafuerte to build that commemorative hilltop chapel for Our Lady. This would explain why the popular tradition made Villafuerte the original owner of the statue.

The chapel soon faded from the Spaniards' memory, but not from that of the local Otomís, who now readily assumed its upkeep, adapted it to their own culture, and told its story in their own way. Later, when the municipal authorities built a regular shrine, the Otomí traditions were picked up by a chaplain named José López, who incorporated them into a series of mural frescoes. These in turn served as a major source for the classic account that Luis de Cisneros was to write in 1616.[11] In those murals, it is not Cortés who orders Villafuerte to construct the original chapel, but rather the Virgin of Guadalupe who gives that order to the Indian discoverer of the statue within the maguey. The Otomís' early upkeep of the shrine would consist mainly in ritual sweeping of the floor and grounds, in continuity with the same services previously rendered to a pagan deity on the same spot. They would also offer candles and incense, as well as the kind of flowers and adornments customary at Guadalupe.

Every shrine presents itself in terms of a popular story in which its location and the origin of its main cult object are steeped in the miraculous. At Los Remedios, as we have seen, the focus was on the maguey, just as at Guadalupe it was on the flowers. From these basic symbols the respective cultures created the meanings the shrines had for them.

Los Remedios Invoked Against Droughts, and Guadalupe Against Floods

Two further factors characterize the difference between the two cults, both involving water. Water has, in fact, always been a problem throughout Mexico, especially in its capital. There has always been the threat of scarcity, with resultant drought, followed by famine and disease, or the possibility of excessive rain resulting in floods, both threatening the very life of the city. When earthly remedies fail, help is sought from Heaven.

Thus, in 1577, when drought threatened to bring famine and disease, recourse turned to the Virgin of Los Remedios and her image was brought into the city. This was repeated in 1597 and in 1616, and for both these latter occasions we have vivid accounts of the people's fervor, and also of their assurance that the rainfall that followed was indeed a miraculous answer to their prayers. It is Luis de Cisneros who offers these eyewitness accounts. Reliance on Los Remedios in the face of drought continued throughout the Colonial Period, and it not only reinforced the people's devotion but also made the municipal and ecclesiastical authorities rise above their frequent disputes and join in organizing the ceremonies. Cisneros's account was printed in 1621 and has remained the chief source on which all subsequent accounts of Los Remedios are based. Moreover, his book was arguably the model that inspired Miguel Sánchez to write the account of Guadalupe, which he published in 1648.

The other aquatic peril threatening Mexico City from time immortal was flooding on account of excessive rain. Already in prehispanic times, around the year 1450, the celebrated King Nezahualcóyotl of Texcoco had ordered the building of a barrage or dike against this danger. In the first century of Hispanic rule, Viceroy Luis de Velasco the elder (1550–64) arranged for that earlier dike to be repaired and extended. Predictably, he made the native authorities supply the labor and also the finances. Even with these improvements there were two further alarms prior to the great flood of 1629: a first one under Martín Enríquez (viceroy from 1568 to 1580) and a second in the early 1600s.

It fell to Luis de Velasco the younger (viceroy from 1590 to 1595) to launch a more definitive solution to the recurrent threat. This consisted of a drainage system, a project that dragged on by fits and starts for the rest of the Colonial Period. Even today the twin tasks of drainage and water supply are among the city's most costly maintenance operations. Meanwhile, until human remedies could prove effective against such flooding, recourse was had to the weapons of faith.

Here is Miguel Sánchez's description of the flood of 1629 and his understanding of the role the Virgin of Guadalupe played in overcoming it:

> It was on Tuesday, the 25th of September, that the flood began, for it was then that the waters started to enter into the city. In the face of this, the Virgin, present in her miraculous Image, made her way from her hermitage of *Guadalupe* [into the city] with many people accompanying her in deep tribulation and affliction, and with the Most Illustrious Lord Archbishop of Mexico City, Don Francisco Manzo y Zúñiga at their head as captain.
>
> She was lodged that night in the palace of this prince, in order perhaps for her to see once more the place and house where she had been born anew amid flowers and had made her appearance depicted on that mantle. [How appropriate it was thus] to call on her to take pity on her own city, her own birthplace.

Next morning [the Archbishop] transferred her to the high altar of the cathedral, where she remained the whole time of the flood . . . Then it was that the embrace and the intercession of the Virgin came to be recognized, and little by little, all quite unnoticed, the waters subsided, leaving the city high and dry—something which neither the stretching out of the years, nor the carrying out of [human] plans had been able to achieve [. . .]

[Four years later, when] Manzo y Zúñiga saw that the city of Mexico was dry, he restored [the image] to its hermitage with all solemnity, adornment and artfulness. [Thus,] on Sunday, the 14th of May, 1634, he took it in procession from the cathedral and down the street named for the clock, making his way as far as the church of St. Catherine the Martyr. There it was afforded hospitality for the rest of the day. Next morning he continued on until he could duly replace it in its shrine.[12]

This same Sánchez is the first to draw the contrast between invoking the Virgin of Los Remedios against drought and the Virgin of Guadalupe in the face of flood. He writes: "the holy Image of Los Remedios . . . had come many times, during season[s] of dryness and sterility, and it was quite evident that it was through her comings that the heavens had been opened for the rain to fall."[13]

A little earlier, when commenting on the Woman of the Apocalypse, with the moon under her feet, he had written: "The Moon is predominant over waters, by way of rains and floods. Hence, to offer defense against the Moon will be to offer defense against the waters, so that the land be not flooded."[14]

The Painter's Art at Los Remedios and Guadalupe

Another art form that takes intimate inspiration from religious devotion is that of painting. It was, in fact, by means of painting that the traditions of Los Remedios took definitive shape when, in 1595, the chaplain José López engaged a painter, Alonso de Villafaña, to depict the various episodes on the walls of the chapel. He also inscribed a series of texts to link each scene to persons and phrases of the Bible or the Liturgy or classical literature. Each ensemble also has a brief caption in verse form, apparently of the chaplain's own making. Cisneros so appreciated these texts that he reproduced them in his book with the following comment:

All these paintings stand in her house in memory of what she has done for her devotees, and they were all done thanks to that devoted chaplain, each one so well adorned with verses, captions and logos. I would do an injustice to his ingenious undertaking and to the whole decoration of the house if I were not to describe these paintings in detail. Thus do I feel obliged to include them, even though it cost me much effort. Indeed, it is from the labor of copying that I have learned to appreciate how diligently the chaplain himself exerted all his ingenuity, his erudition and his scrutiny of sacred literature.[15]

Painting played a similar role in popularizing the Guadalupe story. Around 1650 the chaplain Luis Lazo de la Vega commissioned mural paintings to decorate a chapel he had built over the spring of sulfurous waters where the final apparition of the Virgin is said to have occurred. By way of generalization, Cisneros has the following to say on the role of painting in spreading popular devotions: "Paintings move men to devotion . . . [They constitute] the literature of the illiterate. Those mysteries which cannot be taught to persons unable to read, can be taught by means of painting, which is their equivalent of literature."[16]

On a less official level Guadalupe inspired many other representations: poetry and countless copies of her image, either painted or engraved. And then there were also the other art forms common to all Mexican shrines: music, song and dance, and especially the short-lived art of festive decoration.

Festive Decoration

Mexican shrines are especially noted for the way their devotees adorn their sacred spaces in preparation for a feast day or some special occasion. In ancient times the colorful plumage of birds was used, but nowadays it is mainly flowers. The surface to be decorated might be a triumphal arch, the façade of a building, or the pavement of the courtyard. Indeed, the sacred images themselves are often freshly adorned for a celebration with special garments and drapes, and with the burning of candles and incense before them. Even the sweeping of the floors and courtyards takes on a ritual character.

It is particularly instructive to read what the early missionaries wrote about such ornamentation in prehispanic Mexico. They marvel at the skill with which the natives combine the artificial and the natural into complex varieties of beauty. Cisneros tells of a procession for Los Remedios in 1577 for which, on account of an epidemic, no Indians were available to do the decorating, and he sorely laments how their skills were missed throughout the city.[17]

Decoration of this kind has always been the Indians' chief expression of veneration for the sacred. We think of the floral carpets for the Eucharist in the community of Patamban, Michoacán, on the Feast of Christ the King, or else the Saturday ritual of *enrosamiento* (adorning with roses) in the Lady chapels of villages throughout the Purpecha region of the same state, or, indeed, the very saturation of floral offerings observable any day of the year at the Basilica of Guadalupe itself. The natives' decorative artistry is likewise praised by Bartolomé de las Casas in his *Apologética Historia*, as follows:

> They shape flowers and various herbs into coats of arms and many other objects, quite as skillfully as if they were painting colors with a brush. In fact, some of them so specialize in this task as to have no other work assigned to them. There is such abundance and variety of flowers in this land, and these persons have so subtle a skill in arranging them, that they easily attain a nicety and an excellence of utmost value.[18]

Along with this short-lived decorative artwork, we should mention also the herald's art of oral literature, in the form of announcements chanted in the open squares and responded to by way of dance. This art form is mentioned in the Guadalupan Inquiry of 1666 as having played a key role in the diffusion of the Guadalupe story itself.[19] And, of course, the most characteristic dance of this kind is the Guadalupan procession. Here I could cite Miguel Sánchez' description of Guadalupe's first procession, the one which brought the newly-appeared sacred image back from the city to the primitive chapel at Tepeyac. The text is quoted in the next essay by Martinus Cawley, so I will leave it to the reader to encounter it presently.

Notes

1. Francisco Miranda Godínez, *Dos cultos fundantes. Los Remedios y Guadalupe (1522–1649)* (Zamora: El Colegio de Michoacán, 2002).

2. A handy Guadalupan bibliography for the 1600s is found in Gloria Grajales, Gloria Burrus and Ernest J. Burrus, S.J., *Bibliografía Guadalupana (1531–1984)/Guadalupan Bibliography (1531–1984)* (Washington, DC: Georgetown University Press, 1986), entries ##70–106, 33–39.

3. Jesús García Gutiérrez, *Primer siglo guadalupano. Documentación indígena y española (1531–1648)*, Segunda edición (México, DF: Librería Editorial San Ignacio de Loyola, 1945); Joaquín Antonio Peñalosa, *Poesía gudalupana, siglo XVIII* (México, DF: Editorial Jus, 1988). Idem, *Flor y canto de poesía guadalupana siglo XIX* (México, DF: Editorial Jus, 1985). *Flor y canto de poesía guadalupana siglo XX* (México, DF: Editorial Jus, 1984).

4. This title consists of the first words of the opening rubric of the narrative. See Luis Lazo De La Vega, *Hvei Tlamahvizoltica* (México, 1649). The classic Spanish translation is that of Primo Feliciano Velázquez, *La Aparición de Santa María de Guadalupe* (Tlalpan: Patricio Sanz, 1931). Numerous other Spanish translations have appeared since, but I particularly recommend a translation with commentary by Miguel León-Portilla, *Tonantzin Guadalupe, pensamiento náhuatl y mensaje cristiano en el "Nican Mopohua"* (México, DF: Fondo de Cultura Económica, 2000). The narrative part of Lazo's work is translated from Velázquez in *The Dark Virgin: The Book of Our Lady of Guadalupe*, ed. Donald Demarest and Coley Taylor (Fresno: Academy Guild, 1959), 41–52, and directly from the Náhuatl in Martinus Cawley, *Guadalupe: From the Aztec Language* (Washington, DC: Center for Applied Research in the Apostolate, 1983). A complete translation, made for language students and including the appendices, is offered by Lisa Sousa, Stafford Poole, C.M., and James Lockhart, *The Story of Guadalupe* (Stanford: Stanford University Press, 1998). I use Cawley's translation in this chapter; he uses a quasi-poetic typographic layout to highlight the multiple parallelisms characteristic of Náhua eloquence.

5. The full text (62 stanzas, running to 494 lines) is published in Miranda Godínez, *Dos cultos*, 496–506, with comments on 391–95. There is also an edition of stanzas 39–46, along with an introduction and commentary in García Gutiérrez, *Primer siglo*, 113–17. An English adaptation of parts of those pages is given in Demarest and Taylor, *The Dark Virgin*, 203–7.

6. Copies are extant from more than one early printing, some of which include other short poems, apparently by the same anonymous author. See José Toribio Medina, *La Imprenta en México* (Santiago de Chile: Impreso en casa del autor, 1907–12), entry #447 on 154. The full text of 59 stanzas (236 lines) is given, along with an introduction and commentary, in García Gutiérrez, *Primer siglo*, 125–35. There is no translation of it in Demarest, but a full translation with commentary is given in Martinus Cawley, *Anthology of Early Guadalupan Literature* (Lafayette: Guadalupe Abbey, 1984), 69–80.

7. See *Nican Mopohua*, fol. 1v to 2r, ##18–21, LP 99; TV 291. With so many editions and translations available, it is hard to choose how to refer to the *Nican Mopohua*. First I give the folio of the 1649 edition; then the (quite arbitrary) verse-numbering used by several recent translations; then the page number in León-Portilla (LP), and finally the page number in Ernesto de

la Torre Villar (TV) and Ramiro Navarro De Anda, *Testimonios históricos guadalupanos* (México, DF: Fondo de Cultura Económica, 1982).

8. Ibid., fol. 1v, #8, LP 95, TV 291.

9. Ibid., fol. 1v, #9b–10, LP 95, TV 291.

10. Bernal Díaz del Castillo, *Historia verdadera de la conquista de México*, I:323–35. English-speakers will find an excellent description of the market, partly based on Díaz del Castillo, in Hugh Thomas, *Conquest: Montezuma, Cortés and the Fall of Old Mexico* (New York: Simon & Schuster, 1993), 296–98.

11. Luis de Cisneros, *Historia de el principio y origen, progresos, venidas a México, y milagros de la Santa Imagen de nuestra Señora de los Remedios, extramuros de México* (México, 1621). See my edition under the auspices of El Colegio de Michoacán, printed at Naucalpan in 1999.

12. Miguel Sánchez, *Imagen de la Virgen María. . . . De Guadalupe* (México, 1648), fols. 87v–88v, 251–52. The most readily available modern edition is in Torre Villar and Navarro de Anda, *Testimonios históricos*, 152–267.

13. Miguel Sánchez, *Imagen de la Virgen Maria*, fol. 61r, 223.

14. Ibid., fol. 60r, 221–22.

15. Cisneros, *Historia de el principio*, Book I, chap. xii, fol. 50r, 79. My reference is to the chapter and the folio of the original, and to my own edition of 1999.

16. Ibid., Book I, chap. xi, fol. 45v, 73.

17. Francisco Miranda, "Sobrevivencias de artesanías prehispánicas," in *Manos Michoacanas*, coord. Verónica Oikión Solano (Zamora: El Colegio de Michoacán/Gobierno del Estado de Michoacán/Instituto de Investigaciones Históricas, 1997), 39. The passage in question is in Book II, chap. ii, fol. 86b, 139.

18. Bartolomé de las Casas, *Apologética historia sumaria*, edición preparada por Edmundo O'Gorman, con un estudio preliminar, apéndices y un índice de materias (México, DF: Universidad Nacional Autónoma de México, 1967), chap. lxiii, 327.

19. It is also found in Luis Becerra Tanco, *Origen milagrosa del santuario de Nuestra Señora de Guadalupe, extramuros de la ciudad de México* (México, 1666), fol. 9v–12r; and Luis Becerra Tanco, *Felicidad de Méxic* (México, 1675), fol. 12v–14v; also Torre Villar and Navarro de Anda, *Testimonios históricos*, 324–26.

Municipal Art in Early Guadalupan Processions

MARTINUS CAWLEY

TO ME THE CITYWIDE PROCESSION IS A MOST SIGNIFICANT EXPRESSION of municipal art in colonial Mexico. Moreover, I have long seen California artist John August Swanson's painting *The Procession* as ideally capturing a spirit I find in many early records of Guadalupan devotion.[1] Though the procession in Swanson's painting is actually Eucharistic, for present purposes it serves just as well as would one that was expressly Guadalupan.

In his painting, every face stands out as individual, yet reflects an organic role within the throng. There is no regimentation, yet all gaze and move in the same direction. The whole is laced with the rallying force of confraternity banners and the unifying echo of biblical themes. Individual musical instruments blend with the community bells of the church. Cobblestones underfoot radiate in response to the twin lines of pillars converging overhead on a background replete with biblical scenes.

Processions at Guadalupe?

Guadalupe's twin shrine of Los Remedios is centered on a tiny statue, which lends itself ideally to processional use, but Guadalupe's original image is far too large and awkward to be carried with dignity out-of-doors, except in extraordinary circumstances. On the other hand, throughout the colonial period, the road that led from the city out to Tepeyac was such that any journey on it became something of a Guadalupan procession.

This road consisted largely of a causeway across the lake, such that the waters on either side created a sense of solidarity among travelers in both directions. Add to this that many of these wayfarers bore traditional pilgrim insignia: men and women, rich and poor, singly or in family groups, were conspicuous for going on foot with a recognizable pilgrim's staff in hand.[2] At the Tepeyac end of the causeway various highways radiated out to distant parts of New Spain, but while traversing it all travelers were funneled into close union with the pilgrims. Indeed, public opinion had long held it impious for even the busiest not to step into the sanctuary and ask a blessing on their journey.[3] Moreover, from the 1670s onward, the causeway was adorned with fifteen well-spaced monuments honoring the Mysteries of the Rosary, thereby inviting all to pray to the rhythm of their walk.

Though processions bearing the original Guadalupan image have been rare, derivative shrines have gradually arisen, each equipped with a portable replica for processional use. In any case, to present the role of municipal art in processions I will be drawing not only on the few early descriptions of explicitly Guadalupan processions, but also on the more numerous ones for Los Remedios, the Immaculate Conception, the Rosary, and Corpus Christi.

An Analogy from Modern Literature

Having drawn a lesson from Swanson's recent painting, let me now draw an analogy from the fiction of a modern German author, Herman Hesse. In his story *The Rainmaker*, Hesse depicts a ritual that I like to compare with a Mexican procession. Hesse's rainmaker is the medicine man of an ancient village where a sudden shower of falling stars occurs. Panic among the villagers is setting in, but the rainmaker launches a ritual to rally, first, a few stragglers, and then the entire village. As Hesse puts it:

> [I]nstead of a demoralized horde of madmen, there now [marched] a reverent populace . . . , each one encouraged by having to lock his horror within himself . . . Each now fit[ting] into his place in the orderly chorus of the multitude, keeping to the rhythm of the . . . ceremony . . . The greatest comfort [of such a rite] is its uniformity, confirming the sense of community; its infallible medicine, meter and order, rhythm and music.[4]

A further example of how rituals can play a role in calming panic comes from an account of a ritual for Indian parishes. Whenever hailstones or an infestation of insects threatened the crops, the priest had the village march out in processional form to "conjure" the storm clouds or the insect swarm with prayer, holy water, and an appropriate reading from the Gospel.[5]

Until recent years, it was common practice in Catholic countries to confront wildfire by throwing a relic or a rosary into its path, or by placing a sacred image at a line beyond which the fire should not pass. There are examples of this in the famous diaries of Gregorio M. de Guijo and Antonio de Robles, which cover events in Mexico City in the later 1600s. In reporting a house fire, these diarists include concrete details, such as the cause of the fire and the material loss sustained. More striking, however, is their occasional description of a ritual adopted in response. For instance, the clergy and the confraternities would assemble, each group with its processional cross or the banner of its patron saint. In extreme cases, such as a riot among the citizenry, even the Blessed Sacrament would be brought along and, if the rebels defied so holy a presence, they would tend to lose all credit with the populace.[6]

Question of a Guadalupan Procession in 1556

The unifying power of a Guadalupan procession is forcefully illustrated at an early date. In the mid-1550s, a new archbishop promoted visits to Guadalupe as an aid to moral reform among the Spaniards of his frontier city. He was opposed, however, by leading Franciscans, on the grounds that glib talk of prayers heard and miracles granted would lead their Indian converts to exaggerated expectations, soon to be followed by disappointment and total disillusionment with the faith.[7]

The Franciscans' chief spokesman most dreaded that the archbishop would inaugurate a procession and set the whole city marching out to Tepeyac, thereby canonizing the "upstart" shrine. From the pulpit of the main Franciscan church he urged the viceroy to counter any such move by arranging a rival display in the form of a military pageant out at Chapultepec, a favorite resort for the citizenry, located in a completely different direction from Guadalupe.[8]

Given the close union of church and state, archbishop and viceroy were expected to participate in processions more or less side by side. The good effect of such agreement between both leaders is well illustrated in several processions of Los Remedios,[9] whereas the ugly effect of disagreement between them is vividly seen in certain Eucharistic processions, in which the viceroy disputed the respective place of honor for his own pages compared to those of the Archbishop.[10]

The Tradition of an Inaugural Procession in 1531

At Guadalupe in the early 1600s, the Indians performed an annual dance, which two elders accompanied with a narrative song. It all climaxed when the many participants lined up in procession to reenact the first installation of the sacred image within its newly built shrine. The reenactment seems to have included a miming of the miraculous resuscitation of the Indian killed by a stray arrow during the mock battle.[11] The Basilica museum houses a large painting of this procession, dating from 1653, which was recently studied by Xavier Noguez.[12]

Of course, the choreographers and the painter used artistic license, as do the Evangelists themselves, who canonize the tradition. And so, while caution is needed in treating this tradition as an historical source for the origins of the shrine, the very confidence of these early devotees in taking license shows how familiar the whole city was with the municipal art of processions.

Consider the description of this first procession in the first printed account of Guadalupe, the *Imagen* of Miguel Sánchez.[13] He has no detailed eye-witness account to adhere to, but he waxes lyrically in depicting how the whole city collaborates to plan and execute the rite. In his description, quoted below, notice the wide variety of roles municipal art calls for in organizing the event. In listing them, Sánchez does not ascribe personal names to them, but his imagination readily farms them out to abstract agents.

All prepared themselves . . . , each taking care of the [duty] that fell to him. Fittingness took charge of the bier for carrying [the image], Inventiveness, charge of [its] adornment . . . , Devotion, . . . of the candlelight . . . , Music [took charge of] the canticles . . . , the Public Authorities, of the clarions . . . , Festive Gladness, of the trumpets . . . , Festive Rejoicing, of the wooden flutes. . . , Good Taste prepared the dances; Pleasing Variety, the zarao-displays; the [Indian] Nation, its mitote-dances; the Surrounding Districts, their rhythm-sticks; [The

Element of] Fire [prepared] the salvos; the Air, the perfumes; the Earth, its gardens; the Waters, their canoes. Cleanliness [prepared] the road; Triumph, the arches; Veneration, the awnings; Ingenuity, the bowers; Applause [lined up] the people; Solemnity, the throng.[14]

The Procession Following the Flood of 1629–34

Fourteen years before Sánchez's *Imagen*, a long poem was printed, giving an eyewitness account of the procession that returned the sacred image to its shrine at Tepeyac after its four-year sojourn in the cathedral, occasioned by the flood of 1629–34.[15] The physical causes of that flood were poorly understood but, while various human remedies were being suggested and tried, there remained real doubt whether the city would ever recover, or would rather need to be moved to a safer site. At this point, however, the people drew a lesson from their experience of the opposite danger, drought. For decades it had been the custom to face the prospect of drought by bringing into the city the tiny image from Guadalupe's twin shrine, Our Lady of Remedies, to provide a focal point for citywide prayer. And now the same was done, in the face of flood, by bringing in the image of Guadalupe. During the ceremonies for Los Remedios, time and again, at a key moment, there would come a downpour of rain, which would break the drought so suddenly and effectively that all would see in it Our Lady's miraculous answer to their prayers.[16] The subsiding of the flood was less sudden and less dramatic, but the city was just as unanimous in seeing it as a miracle of Guadalupe.[17] Hence this procession of 1634 was quite ecstatic.

The poet captures the procession's spirit not by cleverness of rhyme or rhythm or figure of speech, but by boldly addressing the image as Our Lady in person. Like the crowd around him, he is full of fervent gratitude for the miracle. While deploring his own inadequacy to express thanks, he takes courage from the sight of his beloved Archbishop Francisco Manso y Zúñiga, who ritually carries the image in which Our Lady is "sacramentally" present. Thus, the poet dares to ask her to accept his fervent tears in lieu of any literary eloquence. In stanzas 12–14, he continues:

But what are words from bards like me,
When men like Manso take the lead?
There he bears thee, there he sings thee,

For all the world to see and cheer.
Songs like his I cannot match;
And yet, my Lady, at thy parting,
At thy leaving of our city,
Can't our tears say as much?
Let them flow, let them flood, let our tears
Be a tide, until our God so willing,
On tear-waves we waft thee homeward,
Who on flood-waves brought thee here.

This custom of addressing an image as Our Lady in person has been studied by David Brading of Cambridge University. He traces it to Amadeus of Portugal, a Franciscan of the late 1400s, whose ideas had considerable impact in Mexico.[18] But whereas Amadeus proposed this doctrine concerning only images involved in renowned miracles, our flood poet partially extends it to replicas made for devotees. And so he continues (stanzas 25–29):

Bitter and sad though thy absence be,
There's still assurance, consolation;
For many copies of thine image
Share they title, stay in our keeping.
These copies too are not diverse;
Extensions, rather, they derive,
And yet remain a single whole,
One image with that selfsame first.
But these are products of human skill,
Earthly the hands that painted these;
Merely men that mixed these colors,
Planned these copies that we keep.
But thou, O Virgin, thou was sketched
By him that limned the Sky and Earth;
Little wonder I should say
That thou art that original!
If such be the hands thou camest from,
What wonder that a world should weep
To be obliged to part with thee,
To see thy portent borne away?

Then, like Sánchez, he describes the whole joyous chaos of sights and sounds that municipal art always produces for city-wide processions: the profusion of candles, bonfires, and sparkling jewels; the tapestries and triumphal arches; the musical instruments and choral hymns (stanzas 31–35).

Yet, for all the diversity, a single unanimity pervades the whole: every individual is loyal to his or her confraternity banner; everyone marches in harmony with peers, from Negro slaves to European-born elites. The Indians, however, with their different language and their special claim on Guadalupe, are to have a separate procession on the morrow. The poet is describing only the first day of the procession, which ends when the city folk lodge Our Lady in a halfway church. Next day her beloved Indians will take her the rest of the way home (stanzas 49–53).

Immediately before that, in stanzas 47–48, the guileless poet expresses regret that the viceroy is not in the procession. But far from disbelieving his official excuse of "sickness," he turns to the image, addresses it as Our Lady in person, and says:

Who is absent from the scene tonight?
Rodrigo the Viceroy! He it is I miss!
How he'd love to march with thee,
If only his sickness would relent!
His excuse is surely valid–
But be a queen and cure him!
What fiestas he shall make
When thou hast healed him entire!

I wonder how true that excuse was.[19] As we have seen, all too often viceroys were at odds with archbishops and at times held up even Corpus Christi processions to dispute placements of honor. Ugly though such disputes were, they show vividly the bond between church and state, and how central processions and their municipal art were in expressing such mutual belonging.

Processions in the Context of Weeklong Pageants

The diaries of Guijo and Robles abound with descriptions of weeklong celebrations for events of church or state, which typically included processions, sermons, and much ringing of bells, but also flowed over into masquerades, dilettante contests between poets, and macho fights with bulls. Also, alas, a devout procession could be followed within days by an auto-da-fé of the Inquisition. Sánchez mentions one of these, but his only comment is to echo his beloved St. Augustine and glory in the fact that none of the accused was Mexican-born.[20] His fellow Guadalupan evangelist, Luis Becerra Tanco, also has a link with the Inquisition, in that a poem of his is given place of honor among commendatory pieces accompanying a work of the Inquisition's prison chaplain, Francisco Corchero Carreño. This saintly priest gave his all in life and death to meet the bodily and spiritual needs of his charges. For his Jewish inmates in particular, he spent countless hours searching the Hebrew scriptures for ways to present Christ to them and then casting his findings into a long Latin poem.[21]

A similarly somber note marked processions honoring the Passion of Christ during Holy Week, and also those held in penitential supplication. In these latter, men would typically intensify their prayer by whipping themselves as they marched,[22] or by pressing on heroically amid clouds of dust under a blazing sun, or through dripping mud under a sudden downpour. Such downpours marked not only the familiar processions of Los Remedios, but also two organized by Juan García de Palacios, who was later to spread Guadalupanism to Puebla and to sponsor a popularized edition of Sánchez's erudite *Imagen*.[23] In 1650, García de Palacios financed from his personal wealth those two Rosary processions in the capital, and the unexpected downpours only intensified the participants' fervor.[24]

Another Rosary procession, more joyous in character, was once held at Christmas, but since it took place in the night hours, it was confined to men only, each with his candle in hand as he marched through the streets. The men's fervor owed much to the fact that their women were admiring them from lighted balconies above.[25]

The Interweaving of Themes in the Municipal Art of Processions

Themes and motifs so intermingle in the processions of Mexico as to remind me of the intertwining lines within the illuminated initials in Ireland's Book of Kells. So, too, in the New Testament, the Gospel intertwines with the Hebrew Scriptures; Christ is glimpsed in the feasts of the Church; Church and State stride side by side; heavenly persons march in their processional banners, and so on.

This is all richly illustrated throughout Cisneros's book on Los Remedios, but one episode in it especially lingers in my mind. Cisneros had heard that the face of the tiny statue often changed its expression in response to individual worshippers. He himself once took a turn at bearing the processional litter, and he deliberately watched as wealthy Spaniards strode up with costly gifts and humble Indians danced up with *tilmas* full of flowers. Only her Indians brought a smile to her face.[26]

Sánchez, too, describes a procession in which he participated personally, one organized by the university in 1653, for renewal of its oath to defend the Immaculate Conception. In earlier times that doctrine had been a favorite topic for recreational disputes among the clergy, but a series of devout kings of Spain had urged that they no longer dispute it, but take their recreation rather in competing to see who could honor the mystery with the finest poetic creation.[27] This oath was in continuity with that royal wish. Sánchez' description of its procession is lyrical, rather than vivid, illustrating another form of clerical recreation, which was in fact his favorite.

Sánchez, for all his humility, had little time for routine homemade poetry, in that the demands of rhyme too easily led to trivial expressions and flattering remarks. Even so, for a few outstanding personal benefactors he was willing to try his hand at an anagram or two, and even at a dedicatory poem.[28] Some clerics of his circle took a keen interest in typesetting and layout for the printing of their works. His fellow evangelist, Luis Becerra Tanco, even did the penwork that was later used to make an engraving in his publications.[29] I doubt that Sánchez himself had much to do with the choice of illustrations for his extant works, except perhaps for a remarkable adaptation of the city's logo, which appears on the title page of his *Imagen*, and a naïve woodcut of his beloved namesake, the Archangel Michael, in his 1665 handbook for pilgrims making novenas. On the other hand, he was clearly knowledgeable about the processes of painting, for he emphatically uses painters' jargon to name the main divisions of his *Imagen*.[30] Moreover, I strongly suspect he was often consulted by persons commissioning copies of the Guadalupan image if they were concerned that they be done as accurately as possible.

What I have called Sánchez's favorite word game comes up in virtually all extant letters in which he commends other men's writings, or they commend his. He gently puns the colleague's baptismal or family name, or playfully applies some biblical theme to his person, his role, or some current event of his. A first prolonged instance comes in Sánchez's first extant sermon, that of 1640, which he preaches at the veiling of a rich criolla widow. With consummate skill he interweaves the story of a biblical widow, Ruth, with that of a criolla saint, Felipe de Jesús (whose feast day it was), and a theme of the Gospel for the day (Sexagesima Sunday). The same kind of word game is central to a report Sánchez wrote in 1653, describing that procession at the university. To me the most beautiful and successful of his biblical applications is in the closing meditations of his *Novenas*, where he offers the parting retreatant a prayer to Our Lady in words adapted from David's address to his bride Abigail (I Sam 25.32–35).

Such playfulness works best when heard aloud in a liturgical setting. Whenever Sánchez's contemporaries praise him, it is as master of the pulpit rather than of the pen, and no one disputes that reading his texts in private is heavy going. That is why García de Palacios engaged Mateo de la Cruz to popularize Sánchez's *Imagen*. On the other hand, though Sánchez loved solitude and study, he was not out of touch with the art forms that delighted the laity. His description of the birdsong of the Guadalupan apparitions, as well as many of his biblical references, reveal a keen ear for music, and show familiarity with its jargon. Though I have little evidence that he was often assigned singing roles at special High Masses, I get the impression that he befriended the musicians and singers whom devotees would hire, both at Los Remedios, where he was chaplain for a time, and at Guadalupe, where he spent so much of his free time throughout his life.

Sánchez's report on that university procession of 1653 is, to my mind, the least successful of his works, and I am not surprised that few modern authors show evidence of having understood it. It was, in fact, meant only as a souvenir for the university personnel. It nevertheless brilliantly illustrates that theme of heavenly persons being quasi-sacramentally present in their liturgical images. Saint Francis marches in person in his processional statue, borne along by his disciples. As Francis sways hither and yon on the friars' shoulders, Sánchez thinks of King David dancing before the Ark (II Sam 6), and just as the stigmatized Francis shares the title *seráfico*, so this dancing Francis becomes what the title of the report names him: *El David Seráfico*. Carrying this lyrical license further, Sánchez also sees the other professors in Davidic terms. Their five academic departments of the university—Theology, Canon Law, Civil Law, Medicine, and Philosophy—become the "five smooth stones" that David chooses from the brook as his ammunition against Goliath (I Sam 17.40–50). These scholars are swearing to defend the title of the Immaculate Conception against any modern Goliath that would dare to deny it. Moreover, in Sánchez's eyes these stones are precious stones, which he identifies, department by department, as "diamond, emerald, ruby, hyacinth, and sapphire." Elsewhere, thanks to his familiarity with the church Fathers, Sánchez sees David's five stones as the five books of Moses's Law, the five wounds of Christ, and the five stigmata bestowed on Francis by the Seraph.[31]

At its outset this procession of 1653 is composed mainly of Franciscan "Seraphim," but on reaching the Jesuit "Professed House," it is joined by other scholars, who are assembled there in robes that remind Sánchez of winged "Cherubim," so that Our Lady and her processional statue now march accompanied by the two loftiest of angelic choirs: the Cherubim and the Seraphim. Further along she is joined by the assembled Cathedral clergy, in whom Sánchez sees not a third angelic choir, but rather the elders of a New Bethulia, who come out to meet their New Judith as she returns from slaying a New Holofernes (Judith 13.14–15).[32]

While most of Sánchez's erudition would be lost on many readers, the procession itself would impress all his contemporaries. Here I think of the response expected by the poet Bernardo de Balbuena when he dedicated his long poem, *Grandeza Mexicana*, to Doña Isabel de Tovar y Guzmán. This devout provincial widow was preparing to leave the world and enter a convent. She would already have high esteem for the parish church of her country town, and for the occasional clergymen she encountered there. Balbuena himself, in contrast, was bored with drab provincial life and yearned for the capital, where everything was on a grander scale. The eighth chapter of his poem climaxes in a review—almost a procession—of the thronging religious communities to be found in that city. To stimulate Doña Isabel's wonderment at all these men and women of outstanding virtue and learning, he begins with the order founded by a kinsman of her own Guzmán clan, namely St. Dominic, whose houses in the capital he describes as:

> Peopled with superhuman giants,
> Giants of letters, holiness and exemplary life,
> Giants of learning, perfection and Christian heart,
> Who stem from a torch kindled in Spain,
> Which lights up the world and reshapes the land,
> Born, like yourself, from the Guzmán line.
> At the blast of whose war cry and trumpet

Hell trembles in fright, Earth cheers and admires,
Lit up with more lights than highest Heaven contains.[33]

The ambitious Balbuena's Baroque triumphalism is not as attractive in our day as is the guileless piety of the anonymous flood poet or the pulpit eloquence of the humble Sánchez. His review of the religious orders would seem more a worldly "parade" for Doña Isabel to admire than a devout "procession" for her to join in, were it not for the fact of her preparing to enter the convent herself.

Conclusion: Processions, Parades and Protest Marches

I began this paper with Swanson's *Procession* and an episode of Hesse's "reverent populace," presenting two communities haunted and dignified by a transcendent presence. I later mentioned a nocturnal procession that had a new element: balconies full of admiring spectators of the opposite sex. I hinted that these last tended to turn the particular procession into a parade.[34] Nowadays, besides processions and parades, we also have protest marches, in which any heavenly presence fades away before a self-assertive "underdog power."

Guadalupe devotion, down the centuries, has undergone many changes, both in its artistry and in its personnel. We know of many touchings-up of the original, many new styles of background, and little narrative vignettes in the corners or pairings with Mexico's national flag alongside. In terms of personnel, Guadalupe has been appropriated by criollos, by Hidalgo's rebels against Spain, by Cristero opponents of the revolution, by Chicano farmworkers, by Chicana feminists, by the Anglo pro-life movement. I would like to end by applying to all such changes in Guadalupan devotion a comment made by Rabbi Gamaliel about the early church. The Jewish authorities were seeking to oppose the nascent church because of its departures from mainstream, but he reminded them of recent similar movements that had gone to excess and had perished of their own accord, whereas no human force could hope to stop a movement that was authentic (Acts 5.38–39). Thus, for instance, if a Guadalupan procession degenerates into a parade or a mere protest march, it will dissipate of its own accord, but if it stays in tune with the real needs of its community and lets the rhythm of its march build trust in the Compassionate Providence that hovers in its midst, no force on earth can stamp it out.

Notes

1. John August Swanson's *The Procession* is available as a poster or card from the National Association for Hispanic Elderly, 2345 East Colorado Boulevard, Suite 300, Pasadena, CA 91101.

2. "*Van descalzas . . . y a pie con sus bordones en las manos*," Ernesto de la Torre Villar and Ramiro Navarro de Anda, *Testimonios históricos guadalupanos* (Fondo de Cultura Económico, México, 1982), sect. Información de 1556, subsect. Testigo Juan de Salazar, 51. For a summary in English, see Martinus Cawley, *Anthology of Early Guadalupan Literature* (Lafayette, OR: Guadalupe Translations, 1982), 28.

3. A very early witness to this is the English pirate Miles Philips, cited at length in Richard Hakluyt, *The Principal Navigations, Voyages, Traffiques and Discoveries of the English Nation Made by Sea or Over-land to the Remote and Farthest Distant Quarters of the Earth at Any Time Within the Compasse of the 1600 Yeeres*; one of many modern editions is that of Irwin R. Blacker (New York, Viking Press, 1965). The Guadalupan text is reproduced in Donald Demarest and Coley Taylor's *Dark Virgin* (New York and Freeport, ME: C. Taylor, 1956), 217–21, and in Cawley, *Anthology*, 66.

4. Hermann Hesse, "The Rainmaker," in *The Glass Bead Game*, transl. Richard Winston and Clara Winston (New York: Holt, Rinehart, and Winston, 1969), 480.

5. *Manual breve, y forma de administrar los santos sacramentos á los indios*, (México, 1640), fols. 33r and 36r.

6. Gregorio M. de Guijo, *Diario, 1648–1664*, 2 vols. (México, DF: Editorial Porrúa, 1952), 2:14 (15 April 1655), and Antonio de Robles, *Diario de Sucesos Notables, 1665–1703*, 3 vols. (México, DF: Editorial Porrúa, 1946), 2:252 (8 June 1692).

7. Fray Alonso de Montúfar, *Información por el sermón de 1556*. This now-famous document was discovered in the archdiocesan archives in the 1880s, and was first published with a false imprint (Madrid, 1888). The second edition (México, 1891) is most readily available in Torre Villar and Navarro de Anda, *Testimonios*.

8. Testimony of Gonzalo de Alarcón, Torre Villar and Navarro de Anda, *Testimonios*, 62.

9. Fray Luis de Cisneros: *Historia de el principio y origen, progresos, venidas a México, y milagros de la Santa Imagen de nuestra Señora de los Remedios, extramuros de México* (México, 1621). This was reprinted with the same title by Francisco Miranda (Zamora, 1999). The harmony of viceroy and archbishop is seen in the processions of 1577 (Cisneros, fol. 86r–88r; Miranda, 139–41), 1597 (Cisneros, fols. 98r and v; Miranda, 154), and 1616 (Cisneros, fols. 124r and v; Miranda, 192–93).

10. The fullest description is found in Guijo, *Diarios*, 1:159–61 (Corpus Christi, 8 June 1651).

11. This dance is described in all three drafts of Luis Becerra Tanco's account of Guadalupe, the third of which is partially available in Torre Villar and Navarro de Anda, *Testimonios*, 326.

12. Xavier Noguez, *Documentos guadalupanos: un estudio* (México, 1991), 111–21 and illustrations 21–25.

13. Miguel Sánchez, *Imagen de la Virgen María* (México, 1648). Available in Torre Villar and Navarro de Anda, *Testimonios*, 152–267. For an English translation, see my bilingual *First Printed Account of Guadalupe: Narrative Sections of the Imagen of Miguel Sánchez (1648) and its Popularization by Mateo de la Cruz (1660), Arranged Synoptically in Spanish and English*, Selected and Translated by Martinus Cawley, ocso, Guadalupe Translations (Lafayette, OR: Our Lady of Guadalupe Trappist Abbey, 2004).

14. Sánchez, *Imagen*, fol. 74r; Torre Villar and Navarro de Anda, *Testimonios*, 236–37; Cawley, *First Printed Account*, 52–53.

15. Copies are extant from several early printings. It is catalogued in José Toribio Medina, *La Imprenta en México* (Santiago de Chile, 1909), tome II, 154, entry #447m, as *Partida de Nuestra Señora*. There are various partial reprints, with a full and annotated reprint in Jesús García Gutiérrez, *Primer siglo guadalupano* (México, 1945), 125–35. There is a full English translation and commentary in my *Anthology of Early Guadalupan Literature*, 69–80.

16. Cisneros, *Historia de el principio*, fols. 86v–87, asserts a miraculous alleviation of the drought of 1577, without specifying at what moment the rain began (Miranda, 139); for that of 1597, see fols. 93r–94r (Miranda, 148–49); for that of 1616, see especially fols. 110v–112v (Miranda, 171–73).

17. The most readily available eyewitness account is Sánchez, *Imagen*, fols. 60v–62r and 87v–88r; Torre Villar and Navarro de Anda, *Testimonios*, 222–24, 251–52. Incidentally, the first of these two passages refers to the flood year 1631 as the centennial of the Guadalupan apparitions. This is the earliest published claim that Guadalupe dates from 1531 instead of the mid-1550s. See Cawley, *First Printed Account*, ix.

18. David A. Brading, *Mexican Phoenix, Our Lady of Guadalupe: Image and Tradition* (UK: Cambridge University Press, 2001). He discusses Amadeus's life (1431–82) mainly on pages 136–37, but treats his ideas on the "sacramentality" of miraculous images mainly on pages 28–29. Amadeus is sometimes referred to by his family name, Joannes Menesius da Silva. Interestingly, Amadeus's blood-sister Beatrice founded the Conceptionist Order, which had a convent in Puebla, whose centennial sermon (1668) was preached by Mateo de la Cruz, popularizer of Sánchez's *Imagen*.

19. Francisco Sosa, in *El Episcopado Mexicano*, 3rd ed. (México, 1962), I:178, tells how both men were very soon to be recalled to Spain, apparently as a result of their inability to cooperate.

20. *Imagen*, fols. 14r; Torre Villar and Navarro de Anda, *Testimonios*, 173–74.

21. Francisco Corchero Carreño, *Desagravios de Cristo* (México, 1649). Becerra Tanco's poem is at the end of the preliminary pages. Medina's notice for this work (*La Imprenta en México*, 267–69) includes a biographical piece quoted from José Mariano Beristáin de Souza. There is also a short obituary for him in Robles, *Diario de Sucesos*, I:52 (16 February 1668).

22. For example, the procession of children thus whipping themselves in Sánchez's *Imagen* (fols. 83r, reproduced in Torre Villar and Navarro de Ands, *Testimonios*, 246).

23. I have never located a copy of the original Puebla edition of 1660, but it seems to have presented Sánchez as its author and García de Palacios as its sponsor, but with no mention of Mateo de la Cruz. The edition I use is that made in Mexico City in 1781, which combines Cruz's account with that of Anastasio

Nicoseli. It has no preliminary pages from 1660. We learn of Cruz's role only from his fellow Jesuit, Francisco de Florencia, in his *La Estrella del Norte de México* (México, 1688), sects. 183–84.

24. Guijo describes this with gusto and in great detail (*Diarios*, I:128–130 [2–10 October 1650]). He explicitly links it to the naval victory at Lepanto, which was universally attributed to group recitation of the Rosary.

25. Ibid., I:188 (Christmas Eve, 24 December 1651).

26. Cisneros, *Historia de el principio*, fol. 46v (Miranda, 74).

27. Sánchez's own contribution, *El David Seráfico* (México, 1653), is presented in Medina, *La Imprenta en México*, II:317, entry #803. A centerpiece of the procession was a book personally sponsored by King Philip IV and entitled *Armamentarium Seraphicum & Regestum [sic] Universale tuendo titulo Immaculatae Conceptionis* (Madrid, 1649) (Reprint, Brussels: Culture et civilization, 1965).

28. At the head of his first extant work, *Sermón de San Felipe de Jesús* (México, 1640), Sánchez sets a (very clumsy) poem, which he composed for the sponsor of the sermon. His attitude to homemade poetry is revealed in the comments of his greatest admirer, Francisco de Siles, in the first of the letters appended at the end of Sánchez's *Imagen*. For his own fullest account of his attitude to poetry, see the long letter he wrote at the end of José López de Avilés, *Poeticum Viridarium* (México, 1669). There he also offers a clumsy poem of his own and some equally clumsy anagrams, but he also offers a fascinating explanation (too detailed to summarize here) of why he broke with his custom and once more tried his hand at poetry.

29. See the annotated poem by the same José López de Avilés, printed at the head of the posthumous edition of Luis Becerra Tanco, *Felicidad de México* (México, 1675), fols. viiir–ixv. And see especially the whole of López de Avilés' own poetic work, *Poeticum Viridarium*. Both works were printed by the Widow of Bernardo Calderón. She was the mother of the founder of Mexico City's Oratory, who was a great friend of this whole circle of devout priests. I suggest she let them do their own typesetting, which is often very complicated, but always astoundingly free from typos. Becerra Tanco mentions preparing a "painting" to illustrate his ideas on how the sacred image was imprinted on Don Diego's cloak, and his posthumous editor, Antonio de Gama, tells of having seen the "lamina" based on this alongside the revised text before the author's death. The print from the lamina is found as a foldout in some of the extant copies. Becerra Tanco had contributed a congratulatory poem for *Poeticum Viridarium* and had allowed López de Avilés to use as his frontispiece a matching pair of illustrations based on his original. This one was signed Antonio de Castro.

30. For fuller details on these sectional titles, and their implications regarding the composition date of Sánchez's central narrative, see my *First Printed Account*, xii–xiii.

31. For the university departments and their precious stones, see Sánchez, *Imagen*, fol. 6v. For the five books, five wounds, and five stigmata, see fols. 2r–3r.

32. Ibid., fols. 12r–14r.

33. Balbuena, Bernardo de: *Grandeza Mexicana*, México, 1604. Two separate editions of that year are described in Medina, II, 14–5, entries ##211 and 212. I have used the university edition prepared by Francisco Monterde, México,

1941. The text quoted is on his p. 110. For the reference to Balbuena I thank my friend William B. Taylor of Berkeley.

34. I owe this distinction of "procession" and "parade" to Flannery O'Connor, though I cannot pinpoint any essay or letter in which she expounds it. Her uses of it that most linger in my mind are throughout "Late Encounter with the Enemy" and in the opening and closing parts of "Displaced Person," in *The Complete Stories* (New York: Farrar, Straus, and Giroux, 1971), 134–44 and 194–235.

Virgin Mary, Guadalupe, and Migration

Images from the Mid-Sixteenth and Late-Twentieth Centuries

LINDA B. HALL

FOR CENTURIES, THE VIRGIN MARY HAS BEEN ASSOCIATED WITH, first, Spanish Christian imperial projects in Reconquest Spain, then in the Spanish discovery and conquest of Latin America, and later in combating and pursuing independence movements in that continent. This association has been both physical—as in the transporting of Marian images ranging from banners of war to tiny personal tokens—and emotional and spiritual, as migrants retained a vivid sense of her presence in their travels. Similar processes continue in the Mexican diaspora into the United States, particularly with images of the Virgin of Guadalupe, and this identification is accelerating as the Latino population here grows ever larger. International agreements such as NAFTA, which increase contact between the two countries, and U.S. immigration policies, in particular the 1986 Immigration Reform and Control Act that provided amnesty to long-term undocumented workers in the United States, have accentuated and accelerated the significance of this cultural and religious icon on this side of the border.

In the cases of the Reconquest, the discovery and conquest, and the independence movements, the image of Mary was used along with military force to impose new political, economic, and social systems in the dominated areas. In the cases of recent immigration into the United States, Mexicans have almost always been relatively disadvantaged in relation to Anglo, Protestant, U.S. citizen populations. Nevertheless, images of Mary and, in particular, though not exclusively, that of the Virgin of Guadalupe, have been key in maintaining a sense of identity, protection, and even power among Mexicans and Mexican Americans in the United States. As early as the seventeenth century, La Guadalupana was seen as especially favoring Mexico through her miraculous appearance at Tepeyac. By the end of the century, the epigraph *Non fecit taliter omni natione*, that is, "It was not done thus to any other nation," was occasionally appearing on engravings and other images of Guadalupe. Taken from Psalm 147, this phrase had been applied to Israel. Thus, the significance of first New Spain and then the nation of Mexico were noted as being of special importance because of the Virgin of Guadalupe's favor.[1] This sense has continued to the present.

And the images are important here. Art historians Hans Belting and David Freedburg have both noted the importance of images themselves in interaction with human beings in spiritual, religious contexts. The figure, according to Belting, becomes more than art and, as he points out, "not only represented a person but also was treated like a person, being worshiped, despised, or carried from place to place in ritual processions: in short, it served in the symbolic exchange of power and, finally, embodied the public claims of a community."[2] He reinforces the significance of community in the interaction he describes, saying "Holy images were never the affair of religion alone, but also always of society, which expressed itself in and through religion. Religion was far too central a reality to be merely a personal matter or an affair of the churches. The real role of religious images (for a long time, there were no other kinds of images) thus cannot be understood solely in terms of theological content."[3] In reference to the Virgin and in particular to her advocation as Guadalupe, I feel that this figure today is just as societally engaged as Belting sees images in the past. Belting himself points out the extraordinary importance of the Virgin in the model of past involvement he draws, in which "Authentic images seemed capable of action, seemed to possess *dynamis*, or supernatural power."[4] Just this kind of power seems to inhere in representations of the Virgin in New Spain and Mexico, in the sixteenth as well as in the twentieth and into the twenty-first centuries, as I will argue below. Further, it seems to mean that there is a continuing sense of Mary's presence within the image, though such a presence is personal and psychological and spiritual, not strictly speaking theological (though this point is, perhaps deliberately, murky). David Freedburg emphasizes the enhanced power of "acheiropoietic images, ones not believed to be made by human hands," among which he particularly points out that of the Mexican Guadalupe—which, according to the legend, appeared miraculously on the tilma of Juan Diego, a representation believed, by some, to have been created by herself. These images, Freedburg asserts, have a particularly strong "supernatural charisma."[5]

Thus, it is worth noting that representations of the Virgin, including figures of both the Spanish Guadalupe and the Mexican one, have appeared miraculously when hidden or have seemed to be miraculously created. Duplication has extended their power, and these images, large and small, have accompanied migrants for a very long time.[6] The mechanisms and significance of Mary's travels with migrants are similar over the centuries, although there are important differences. In Reconquest Spain, the Virgin became closely associated with differentiation between Christians and people of other faiths, particularly Muslims and Jews. The fact that Muslims held peninsular territory that Christian princes desired made this distinction more significant, as Nuestra Señora developed into a kind of warrior goddess leading Christian forces forward. Although Muslims accepted Mary in the Koran as the Virgin Mother of Jesus, the idea that she was virgin both pre- and postpartum was more than their theology could permit. This viewpoint was seen by Spanish Christians as a slight, and the Reconquest was in some sense envisioned as a defense of this view of Mary's purity. At the same time, the Virgin Mother of God, in various manifestations and advocations, was seen as bringing a nurturing and protective presence into the dangerous, liminal areas retaken from the Moors. The battle of Las Navas de Tolosa in 1212, unquestionably the key to the retaking of the South below Toledo, featured the use of a banner of the cross and another of St. Mary. The story goes that during the battle, the banner of Mary was attacked with stones and arrows. The king of Castile, seeing the Virgin attacked, redoubled his efforts and forced the Muslims to flee. This standard, it was later noted, miraculously escaped damage, and the way to the South was opened. Fernando III, the great reconqueror who continued the sweep south below Toledo to Seville in the thirteenth century, was highly reverent to Santa María and, according to legend, carried an image of the Virgin on his saddle. After taking both Córdoba and Seville, he appropriated the great mosques, later using these sacred spaces for churches dedicated to Mary in a direct assertion of the new Christian dominance.

It is important, however, to keep in mind the second aspect of the Virgin's power for Spanish Christians: her ability to nurture and protect. Fernando III's son, the great lawgiver and patron of arts and literature Alfonso X, directed the creation of the largest compendium of Marian miracles in the medieval period, the *Cantigas de Santa María*. Notably, the stories included both illustrative art and music for performance. The *Cantigas* combined well-known Marian stories from Europe more generally with rescues, healings, and other helping miracles quite specific to the case of the Spanish Reconquest. In particular, stories emphasizing the aid she provided to those moving into the frontier areas of the south were recorded. Notable among these are the series related to the Puerto de Santa María on the Gulf of Cádiz, an area Alfonso was eager to populate as a base for further conquests in northern Africa. In 1260, he fortified and developed the town as a base for naval operations, changing its name from the Muslim one of al-Qanatir to the one it holds to this day. The Port of St. Mary, close to the southern extreme of Castilian holdings and almost on the frontier of Christian and Muslim territories in land still disputed, would distinguish the Christian realm from that of the infidel. The name was by no means capriciously chosen, and Muslim populations were offended and objected, though ultimately they acquiesced. Legends developed around the miraculous recovery of an image of Mary discovered when she appeared to Alfonso and directed him to the location where it was buried. Other stories recounted in the *Cantigas* differentiated Christian from Muslim and Jewish populations, encouraged conversion, and emphasized the safety of Christian populations moving into newly conquered territories of the frontier, all under the watchful eye of the Virgin. As Maricel Presilla has pointed out, the *Cantigas* used Marian stories as one component "of a highly structured theological model aimed at the reorganization of thirteenth-century Spanish society. Such an attempt indicates that Alfonso was consciously reacting to the immediate challenges presented by the halt of the Reconquest in the middle of the thirteenth century and to the long-term consequences of the process of territorial expansion such as: inflation, intragroup violence, population shifts, religious diversity, a frontier mentality, and acute cultural dissonance."[7]

Alfonso's inclusion of the stories of the miracles of the Virgin that he personally experienced indicates to me, at least, that although he was aware of the way he was using her to cement and consolidate Spanish imperial power, his own personal faith in Mary was strong. Indeed, the

Virgin accompanied him in his imperial task. Again, as Presilla notes, "One has to bear in mind that Alfonso X was a culture-hero engaged in an almost messianic process of state-building. His efforts required, above all, a consensus both at the secular and religious levels. The cult of Mary, which was the most deeply rooted form of religious expression in the popular mind, provided Alfonso with all the means he needed to achieve symbolic consensus."[8]

The fervor for Mary continued through the Reconquest, as did the profound reverence for her on the part of the Spanish rulers. At the time of the victory over Granada in 1492, both of the Most Catholic Monarchs, Fernando and Isabel, were devoted to Mary and associated their victory and other important imperial issues with her presence. Fernando's sword was inscribed with a plea to the Virgin to protect and aid him. Isabel, on her part, seems to have identified strongly with Mary as Mother, seeking the help, both spiritual and medical, of the monks of the Marian sanctuary of Guadalupe when she was hoping to conceive a son. In fact, in the year after her visit to the shrine in 1477, she gave birth to Prince Juan. She is reported to have cried, "Oh, Sweet Mary," at the moment of birth—or at least so it was reported by writers in her service.[9] Isabel was particularly devoted to the doctrine (not to become Roman Catholic dogma until the middle of the nineteenth century) of the Immaculate Conception, a doctrine emphasizing the purity of Mary from the moment of her conception. Isabel's emissary, sailing west into the unknown ocean, Christopher Columbus, shared her devotions to St. Mary. In designing his signature, he indicated his reverence for the Virgin, and the second island he encountered in what he supposed to be the Indies was named Concepción. He himself later carried out a pilgrimage to the monastery of Guadalupe to fulfill a vow he had made when Mary miraculously saved the Niña from high winds and seas on the return trip of his first voyage.[10]

The best evidence for the mechanisms for imprinting the Virgin on the landscape and layering it onto indigenous religious practice comes from Cortés's conquest of Mexico, and here actual physical representations were of utmost importance. From the earliest contacts with indigenous peoples on the island of Cozumel straight through to Tenochtitlan, Cortés insisted on the replacement of native gods by images of the Virgin Mary and the cross. While the documents indicate that the crosses were often constructed at the sites where they were erected, the images of Mary—both statues and paintings—seem to have been carried with his expedition. There is no doubt that the Spanish were shocked by native religious practice, particularly by human sacrifice, and the documents are full of distress at sacred sites and their caretaker priests covered by blood. Cortés made a habit in his march through Mexico of presenting the Christian religious figures to native rulers and then enjoining their priests to clean and whitewash their own altars, often on pyramids, to provide a suitable place where the Christian images could be revered. The reader will recognize the similarity to the Spanish practice of putting churches dedicated to Mary precisely on the locations of the principal mosques. Indeed, even the wording in the documents was similar; indigenous places of worship were often referred to as *mezquitas*, the Spanish word for mosques. It should be remembered that Cortés began his *entrada* only twenty-six years after the triumphal Spanish entry into Granada. The sense of being Spanish faced with hostile or at least very different peoples seems to have been closely associated with Mary. When Jerónimo Aguilar, who had been stranded by an earlier expedition to Yucatán and who would later serve Cortés as interpreter, leapt out of his canoe to encounter Cortés's men on the island of Cozumel, they took him for an Indian because of his ragged clothes and darkened skin. He identified himself by crying, "Our Lord, St. Mary, and Seville," connecting himself with Mary and her Son and the city where most expeditions to the Indies were prepared.[11]

The difficulties caused Cortés by his insistence on the destruction of local idols and the imposition of Spanish substitutes were significant; still, he persisted until Saint Mary, the cross, and St. Christopher were ensconced on the great pyramid in the center of Tenochtitlan, the Aztec capital. By this time, the supply of suitable images was running low, and the image there of Mary may have been a painting rather than a statue. Although subsequent historians have puzzled about the inclusion of St. Christopher in this extraordinarily important space, it seems likely that Andrés de Tapia, one of Cortés's closest friends on the expedition, reported accurately when he said that they had run out of other images.[12]

Precisely this imposition of the image of the Virgin and the removal of the idols of Huitzilopochtli and Tezcatlipoca from the top of the Great Temple led to great agitation among Montezuma's followers. In fact, at the time that Cortés had to return to the coast to meet the forces sent after him by the governor of Cuba, Diego Velásquez, Montezuma was having serious second thoughts about having permitted the Spanish to install her there in the first place. Sometime in March of 1520, Montezuma complained that he was now in touch with his gods. They had told him, he told the Spanish leader, to make war on these foreigners who had stolen his valuables, imprisoned him and other nobles, and especially had imposed Mary and the cross where they themselves belonged. Montezuma then urged Cortés and his men to depart.

In fact, Cortés did leave the city, but without backing down on the issue of Mary's preeminence in the sacred landscape. When he left to make his way to the encounter with the force that Velásquez had sent, he rather extraordinarily asked Montezuma's priests to care for the image and to be sure that she was always surrounded by flowers and wax candles.[13] On his return to Tenochtitlan, he found the Spanish troops that he had left under Pedro Alvarado living virtually under siege after they had perpetrated a massacre against Aztec warriors celebrating a major ritual. When he upbraided Alvarado for his actions, the offender replied that his hand had been forced by the attempts of the Aztecs to remove Mary and the cross from the Great Temple (which, according to the story, they had had great difficulty achieving). Cortés, though still angry, dropped the matter.[14] Such a threat to an *image* of the Virgin, apparently, was sufficient reason for widespread killing and thus putting Cortés's entire mission in peril. The night before the Spanish retreat from Tenochtitlan, Cortés is reported to have prayed to the Virgin of Remedios for his salvation and that of his forces; later he would erect a church in her honor in the town where they rested after their escape.[15]

It should be emphasized, however, that Cortés was not exclusive of other advocations in his devotion to Remedios. When bitten by a scorpion and fearing death from the venom, he committed himself to the Virgin of Guadalupe, the same Virgin of Extremadura whom Columbus had invoked on his voyage home on the Niña. Cortés, surviving this unfortunate incident, ordered the goldsmiths of Azcapotzalco to prepare a votive offering containing forty emeralds and two pearls in a gold box, in which the remains of the offending insect were kept as well.[16] Moreover, in his will he indicated his devotion to the purity of Mary by endowing both a hospital and a convent to the Immaculate Conception. This latter was a favored doctrine rather than an advocation; many of the advocations of Mary bore elements of the standard iconography recognized as conveying this idea.[17] This iconography was associated with the Woman of the Apocalypse and conflated with the Virgin of the Assumption. Mary was pictured standing on the moon, which might be either full or crescent, surrounded with the aureole of the sun, usually without the Christ Child, often crushing serpents or dragons or devils beneath her feet. The acknowledgment of the debt to the Virgin and of her purity through a bequest to the Immaculate Conception seems to have been common in the sixteenth century. Columbus had earlier left money for a church dedicated to this doctrine; the conqueror of Peru, Francisco Pizarro, also left money to build a church dedicated to the Immaculate Conception in his hometown of Trujillo. Further, he instructed that it be placed as close as possible to his brother's and father's homes, which would put them in the shadow of the protection the Virgin.[18] Although bequests of this nature and magnitude are uncommon today, the willingness to call on different advocations of the Virgin until one or the other responded and to be grateful to more than one idea of the Virgin was common in the fifteenth and sixteenth centuries, as it is now.

The centuries of the colonial period in Latin America saw the development of a number of advocations of the Virgin that eventually began to be seen and sometimes officially recognized as the national patronesses of the regions and later nations involved. Sometimes legends involving the particular advocation stretched back to the sixteenth century, but in general the documentary evidence appears in the seventeenth. In the case of the Virgin of Guadalupe in Mexico, the 1531 appearance to the Indian Juan Diego provides no contemporary documentation, despite efforts in the seventeenth century to trace the story.[19] Still, we know that the Virgin of Guadalupe in Spain was dear to the early Spanish arrivals, as we have noted above. By the middle of the seventeenth century it is clear that the devotion to the Mexican image was beginning to spread, but mostly among the Spanish and only, perhaps, later to indigenous populations. Significantly, the iconography of this image is that of the Immaculate Conception.

Another fascinating image, a stone sculpture that *has* been authoritatively dated to the early post-conquest period, is also a traditional representation of the Immaculate Conception. This sculpture may be a precursor image to the tilma, though she is represented a bit differently and carries a hidden message. Her heavy cape forms a triangle; her head above is crowned and surmounted by a cross and surrounded by a spiked aureole.[20] Her face is rather masklike. She is standing on the moon, with one tiny foot emerging—a feature that appeared not infrequently in European sculptures, where it could be kissed by the faithful. Her mouth is open, quite uncharacteristically for European representations, and may have referred to speaking or singing, speaking in pre-Cortesian Mexican societies being characteristic of the connection between sacred and human power.[21] The style itself is quite consistent with Aztec pre-Cortesian sculptures. She greatly resembles a cornstalk-paste figure, La Virgen de la Salud (the Virgin of Health) de Pátzcuaro, an image commissioned in 1540 by Bishop Vasco de Quiroga and revered to this day at the Pátzcuaro Basilica in Michoacán in western Mexico. Cornstalk-paste was also a pre-Columbian technique used by Mexican artists to produce light but lasting figures. Fred Kline, the discoverer of the stone sculpture, which he has named the Virgin of the New World, hypothesizes that both were probably modeled on the same engraving or woodcut, perhaps from a fifteenth- or sixteenth-century prayer book. The four tassels that hang from the top of her cloak may be taken from the European model, or they may be bells, ubiquitous and significant in pre-Hispanic religious images. There are two dramatic striated circles on each side of her cape, with what may be flowers inside them. The circles also, rather ominously, are characteristic of Tezcatlipoca, the Smoking Mirror, the mysterious Aztec figure associated with the night wind, a trickster who introduced the random and the unexpected into the cosmos. Some authorities believe, following testimony by Aztec notables in the second half of the sixteenth century, that Tezcatlipoca was actually the "supreme power, omnipresent and omnipotent."[22] The specific iconography of the rosette is similar to that of the mirror, "a sacred means of understanding the universe and man himself."[23] The Virgin's gown drapes in folds that look very much like feathers, highly reminiscent of Aztec representations of Quetzalcóatl, the culture hero/feathered serpent. The framed rectangular platform on which she stands is characteristic of both sixteenth-century Renaissance style and the decoration of some of the pyramids at Teotihuacán. Probably this figure was carved by an indigenous artist, possibly for an outdoor niche or an open chapel, that is, a balcony from which priests delivered sermons to indigenous audiences in the early colonial period, when adequate indoor accommodations were insufficient.

But more than the Christian message is quite likely here. From the front, if the section with the Virgin's head and nimbus are obscured, the feathers of the gown and the crescent moon become a beak, while the rosettes are eyes for the face of an owl. Even more strikingly, if the image is turned to its very plain back, the holes in the aureole become the eyes of the owl, the striated nimbus itself the feathers of its head, the cape its wings. This feature is particularly noticeable in the shadow cast through the image if candles are positioned in front of it—as they would have been reverently placed in the immediate post-Conquest period. Among the Nahua, the owl was very important, strongly associated with death and also with protection. The early missionaries connected the owl with native religion, leading them to use the word *tlacatecolotl*, meaning "owl man," as an expression for the devil. This term was also used by the indigenous for a particularly dangerous nahualli, that is, a shaman who, in trance states, took the form of an animal. This being, in its owl shape, would inflict illness and death. Moreover, the owl, in Mesoamerican religion, was an emissary from the underworld.[24] Interestingly, later in the colonial period blacks and mulattoes sometimes used tattoos of owls to signify a diabolical resistance to Christian and Spanish authority.[25] As this information comes from Inquisition records, from which the indigenous population was exempt, it is possible that these groups also used tattoos as resistance and we simply lack the data that would confirm the practice. The owl tattoos that we know of certainly evidence the continuing interpenetration of indigenous, Spanish, and African cultures in Mexico in this form of body art.

This stone image of the Virgin Mary, then, may be read as the force of Christianity in opposition to the power of the old religion; or as a combination of the power of both the Christian and the indigenous sacred, with the shadowy figure of Tezcatlipoca present in the eyes of the owl. It is also possible to read it as showing the power of Mary defeating and obliterating the traditional religion; the owl is hidden, subsumed in the figure of the Virgin. Yet another reading is to associate Our Lady with the enormous wave of death and illness brought by the Spanish, with St. Mary as destroyer rather than protector. Or perhaps it implied her power to save the indigenous peoples—and possibly, the Spanish—from these disasters.

This Virgin of the New World exhibits iconography showing she is a representation of the Immaculate Conception. The Mexican Virgin of Guadalupe reflects similar moon iconography, which is certainly understandable in view of her importance to the Spanish conquerors. It is no surprise that the new Guadalupe would appear in the Spanish New World, and that she was very important to the Spanish and later to the creole population. It would be a mistake, I think, to imagine that she was immediately important to the indigenous population, despite the fact that she appeared on a pre-Columbian sacred site that was significant to Nahua feminine deities.[26] Despite later constructions, most historians working today believe that the indigenous interest in Guadalupe specifically came after that of the Spanish and the creoles, and widespread devotion among native peoples probably dates no earlier than the eighteenth century.[27]

The appropriation of the image of Guadalupe by one group or another was by no means uncontested. An example appears in the Mexican independence movement from Spain. Though Father Hidalgo's creole and Indian forces carried the banner of the Virgin of Guadalupe into battle, the Spanish claimed her as well. In comments on an 1811 sermon by Josef Mariano Beristáin de Souza, the Marqués de Castañiza, rector of the Church of San Ildefonso, declared that, "He shows that the taking of the sweet name of María of Guadalupe in order to promote subversion, theft, homicide, and everything that the Revolution has brought with it, is a horrible sacrilege that tries to make the Mother of God the protector of the excesses and the horrors that are prohibited and condemned by the Holy law of her Son, which she herself came to these kingdoms to establish."[28] Beristáin himself emphasized that María had always been the protector of the Spanish in their endeavors, from the time that the Virgin of Pilar had appeared to St. James (Santiago) during his effort to evangelize the Spanish to the victory at Covadonga, with which the Reconquest against the Moors began in earnest; and, to the conquest of Mexico. She had then appeared at Tepeyac to assure Mexico for her Son for all centuries. He went on to emphasize that Mary could be the Mother of Indians only if they were united with the Spanish.[29] Nevertheless, despite Loyalist protests, Guadalupe continued to be associated with the insurgents and then with the new, independent nation of Mexico.

The movement of the images and presence of La Guadalupana into what is now the southwestern United States is longstanding. We know from Josephine Dunnington's work that a mission was dedicated to her at what is now El Paso, Texas, in 1659. The mission church was completed nine years later and was clearly dedicated to the Virgin of Tepeyac as opposed to the Spanish Guadalupe. Celebrations in front of this Christian church on Guadalupe's Day continue in the present. The inventory of New Mexico missions prepared in 1776 by Fray Francisco Atanasio Domínguez shows that, by the latter part of the eighteenth century, representations of the Virgin of Guadalupe were on wide display, with fully half of the then-extant pueblo missions having images of this figure.[30]

Father Thomas J. Steele, who has made an extensive study of religious folk art in New Mexico, believes that this advocation was extremely popular prior to 1850. In fact, he has found almost as many images of Guadalupe for this period as of Nuestra Señora de los Dolores, which was extremely important to the regional sect of the Penitentes. Yet another study cited by Father Steele indicates that among place names in the region honoring the Mother of God, the largest number for any one advocation (eight) are known as Guadalupe. This devotion was renewed in New Mexico, as indeed it was throughout the Southwest, during the period of the Mexican Revolution, when more than one million Mexicans spent a significant amount of time on the U.S. side of the border, and during the 1920s, when many more came and stayed.[31]

Other waves of Mexican migration have continued this renewal, up to and including the present. Images of Guadalupe abound throughout the U.S.-Mexican borderlands and wherever there are large Mexican and Mexican American populations. Youth programs reinforce her connection with physical power. In a vivid example, at the Chávez Gym in Albuquerque, New Mexico's South Valley, teenagers, both male and female, engage in rigorous physical training in front of the image of the Virgin. Some representations are even inscribed on the bodies of the faithful; images of Guadalupe are now particularly popular in tattoos (almost always on males). The Chicano boxer, Johnny Tapia, protects his torso with a representation of this advocation of the Virgin.

In a more troubling development, La Guadalupana has become a symbol and a presence for some prison and street gangs and important in prison art. Only further research can clarify this point, but I suspect that both her power and her protection are being invoked in these latter cases. I believe that the Virgin of Guadalupe indicates not only a strong connection between gang members, but also underlines their emotional links with Mexico and, perhaps, with Latin America more generally. At the same time, identification with her differentiates them from Anglos and other groups, although even some Anglos are adopting the devotion. In fact, it does not seem to be only Mexicans who are attracted to her image. A sort of pan–Latin American nationalism among Latinos in the United States, particularly in large cities such as Los Angeles that harbor immigrants from many nations of origin, seems to be developing around this figure.

Jeanette Rodríguez, in her remarkable study of the reverence for Guadalupe among Mexican American women, emphasizes the sense that these women have about the power of the image. Despite the falling off of direct connections with the hierarchical church within the second generation, the tie to Guadalupe remains very strong.[32] And strength, precisely, is what these women characteristically draw from her. As Rodríguez explains,

> Assumptions are tied to beliefs. For these women, the world is ordered. There is a God. God cares for them. God works through Mary/Our Lady of Guadalupe. More importantly, Mary is accessible. She is approachable, and because we can approach her, we can approach God.[33]

Rodríguez's study emphasizes the connections these women devoted to La Guadalupana feel. These associations are with mothers and motherhood and children, with power, with loyalty and support for family, with the strength to defend oneself, with light, with one's Mexican identity. They say "She has more leverage. . . . Well, I pray to the Virgin like I say the 'Our Father,' but I speak to the Virgin, and you know, like as if she's my mother"; "She's always been there for me, but then again she's always been there for God, she's always represented him"; "When I pray to her I feel like she's really listening to me"; "Because she was Mexican and I am Mexican"; "I think that I have always had her like a torch in my life, the torch that keeps burning, and there is nothing that can turn it off"; "I feel proud that we have the Virgin of Guadalupe on our side"; "Our Lady of Guadalupe represents to me everything we as a people should strive to be: strong yet humble, warm and compassionate, yet courageous enough to stand up for what we believe in." Rodríguez believes, as I do, that "Our Lady of Guadalupe is viewed as having achieved something, as being competent, as in control, and as having power." She further emphasizes that she is "a 'felt presence.'"[34] These women reflect a powerful, assertive view of Mary. An article several years ago in the *New York Times* gives an indication of what Mexican men in the United States think, as well. As a group of Mexican runners in Brooklyn were about to undertake "a speed workout of laps and sprints," one of them crossed himself and asked the Blessed Mother to take care of his legs.[35] For him, as for the women, the Virgin is associated with strength, power, and endurance, not passivity.

Yet the image of Guadalupe, as other images of Mary, carries different meanings for different people, and the use and interpretation of the image continue to be contested. An example was the Guadalupe T-shirt controversy that erupted in April 1998, in Santa Fe, New Mexico, when elementary school principal Bobbie Gutiérrez sent a letter to parents reminding them that "Any outerwear that is deemed gang-related, for example, Our Lady of Guadalupe shirts" would not be tolerated. One outraged parent, Leonard Gómez, protested that the order was "basically violating my freedom of religion." Gutiérrez, who is Catholic, responded that experts had informed her that the T-shirts were gang attire, as were sagging pants and the like. While she said that she had never sent home an elementary school student, in her former position as a teacher at DeVargas High School, she knew of students either being sent home or forced to turn their Guadalupe shirts inside out.[36] Both the American Civil Liberties Union of New Mexico and Archbishop of Santa Fe Michael Sheehan immediately objected. The ACLU offered to represent any student told to change their clothing; the Archbishop demanded that Gutiérrez apologize. The spokesperson for the ACLU opined that the policy was "terrible for those little kids who just love the Virgin"; Archbishop Sheehan offered that "Mary is Our Lady of Peace, not Our Lady of the Gang, and I think we shouldn't allow gang members or anyone else to take away the symbols that are sacred. I don't think that this sacred image, which is so important to Catholics, should be discouraged because a few people abuse it."[37] Police spoke in favor of the anti-Guadalupe T-shirt policy, warning the Santa Fe public of a "rude awakening" if they continued to permit the wearing of such images of the Virgin. Still, public school authorities hastened to plan a meeting with the archbishop. The policy was quickly rescinded.[38]

A particular venue for these representations on the U.S. side of the border in recent years has been in public murals in Mexican and Mexican American neighborhoods. These murals have been appearing at least since the 1970s. El Paso, Texas, on the border with Mexico, has a number of examples of this public art; it is in the neighborhoods closest to the border that the largest numbers of murals—and the largest proportion of Mexicans among the residents—coincide. Most of these are the usual more or less accurate duplications of the famous representation on the tilma of Juan Diego that hangs in the Basilica of Guadalupe in Mexico City. A particularly large one that appears in a housing project just at the edge of the border shows the apparition of Mary with Juan Diego hovering in reverence. Another appears at the side of a house, framed in stones with plastic flowers in front of the image, a site clearly meant as a private shrine but available for public devotion.

The association of the Virgin Mary with the deceased is shown in yet another, dedicated to the son of the artist after the younger man's untimely death in his twenties. This image appears in the Spaghetti Bowl area of the city, underneath the freeway, close to the Chamizal. The murals in this area are painted on the supports of the freeway, and the location itself is significant. The Chamizal is an area where the Rio Grande River shifted course a number of years ago, adding territory to the United States and taking it away from Mexico. This area was restored to Mexico during the administration of Lyndon Johnson, so this part of El Paso is very close to that previously disputed territory, which has acquired strong symbolic content associated with Mexican nationalism.

Another powerful image of Guadalupe appears just across the street from the one commemorating the life and death of the artist's son. This second image was painted in the summer of 1999 by high school students working under the direction of Carlos Callejo, who designed the mural.[39] It occupies the entire freeway support, both the central upright and two flying panels at each side. Guadalupe's power is shown clearly, as she emerges boldly out of her blue cloak, clad in bright red rather than the muted pink of the original tilma, her hands spread wide apart rather than together in prayer. The representation reflects a dual loyalty, as on one side panel, a cherub unfurls a Mexican flag, while on the other, another cherub unfurls the Stars and Stripes of the United States. Below the Virgin's feet is written, "Nuestra Reina de El Paso Ombligo de Aztlán"—"Our Queen of El Paso Navel of Aztlán." This mural, it seems to me, expresses interacting allegiances. The term Aztlán indicates the ancient homeland of the Aztecs, mythologically located in what is now the U.S. Southwest, thus symbolically connecting that region with Central Mexico, with the place of the mural, El Paso. No longer a liminal border space belonging completely to neither country, it is at the very center of the Mexican homeland. Mexican Americans and Mexicans living in the United States, united in devotion to Guadalupe, are no longer seen as being only Mexican or some kind of subset of Mexican, but also as American, with connections—and homes—on both sides of border. Pride in both nations and in this dual identity, it seems to me, is indicated here.[40]

The Virgin Mary has been a powerful and reassuring presence in Spanish expansion during the Reconquest and Conquest, differentiating Christian populations from Muslims, Jews, and indigenous peoples. Her power continued through the independence period in Latin America, but it was contested between those who supported continued Spanish control and the forces fighting for separation. The vision of Mary as protective, nurturing, and powerful has maintained its psychological resonance for those Latin Americans coming into the United States in the nineteenth and twentieth centuries, this time without the support of Spanish or any other military force. The images of Mary—in sculptures, paintings, murals, tokens, and even body art—have been associated with manifest expressions of nationalism, and this nationalism is Mexican, Mexican American, and now possibly even pan–Latin American. In the immediate wake of NAFTA (North American Free Trade Agreement), it seems that at least to some in El Paso, Mary in the form of Guadalupe may be beginning to stand for a dual Mexican/American identity. But these allegiances should not surprise us. The image, and the presence for believers, of Mary, the Mother of God, has been spur, solace, and expression of identity—perhaps both national and transnational—to migrants for centuries.

Notes

1. D. A. Brading, *Mexican Phoenix: Our Lady of Guadalupe: Image and Tradition across Five Centuries* (Cambridge: Cambridge University Press, 2001), 99. Translation my own.

2. Hans Belting, *Likeness and Presence: The History of the Image before the Era of Art* (Chicago and London: The University of Chicago Press, 1994), xxi.

3. Belting, *Likeness and Presence*, 3.

4. Ibid., 6.

5. David Freedburg, *The Power of Images: Studies in the History and Theory of Response* (Chicago and London: The University of Chicago Press, 1991), 110.

6. See Belting, *Likeness and Presence*, 6, for a discussion of the significance of duplication.

7. Maricel Presilla, "The Image of Death and Political Ideology in the *Cantigas de Santa María*," in *Studies on the Cantigas de Santa María: Art, Music, and Poetry*, ed. Israel J. Katz and John E. Keller (Madison: The Hispanic Seminary of Medieval Studies, Ltd., 1987), 427.

8. Ibid., 424–25.

9. Peggy K. Liss, *Isabel the Queen: Life and Times* (New York: Oxford University Press, 1992), 160.

10. See Samuel Eliot Morison, *Admiral of the Ocean Sea: A Life of Christopher Columbus* (Boston: Little, Brown and Co., 1946), 326–35. Columbus's own account is in Christopher Columbus, *Journals and Other Documents on the*

Life and Voyages of Christopher Columbus, translated and edited by Samuel Eliot Morison (New York: The Heritage Press, 1963), 163–66.

11. Bernal Díaz del Castillo, *Historia Verdadera de la Conquista de Nueva España* (Guatemala: Biblioteca Guatemalteca de Cultura Popular, 1964), 77.

12. See Salvador de Madariaga, *Hernán Cortés* (Buenos Aires: Editorial Sudamericana, 1941), 396.

13. Hugh Thomas, *Conquest: Montezuma, Cortés, and the Fall of Old Mexico* (New York: Simon & Schuster, 1993), 370. Díaz del Castillo, *Historia verdadera*, 375.

14. Thomas, *Conquest*, 396.

15. Ibid., 423.

16. Jorge Durand and Douglas S. Massey, *Miracles on the Border: Retablos of Mexican Migrants to the United States* (Tucson and London: University of Arizona Press, 1995), 11.

17. Hernán Cortés, *Testamento de Hernán Cortés* (Mexico: Imprenta del Asilo "Patricio Sanz," 1925), 14–17, was discovered and annotated by Father Mariano Cuevas, S. J.

18. Francisco Pizarro, *El Testamento de Pizarro*, prologue and notes by Raul Porras Barrenechea (Paris: Imprimeries Les Presses Modernes, 1936), 22.

19. See the essay by Stafford Poole in this volume.

20. The discussion of this image of the Virgin is based on Fred R. Kline, "The Lost Virgin of the New World: The Discovery of a Marian Sculpture of First Contact," unpublished paper, 1998, although I have added to Kline in my interpretation. The figure is dated by Constantino Reyes-Valerio, the preeminent authority on Mexican Indo-Christian art, in his unpublished "Opinion," April 15, 1996. Reyes-Valerio indicates his belief that it was probably made before the middle of the sixteenth century, and it is "one of the early rare examples of religious art made in the New World and one of the finest Mexican Colonial 'Indian Madonna' single-figure sculptures known to exist."

21. Burr Cartwright Brundage, *The Jade Steps: A Ritual Life of the Aztecs* (Salt Lake City: University of Utah Press, 1985), 105.

22. Inga Clendinnen, *Aztecs: An Interpretation* (Cambridge and New York: Cambridge University Press, 1991), 299. Quote is from Clendinnen. See also Fernando Cervantes, *The Devil in the New World: The Impact of Diabolism in New Spain* (New Haven and London: Yale University Press, 1991), 41, 54; and Jill Leslie McKeever Furst, *The Natural History of the Soul in Ancient America* (New Haven and London: Yale University Press, 1995), 90–93.

23. Luis Barjau, *Tezcatlipoca: Elementos de una teología nahua* (Mexico: Universidad Nacional Autónoma de México, 1991), 93–94. Spanish reads, "un medio sagrado de conocimiento del universo y del hombre mismo."

24. Louise M. Burkhart, *The Slippery Earth: Nahua-Christian Dialogue in Sixteenth Century Mexico* (Tucson: University of Arizona Press, 1989), 40–41.

25. Solange Alberro, *Inquisición y sociedad en México, 1571–1700* (Mexico: Fondo de Cultura Económica, 1988), 463, 475; Serge Gruzinski, *La guerra de las imágenes de Cristóbal Colón a 'Blade Runner' (1492–2019)* (Mexico: Fondo de Cultura Económica, 1994), 163.

26. See the interesting discussion of these points in Solange Alberro, *El aguila y la cruz: Orígenes religiosos de la conciencia criolla, México, siglos XVI–XVII* (Mexico: Fondo de Cultura Económica, 1999), 128, and Johanna Broda, "The

Sacred Landscape of Aztec Calendar Festivals: Men, Nature, and Society," in *To Change Place: Aztec Ceremonial Landscapes*, ed. David Carrasco (Niwot, Colorado: University Press of Colorado, 1991), 89–92.

27. In particular, see William Taylor, "The Virgin of Guadalupe: An Inquiry into the Social History of Marian Devotion," *American Ethnologist* 20 (1986): 9–33, and the discussion in Stafford Poole, C.M., *Our Lady of Guadalupe: The Origins and Sources of a Mexican National Symbol, 1531–1797* (Tucson and London: The University of Arizona Press, 1995), 1–3.

28. Josef Mariano Beristáin de Souza, "Declamación que en la solemne función de desagravios a María Santísima de Guadalupe" (Mexico: Imprenta de Arizpe, 1811), foreword. The Spanish reads, "El hace ver que el tomar el nombre dulcísimo de María de Guadalupe para promover insubordinación, el hurto, el homicidio, y quanto [sic] ha traido consigo la revolución, es un horrendo sacrilegio que quiere hacer a la madre de Dios protectora de los excesos y horrores que proibe [sic] y condena la ley santa de su hijo, que vino la Señora a establecer en estos reynos."

29. Beristáin, "Declamación," 12–17.

30. Jacqueline Orsini Dunnington, *Guadalupe: Our Lady of New Mexico* (Santa Fe: Museum of New Mexico Press, 1999), 49.

31. Thomas J. Steele, S. J., *Santos and Saints: The Religious Folk Art of Hispanic New Mexico* (Santa Fe: Ancient City Press, 1974), 98–109.

32. Jeanette Rodríguez, *Our Lady of Guadalupe: Faith and Empowerment among Mexican-American Women* (Austin: University of Texas Press, 1994), 98.

33. Ibid., 122.

34. Ibid., 122–34.

35. *New York Times*, 21 July 1996.

36. *Santa Fe New Mexican*, April 17, 1998.

37. *Santa Fe New Mexican*, April 18, 1998.

38. *Santa Fe New Mexican*, April 23, 1998.

39. Callejo was aided in the supervision of this project by Steve Salazar and Fabián Araiza, working with students Daniel Hernández, Gregorio García, Mike Vargas, Janet Becerra, David Ramírez, Gilbert Chen, Christián Hernández, Arlene Caudillo, Beatriz Moreno, Yvonne Ortega, Liz Landeros, and Irene Juárez.

40. The discussion of the murals of El Paso is based on personal observation by the author, October 14–16, 1999, and telephone conversations with Carlos Callejo, January 2004.

Our Lady of Guadalupe
in Historical Perspective

STAFFORD POOLE, C.M.

⮒ IN THE PROSPECTUS FOR THE CONFERENCE THAT GAVE RISE TO THE essays in this volume, there are references to the fragmentation of knowledge in the western world. In my own field of history the proliferation of specialties and subspecialties is a rapid and apparently never-ending process. Among historians of Mexico in the colonial period alone we find scholars who have devoted themselves to highly specialized topics, often at the price of synthesis or an overarching view that would place those topics in a larger historical context. Again, on looking over this prospectus, I realize that this fragmentation or separation applies to the questions surrounding the tradition of and devotion to Our Lady of Guadalupe. Specifically, I am speaking of the gap between the many interpretations of the Guadalupan event and the historical fact on which they are supposedly based.

The purpose of this essay is to survey the historical problems involving Guadalupe and, if possible, to see what impact they have on these various interpretations.[1] I seek to address the question of whether the historical reality or nonreality of Guadalupe is of any importance. More than a few modern interpreters have answered that question in the negative. But can their interpretations be accepted uncritically? And, if not, why not?

From the beginning the major difficulty with the Guadalupe tradition has been the lack of any documentation or witness that is contemporary with the accepted date of the apparitions, that is, December 1531. It was only in 1648 that the story of the apparitions was made known by the creole priest Miguel Sánchez in his book *Imagen de la Virgen María, Madre de Dios de Guadalupe, milagrosamente aparecida en la ciudad de México*.[2] Hence there is a gap of 117 years in which there is no evidence whatever for the reality of Juan Diego and the apparitions at Tepeyac. Let me explain this in more detail.

There is general agreement that the missionary enterprise in New Spain formally began in 1524 with the arrival of the twelve Franciscan friars led by Martín de Valencia. From the beginning these missionaries made a conscious decision to evangelize the natives in their own languages, a decision later accepted by the diocesan church structure. No serious thought was given to compelling the Indians to learn Spanish or to use Spanish as the instrument of evangelization. To this end the Franciscans devoted themselves to adapting the native languages, especially Náhuatl (Aztec), to the Latin alphabet, and then to producing grammars and dictionaries. In the sixteenth century alone they published catechisms, confessional manuals, sermons, rituals, devotional books, and even catechetical dramas. Yet amid this plethora of writings and publications, between the years 1531 and 1648 there is not one single mention of Juan Diego nor a single unequivocal reference to the apparition tradition. They simply do not exist.

Adding to the impact of this silence is the fact that when Sánchez published the first account of the apparitions, it came as a complete surprise to his contemporaries. Sánchez himself was maddeningly vague about where he got the story.[3] Juan de Poblete, one of the censors of the book, spoke of the carelessness that had prevented the publication of the apparition account until such a late period after the events. "With special attention and more than human disposition, the great enterprise has been reserved after 116 [*sic*] years to the superior genius, sharp intelligence, eloquent speech, and delicate pen of the author."[4] Fray Pedro de Rozas, professor of theology at the Augustinian convent in Mexico City, asked "Should this prodigy remain in silence? No, for such a singular favor was reserved to a careful preacher, to the licenciado Miguel Sánchez, whose rare devotion has raised him up to understand the miracle and, profiting from it, to declare it to us to our profit. Let all New Spain thank him that after 116 [*sic*] years he took up his pen in order that what we knew only by tradition, we may understand without distinction, in its details and defined with authority and foundation."[5] Francisco de Siles, a member of the cathedral chapter of Mexico, wrote that Sánchez "made known the apparition, forgotten in the course of more than a century and rescued by his effort from the lack of care within a brief time; a book so profitable that I do not know if before he gave it to the press this miracle was well known, even in our America."[6] In an obituary written at the time of Sanchez's death, Antonio de Robles wrote "He wrote a learned book about her apparition, which seemingly has been the means by which devotion to this holy image has spread throughout all Christendom. It had been forgotten, even by the citizens of Mexico, until this venerable priest made it known."[7]

In a letter of praise appended at the end of the book, the vicar of Guadalupe, Luis Laso de la Vega, wrote that he and all his predecessors had been like Adam sleeping next to Eve in the Garden of Eden, not knowing what a treasure they had at their very side. This same Laso de la Vega published his own account of the apparitions in 1649 in the Náhuatl language. In it he also testified to the fact that the account was unknown until Sánchez's book appeared. He spoke of God's charitable acts to his people as having been "lost according to the nature of time's passing." Later he wrote, "A great deal has been left out, which time has erased and no one at all remembers any more, because the ancients did not take care to write it down when it happened."[8]

There are indications implicit in Guadalupan writings after 1648 that objections were raised because of this lack of evidence. Defenders of the tradition then brought forth a number of arguments. The first was that of tradition, a longstanding oral tradition that extended back to the time of the apparitions themselves. Second, there was the appeal to the image itself, that is, its miraculous preservation in the humid and salty atmosphere of Tepeyac. Third was an appeal to authority, specifically Roman authority. According to this argument Rome's approval of the devotion and the granting of a proper mass, office, and feast day was sufficient proof or guarantee that the tradition was true. The nineteenth-century Jesuit Esteban Antícoli, one of the most fervent and intemperate defenders of the Guadalupe tradition, wrote "If such a one denies the competence of the Roman Pontiff in judging about the historical fact linked with the cultus, specifically, a limit is placed on the extent of the Church's magisterium, such a one is a *heretic*, at least objectively."[9] During the controversy over the canonization of Juan Diego, the assertion was made that it was lawful to deny his existence prior to the canonization but not after, because "Roma locuta es, causa finita est" (Rome has spoken, the case is closed). Finally, the argument comes full circle, saying that, yes, there is documentary proof of the tradition, most especially the *Nican mopohua*, the Náhuatl language account of the apparitions written and published by Luis Laso de la Vega in 1649, which they retrodate to the sixteenth century. All of these arguments are still used today, as can be seen in the process that led to the canonization of Juan Diego in 2002.

Defenders of the apparition tradition frequently point out that the argument from the lack of documentation is actually an argument from silence, something that is not of strong probative force in history. It should be noted, however, that it is not a question simply of silence, but of silence on the part of persons who would be expected to mention the apparitions. This begins with Archbishop Juan de Zumárraga himself, the man to whom Juan Diego was said to have brought the news of the apparitions. There is nothing about Guadalupe in any of his known correspondence. It can be argued, and has been, that not all of it has survived. True, but more surprising is his failure to mention the devotion or the shrine in his will. Any Spaniard of the sixteenth century who founded a chapel or church would have made provision for its support in his will and would have specified how the pastor or vicar was to be chosen and paid. Zumárraga's will is completely silent on these points, nor did he ask to be buried there.[10] Equally silent are Gerónimo de Mendieta, Bernardino de Sahagún, Toribio de Motolinía, and Bartolomé de las Casas, all of whom would have been expected to invoke Guadalupe in their writings about the spiritual favors that God had granted to the Indians.

One of my favorite ways of illustrating this point is to be found in Arthur Conan Doyle's story "Silver Blaze." Sherlock Holmes and Doctor Watson are in the country, investigating the disappearance of a champion race horse. As they get into a carriage with two local policemen, one of the latter asks Holmes, "Is there any point to which you would wish to draw my attention?" Holmes replied, "To the curious incident of the dog in the night-time." Watson said, "The dog did nothing in the night-time." "That was the curious incident," remarked Sherlock Holmes. Even more pertinent is the story of the famed Mexican historian Joaquín García Icazbalceta, one of the greatest scholars that nation has produced and also, I might add, a devout and conservative Catholic. In 1881 he published a landmark biography of Juan de Zumárraga.[11] The book caused an immediate uproar. Why? Because it made no mention of Guadalupe. A simple explanation of this was that there was no mention of Guadalupe in Zumárraga's life or writings. García Icazbalceta was viciously attacked by defenders of the tradition and denounced as a heretic. An article in *La Patria*, 16 February 1884, neatly summarized the reasons for the outcry. "Señor Icazbalceta is a very illustrious person, and his silence on the apparition of the Virgin of Guadalupe is more significant than anything we could say against it." A similar opinion was voiced by the liberal politician and writer Ignacio Manuel Altamirano. "In his authoritative book he does not say a single word about the apparition of the Virgin of Guadalupe of Mexico, and although such a silence constitutes only a negative argument, it is worthy of the greatest attention in the case of a writer as scrupulous as Señor García Icazbalceta, of a book as meticulous and researched as his, and of a tradition as interesting as that of the Virgin of Guadalupe."[12] Esteban Antícoli wrote, "that author did not show himself a Catholic, much less a good Catholic, who, purposely writing the life of Venerable Zumárraga, first bishop and archbishop of Mexico, in the work that he published in 1881, completely left out everything that referred to the apparition. . . . So then, to speak objectively, the author of the biographical study of Venerable Zumárraga did not write as a Catholic writer when he said nothing about the apparition of the Virgin at Tepeyac."[13] In this can be seen the real significance of the so-called argument from silence.

The question remains: does all this make any difference? For some, the answer is no. There are those who would remove Guadalupe from any historical consideration whatever. Antícoli asserted that Guadalupe was not subject to historical judgment because it was an intrinsically supernatural or miraculous event. During the controversy over the canonization of Juan Diego some clerics made a similar assertion, saying that it was a "salvific event." According to the feminist theologian Jeannette Rodríguez, "The question as to whether the apparitions did in fact occur is inconsequential."[14] The German lay theologian Richard Nebel, declared, "What we do want to do is to emphasize as a notable fact that the veneration of this image has inspired a cultus of such great scope as is the cultus of the Virgin of Guadalupe and Mexico, and therefore the question of whether the image was created by human hands or is of divine origin is totally irrelevant."[15]

The Jesuit Allan Figueroa Deck, in a review of my book on Guadalupe, wrote that "for Catholics of the Americas, for whom this devotion is paramount, no ultimately satisfactory assessment of the Guadalupe phenomenon can be made outside the framework of faith."[16] David Brading, in a recent and highly praised work makes the assertion, odd for an historian, that the current controversy "derives from a nineteenth-century concern with 'historicity' and is animated on both sides of the debate by a latter-day positivism which impels apparitionists to insist on 'the Guadalupan Fact,' and their opponents to hint at forgery and condemn error."[17] Ultimately, Brading appears to side with those who would divorce theology from history and thus would take theology into the realm of the subjective. In an earlier chapter of the same work, when discussing Nebel's book, he observes "For Nebel, the truths of theology soared far above any concern with mere historicity."[18] Yet Brading does the very same thing.

Let me give a concrete example of how this divorce of history and devotion can lead to questionable conclusions. In the prospectus for this conference there are references to Guadalupe as the avatar of the Aztec goddess Tonantzin. The Mexican Guadalupe is viewed as a syncretic or Christianized version of the mother goddess of the Aztecs (or Mexica, to put it more correctly). The prospectus puts it this way, "What has happened here is not so different in concept than what happened in sixteenth century Mexico, where the indigenous Náhuatl language was adapted to western-based polyphony sung by Indian choirs in honor of La Virgen de Guadalupe as equated with *Tonantzín* (sic), the indigenous mother spirit of the Aztecs. . . . The above-cited equation of Tonantzín represents a dynamic example of a conceptual and cultural mestizaje that would begin to characterize Mexico since the sixteenth century."

The classic expression of this idea has been given by Carlos Fuentes:

> In early December 1531, on Tepeyac Hill near Mexico City, a site previously dedicated to the worship of the Aztec goddess Tonantzin, the Virgin of Guadalupe appeared, bearing roses in winter and choosing a lowly *tameme*, or Indian bearer, Juan Diego, as the object of her love and recognition. In one fabulous stroke, the Spanish authorities transformed the Indian people from children of violated women to children of the pure Virgin. From Babylon to Bethlehem, in one flash of political genius, whore became virgin and Malinche became Guadalupe. Nothing has proved as consoling, unifying, and worthy of fierce respect since then as the figure of the Virgin of Guadalupe in Mexico . . . The conquered people now had a mother.[19]

This facet of Guadalupe has been aptly summarized by William B. Taylor:

The story of the apparition in 1531, just ten years after the Aztec capital at Tenochtitlan fell to Cortés, *is* rich in providential possibilities—a dark-complected Virgin Mary appears to a lowly Indian at Tepeyac, the sacred place of a pre-Columbian mother goddess, leaving her beautiful image on the Indian's cloak. Then, in a spontaneous surge of Indian devotion, natives flock to the site of the miracle, embracing her image in their spiritual orphanhood as if she were a new mother restoring order in the supernatural world as well as in the here and now. She combines the Indian past with the Spanish present to make something new, a proto-Mexican Indian madonna who will gradually be accepted as well by American Spaniards and *mestizos* as their own, thus forming the spiritual basis of a national independence movement in the early nineteenth century.[20]

This association of Tonantzin/Guadalupe is now so widely accepted as to appear to be established fact. Nebel used it in the title of his book, as did Miguel León-Portilla in his version of the *Nican mopohua*. Yet what is the basis for it? Where did it come from? Prior to the last quarter of the sixteenth century there is no reference to Tonantzin in relation to Guadalupe. In 1556 the Franciscan provincial in Mexico, Francisco de Bustamante, delivered a fiery sermon condemning the devotion at Guadalupe as crypto-idolatry (remember, this was before the story of the apparitions, of which Bustamante said nothing, became attached to the shrine and devotion). He said that the Indians were worshipping the image just as they had worshipped idols in pre-Columbian times.[21] If Tepeyac had been the site of a pre-Hispanic shrine to the mother goddess Tonantzin, it seems reasonable that Bustamante would have mentioned this fact, which would have bolstered his case immeasurably. He did not.

The association of Guadalupe with Tonantzin came with the famed Franciscan missionary and ethnographer Bernardino de Sahagún, writing about the year 1576. In a frequently quoted passage he declared:

Near the mountains are three or four places where they used to offer very solemn sacrifices, and they would come to them from very distant lands. One of these is here in Mexico [City], where there is a hill that is called Tepeyacac and the Spaniards call Tepeaquilla and is now called Our Lady of Guadalupe. In this place they used to have a temple dedicated to the mother of the gods, whom they called Tonantzin, which means "our mother." . . . The gathering of people in those days was great and everyone would say "let us go to the feast of Tonantzin." Now that the church of Our Lady of Guadalupe has been built there, they also call her Tonantzin, taking their cue from the preachers who call Our Lady, the Mother of God, Tonantzin. What may be the basis for this use of Tonantzin is not clear. However, we know for certain that the original use of the word means that ancient Tonantzin. It is something that should be remedied because the proper name for the Mother of God, Our Lady, is not Tonantzin but Dios inantzin. This appears to be an invention of the devil to cover over idolatry under the ambiguity of this name Tonantzin. They now come to visit this Tonantzin from far away, as far as in former times. The devotion itself is suspect because everywhere there are many churches to Our Lady and they do not go to them. They come from distant lands to this Tonantzin, as they did in former times.[22]

Though this testimony seems straightforward, it should be examined closely. For one thing it came toward the end of Sahagún's life, when he and other Franciscans were suffering disillusionment over what seemed to be the limited success of the missionary enterprise. Fray Bernardino, like other missionaries, tended to blame this on the devil or the character flaws of the natives, but he also tended to see heresy and idolatry everywhere. Sahagún was writing over half a century after the fall of Tenochtitlan and, more importantly, he was the only person ever to have made this association. His primary concern was linguistic, that is, the use of Tonantzin as a term for the Virgin Mary. Others who made this same association, such as Juan de Torquemada and Martín de León, were following Sahagún, sometimes verbatim.[23] Rather little is known about the Nahua goddess Tonantzin and what is known is confusing and contradictory. Louise Burkhart, one of the foremost authorities on Marian devotion among the natives, rejects the association. She bases this in part on the fact that Tonantzin was not a proper name but rather a respectful form of address that was generally used in the sixteenth century not only for the Virgin Mary but also for the Church. Sahagún himself had used the term for the Virgin in some sermons he wrote in the 1540s. She also points out that Sahagún's native informants never mentioned a preconquest shrine at Tepeyac. "The Indians were not perpetuating memories of precolumbian goddesses but were projecting elements of their Christian worship into their pre-Christian past, conceptualizing their ancient worship in terms of Mary. . . . There is no evidence that Tepeyacac held any special meaning for sixteenth-century Indians."[24]

I am not saying that the Tonantzin/Guadalupe association is totally false. I am saying that it is based on the feeble evidence of one statement by one man, evidence that does not justify the exaggerated interpretations that have been given to it.

Can Guadalupe be judged merely as a historical fact apart from any religious or national significance that it may have? I believe that it can. There is no law that exempts it from examination as an historical phenomenon. It is precisely the failure to take into consideration the historical reality of Guadalupe that has warped so many interpretations of it and, if I may speak frankly, rendered them useless. Once the link with the historical foundation is severed and Guadalupe is removed from empirical investigation, then people are free to spin the most outlandish theories and manufacture extravagant and fanciful interpretations without having to prove them. That is precisely what has happened with Guadalupe and Juan Diego during the past twenty to thirty years, especially during the course of the recent canonization. It has been asserted that he was a Chichimeca (that is, a member of one of the nomadic and semibarbarous tribes to the north of Mexico City), a leader (*principal*) of his village, that he was descended from the royal house of Texcoco, that he had had two wives before his conversion, that he had fought against the Spaniards, that he was a poet and philosopher, and that his numerous descendants live in Mexico today.[25] The claim has also been made that it was his high-born status that gave his message credence among the Indians. There is no evidence for any of these assertions, which seem to have been made up out of whole cloth. Further, they miss the central point of all apparition stories, that Mary comes to the poor, the helpless, and the marginalized in society. She is their special defender. In the *Nican mopohua* Juan Diego asks, "I greatly implore you, my patron, noble Lady, my daughter, entrust one of the high nobles, who are recognized, respected and honored, to carry and take your message so that he will be believed." The Virgin responds, "Be assured that my servants and messengers to whom I entrust it to carry my message and realize my wishes are not high ranking people. Further it is highly necessary that you yourself be involved and take care of it. It is very much by your hand that my will and wish are to be carried out and accomplished."[26]

It is only when that history is well established that we can evaluate so many of the claims, interpretations, and legends about Our Lady of Guadalupe.

Notes

1. There have been a remarkable number of studies of the historical questions surrounding Guadalupe in the last few years, especially in the period immediately preceding the canonization of Juan Diego in 2002. Principal among these are Stafford Poole, C.M., *Our Lady of Guadalupe: The Origins and Sources of a Mexican National Symbol, 1531–1797* (Tucson: University of Arizona Press, 1995); D. A. Brading, *Mexican Phoenix: Our Lady of Guadalupe: Image and Tradition across Five Centuries* (Cambridge: Cambridge University Press, 2001); Fidel González Fernández, Eduardo Chávez Sánchez, and José Luis Guerrero Rosado, *El encuentro de la Virgen de Guadalupe y Juan Diego* (Mexico City: Editorial Porrúa, 1999); Jacques Lafaye, *Quetzalcóatl et Guadalupe: La formation de la conscience nationale au Mexique (1531–1813)* (Paris: Éditions Gallimard, 1974), and its English translation *Quetzalcoatl and Guadalupe: The Formation of Mexican National Consciousness, 1531–1813*, trans. Benjamin Keen (Chicago: University of Chicago Press, 1976); Francisco Miranda Godínez, *Dos cultos fundantes: los Remedios y Guadalupe (1521–1649). Historia documental* (Zamora: El Colegio de Michoacán, 2001); Richard Nebel, *Santa María Tonantzin: Continuidad y transformación religiosa en México*, traducción del alemán por el Pbro. Dr. Carlos Warnholtz Bustillos, arcipreste de la Insigne y Nacional Basílica de Guadalupe, con la colaboración de la señora Irma Ochoa de Nebel (Mexico: Fondo de Cultura Económica, 1995); Xavier Noguez, *Documentos guadalupanos: Un estudio sobre las fuentes de información tempranas en torno a las mariofanías en el Tepeyac* (Mexico: El Colegio Mexiquense, A. C. Fondo de Cultura Económica, 1993); Joel Romero Salinas, *Eclipse guadalupano, la verdad sobre el antiaparicionismo* (Mexico: Editorial El Nacional, 1992).

2. Mexico: Imprenta de la Viuda de Bernardo Calderón, 1648. It is reprinted in *Testimonios históricos guadalupanos*, edited by Ernesto de la Torre Villar and Ramiro Navarro de Anda (Mexico: Fondo de Cultura Económica, 1982), 152–281.

3. "With determination, eagerness, and diligence I looked for documents and writings that dealt with the holy image and its miracle. I did not find them, although I went through the archives where they could have been kept. I learned that through the accident of time and events those that there were had been lost. I appealed to the providential curiosity of the elderly, in which I found some sufficient for the truth. Not content I examined them in all their circumstances, now confronting the chronicles of the conquest, now gathering information from the oldest and most trustworthy persons of the city, now looking for those who were said to have been the original owners

of these papers. And I admit that even if everything would have been lacking to me, I would not have desisted from my purpose, when I had on my side the common, grave, and venerated law of tradition, ancient, uniform, and general about that miracle." Miguel Sánchez, *Imagen de la Virgen María*, unpaginated; Torre Villar and Navarro de Anda, *Testimonios*, 158. In the eighteenth century the priest/scholar Patricio Fernández de Uribe criticized Sánchez for his lack of precision. "This respectable author would have done a great service for posterity if he had left us a precise notice of those documents that he used for his work. But either because he did not judge this useful work necessary for proving a tradition that he found universally accredited in the common and general concept of the miracle or because his design (as it is explained) was more to proclaim it as an orator of the apparition than to detail it as an historian, he contented himself with just the common notice and with assurances that he had before him ancient and curious documents, examined well and at length, in agreement with the information in the most ancient and trustworthy and sufficient ones in order to go forward in security with the historic eulogy that he contemplated" (*Disertación Histórico-crítica en que el autor del sermón que precede sostiene la celestial imagen de María Santísima de Guadalupe de México, milagrosamente aparecida al humilde neófito Juan Diego escribiase por el año de 1778* [Mexico: En la Oficina de D. Mariano de Zúñiga y Ontiveros, 1801], 71).

4. Sánchez, *Imagen*, unpaginated; Torre Villar and Navarro de Anda, *Testimonios*, 153.

5. Sánchez, *Imagen*, unpaginated; Torre Villar and Navarro de Anda, *Testimonios*, 155.

6. Quoted in Joaquín García Icazbalceta, *Carta acerca del origen de la imagen de Nuestra Señora de Guadalupe de México* (Mexico, 1896), 112, n. 5.

7. Antonio Robles, *Diario de sucesos notables (1665–1703)*, edición y prólogo de Antonio Castro Leal, 2 vols. (Mexico: Editorial Porrua, 1964), 1:145. Writing in the following century Julián Gutiérrez Dávila, who borrowed much of his material verbatim from Robles, expressed surprise that such a great event could have been forgotten. "The forgetting of such a great benefit that the Empress of Heaven did for our America, and especially for Mexico, was certainly something worthy to be pondered" (*Memorias historicas de la Congregacion de el Oratorio de la Ciudad de Mexico . . . recojidas, y pvblicadas por el P. Julian Gutierrez Davila, Presbytero Preposito, que fue, de dicha Congregacion del Oratorio de Mexico* [Mexico: En la Imprenta Real del Superior Govierno, y del Nuevo Rezado, de Doña Maria de Rivera: 1736], 254).

8. *The Story of Guadalupe: Luis Laso de la Vega's* Huei tlamahuiçoltica *of 1649*, ed. and transl. Lisa Sousa, Stafford Poole, C.M., and James Lockhart (Stanford: Stanford University Press, 1998), 55, 117.

9. *El magisterio de la Iglesia y la Virgen del Tepeyac, por un sacerdote de la Compañía de Jesus* (Querétaro: Imp. de Bellas Artes, 1892), 75. Emphasis in original.

10. The will can be found in Joaquín García Icazbalceta, *Don Fray Juan de Zumárraga, primer obispo y arzobispo de México*, edición de Rafael Aguayo Spencer y Antonio Castro Leal, 4 vols. (Mexico: Editorial Jus, 1947), 3: 385–94. See also *Zumárraga and His Family: Letters to Vizcaya, 1536–1548: A Collection of Documents in Relation to the Founding of a Hospice in His Birthplace*, transcribed and edited by Richard E. Greenleaf, Trans. Neal Kaveny, O. F. M. (Washington, DC: The Academy of American Franciscan History, 1979), throughout.

11. Joaquín García Icazbalceta, *Don Fray Juan de Zumárraga*.

12. *Paisajes y Leyendas. Tradiciones y Costumbres de México* (Mexico City, 1884), 317–18; Torre Villar and Ramiro Navarro de Anda, *Testimonios*, 1156.

13. *Defensa de la aparicion de la Virgen Maria en el Tepeyac, escrita por un sacerdote de la Compañia de Jesus contra un libro impreso en Mexico el año de 1891* (Puebla: Imprenta del Colegio Pio de Artes y oficios, 1893), 108.

14. Jeanette Rodríguez, *Our Lady of Guadalupe: Faith and Empowerment among Mexican-American Women* (Austin: University of Texas Press, 1994), 127.

15. Richard Nebel, *Santa María Tonantzin: Continuidad y transformación religiosa en México* (México: Fondo de Cultura Económica, 1995), 126–27.

16. *America* 173, no. 9 (September 30, 1995): 25.

17. Brading, *Mexican Phoenix*, 361.

18. Ibid., 345.

19. Carlos Fuentes, *The Buried Mirror: Reflections on Spain in the New World* (Boston: Houghton Mifflin, 1992), 145–46. Fuentes is in error when he says that Juan Diego was a *tameme* or Indian porter. No such assertion is to be found in any of the sources.

20. William Taylor, "The Virgin of Guadalupe: An Inquiry into the Social History of Marian Devotion," *American Ethnologist* (1986): 9–10. Emphases in original.

21. On this sermon and the reaction it provoked, see Poole, *Our Lady of Guadalupe*, 58–64.

22. Bernardino de Sahagún, *Historia general de las cosas de la Nueva España escrita por Bernardino de Sahagún y fundada en la documentación en lengua mexicana recogida por los mismos naturales; la dispuso para la prensa en esta nueva edición, con numeración, anotaciones y apéndices, Angel María Garibay K.*, 4 vols., 4th ed. (Mexico: Editorial Porrúa, 1981), 3:352.

23. Juan de Torquemada, *Monarquía indiana*, Introducción por Miguel León-Portilla, 3 vols. (México: Editorial Porrúa, S.A., 1969), book 10, chap. 8, 245–46; Martín de León, *Camino del cielo en lengva mexicana, con todos los requisitos necessarios para conseguir este fin, co[n] todo lo que vn Xpiano deue creer, saber, y obrar, desde el punto que tiene vso de razon, hasta que muere. Co[m]puesto, por el P. F. Martin de Leo[n], de la Orde[n] de Predicadores.* (Mexico: En la emprenta de Diego Lopez Daualos y a costa de Diego Perez de los Rios, 1611), fol. 96r.

24. Louise Burkhart, "The Cult of the Virgin of Guadalupe in Mexico," in *South and Meso-American Native Spirituality: From the Cult of the Feathered Serpent to the Theology of Liberation*, ed. Gary H. Gossen in collaboration with Miguel León-Portilla, Vol. 4 of *World Spirituality: An Encyclopedic History of the Religious Quest* (New York: The Crossroad Publishing Company, 1993), 208.

25. *Positio* for beatification, Congregatio pro causis sanctorium officium histori-cum, 184, Mexicanas canonizationis servi dei ioannis didaci cuauhtlatoatzin vivi laici (1474–1548), positio super fama sanctitatis, virtutibus et cultu ab immemorabili praestito ex officio concinnata (Rome: 1989); Luis Guerrero Rosado, *El "Nican Mopohua": un intento de exégesis* (Mexico City: Universidad Pontificia de México, 1996), 102.

26. Sousa, Poole, and Lockhart, *Story of Guadalupe*, 68–71.

PART II

Visual and Poetic Art

History, Aesthetics, and Religion

From Merriam to Guadalupe

Toward a Theory
for Religion as Art

STEVEN LOZA

It is said in intellectual lore that Mexican artist Diego Rivera was once asked if he believed in God. His answer was no. He was then asked if he believed in the Virgen de Guadalupe. His answer was yes.

☞ MY PURPOSE IN THIS ESSAY IS TO CRITIQUE THE INTELLECTUAL philosophy of Alan Merriam, one of the classic scholars of ethnomusicology, in terms of a pervading positivism that has largely characterized ethnomusicological research and scholarship, especially in the United States. In the second portion of the essay, I propose an approach diametrically opposed to the concepts of Merriam, suggesting an aesthetic paradigm invoking our inevitable dependence on subjectivity, art, the metaphysical, morality, religion, and faith in the infinite. Through a conceptualization of "religion as art," I develop some theoretical possibilities using the religious experience of La Virgen de Guadalupe as a case study for further cross-cultural analysis.

Thoughts on Ethnomusicology and Alan Merriam

In our often isolated field of ethnomusicology, purportedly the cross-discipline of musicology and ethnology, it is my belief that we have certain salient problems. All academic disciplines have problems of methodology and conceptualization. But I feel that our field especially has some problems that are not only unique when compared to many other academic disciplines, but are unique in and of themselves. Foremost is our encounter with the art versus science dilemma. I feel that many of us engaged in ethnomusicology are still largely artistically inclined, yet still dedicated to the pursuit of strongly conceptualized approaches in research methodology, theoretical notions and their applications, and broad planes of analysis in general. Our role as artists has, in fact, been one of the greatest opportunities to enhance our research and scholarship and to adapt our insight and intuition as musicians and scholars in joint practice. But the academy we work in has largely ignored this blessed vocation when the science is overvalued and the art undervalued. Charles Seeger spoke of the problem of speech communication in our field (1961). Little did he know that not only would we become obsessed with words and vogue theories expressed only literally, but that we would become almost totally dependent on analytical ideas emanating almost exclusively from other disciplines.

I also feel that our obsession with definitional words often leading nowhere can be traced back some time, notably to the 1960s, partly personified through the often frustrating debates of Mantle Hood and Alan Merriam (Hood 1957, 1963; Merriam 1960, 1963, 1964, 1966, 1974). More of the same would eventually follow, and can be traced through Lomax (1968, 1971), Herndon (1974), Kolinski (1967, 1976), and others. I must resolutely agree with the *words* of Nettl (1990, 1) originally written in 1980: "I have not encountered an academic field or discipline whose members spent as much time worrying about defining themselves as ethnomusicology. Definitions abound and they can be discussed historically, something done by the late Alan P. Merriam in one of his last articles" (Merriam 1976).

Merriam had become obsessed with the idea that ethnomusicology is the *dual* discipline, the fusion and welding of ethnology and musicology, of the social sciences and the humanities, and he understated the arts and the artistic aspects. Agreeing with the perspectives of Harold Cassidy, who drew ideas from Bertrand Russell, and who considered the context of an artist conveying knowledge as a "bonus" (Cassidy 1962, 14), Merriam (1964, 19–20) thus wrote the following:

> If we accept this point of view [Cassidy's], it is clear that in ethnomusicology the basic problem is not the artist versus the social scientist, for since the artist is not concerned primarily with communicating knowledge,

he is not concerned primarily with ethnomusicology. Ethnomusicology is not creative in the same sense that the artist is creative; it does not seek to communicate emotion or feeling, but rather knowledge . . .

The artist as such, then, plays little part, so far as his creative capacities are concerned, in ethnomusicology, for it is not involved in creating works of art. Its concern lies in the problems of the artist, in how he creates the work of art, the functions of art, and so forth. Thus the process of creating art differs from the study of that process, and ethnomusicology is concerned with the latter—the accumulation and communication of knowledge about music. In this sense, its studies fall on the scientific rather than on the artistic side . . .

The conclusion is almost inescapable, that what the ethnomusicologist desires is not the subjective, qualitative, discursive, aesthetic and so forth but rather the objective, quantitative, and theoretical, wherever this is possible. There is a valid distinction to be drawn between the process of creating art and the artistic outlook, as opposed to the study of such processes. The ethnomusicologist seeks knowledge and seeks to communicate that knowledge; the results for which he aims are more scientific than artistic.

Herein is a pernicious, positivist notion of knowledge and a Pharisean attitude toward art and the artist. And what of musicology? Did Merriam ever respond to Seeger and Hood, who both desired to witness the various facets and branches of the discipline of musicology incorporated into the field of ethnomusicology? And I mean *really* respond. Whatever went on in the laboratory portion of analysis that Merriam incessantly referred to? He saw no point in pragmatically defining that part, for, as he explained, "The second, or laboratory, phase of ethnomusicological investigation need not concern us here; in this phase the investigator turns to the transcription and structural analysis of the materials he has recorded in the field, and is, of course, basic in the field and this is, of course, basic in establishing the taxonomy essential to the study" (1964, 107–14). In other words, Merriam seemed to like the idea of defining ethnomusicology the way he wanted. He actually wanted us to accept the musicological norms of doing musical analysis of the time. How, then, was this a welding, a fusion of the ethnologist and the musicologist?[1] It wasn't. And it is still not. And one of Merriam's last contributions to this debate? A compendium of more definitions (Merriam 1977).

I do not note these things out of disrespect for Merriam. In my seminars surveying the field of ethnomusicology, Merriam's writings are referred to. I do believe Merriam was certainly a field eulogist. But he was not an artist, and for that reason I have found his methodological ideas difficult to accept.[2] Also the obsession with definition has been a characteristic of not only Merriam's thinking. It can be located in much of the ethnomusicological literature. Someone may call me on the fact that I am so audacious as to criticize scholars because they wanted to define something the way they wanted. Well, I feel that is part of the whole problem. We are not here merely to do what we want. We are here (and especially in academia) because of moral responsibilities and ideals. We are here for many reasons, most of them metaphysical, spiritual ones. I was quite inspired by something that anthropologist Sir Edmund Leach wrote in 1977. It is not a definition; it is an idea.

> Social anthropology is not, and should not aim to be, a "science" in the natural science sense. If anything it is a form of art . . . Social anthropologists should not see themselves as seekers after objective truth; their purpose is to gain insight into other people's behavior or, for that matter, into their own. "Insight" may seem a very vague concept but it is one deep understanding which, as critics, we attribute to novelists, composers; it is the difference between fully understanding the nuances of a language and simply knowing the dictionary glosses of the individual words. (Leach 1977, 48)

In sum, it is my estimation that contemporary research and scholarship, especially in the field of ethnomusicology in the United States, is pervaded by a psychological complex that can be loosely conceptualized as a dialectical paranoia. As artists, not only have we largely discarded our intuition in our role as scholars, but we have also chosen to ignore the metaphysical and its extreme potential in being at least a reference block in our research, a philosophy. Perhaps discarding intuition inevitably corresponded to ignoring the metaphysical (here, I am directly influenced by the writing of Benedetto Croce (1952), who defined art as "intuition").[3]

But the real gist of this dialectical paranoia goes even beyond the above contradiction. Academia, with its various aesthetical and political dimensions, has become our religion. All of the characteristics are there. Yet we shun religion and the reason for which it was created, much longer ago than the scientific quest for knowledge superseded religion's social meaning in our society. Religion, humankind's socially organized structure serving various pursuits of the spiritual and metaphysical has been thrown by the wayside—cast away from the very structure it was so instrumental in formulating, molding, and socially renovating. Certainly this was not a historical model of error-proof idealism. But it was certainly socially idealistic, for it chose not to censure the concepts of metaphysical and thus religious inquiry. The idea of learning and acquiring knowledge and developing it was more than a concept. The concepts were only tools to be applied to quite lofty questions, but questions that were based on the intangibles of hope, faith, and morality. We are uncomfortable communicating with each other what it is that we believe and hesitate to be human with the grace and honesty of the believers we scrutinize.

It is at this point that we should perhaps ask whether we should make professions of faith in our role as academics. Should I, at this point, make the rhetorical and professional (as in "to profess") statement, "I believe in Christ?" Should others say they believe in the God of Abraham, of Mohammed, in the Orishas of the Yoruba tradition, the teachings of Buddha, the Great Spirit of the Native American? Or all of the above?

Religion as Art: The Aesthetics of Guadalupe

The case study I will refer to is one I am currently developing, based on a study of La Virgen de Guadalupe (the Virgin Mary of Guadalupe) as related to the arts. The study is part of a larger, ongoing research project focusing on a diversity of religious traditions and their relationships to the arts.

The rationale for conducting interdisciplinary research for this project is an essential factor in its planned framework. As an ethnomusicologist, I have found it increasingly difficult and contradictory to segment musical activity out of the various artistic contexts that I have studied and taught. It is especially in the arts that interdisciplinary work is needed, and especially so in the intensive character of topics such as religion and its relationship to the arts. Illustrative of this interdisciplinary need and growing interest in world religions and their relationship to the arts are the recent World Festivals of Sacred Music in Los Angeles (1999 and 2002). Reflective of this intercultural spirit was the participation of the music directors of various churches, synagogues, and temples. An excerpt from the *Los Angeles*

Times coverage of one of the festivals also reflected the diversification of sacred music in a diverse city:

> A number of religious leaders see their community as a mirror of the city's ethnic diversity and the festival as an opportunity to show that peaceful coexistence is possible. The cross-cultural Buddhist chanting of the Shinshin Temple in Los Angeles melds the voices of the temple's 400 Japanese American members with sacred texts written in Chinese. "The sound becomes effective, more so than the words," says the Rev. Masao Kodani, who oversees the Shinshin community. "Oneness is achieved through the sound." (Rourke 1999)

What has happened here is not so different in concept than what happened in sixteenth-century Mexico, where the indigenous Náhuatl language was adapted to Western-based polyphony sung by Indian choirs in honor of La Virgen de Guadalupe as equated with Tonantzin, the indigenous mother spirit of the Aztecs. The concept of mestizaje in Mexico and Latin America has been developed by a number of Mexican philosophers (e.g., Vasconcelos, Pompa y Pompa), and its place in this study will be an essential link to Mexican perspectives and contemporary views in the United States on multiculturalism.

Toward a Theory for Religion as Art

In his study of the Japanese poetic art of *haiku*, Kenneth Yasuda (1957) conceptualizes three levels of analysis—those of the economic, the scientific, and the aesthetic. Yasuda coincides with many of the aesthetic theories of Croce (1952), who not only defined art as intuition but also critiqued at length the issue of art and morality.

In conceptualizing the art of Our Lady of Guadalupe, we are able to ask some philosophical questions based on Yasuda's framework. First, is the tilma (the Virgin's cape enshrining her image) of Guadalupe socially or otherwise based on economic value?[4] Second, is the belief of Guadalupe based on scientific data or analysis? Third, is there a relationship of the belief in Guadalupe to her artistic presence and quality as related to meaning and experience, and is this meaning and experience the essential factor of the belief system? I propose that the answer to this third question is *yes*.

The concept of truth can easily and rationally be separated from scientific or social fact. Whether the tilma is painted by human hands is not the basis of meaning for belief in Guadalupe, nor are such facts in such a case the basis for the issue of truth in an experiential context.[5] This is certainly neither a recent idea in the history of ideas nor of art criticism. In 1932 the poet T. S. Eliot recognized this paradox by expressing the notion that when philosophical theories enter the realm of art (e.g., poetry), "its truth or falsity in one sense ceases to matter, and its truth in another sense is proved" (248). S. K. Langer also differentiated the interpretation and experience of truth, especially as related to art where factual truth is not artistic truth. "Artistic truth does *not* belong to statements in the poem or their obvious figurative meanings, but to its figures and meanings *as they are used*, its statements *as they are made* . . . in short, to the poem as 'significant form'" (1942, 26).

The "significant form" of Guadalupe does not lie in its factual truth, its physical origin and material analysis, or its financial value. The significance of Guadalupe is a belief, concept, and practice associated with that belief. The *experience and meaning* of devotion to the Virgin denote what believers know as truth—a truth not based on materialist truth but on metaphysical truth.

The art signifying Guadalupe is primarily visual—that of the tilma; but an extended repertoire of art is also closely associated and experienced through various practices, as in the case of musical expression. Hundreds of hymns performed by various types of folk ensembles exist in addition to a rich repertoire of sacred music composed for ecclesiastic purposes (e.g., Hernando Franco's sixteenth-century piece composed as homage to Tonantzin). Additionally, a complete archive of symphonic and chamber works composed during the nineteenth century is currently being catalogued by musicologists in Mexico. In the basilica where the tilma is enshrined, indigenous dance troupes periodically dedicate intricate choreography and music in commemoration of feast days. The mixing of indigenous and Christian concepts continues to characterize the mestizaje of the numerous artistic expressions dedicated to the Virgin.

On another level of theoretical orientation, G. Bachelard has suggested that various contradictions in the history of science represent certain "epistemological breaks" (see Certeau 1971). Michel de Certeau (1971) extends this perspective by suggesting that various contradictions call "permission" into question. Permission can refer to "experiences" or to "event." Certeau posits that "Christianity implies a relationship to the event which inaugurated it." The series of intellectual and historical social forms transpiring since the inaugurative event, that of Christ on earth, have taken shape through "two apparently contradictory characteristics: the will to be *faithful* to the inaugural event; the necessity of being *different* from these beginnings" (142).

La Virgen de Guadalupe and her role in Mexican and world history fit well into the conceptualizations of Bachelard and Certeau. As both an epistemological break and a contradiction to the inaugural event, La Virgen has changed certain aspects of earlier Christian concepts while also maintaining and even reinforcing much of Christianity's basic dogma. Both contradiction and resolution lie in the fact that La Virgen appeared on a hill associated with the indigenous belief and cosmology of the Náhuatl-speaking inhabitants of the Aztec (Mexica) sphere of culture and life in Mexico City (Tenochtitlan). The above-cited equation of Tonantzin represents a dynamic example of a conceptual and cultural mestizaje that would begin to characterize Mexico since the sixteenth century.

Another theoretical shift that might be developed through the proposed study is what I refer to as the verb/icon dichotomy, which to my knowledge has not been formally presented in the related scholarship. It is appropriate to this study to compare the types of belief systems largely (but not solely) based on expressive, artistically conceived icons versus other belief systems largely based on the written word (e.g., the Bible). A good comparative example would be that of fundamentalist Christian movements versus traditional Catholicism, especially as associated with Guadalupe. A strong argument can be made that a major aesthetic/devotional difference exists between the two general categories of "Christians." One group is largely reliant upon the written-word concept of the Bible, literally defined as the "word of God." Icons such as that of Guadalupe are condemned by much of this constituency as idol worship, demonic, and as false gods, due to literal and often dogmatically irresponsible interpretation. One critique of this perspective is that the Bible is largely poetic and thus artistic in form; numerous fundamentalists, however, would argue and resist the "artistic truth" meaning of much of the Bible's allegories and metaphors. Believers of Guadalupe, on the other hand, represent a constituency and philosophy that would support many of the theoretical notions presented above, for example, significant form, experience and meaning as a mode of understanding, theory, and faith, and the will to be faithful to the inaugural event while simultaneously requiring a difference (and thus, resolution) from these beginnings. Dorothea Olkowski-Laetz's position (1990, paraphrasing Steiner 1982) on the contradiction of rhetoric versus art lends itself well to the conceptualizations I present above:

> Prose stresses the already established signifying system, while painting stresses the work of art as a thing. The more it is a thing, the more trouble it has being meaningful within the system of the signifying norm. This is because structuralism has made language the model for understanding all cultural phenomena, even though the structure of painting is not dependent upon the phonemic-morphemic relation, nor upon the rules of syntax. (108)

Thus, notwithstanding the issue of whether Guadalupe is a human painting or not, there is a clear distinction within this verb/icon polarity in terms of experience based on meaning and interpretation. The experiences of Guadalupe devotion versus fundamentalist biblical interpretation do provide profoundly different human acts and practices, both resulting in radically opposing world views, philosophies, and aesthetic/spiritual mentalities. Do they, therefore, represent the same religious belief?

Some basic research questions in conducting work on the issue of religion, morality, and the arts have been raised by some scholars attempting to negotiate the problem. Yasuda (1957) has critiqued at length the question of morality in art and has expressed the viewpoint that many Western critics have eluded the "relationship between an artist's mode of life or sense of artistic morality and his [her] works" (18). He proceeds to remark that "students of art have also tended to feel that the matter lay outside of their area, which is perhaps another instance of the fragment of learning in the West." Although a number of scholars have addressed the issue since the 1950s (Sowande 1972; Ricouer 1991; Loza 1994; Sancho Velásquez 1994), it still remains largely a speculative issue. Champaign (1989) has been critical of what he refers to as the "compartmentalization" of culture concepts and the disciplines in general (e.g., separating religion from other cultural practices, which becomes highly superficial and contradictory in the American Indian context). Susan McClary, who has called for a radical reevaluation and practice of the field of musicology, has unabashedly dismissed "the neat ordering of institutionalized music scholarship, especially as it is practiced in the United States" (1985, 149). McClary has shared with me her personal observations and experience similar to mine on the difficulty in teaching to U.S. student seminar topics addressing music and religion, which unfortunately, perhaps due to U.S. diversity, becomes an over-subjectivated and culturally conflictual context for study. McClary foresees a much more relative and useful approach to research in musicology as a response to what she witnesses as "the rise of positivistic musicology and pseudoscientific music theory, both of which depend upon and reinforce the concept that music is autonomous, unrelated to the turbulence of the outside, social world" (149).

My methodological goal, therefore, includes going even beyond the problem of musicology by incorporating an interdisciplinary approach as described at the outset of this essay. Although ethnomusicology is an interdisciplinary approach combining the techniques of the humanities and the social sciences (more specifically, musicology and ethnology), the field has yet to incorporate much scholarship from the other art disciplines (e.g., art history and criticism, film and television studies, theater, dance, visual and plastic arts, literary studies, and architecture). This research project centering on La Virgen de Guadalupe necessitates such interdisciplinary methods because of the intercultural relationships represented by her and the interactive and diverse means and practices of individuals devoted to her. To many, La Virgen transcends the issues and categories of class, ethnicity, gender, age, ideology, and even religion. As scholars, how do we account for such social possibilities? In my estimation, we cannot rely on preconceived methodologies or theory, especially in the type of study I am proposing here.

The Larger Picture

In this essay it has been my aim to examine two worlds of thought as related to the arts, and to propose a more humanistic, interdisciplinary, and philosophical base for the field of ethnomusicology. Croce's concept of art as the imaging of a superior dimension of our existence permits us to think of the arts as a "supreme" channel to an intuitive level—one higher than the intellectual. This differs radically from Merriam's consideration of the scholar's role as a scientist, not an artist.

Assessing the arts from a unified approach, instead of the separate disciplinary modes of music, dance, visual art, theater, and so on, enables us to comprehend the unity of the arts and artists as a basic catalyst through time and space. In his *Phenomenon of Man* (1965), Pierre Teilhard de Chardin wrote of infinity as both outward and inward, and he recognized evolution as both a physical and metaphysical process; in fact, in his conceptualization of these two planes, Teilhard de Chardin perceived no separation. Only our present perception and stage of evolution limits our abilities to understand on a larger or more prolific level. With time we may proceed to understand more, but as long as we are living the human condition, we will never arrive at a complete understanding of a constantly evolving infinity.

Why do so many artists throughout the world base so much of their work on themes, experiences, meanings, and perceptions (or feelings) pertaining to theologies? If one adapts the ideas of Croce and Teilhard de Chardin to the study of music as an essential element of culture in addition to being infinitely linked to art in general, it is possible to conceptualize a theology of art. Through a plethora of world religions, past and present, humankind has participated in the ingenious act of achieving belief, hope, and faith by creating art—the closest and most illuminating bridge that has existed to Croce's "supremely real," or to what so many have described as the spiritual realm or another dimension. But there are no "other" dimensions. We live the all-encompassing dimension of infinity—one where art has emerged as the one lasting component of this mysterious, yet fulfilling phenomenon.

Notes ————————————————————————————

This chapter has evolved from a paper presented at a UCLA conference on musicology in 1999. Portions of the first section of the chapter have been adapted from a previously published article (Loza 1994).

1. I should point out that Merriam did defend himself on this one. Responding to reviews by Codere, Graf, Hood, Maceda, Nettl, and Nketia (Merriam 1966, 217–30), he pointed out that he had written, "Both groups [anthropologists and musicologists] agree, however, that the ultimate objective is the fusion of the two as an ideal inevitably modified by practical reality." The reviews, however, testify that this was not a consensus ideal. Merriam later proceeds in his defense as follows:

> Thus the point of the book is not to attempt the synthesis of the two approaches—indeed, I am not sure any of us yet knows how—but

rather to clarify one approach in order that the task of synthesis, which is clearly the next step, may possibly, be more readily achieved. (1966, 229)

It is this "task of synthesis" that I have resisted and considered an unnecessary, dialectically constrained ideal.

2. Some might cite the fact that Merriam was a musician. But to me he did not write as an artist.

3. For the reader, I cite the fact that although Croce refers to the concept of image in his references to art, he considers music as a part of this imaging process, or intuition, in that the reproduction of images involves the "apparent transformation of intuitions into physical things" (1979, 36–37). In the case of music, this process involves tonal, aural, physical properties. It is thus that Croce differentiates between the theoretical and the physical. In my estimation, this concept of intuition also refers to the balance of metaphorical (or in Croce's term, "conceptual") knowledge and the various forms of conscience (including Croce's notion of intuitive knowledge), which in his view did not "enjoy the same cognitive status as 'conceptual knowledge,' which operates with 'concrete universals.'" (1979, xxv).

4. Here I refer to the tilma itself, not to the industry that markets innumerable images or representations of it.

5. There have been numerous scientific studies of the tilma, attempting to determine if the image is composed of paint. Here again lies the problem of materialist view versus spiritual possibilities, or the concept of "truth." One view has questioned that even had the image been painted by the hands of an Indian, who are we to say that the act itself was not a miracle? Furthermore, should the scientists prove that the image is composed of paint, does such evidence prove that human hands painted it? My response to this paradox has been that if I were God, the supernatural being, or merely a mystic, I would certainly not create a miracle leaving supernatural substances to capture the dubious faith of my mortal human subjects. In other words, what do the scientists expect to find? If I were God, I would use paint.

References

Cassidy, Harold Gomes. 1962. *The Sciences and the Arts: A New Alliance*. New York: Harper.

Certeau, Michel de. 1971. "How is Christianity Thinkable Today?" *Theology Digest* 19:334–45. Reprinted in *The Postmodern God: A Theological Reader*, ed. Graham Ward, 142–58. Oxford and Malden: Blackwell Publishers.

Champagne, Duane. 1989. *American Indian Societies: Strategies and Conditions of Political and Cultural Survival*. Cultural Survival Report no. 32. Cambridge, Mass.: Cambridge University Press.

Croce, Benedetto. 1979 [1952]. *Guide to Aesthetics (Brevario de estetica)*. Translated by Patrick Romanell. South Bend: Regnery/Gateway Inc.

Eliot, T. S. 1932. *Selected Essays*. New York: Harcourt Brace.

Firth, Rosemary. 1971. "From Wife to Anthropologist." In *Crossing Cultural Boundaries: The Anthropological Experience*, ed. S. T. Kimball and J. B. Watson, 10–32. San Francisco: Chandler Pub. Co.

Herndon, Marcia. 1971. "Analysis: Herding of Sacred Cows?" *Ethnomusicology* 18, no. 2:219–62.

Hood, Mantle. 1957. "Training and Research Methods in Ethnomusicology." *Ethnomusicology Newsletter* 1, no. 11:2–8.

———. 1963. "Music the Unknown." In *Musicology*, ed. F. Harrison, M. Hood, and C. Palisca, 215–326. Englewood Cliffs: Prentice-Hall.

Kolkinski, Mieczyslaw. 1967. "Recent Trends in Ethnomusicology." *Ethnomusicology* 11:1–24.

Langer, S. K. 1942. *Philosophy in a New Key*. Harvard University Press.

Lewis, I. M. 1984. *Religion in Context: Cults and Charisma*. Cambridge: Cambridge University Press.

Lomax, Alan. 1967. *Folk Song Style and Culture*. New Brunswick: Transaction Books.

———. 1971. "Song-Structure and Social Structure." In *Readings in Ethnomusicology*, ed. David P. McAllester, 227–51. New York: Johnson Reprint Corporation.

———. 1974. *Cantometrics: A Method in Musical Anthropology*. Berkeley: University of California Press.

Loza, Steven. 1994. "Fantasmas Enmascarados: Pensamientos Sobre Nuestra Investigación y lo Académico en Etnomusicología." *Heterofonía* 109–110:4–16.

McClary, Susan. 1985. "Afterward." In Jacques Attali, *Noise: The Political Economy of Music*. Minneapolis: University of Minnesota Press.

Merriam, Alan P. 1960. "Ethnomusicology: Discussion and Definition of the Field" *Ethnomusicology* 4:107–14.

———. 1963. "Review of Harrison, Hood, and Palisca." *Musicology*. *Ethnomusicology* 8:179–85.

———. 1964. *The Anthropology of Music*. Evanston: Northwestern University Press.

———. 1966. "A CA Book Review: The Anthropology of Music." *Current Anthropology* 7:217–30.

———. 1974. "Definitions of 'Comparative Musicology' and 'Ethnomusicology': A Historical-Theoretical Perspective." *Ethnomusicology* 21, no. 2:189–204.

Nettl, Bruno. 1964. *Theory and Method in Ethnomusicology*. Glenco: Free Press.

———. 1983. *The Study of Ethnomusicology: Twenty-Nine Issues and Concepts*. Urbana: University of Illinois Press.

———. 1989. "The Ethnomusicologist and Black Music." *Black Music Research Journal* 10, no. 1:1–4. Originally published in *Black Music Research Newsletter* 4.2 (fall 1980): 1–2.

Nketia, J. H. Kwabena. 1990. "Contextual Strategies of Inquiry and Systemization." *Ethnomusicology* 34, no. 1:75–97.

Olkowski-Laetz, Dorothea. 1990. "A Postmodern Language in Art." In *Postmodernism-Philosophy and the Arts*, ed. Hugh J. Silverman, 101–19. New York and London: Routledge, Chapman and Hall, Inc.

Pompa y Pompa, Antonio. 1981. *El Tercer Hombre*. Editorial Libros de México.

Ricouer, Paul. 1989. *A Ricouer Reader*, ed. Mario Valdés. Toronto: University of Toronto Press.

Rourke, Mary. 1999. "What Religious Diversity Sounds Like." *Los Angeles Times*, August 25.

Sancho Velásquez, Angeles. 1994. "Interpreting Metaphors: Cross-Cultural Aesthetics as Hermeneutic Project." In *Selected Reports in Ethnomusicology (Vol. 10): Musical Aesthetics and Multiculturalism in Los Angeles*, ed. Steven Loza, 37–50. Los Angeles: Ethnomusicology Publications, Dept. of Ethnomusicology, University of California, Los Angeles.

Seeger, Charles. 1960. "Semantic, Logical, and Political Considerations Bearing Upon Research in Ethnomusicology." *Ethnomusicology* 5:77–80.

Sowande, Fela. 1972–73. "Le role de la musique dans la société africaine tradition-elle." *La revue musicale* Issue No. 288–89:57–68. Also published in English in 1972 as "The Role of Music in Traditional African Society." In *African Music*, UNESCO, 59–69. Paris: La revue musicale.

Steiner, Wendy. 1981. *The Colors of Rhetoric: Problems in the Relation Between Modern Literature and Painting*. Chicago: University of Chicago Press.

Teilhard de Chardin, Pierre. 1965. *The Phenomenon of Man*. New York: Harper and Row.

Vasconcelos, José. 1997 [1925]. *La Raza Cósmica*. Introduction by Didier T. Jaen. Afterward by Joseba Gabilondo. Baltimore: John Hopkins University Press.

Wimberly, Richard E. 1988. "Prophecy, Eroticism, and Apocalypticism in Popular Music: Prince." *Black Sacred Music* (special issue: *The Theology of American Popular Music*) 3, no. 2:125–32.

Yasuda, Kenneth. 1957. *The Japanese Haiku: Its Essential Nature, History, and Possibilities in English, With Selected Examples*. Rutland: Charles E Tuttle Company.

"Maravilla Americana"

The Virgin of Guadalupe
and the Ideal Spectator

RAY HERNÁNDEZ-DURÁN

Introduction

☞ IN SPRING 2001, THE BBC NEWS REPORTED A STORY INVOLVING AN art exhibition in Santa Fe, New Mexico. The following is an excerpt from that article: "Catholic activists have described the digital collage by Los Angeles artist Alma López as disgusting and insulting and said they want it removed . . . Archbishop Michael Sheehan said the work . . . depicts Mary 'as if she were a tart.'"[1] The work in question, titled *Our Lady*, was a digital image of the artist, wearing a two-piece, floral bikini and surrounded by Marian iconographic elements. The image was included in the exhibition "Cyber Arte: Tradition meets Technology" held at the Museum of International Folk Art in Santa Fe in 2001–2002. As a result of this work's presence in the show, protesters picketed and gathered in a town meeting. A committee was formed by the museum to discuss the incident. The committee members ultimately elected to keep *Our Lady* in the show; however, the exhibition's run was shortened as a result of this decision and the perceived need for a compromise.

As a canonical work that is widely recognized by millions of faithful worldwide, the painting of the Virgin of Guadalupe belongs to the public domain and inevitably experiences duplication as a form of veneration and as a subject of investigation and expression. The conflicted response to López's image, which was evidently inspired by and thus shares superficial formal elements with an original—the devotional image of the Virgin of Guadalupe located in Mexico City—points to a constellation of perceptions and responses that motivate a central question: how can we discuss such a sacred icon in art historical terms, that is, as a work of art with a definable iconographical lineage and a social biography, given its allegedly divine and spontaneous origin?

This question raises a number of issues regarding the complex network formed by artist, patron, work, spectator, site of display, and reception. The latter factor, reception, engages two important elements in the perception of an image—interpretation and meaning—elements that tend to be historically and culturally specific, and thus diachronically protean.[2] The act of interpretation—how a work of art is actively perceived and understood—varies from one region to another, from one class of viewer to another, and shifts, furthermore, over time. The hermeneutic act, not surprisingly, defines modern art historical practice, which is based on the deciphering of meaning via formal and iconographical analysis, as well as the historical, cultural, and social contextualization of a work or a body of works. The content of art history is thus not actually anchored solely to objects or images, or even to reproductions of privileged examples, per se, but to texts, which themselves are interpretations of interpretations, forming a concatenation of verbal and written responses to images and objects. Our understanding of works of art, especially those that predate our contemporary setting by significant amounts of time and whose cultural-viewing contexts are equally as distant, is based on how selected works have been experienced, on one hand, and qualified in writing by experts and various authority figures on the other. Such texts can take a number of forms; for example, mediating performances (such as sermons and plays), chronicles (such as historical accounts or journals), literary works (such as poetry), as well as more recent "objective," methodologically structured, academic analyses. What is said about art objects thus changes over time, reflecting shifts in the idea of art, its meaning, and the language that names and explains it.

It is important to understand that a work of art exists on various levels beyond the purely material or visual; a work of art takes form in our consciousness based on information accumulated over time from various sources. Texts—written and verbal—constitute a significant part of our understanding of any given image-object. Therefore, any attempt to map the development of our knowledge of an art object should take such documents and practices into account. With this perspective in mind,

I will look at a number of texts that address the image of the Virgin of Guadalupe to emphasize two primary things: one, that the manner in which the image has been qualified textually has varied due to contextual and epistemological shifts and practices and, two, that in spite of historical developments (such as the emergence of modern art historical practice), the image continues to be a multivalent symbol that resists a solely modern mode of art historical qualification. As such, it can be viewed as a powerful cipher, which draws attention precisely for its ability to draw empathy and express identity, thus provoking intense reactions.

Archaic Reception: The Virgin of Guadalupe in Early Colonial Texts

The question of how knowledge and familiarity with the image of the Virgin of Guadalupe has been constructed textually can be addressed in preliminary form by considering a select number of texts from Mexico dating from the sixteenth century onward. The earliest textual reference to the Virgin can be found in early colonial documents, such as *Relación primitiva* and *Nican mopohua*, dated 1531–33 and 1552–60, respectively.[3] These early texts were written in Classical Náhuatl and in Castilian translation, and describe, in narrative form, the sequence of events surrounding the apparitions of the Virgin. References to the image are embedded within the narrative as one of various elements that, like a formula, serve as points of emplotment in the story, recreating the events for the reader and verifying the apparition in the process. An excerpt from the earlier source reads: "Truly, the same image of the child Queen was miraculously painted on this poor man's mantle, where it is placed as a beacon for the entire universe."[4] Although a clear reference is made to the presence of an image on the mantle and to the act of painting, the reader is not presented with an exact description of the image itself.[5] Lacking any prior experience with the image, the unfamiliar reader would have no idea what it looks like—that familiarity is presumed. Shortly after these works were written, the creole intellectual, Carlos Sigüenza y Góngora, wrote the poem *Primavera indiana*, published in 1662. Praising the wonders of the Americas in a literary form drawn from classical models, he listed the marvelous attributes of his native soil, high among these being the Virgin's privileging of his homeland through her apparition and the presence of her cult shrine north of Mexico City. References to the image consist of fictive dialogue and comments the Virgin may have uttered to Juan Diego, such as the following: "I am Mary, humble mother of the omnipotent God, sovereign virgin, torch whose brilliant light illuminates humanity's hope."[6] Although in this phrase there is a clear reference to vision via light and illumination, the image's exact appearance still remains a mystery. Other colonial texts, such as *La estrella del norte de México*, by Father Francisco de Florencia from 1688, similarly acknowledges the presence of the image as he recounts the unfolding of events surrounding the appearance. In this text, providing an exact description of the image is clearly secondary to the careful emphasis of the pivotal episodes structuring the story. During this earlier American historical period, textual references to an image never focus on the image independently of the narrative in which it is embedded. It is not isolated or extracted from its narrative matrix, described in detail, or discussed as an object. It is acknowledged as one miraculous element that proves the divine status of the apparition and the special significance of that apparition to the Americas. This approach to the image recalls the ideas of scholars such as Hans Belting and David Freedberg, who have discussed the symbolic power of images throughout history and the pivotal epistemological shifts that occurred in traditional perceptions of sacred images following the Protestant Reformation in sixteenth-century Europe.[7]

A common concern, in spite of regional differences, dealt with the status of figural images within the church space and its rituals, specifically in relation to the spectator and his/her perception of and response to the painted and/or sculpted figure. Church officials expressed concern that worshipers were confusing the constructed image with the actual sacred entity, a misperception that suggested idolatry, a sin according to Christian dogma. As a result of various leaders' remarks and activities, numerous religious works of art were destroyed. This response motivated the gradual removal of images in Protestant religious practice and an intensified focus on scripture, that is, the word of God. In the southern Catholic countries, the church and its followers responded by arguing for the continued use of images, in a movement known as the Counter-Reformation. Two outcomes of this reaction included a series of justifications for the presence of imagery in religious settings and an augmentation in the production of religious images and their incorporation into church ceremonial practice. In the mid- to late sixteenth century, ecclesiastics gathered in a series of sessions commonly known as the Council of Trent, where this matter was deliberated.[8] A set of edicts, called the Tridentine Edicts, which addressed the nature of images and their utility, was drafted at this council and publicized in 1563. These edicts were, in turn, used to determine a codified set of criteria for the representation of religious iconography and disseminated in the form of painting treatises.[9] Artists were required to stress the mnemonic and didactic functions of religious images, which had to be easily legible and had to glorify the sacred figures represented. An argument in defense of the continued use of images was that they reminded the faithful viewer of the sacred referent; thus, prayers directed to the image were believed to be transmitted directly to the holy original and not to the representation itself. What we see at this moment in history is an epistemological shift in the Western perception of the religious image, which spilled over into the realm of secular works as well, a transition from the perception of the devotional image as an actual sacred presence to the recognition of its status as a manmade object, a representation, and thus, artifice.

This change in perception and practice possessed a slightly different valence in the Counter-Reformation Catholic regions where sacred images continued to retain a special significance at all societal levels and, later, to developing national, political identities. In the Americas, as in Europe, this shift was not monolithic or uniform. Outside of a presumably enlightened, elite minority, the mass population continued to preserve more traditional ideas and practices, especially in the realm of devotional images. Thus, we see the coexistence of a premodern perception alongside the modern. In Mexico City, for instance, even among progressive, literate elites, this movement toward a modern approach in the reception of religious images made its mark on subsequent readings of the Virgin image; however, this did not mean that elites had abandoned their faith. If not significantly impacting the perception of the Guadalupe image, this shift yielded some curious responses, which appear to bridge supposedly incommensurable receptions.

The presence of recorded sermons that address such images engages the issue of the context in which the image was experienced, that is, its display site, the subject of the painting, and its audience(s). In-situ works, such as religious images framed by larger altarpieces in church interiors, are viewed differently than when extracted from such contextualizing frames and placed in a secular museum space. In the church, those images were/are impacted by their immediate environment, in terms of lighting, sound, smell, location, surrounding images, the accumulation of detritus (dust, candle smoke, etc.) on the picture surface, intermittent and regulated viewing, and the mental or emotional state of the spectator when viewing takes place. As the embodiment of a sacred presence, such factors, some of which actually endanger the object's physical integrity, are irrelevant, as Krysztof Pomian suggests.[10] In the museum setting, where viewing rituals and the perception of the painting as an object with historical and physical values are different, the preservation of the object becomes of utmost import. The act of preservation itself can be viewed as an interpretive act in the ideas it conveys about the object's historical and cultural value, and in its intended appearance and meaning as the object is cleaned, and thus altered, installed, exhibited, stored, and described in object labels or catalogues.[11]

This reality of the modern work of art brings up the issue of the artist's intention and the image's original objective. Were such works meant to experience a church environment in perpetuity, which we today would, in many cases, consider to be problematic in terms of viewing and preservation? In those original sites, furthermore, the ideal spectator would have been an individual who believed religious dogma and who approached the image with faith, passion, and need, and not necessarily an interest in or awareness of (art) history or the processes of art making. In the museum setting, how does a nonbelieving, modern consciousness determine that viewing experience? David Carrier addresses the same question when he states:

> Surely Titian envisaged the ideal spectator of his Assumption as a believer who saw the Holy Virgin rising upwards . . . This much could have been seen only by an unusually erudite contemporary of the artist. Even so, that person, like his less erudite contemporaries but unlike most art historians, who are nonbelievers, would have seen moving sacred scenes, whereas most of us see a complex grouping of artworks illustrating beliefs we cannot share. The "ideal spectator" of the work does not simply view the Assumption aesthetically, but also sees it as a sacred work. But how is that possible for a nonbeliever?[12]

This question emphasizes the disjuncture in the viewing of a religious image between the recognition of and belief in the sacred aspect of an image's subject versus its physical presence as a manmade object in time, and in particular, the gradual layering, even displacement, of the former by the latter.

Early American Modernity:
Miguel Cabrera's *Maravilla Americana*

Illustrative of a stage in this gradual conceptual transition as it appears to have occurred in the Americas was a pivotal event that took place in mid-eighteenth-century Mexico City. The issue of physical and mnemonic preservation leads us to a specific novohispanic document. The text in question, titled "*Maravilla americana, y conjunto de raras maravillas, observadas con la dirección de las reglas de el arte de la pintura en la prodigiosa imagen de Nuestra Sra. de Guadalupe de México,*" was written by the novohispanic painter Miguel Cabrera and published in 1756 by the press at the Real y Mas Antiguo Colegio de San Ildefonso in Mexico City.[13] In the foreword to the text, "The Motive for this Inscription," Cabrera recounts how this project took form. According to the author, on October 22, 1750, following the installation of a new administrative directorate at the Collegiate of the Sanctuary of Our Lady of Guadalupe, the most prestigious painters in Mexico City were invited to participate in the evaluation of the image of the Virgin of Guadalupe to determine, through close examination of its material and representational properties, the image's rare (i.e., divine) origin and whether or not it could have been the product of human manufacture. This concern about proving the image's divine origin was motivated, in part, by political and economic interests, such as the concurrent expansion of the sanctuary complex, an interest in further promoting Marian cult worship, and, possibly, as has been generally recognized, a desire to augment this image's status as a creole proto-national symbol. The selected artists gathered at the sanctuary on April 30, 1751, were permitted to carefully review the image without its protective glass covering. Observations and conclusions were then recorded by Cabrera in narrative form and submitted for approval before they were sent for publication.

Cabrera's testimony is divided into eight paragraphs; each section addresses a different aspect of the image in question. For example, the introductory sections consider the local climate and the physical components of the canvas upon which the image is painted. The material is identified as *ayate*, from the Náhuatl *ayatl*, a plant fiber obtained from the native succulent called maguey. The thick fiber produces a rough textile that imbues any image applied to its face with a textured, uneven surface, while its organic nature renders it susceptible to environmental corrosion, especially in the humid, saline, lacustrine setting that surrounded Mexico City at that time. Cabrera noted the image's smooth surface and pristine condition, in spite of the vulgar material and the damaging atmosphere, attributing its preserved quality to its miraculous nature. He wrote that "we should attribute this rare preservation to special privilege, which it enjoys due to the presence of this Sacred Image."[14] To the observation of the image's resistance to its toxic natural environment, he added the innumerable occasions when the image had been removed from its vitrine and made physically accessible to countless worshippers. He stated the following: "The same fragile threads have resisted the damage which all painted canvases, and other cult objects, suffer when touched, and have touched the Sacred Image on the occasions when the vitrine is opened; although this does not occur on a daily basis, it must have taken place, at the very least, numerous times in over 200 years."[15] In response to the image's unsullied appearance, he concluded that "this canvas, and its celestial painting, appears to be exempt from the common laws of nature."[16] The narrative continues in this manner, by focusing on the image's composition and, most interestingly, the quality of the drawing. Cabrera's commentary demonstrates clear academic criteria, not surprisingly, given his concurrent interest in founding the first academy of art in New Spain. In his comments, he does not provide an accurate description of the figure but qualifies each of the pictorial elements individually, utilizing such general terms as symmetry, outline, and proportion, with special interest on the figure's construction. Cabrera estimated the measurement of the body of the Virgin as consisting of $8^2/_3$ heads in length, attributing her delicate stature to the approximate age of the representation as that of a fourteen- or fifteen-year-old girl. In conjunction with his contemporary José de Ibarra, another participant, Cabrera referenced artists from previous historical and cultural periods, such as Apelles, Phidias, Lyssipus, Juan de Arfe, Gaspar Becerra, and Albrecht Dürer, as well as earlier colonial painters of renown, such as Baltasar de Echave, Sebastián López de Arteaga, Luis and José Juárez, Alonzo Vázquez, and Juan Correa, as a way to contrast their work with the image, emphasizing its inimitable character and uniqueness in the incapacity of other artists to reproduce it, or as "proof that it is so unique and strange that it is not an invention of human artifice but of the All Powerful."[17] This process, although intending to resist historicizing the image, inevitably placed it as one link in a longer painting tradition, beginning in the ancient classical world through recent history.

Although a self-professed "imperfect" print copy by Cabrera is included with the text as an illustration, no part of this document provides an exact description of the image of the Virgin of Guadalupe, since any successful attempt at capturing its appearance, whether textual or visual, would be copying it. The replication of the icon would undermine the argument that it was an impossibility given its alleged divine origin and sacred status. The most fascinating aspect of this text is the participants' attempt at proving divine status, an otherwise ineffable, indefinable quality, by examining the image's physical-visual properties via the application of academic criteria and by making historical references, thus locating the holy image in an identifiable pictorial tradition. The argument over this image's ontological status embodies a conceptual interstice where a pre-modern conception of the image as an incarnation of a sacred presence, which exists outside of the temporal continuum, and the modern perception of such a construct as consisting of the very same qualities identifying manmade painted images, which can be historically and culturally specified, are located. The provocative nature of this eighteenth-century exposition—the integration of mutually exclusive ideas and forms normally identifying distinct historical periods and shifts in the development of Western thought—can be seen as representing one of the fundamental qualities of the American context. It represents an intermediary space, within the realm of early American visual culture, which has been normally configured as a transitional moment linking a linear shift from pre-modern to modern perceptions of the image-object.

In Cabrera's preliminary statements, we find various references to the commensurability of text and image, manifesting an early recognition of the interpretive nature of text in relation to a pictorial source. Preceding Miguel Cabrera's foreword to the text, there are two introductory sections that present the approval and acknowledgment of this report by two senior ecclesiastic officials. In the *Aprobación*, Dr. Joseph Gonzáles del Pinal, Canonical Magistrate of the Insigne y Real Colegiata de Nuestra Señora de Guadalupe, added that, "the painting which he [Cabrera] addresses in his paper is greater still, since it is not so dissimilar to call painting what is written, since his Divine Majesty, in order to console his elected few in their tribulations, assures them that he has them written down—*Ecce in manibus meis descripti te* . . . (this means to be painted)—*de pinti*—I could very well say that when his (i.e., Cabrera's) pen's description is clear, his painting is more alive or clearer still."[18] In the conclusion to this section, Gonzáles del Pinal references a well known Spanish treatise of the time, providing another analogy between writing and the painted image. He wrote: "Give this honor to the author so he can receive the accolades that Don Antonio Palomino, painter to our King and Lord, Philip V, offers to other artistic talents; in volume one of his authoritative *Museo Pictórico*, he declares that painting is not only a universal language, but also angelic, since angels, simply at a glance, communicate ideas one to another, just as painting manifests, at a glance, what would waste many pages in a book to explain."[19] Gonzáles del Pinal's focus appears to be on the painted image as the primary vehicle for meaning, aspects of which are referenced and clarified by writing, by relation, and by verbal articulation. In contrast to such statements, the second preliminary text by the Jesuit Father Francisco Xavier Lazcano, Prefect of the Congregation of la Purísima at the College of Saints Peter and Paul in Mexico City, presents the text as the principal vehicle for understanding an image. He wrote: "the celebrated painter, Don Miguel de Cabrera, sweetly enticed my fantasy and sublimated all of my admiration concerning the brush transformed into pen, and the friendliest object of vision, exalted to the most harmonious concept of understanding . . . we can truly say that Don Miguel Cabrera has placed finely focused lenses before our eyes."[20] Such statements, which qualify the relationship between image and text, clearly privilege the interpretation of the image, that is, its meaning, not the visible pictorial elements.

Cabrera does not attempt to provide a mimetically exact description of his pictorial subject. Although the primary intention did not include defining style as a historical-cultural marker or creating an exact textual parallel to the image's formal aspect, Cabrera does just that in his discussion. Given the image's status as an integral element in the larger novohispanic pictorial field, an authoritative voice had to be brought in to articulate the expertise of painters in order to corroborate what exactly about the image's formal qualities could be interpreted as anomalous and inexplicable, thus proving its wondrous nature. The only method to accomplish this task was to work with the image's physical attributes as a painting that exists in time and space. The text provided a site for the merging of the sacred and miraculous into a modern, increasingly secular environment. In *Maravilla americana*, an aspect of modern art historical and museum practice confronted the presence of what would become configured in the modern period as an archaic form of expression with roots in "Old World" medieval practice.

Modern Reception: The Virgin and Colonial Art History in the Nineteenth Century

In nineteenth-century, postindependence Mexico, the conflict between an increasingly secular context and a continuing faith in the mystical among the Mexican populace is clearly evidenced, specifically in relation to the Virgin of Guadalupe, in its treatment, or rather lack of treatment, in the first book devoted to the history of painting in Mexico. As an image that allegedly surfaced in the sixteenth century, the Guadalupana, historically and stylistically, belongs to the early colonial period of Mexican history. Although we note the emergence of a colonial art history by the mid-nineteenth century, the Virgin image curiously remains absent from this development. It is not addressed in the same manner as other religious images, representing what was then termed the "old school" of Mexican painting. The text that serves as an ideal next step after Cabrera's contribution is the first Mexican publication devoted to colonial painting from an art historical perspective. The text in question is titled *Diálogo de la historia de la pintura en México*, written by the president of the Academy of San Carlos, don José Bernardo Couto, in 1862 but published posthumously in 1872.[21]

Responding to a presidential decree requesting the creation of a gallery of paintings by national masters, Couto began to collect what he judged to be the finest examples of painting from the old Mexican school. These included works from existing monasteries and churches, as well as from collections of confiscated properties warehoused in closed convents under the government's jurisdiction. The first version of the old school Mexican painting gallery was open to the public by 1857. The collection was then augmented and reinstalled in 1861. Although there is no known record documenting the content and/or configuration of the initial installation of colonial painting in the academy, reviews of the display, published in local newspapers, provide the names of some of the painters who were represented. These include: Sebastián López de Arteaga, Baltasar de Echave (Orio?), Luis and José Juárez, Miguel Cabrera, and Juan Rodríguez Juárez.[22] Given space restrictions in the academy building and the single space devoted to colonial painting at that time, not all works in the academy's holdings could be exhibited; thus, an extremely edited version was displayed in light of both spatial constraints and the formative status of the collection.[23] The "best" paintings appear to have been out of the academy's reach in 1861, yielding a gallery installation with huge representative lacunae. In selecting the works to be installed, the academy president presumably looked for classical qualities in viceregal works—naturalism, decorum, correct drawing, chiaroscuro, perspective, anatomical accuracy—characteristics that would imply a commensurability between the older material's formal elements and the rules propagated by the Academy of San Carlos in the mid-nineteenth century.[24] Although Couto included a few secular paintings, such as the self-portrait by Juan Rodríguez Juárez, the exhibited body of works displayed an evident tendency toward the religious.

In 1862, Couto began writing a text, which may have drawn inspiration from the later, expanded version of that initial gallery display. The narrative begins with Couto and his cousin José Joaquín Pesado entering the galleries in the Academy of San Carlos as they are being reinstalled one unidentified morning in the final months of 1860. In the galleries, they encounter Pelegrín Clavé, the Catalán director of painting.[25] Clavé takes the opportunity to return a document to Couto, which lists the names of old school Mexican painters, as well as the titles and dates of some identified and/or attributed canvases.[26] Since all three men are gathered in the gallery, Pesado suggests using the inventory as a guide to the installation that is in the process of being hanged, given that many of the artists noted on the list are also represented by those works.[27] At the very beginning of the narrative, the speakers set the stage for the works to be discussed. It is Pesado, the first person to speak, who, in his introductory comments, identifies colonial painters as *maestros nacionales* and colonial painting as *la antigua escuela mexicana*.[28] He continues by stating the three primary criteria for inclusion in this collection: (1) that works had to be by national masters of great renown, (2) these works were gathered in order to preserve their memory, and (3) to provide models for academy students.[29] In other words, important factors included a painter's reputation, determined by a substantial and/or identified oeuvre, the perception of novohispanic artists as already belonging to some geographical idea of nation, an interest in rescue and preservation, and a projected didactic function.[30] Pesado lists the following criteria that, according to his conservative, academic opinion, qualified a true work of art: "correct" drawing, chiaroscuro, perspective, and a taste for "beauty" and "grace." To this, Clavé added that most important for an artist were regularity and beauty, and that "deformed" paintings were repugnant (i.e., an anti-aesthetic from the academic perspective, which I believe may have also been a veiled critique of colonial Baroque painting, in addition to its reference to prehispanic painting).

In the rest of the text, Couto reaffirms the emerging national-historical configuration—prehispanic, colonial, and modern—by describing the character of colonial art and culture as an intermediary stage between the pre-contact cultures and his current mise-en-scène. The modernity of his interpretation lies in his perception of distinct historical periods as empty categories to be filled and defined by specific artifacts, followed by an explanation in narrative form. The curatorial process entailed gathering exemplars from material culture, spatially arranging these selected objects in a designated display site, and establishing a new coherence for the exhibited corpus by interpreting the material in didactic texts generated by connoisseurs or "experts." Couto's dialogue could not have been possible without an actual collection of objects that could serve as a reference point for the text's subject matter.[31] Given the text's relative permanence and facile dissemination, it experienced a greater circulation and longevity than the installation, which permitted its status as a literary exemplar. This process corroborates current theories regarding the origins of canon formation, which suggest that, "a canon is not made up of the actual objects but only of representations of those objects . . . art historical canons, as constituted by a set of predetermined, isolated images of 'great works' reproduced or in a series of more complex institutional replicas . . . are thus, like writing, supplemental and secondary."[32]

These observations lead me to believe that Couto was able to construct, in the text, an ideal version of the colonial painting collection and its most effective presentation in the face of noted limitations.[33] Although Couto was able to present what he judged to be the ideal colonial painting collection by referring to works that were still in-situ at the time of the text's writing, he did not include or reference the image of the Virgin of Guadalupe. Couto mentions Miguel Cabrera and *Maravilla americana*; however, he does not describe or make any detailed references to the painting of the Virgin of Guadalupe as he does with other colonial religious images, such as those by Cabrera's hand and others.[34] The absence of the Guadalupe painting is glaring, given its widespread, popular recognition in the Americas, as well as its importance to national identity in New Spain and, later, Mexico. Was it the image's divine status that impeded its inclusion in a historical discussion of national masters? It is plausible to suggest that he omitted placing the miraculous image within the same context as other paintings in the dialogue, which were recognized as manmade artifice, given its permanent site of display (the academy would never acquire it) and as an expression of his own faith and political concerns, that is, to avoid conflicting with the narrative recounting its origin and character. In other words, the Guadalupe image was eternal, universal, and unique and could not be viewed in relation to either other mundane works of art nor the museum-based national-historical narrative that was taking form at that time. It could be read only in relation to its founding myth and on its own terms. The exclusion of that particular religious image, whether executed by human hands or not, from such a groundbreaking text on Mexican painting indicates the influence of current cultural politics and of the continued presence of faith among Mexican elites, in spite of the more secular context surrounding them. It is this same perception of the Guadalupe icon, as removed from the mundane and untouchable, in spite of its clear physical qualities that informs more current responses to its interpretation in contemporary works of art and in art historical analyses.

Concluding Remarks

Images in and of themselves are incapable of holding meaning. Their meaning, tied to external cultural conventions and related symbolic systems, is ultimately generated by viewers at the time of observation and contemplation. Although the subject and composition of art objects, both two and three dimensional, derives from an artist's understanding and manipulation of preexisting signs, and thus have a specific value to the author, this value may or may not be recognized or shared by others. Without the author's mediation, meaning is ultimately read into works of art and/or constructed by the spectator at the moment of viewing. Since each individual is unique and has a distinct and changing understanding of signs based on their sociocultural identity and experience, the interpretive act will vary. An image, therefore, may signify on many levels at any given moment in time. Adding to the complexity of the reception of such constructions, cultural contexts and conventions change, impacting the reception of images in turn. Recognition of the protean nature of reception suggests that there has to be room for this protean quality in the study of images. The concept of the "ideal spectator," as proposed by Carrier, consequently, needs to be refined to more accurately capture or reflect the changing viewing contexts that determine the meaning ascribed to images. As former University of Chicago medieval art historian, Michael Camille stated: "to ask these questions is to seek meaning in artistic production and point of origin, which is much less important than plotting those meanings constituted outside the artist's power."[35] Perhaps a distinction between "original" or "primary" spectators and "secondary" spectators would provide a more functional approach to establishing and understanding the multiplicity of viewers of an image and their consequent interpretations.

The issue of audience is quite significant. How can the quotation of and/or reference to a work of art by artists and art historians be studied, especially when such appropriations or interpretations may yield negative responses, even censure and the withdrawal of financial support? How should artists and scholars negotiate an image's larger significance to nonacademic communities? Typically, it is precisely an image's symbolic charge that motivates its appropriation and manipulation. However, what are the political ramifications of such actions? Alma López's work is not an image of the Virgin of Guadalupe, per se; that much is evident. The artist appropriated certain compositional elements associated with the virgin image, in order to make a statement concerning gender and politics in contemporary U.S. society. Those elements appear to have been enough to elicit a strong reaction from individuals who continue to feel the original image's impact, even in reinterpreted or veiled references. The image of the Guadalupana, to her followers, most of whom, curiously, know not the original but copies, is undeniably of divine origin, and thus untouchable. Responses to such works and the events surrounding them, such as the news articles that reported the protests in Santa Fe, add to the accumulated knowledge of the Virgin, just as earlier texts, sermons, and folkloric anecdotes have done. Significance and meaning aren't erased but continue and are augmented by these added evaluations. The image of the Virgin of Guadalupe, as it always has, signifies on various levels—culturally, politically, as well as religiously. In conclusion, I suggest that recent responses should be accepted as current interpretations of a still potent image in our culture, an image that elicits archaic forms of reception among many viewers, demonstrating that in our contemporary media-inundated, increasingly cosmopolitan societies, there are no ideal spectators, but simply spectators.

Notes

1. BBC News, online edition, April 5, 2001, Americas section, http://news.bbc.co.uk/2/hi/entertainment/1261720.stm (accessed January 16, 2009).
2. Michael Camille described the outcome of a diachronic investigation, such as the one proposed in this paper. His statement, therefore, can effectively serve as a thesis. He stated that, "Charting the changes an image undergoes in being viewed and used in different contexts will challenge the idea that subjectivity is embedded only in the artist and instead will locate meaning in the various audiences of the image up to and including ourselves." See Michael Camille, "The Abject Gaze and the Homosexual Body: Flandrin's Figure d'Etude," in *Gay and Lesbian Studies in Art History*, ed. Whitney Davis (New York: Harrington Park Press, 1994), 162–63.
3. More recent editions of these early texts were published in 1999 in an anthology that gathers all extant documents related to the apparition and to subsequent discussions regarding her status and significance. See Ernesto de la Torre Villar and Ramiro Navarro de Anda, *Testimonios Históricos Guadalupanos*, 2nd ed. (Mexico City: Fondo de Cultura Económica, 1999).
4. Ibid., 25, in "Relación primitiva."
5. There are different kinds of interpretations of an image that can be viewed as ranging from point-by-point verbal descriptions of the work's appearance— called *ekphrasis*, which allows someone to recreate in his/her mind an image of the work without ever having seen it—to more subjective interpretations of the meaning of the pictorial elements in an image, elements normally figurative and referencing some kind of external textual or cultural source.
6. Torre Villar and Navarro de Anda, *Testimonios*, 349, "Primavera indiana" (1662).
7. See Hans Belting, *Likeness and Image: A History of the Image before the Era of Art*, Trans. Edmund Jephcott (Chicago: The University of Chicago Press, 1994); and David Freedberg, *The Power of Images: Studies in the History and Theory of Response* (Chicago: University of Chicago Press, 1989).
8. For a more thorough historical discussion of idolatry and iconoclasm, see Freedberg, *Power of Images*, 378–428.
9. In Spain, the most significant painting treatises were produced by Vicente Carducho, Francisco Pacheco, and Antonio Palomino. Their ideas, in turn, circulated in the Americas where they impacted art production. See Jonathan Brown, *Images and Ideas in Seventeenth-Century Spanish Painting* (Princeton: Princeton University Press, 1978).

10. Krzysztof Pomian distinguishes the ontological status of the image in sacred and secular spaces by focusing on the nature of time in each context. In the first, time is eternal and the image is an actual sacred presence; consequently, the preservation of the material of the image is insignificant. In the latter, where time is terrestrial, the image is recognized as a manmade object, motivating historical and stylistic awareness and the need for preservation. See Krzysztof Pomian, "Le Musée et le Temps," in *Curiosité: Études d'histoire de l'art en l'honneur d'Antoine Schnapper*, ed. Olivier Bonfait et al. (Paris: Flammarion, 1998), 431–47.

11. See David Carrier, "Chapter one: Preservation as Interpretation," in *Principles of Art History Writing*, 4th ed. (University Park: Pennsylvania State University Press, 1997), 13–26.

12. Ibid., 21.

13. Torre Villar and Navarro de Anda, *Testimonios*, 494–528; see also Miguel Cabrera, *Maravilla americana*, Vol. 3, Serie Documentalia Poblana (Puebla: Editorial Nuestra República, 1998 [1756]).

14. Cabrera, *Maravilla americana*, 25. In the original: *debemos atribuir esta rara conservación a especial privilegio, que goza por estar pintada en él la Sagrada Imagen.* English translation mine.

15. Ibid., 25. In the original: *El mismo fragil hilo ha resistido a los embates, que padece todo el Lienzo en las innumerables Pinturas, y otras alhajas piadosas, que se tocan, y han tocado a la Sagrada Imagen en las ocasiones, que se abre la vidriera: que aunque esto no se executa todos los dias; no puede menos, que aver sido muchas al cabo de mas de docientos años.* English translation mine.

16. Ibid., 26. In the original: *parecer essento este Lienzo, y su celestial Pintura de las comunes leyes de la naturaleza.* English translation mine.

17. Ibid., 33–34. In the original: *prueba, de que es tan unica, y tan estraña, que no es invencion de humano Artifice, sino de el Todopoderoso.* English translation mine.

18. Ibid., 13–14. In the original: *pero la pintura mayor es, la que oy nos hace en su papel: que no es muy desemejante llamar pintura a lo que se escribe; pues si quando la Magestad Divina, para consolar en las tribulaciones a sus escogidos, les asegura tenerlos escritos: Ecce in manibus meis descripti te: segun la version de los Setenta, es estar pintados: de pinxi: bien puedo decir que quando aora tan clara la descripcion con su pluma, es quando mas al vivo nos la pinta.* English translation mine.

19. Ibid., 15. In the original: *Hazele este digno a su Author de que logre de los elogios, que a otros peritos de el arte da Don Antonio Palomino, Pintor que fue de Camara de Nro. Rey, y Señor, Don Phelipe V: en el tomo I. De su doctisimo Museo Pictorico declara, que no solo es la pintura universal idioma, sino lenguage Angelico, pues si los Angeles con una vista manifiestan los conceptos unos a otros, la Pintura manifiesta luego a el punto lo que gastara muchas ojas un libro para explicarlo.* English translation mine.

20. Ibid., 17–18. In the original: *el celebrado Pintor D. Miguel de Cabrera, lisongeó dulcemente mi fantascia, y sublimo toda mi admiracion respectando al Pincel transformado en pluma, y al amabilissimo objeto de la vista, exaltado al mas harmonioso concepto del entendimiento . . . verdaderamente podemos affirmar, que D. Miguel Cabrera ha puesto en nuestros ojos unos bien graduados cristales.* English translation mine.

21. We must make brief note of an article by Dr. Rafael Lucio, which immediately preceded Couto's project. Lucio's article was first published in *Boletín de la*

Sociedad Mexicana Geográfica y Estadística (Mexico City, 1863). The text was later published as *Reseña histórica de la pintura mexicana en los siglos XVII y XVIII* (Mexico City: J. Abadiano, 1864). Lucio was a collector of viceregal paintings who traveled around Mexico studying works of art located in different churches and other collections. He compiled a list of artist's names that was limited to those on canvases that had been signed. Comments in his text concerning colonial painting were based on his personal observations, and thus illustrate a lack of knowledge and personal biases. His publication lacked a historical or narrative component; the main body of his text consists primarily of an inventory of artist's names and known work titles. The nature of Lucio's article, composed of a dispersed, fragmented, and/or unrelated body of objects presented in an uncritical, nonhistorical, decontextualized format, highlights what would be Couto's innovative treatment of the same material. The earliest postindependence publication, however, known to treat the subject of colonial art was written by the Italian traveler J. C. Beltrami, who published a travelogue of his visit to Mexico titled, *Le Mexique* (Paris 1830).

22. See "La pintura mexicana," *El Monitor* year XII, number 3,444, (February 1, 1857), 4.

23. An inventory dated 1862, the year in which Couto wrote his dialogue, indicates a total of 105 paintings in the academy collection. See Eduardo Báez Macías, *Archivo de la Antigua Academia de San Carlos* (Mexico City: Universidad Nacional Autónoma de México, 1976), doc. 6541.

24. Interestingly, many of the academic qualities deemed as comprising an acceptable work of art were the exact same elements that Cabrera saw in the image of the Virgin of Guadalupe, further motivating the question of why it was omitted from Couto's text.

25. Since we know that Couto began collecting numerous paintings from various churches and monasteries in 1855, five years before this account allegedly takes place, we can assume one of two things: first, that not all of the works acquired from 1855 to 1857 were exhibited due to spatial limitations, indicating that the reinstallation in the dialogue describes a rotation of works or the probable addition of such in an expanded space, or, second, that the probable addition of works may have included, by this time, examples drawn from the collection of confiscated paintings warehoused in the former convent of La Encarnación.

26. I wonder if the inventory cited in this section may actually be a reference to the list of artists and works originally gathered by Rafael Lucio. Lucio's directory of artists was the first known collection of that sort at the time. It is not improbable that Lucio might have shared his work with Couto. If the list Couto refers to is Lucio's, it could have been an early version that may have circulated within Mexico City's intellectual circles, before its publication in 1863, then again in 1864. See Lucio, *Reseña histórica*.

27. It is unclear whether this conversation actually occurred, although it is suspected that Couto may have visited the galleries on various occasions with the other two, either together or on separate occasions. It is probable that Couto did participate in conversations with Pesado, Clavé, and perhaps even others, and later reviewed notes, cutting and pasting sections as he constructed his narrative, following a personal vision accommodated to traditional dialogic rules.

28. See José Bernardo Couto, *Diálogo sobre la historia de la pintura en México*, Introduction by Juana Gutiérrez Haces (Mexico City: Cien de México, 1995 [1872]), 67.

29. Ibid., 67.

30. These factors mirror the criteria noted in a letter dated 1855, directed by Couto to a monastery, and used to determine which paintings religious orders were to select from their collections for the consideration of the academy representatives.

31. The production of a canon is not an operation that can be carried out in thought alone but must be accompanied by the physical manipulability of selected objects being classified and viewed in relation to one another; only then are they resonant with the requirements of canon construction. The desire to create a totality of Mexican history, specifically a colonial phase, necessitated the imposition of a logic of classifications, relations, and propositions within the whole system, a synecdochic operation through which discrete objects were presented as parts of a whole.

32. Michael Camille, "Rethinking the Canon: Prophets, Canons, and Promising Monsters," *The Art Bulletin* 78, no. 2 (June 1996): 198–201.

33. Paintings noted as not belonging to the academy in 1861 but which were later added include the following canonical works: *Los santos niños Justo y Pastor* (José Juárez), *San Alejo* (José Juárez), *La incredulidad de Santo Tomás* (Sebastián López de Arteaga), and *La oración en el huerto* (Luis Juárez). These paintings, interestingly, are works that turn up on the inventory of missing items from the warehoused collections of confiscated properties in 1865. Based on the gallery photographs from 1898, we note that these canvases had already been added to the academy collection and installed in the gallery. See Báez Macías, *Archivo*, doc. 6541.

34. Couto noted comments by another Mexican scholar, José Ignacio Bartolache, who believed Cabrera had carefully studied the Guadalupe image more through the eyes of devotion than of art. He stated: "Respecto de su sustancia, el mismo Bartolache daba a entender que a su juicio Cabrera había registrado la imagen, más con los ojos de la devoción, que con los del arte." See Couto, *Diálogo*, 114.

35. Camille, "The Abject Gaze," 168.

Bibliography

Anonymous. "La pintura mexicana." *El Monitor* year XII, number 3,444, February 1, 1857, 4.

Báez Macías, Eduardo. *Archivo de la Antigua Academia de San Carlos*. Mexico City: Universidad Nacional Autónoma de México, 1976.

BBC News, online edition, April 5, 2001, Americas section, http://news.bbc.co.uk/2/hi/entertainment/1261720.stm.

Belting, Hans. *Likeness and Image: A History of the Image before the Era of Art*. Trans. Edmund Jephcott. Chicago: University of Chicago Press, 1994.

Beltrami, J. C. *Le Mexique*. Paris, 1830.

Brown, Jonathan. *Images and Ideas in Seventeenth-Century Spanish Painting*. Princeton: Princeton University Press, 1978.

Cabrera, Miguel. *Maravilla Americana, y conjunto de raras maravillas, observadas con la dirección de las reglas de el arte de la pintura en la prodigiosa imagen de Nuestra Sra. de Guadalupe de México*, Vol. 3. Documentalia Poblana Series. Puebla: Editorial Nuestra República, 1998 [1756].

Camille, Michael. "The Abject Gaze and the Homosexual Body: Flandrin's Figure d'Etude." In *Gay and Lesbian Studies in Art History*, edited by Whitney Davis, 161–88. New York: Harrington Park Press, 1994.

———. "Rethinking the Canon: Prophets, Canons, and Promising Monsters." *The Art Bulletin* 78, no. 2 (June 1996): 198–201.

Carrier, David. *Principles of Art History Writing*. 4th ed. University Park: Pennsylvania State University Press, 1997.

Couto, José Bernardo. *Diálogo sobre la historia de la pintura en México*. Introduction by Juana Gutiérrez Haces. Mexico City: Cien de México, 1995 [1872].

Freedberg, David. *The Power of Images: Studies in the History and Theory of Response*. Chicago: The University of Chicago Press, 1989.

Lucio, Rafael. *Reseña histórica de la pintura mexicana en los siglos XVII y XVIII*. Mexico City: J. Abadiano 1864. First published in *Boletín de la Sociedad Mexicana Geografía y Estadística*, 1863.

Pomian, Krzysztof. "Le Musée et le Temps." In *Curiosité: Êtudes d'histoire de l'art en l'honneur d'Antoine Schnapper*, edited by Olivier Bonfait et al., 431–47. Paris: Flammarion, 1998.

Torre Villar, Ernesto de la, and Ramiro Navarro de Anda, *Testimonios históricos guadalupanos*. 2nd ed. Mexico City: Fondo de Cultura Económica, 1999.

Editing the Anthology
Renaming Ecstasy: Latino Writings on the Sacred

ORLANDO RICARDO MENES

☞ PRESENTED IN THIS ESSAY ARE VARIOUS REFLECTIONS ON MY anthology *Renaming Ecstasy: Latino Writings on the Sacred*, published in 2004 by Bilingual Press/Editorial Bilingüe at Arizona State University.

The conference that gave rise to this essay has truly been an educational experience for me. I had never encountered the fervor for the Virgin of Guadalupe firsthand. I had read about it but never witnessed it. And I find it transformative.

Editing the anthology was also transformative for me. I began to edit *Renaming Ecstasy* six years ago, and at the time I was doing my Ph.D. in creative writing at the University of Illinois, Chicago. I was also writing poems that were inspired by Santería, a religion I had not grown up with but had discovered through books. This syncretic religion called Santería inspired me to write many, many other poems that make up *Rumba atop the Stones* (my first full-length poetry collection). My advisor at the time, the poet Michael Anania, suggested I edit an anthology. I said, "Sure! I'll do that." "What will I edit?" I thought aloud. "Oh, writings on the sacred, since I write poems inspired by the sacred. Latinos, yeah, let's see. I haven't read any poems by Chicanos. I think I will have to look up poems by Chicanos."

I went to the library and checked out all the books I could find by Puerto Rican writers and other Latino poets. It educated me, and, in fact, now I teach Latino poetry. But, six years ago, I had no idea what it was.

I also want to point out that the anthology is one that aims to define the sacred and the spiritual based on the poets themselves—in other words, how they culturally contextualize sacredness, how they create a language of the sacred, how they experience the sacred in the heart and in the mind. The anthology, then, is divided into five sections. Two sections encompass mestizo sacredness, consisting of various poets who are inspired by cultural and spiritual hybridities, especially those between Catholicism and either Aztec or Afro-Caribbean religions. Another section is devoted to a poet who alludes to shamanistic spirituality; and then there is, of course, the section on Catholic groups, while the fifth and last one is composed of poets who are inspired by nature and art.

Here I discuss two poets in particular. The first is Pat Mora and her poem "Consejos de Nuestra Señora de Guadalupe: Counsel from the Brown Virgin," which belongs to the Cuarteto Mexicano (the Mexican Quartet) in her book *Agua Santa/Holy Water*.[1] Indeed, the Mexican Quartet is a remarkable matriarchal exploration of Mexican identity at the level of the mythic. It gives a personal and authorial voice to four women (the Virgin of Guadalupe, La Llorona, Coatlicue, and La Malinche) who are, in essence, the foundation of the Mexican identity, its soul and its psyche. From this grouping one can tell that in Pat Mora's mind there is no clear separation between the sacred and the secular, the historical and the mythic, the European and the indigenous. Indeed, it is this collapsing of borders that best characterizes Mexican identity. No doubt these are complex mother figures, conflicted mother figures. La Llorona is guilty of infanticide, La Malinche is a traitor, and Coatlicue is a victim of matricide. As Pat Mora addresses this as follows:

Consejos de Nuestra Señora de Guadalupe:
Counsel from the Brown Virgin

You seem surprised that I've appeared.
You gape like Juan Diego as I hovered in a cloud
that December morning above dry Tepeyac. Mortals lack faith
and imagination, fear flying. Hijas, be unpredictable.

> Como la flor de rosa.
> Como el arco iris.
> Como las nubes de gloria.
> Como la luna espléndida.

Do not be insistent. I raise neither my voice nor eyes—
yet. Bodies, even celestial, are creatures of habit.
Hijas, what we repeat becomes our nature. Beware.
Goddesses fade in and out of fashion.

> Como la flor de rosa.
> Como el arco iris.
> Como las nubes de gloria.
> Como la luna espléndida.

Names and images are converted. Now I'm moon-rider
in repose, body concealed in flowing cocoon,
hands, mouth, eyes folded, cloaked in stars.
Hijas, consistent trappings can release us for internal work.

> Como la flor de rosa.
> Como el arco iris.
> Como las nubes de gloria.
> Como la luna espléndida.

You analyze the persistence of my image, how I don't fade.
Too much analysis inhibits wisdom, hijas. You fear
flying. A muse amused, I am used everywhere, auto-shops,
buses, bars, slender mother but virgen pura, no Malinche.

> Como la flor de rosa.
> Como el arco iris.
> Como las nubes de gloria.
> Como la luna espléndida.

Hijas, beware of altars and rumors of legends.
Holy men altered me, Aztec goddess to Reina de Las Américas,
pyramid to cathedral. They say I called sweet as birdsong
to Juan Diego rushing to the curling hum of holy incense.

> Como la flor de rosa.
> Como el arco iris.
> Como las nubes de gloria.
> Como la luna espléndida.

Send men clear signs. They need them, hijas.
In deserts, I favor scarlet roses. Come.
Rise. Practice solitary levitation. Rise,
but ignore halos, hovering men who look like angelitos.

> Como la flor de rosa.
> Como el arco iris.
> Como las nubes de gloria.
> Como la luna espléndida.

Hijas, value contemplation. Alone, I write
my own legends. My lines improve. Play the symbols.
I loan my cape to women in tennis shoes who fly
back and forth across the Rio Grande.

> Como la flor de rosa.
> Como el arco iris.
> Como las nubes de gloria.
> Como la luna espléndida.

Listen to this buzz of litanies. Endless praise inhibits musing.
Hijas, silence can be pregnant. My voice rose like a beam
of sunlight, entered Juan. Remember, conceptions,
immaculate and otherwise, happen. He knelt, full of me.

> Como la flor de rosa.
> Como el arco iris.
> Como las nubes de gloria.
> Como la luna espléndida.

I love that last part where she who is impregnated does the impregnation. It is a beautiful moment of empowerment for a female. Of course it is much more complex than that, but I wanted to repeat a recurring theme of the essays in this volume: although the Virgin of Guadalupe represents the confluence of two cultures, she also constitutes a locus of contention—cultural, sexual, and so on—and we certainly see that contention in Chicano art (e.g., the prisoner's tattooed back). The Virgin of Guadalupe is an object of continual reinterpretation, reinvention; she is a figure in flux.

I am reminded of the idea from the deconstructionists that the sign resists signification, that the sign is unstable. I think we are seeing an expression of that in the Virgin of Guadalupe. As both a virgin and a mother, she reflects a profound paradox of identity. It is a paradox that we live with all the time and that we accept through faith rather than reason. But it seems to me that in Chicano art the Virgin of Guadalupe is more the mother than the virgin proper; in other words, her virginal aspects of identity are displaced, while the motherly aspect has been pushed to the foreground in this process of defining the Mexican cultural identity. The other three mother figures that I mentioned also create a web of complexity that to my Cuban-American mind is astounding. I am reminded of an important idea in Gloria Anzaldúa's book *La Frontera/The Borderlands* that the mestiza consciousness is one that not just tolerates contradiction but actually embraces it, and thus the mestiza can exist in simultaneous worlds.[2] In addition, the Virgin of Guadalupe, at least in Chicano art, similarly becomes a vessel of contradictions—contradictions of identity, contradictions of history, contradictions of the sacred.

I also did a bit of etymological research into the name of Guadalupe. It appears that it is a hybrid Arabic/Latin place name for the River of the Wolf, which does not necessarily mean that she is a hybrid figure in her region of origination, Extremadura, in west-central Spain. To my mind that would be an erroneous conjecture. This hybridity might, in fact, constitute an appropriation of the Arabic to express a certain dynamic of power by the Spanish (Ibero-Roman) Christians. As land was reclaimed during the Reconquista, so did Arabic culture and language become usurped and reconstituted to express domination rather than valorization. While this local appellation might well be problematic, the Spanish Virgin of Guadalupe, when she arrived in Mexico in the sixteenth century, undoubtedly underwent complex processes of hybridity, and it is fascinating how she is continually or periodically being reinterpreted and reappropriated.

Now I turn to one of my own poems, titled "Fish Heads." In this poem, I aim to fashion a language of sacredness through images or figures of hybridity, in addition to surrealism and the Afro-Cuban religion of Santería.

Fish Heads

A glowing crucifix (five
flashing lights) atop the lobster trap,
a rosary of papaya seeds,
a clock like a flaming heart
that shudders every hour;
the heart speaks: *I thirst,
It is finished, etc.*

The fisher's son, an acolyte,
sleeps cuddled up in his canoe
of mist, rocking like censer
or bell buoy. Child of the sea,
river, lagoon—Antillean *querubín,*
who drools rose water on the pillow,
commands dolphin and barracuda
to weave arabesques of crown, cross, and pike,
boats skimming with sails of flogged skin.
Inside a pelican's pouch he flies from island
to island, wreathing with rain-lilies
light houses, masts, and campanili.

In their shack of tamarind wood,
a chapel on stilts, the smoke of candles
vivifies fish heads (nailed to the wall)
to bleed, quiver, turn east at cock-crowing;
a procession of ants will then surrender
to the flames. Lye falls
from clouds of ash. Lenten night:
the resurrection ferns will again be lush

and green. Yesterday the sea was vinegary,
less brackish than customary for baptism.
Waves release rosaries gnarled
with bladder wrack that village youths
unravel to mourn another acolyte.
Fragrant as sweet plantain, three mulatas—
fishnet menders—sing a dirge in Lucumí,
pantomime the hammerhead's thrust
and thrash to sign the boy's martyrdom.

Yemayá, Lady of the Sea, spawned
without sin, light from darkest water,
spare the fisher's son, swaddle him with fish
guts, brood him under your manta wings.
That blinding aureole will forever
burn above your shark's-jaw crown.

You can see that in the body of the poem I have tropicalized Catholic iconography, but it also follows the tripartite structure of the Jesuit meditation: (1) place, (2) meditation, and (3) prayer. I was reading a lot of John Donne at the time, as well as Louis Martz's seminal study *The Poetry of Meditation*,[3] and that tripartite structure stuck to me.

I want to address the last stanza of my poem, where I invoke the orisha, or Yoruba deity, named Yemayá. Doing so troubled me tremendously at the time. As I was finishing the poem over a period of many weeks, I struggled with whether to make her Catholic or Yoruba. And even after I had taken that leap of faith into Santería, I still agonized over this decision, one that I characterize as aesthetic rather than personal. I was not raised with that religion; indeed, my two grandfathers were Spaniards, so I was brought up to view myself as a defender of Spain, which seems comical to me, yet I realize that our identities are forged less by reason and more by unquestioned, or even irrational, beliefs and mores. Thus taking such a leap into Africa was wrenching, and I felt like I was betraying my heritage. But then I allowed the imagination to take control. I allowed the intuitive faculty, in the sense of Croce's aesthetic philosophy,[4] to command the reins, and yes, I surrendered to the orisha. I did not believe in her, but I surrendered nonetheless. I did it for the sake of the poem. I still do not understand exactly what happened in my own mind, but I am continually returning to that epiphanic moment where, in my poem, I became someone other than who I am in real life.

Notes

1. Pat Mora, "Consejos de Nuestra Señora de Guadalupe: Counsel from the Brown Virgin," in *Agua Santa/Holy Water* (Boston: Beacon Press, 1995).

2. Gloria Anzaldúa, *Borderlands/La Frontera: The New Mestiza* (San Francisco: Aunt Lute Books, 1987).

3. Louis Martz, *The Poetry of Meditation*, 2nd ed. (New Haven: Yale University Press, 1962).

4. Benedetto Croce, *Guide to Aesthetics (Brevario de estetica)*, translated by Patrick Romanell (South Bend: Regnery/Gateway, 1979).

PART III

Musical Relationships of Faith and Art in Celebrating the Guadalupe Tradition

The Presence of Miguel Bernal Jiménez in the Fiftieth Anniversary of the Coronation of the Virgin of Guadalupe

LORENA DÍAZ NÚÑEZ[*]

Introduction

☞ THE RICH MUSICAL LANDSCAPE OF MÉXICO HAS NOT BEEN EXPLORED in its entirety, and one of its less recognized aspects is Catholic sacred music of the twentieth century. I offer the hypothesis that this is due to the political conflict that existed between the state and the church—inherited from the previous century—as with the anticlericalism of the 1910 Revolution, in force during most of the first half of the twentieth century. As a consequence, biases born of political, ideological, cultural, and artistic hoaxes and phobias led to the near exclusion of twentieth-century issues related to the sacred in the historiography of Mexican music. A review of the related bibliography alone reveals this omission. For these reasons, we have had to settle for a limited number of catalogued materials, monographs, and recordings of sacred music of this period.

After many years of tension, the beginning of a new modus vivendi between the church and state—an agreement reached in 1938, thanks to the nationalist interests of both—provided for a better diffusion of sacred music and the organization of conferences and concerts, the publication of journals, books, and musical scores, as well as the founding of schools of sacred music. Before 1938, religious intolerance and persecution—armed

---

*English translation by Steven Loza

or not—obligated musicians of sacred music to express themselves more or less in a clandestine manner, in conformance with the political climate of the country.

This essay attempts to clarify the participation of composer Miguel Bernal Jiménez, from the state of Michoacán, in an event of great significance that marked the apogee of a new modus vivendi: the commemoration of the fiftieth anniversary of the coronation of the Virgin of Guadalupe originally carried out in 1895 in the city of Mexico. The magnificent Guadalupan celebrations of 1945, organized by the Mexican episcopate, included pontifical masses, pilgrimages, and the premiere of various masses composed for the occasion. Among the masses that were premiered was *Misa guadalupana Juandieguito* (1945) by Bernal Jiménez.

The importance of the celebrations of the fiftieth anniversary was marked by the presence of the representative of Pope Pius XII, Rodrigo Villenueve, cardinal of Quebec and the first official of the Vatican to visit Mexico. Representatives of all the Mexican archdioceses attended, in addition to representatives from the United States of North America, Canada, Guatemala, Peru, Cuba, Colombia, and Ecuador. In sum, the commemoration of the fiftieth anniversary of the coronation of the Virgin of Guadalupe was a continental event that united thousands of people in the Basilica of Guadalupe in Mexico City who, without fear of repression, celebrated the *Guadalupana*, who in 1895 had been crowned in the same city as Queen of America.

Miguel Bernal Jiménez

Miguel Bernal Jiménez was a composer, organist, choral and orchestral conductor, scholar, and educator. Born in Morelia, Michoacán, on February 16, 1910, he died in León, Guanajuato, on July 26, 1956. During his short life of forty-six years, he authored or composed ten books, 250 musical compositions, and 150 articles. He founded the music conservatory Conservatorio de las Rosas, the childrens' choir Niños Cantores de Morelia, and the journal of sacred music culture *Schola Cantorum*. He was, likewise, a research pioneer on the music of New Spain, and he organized the first concert of viceroyal music produced in Mexico during the twentieth century. He also had a family of eleven children.

At the age of seven, Bernal Jiménez began school at the Colegio de Infantes de la Catedral de Morelia, and at the age of ten he entered the school Orfeon Pio X, which in 1921 became the Escuela Oficial de Música Sagrada of the archdiocese of Michoacán. Due to his excellent musical talent, at the age of eighteen he was sent to Rome to study at the Pontificia Scuola Superior di Musica Sacra, where he remained for five years (1928–33) and earned the degrees Maestro of Organ, Maestro of Sacred Composition, and Doctor of Gregorian Chant. Upon his return to México he became artistic director of the Escuela Superior de Musica Sagrada de Morelia, founding director of the journal *Schola Cantorum* in 1939, and founding director of the Conservatorio de las Rosas in 1945. From Morelia he headed the national movement of restoration, renovation, and reform of sacred music, inspired by the 1903 publication of *Motu proprio* by Pius X. Finally, from 1953 to 1956, Bernal Jiménez served as Dean of the College of Music of Loyola University in New Orleans.

Miguel Bernal Jiménez was a fascinating personality and one of the principal architects of the movement that I call, in the case of Mexico, the "new sacred music," beginning with Pius X's *Motu proprio*. The pen of Bernal Jiménez tells us about the diverse aspects of sacred music, and his life and work reflect, without a doubt, the artistic and spiritual intersection of his era. I should make note of the fact that a great part of Bernal Jiménez's life traversed an atmosphere of religious conflict, since he was the object of a certain marginalization within the official artistic world of Mexico. Nevertheless, both nonsectarians and Catholics recognized the great quality of his work. He and many other Catholic artists of his era have enriched our cultural heritage.

It is important to mention that Bernal Jiménez was an attentive composer within at least two musical tendencies and, as such, participated as a central figure in the two most important nationalist movements of the first half of the twentieth century: the "sacred" and the "secular" (named thusly for the nationalism that embraced plural music in tendencies and styles, among which composers we can mention Manuel M. Ponce, Silvestre Revueltas, Carlos Chávez, José Pablo Moncayo, and Blas Galindo, among many others). It would not be an exaggeration to state that, among the national composers of his time, Bernal Jiménez was the only one who explicitly incorporated into his work the Hispanic watershed of our roots as represented through the Catholic religion.

Among Bernal Jiménez's works representing Hispanic nationalism are, for example: the opera *Tata Vasco* (1940–41), which alludes to the evangelical work of Vasco de Quiroga, first archbishop of Michoacán; the *Gran corrido a la Virgen de Guadalupe* (1941), which sings the apparitions of the Virgin; the choreographed retable (story) *Los tres galanes de Juana* (1952), which alludes to the decision of Sor Juana Inés de la Cruz to accept religious orders; the *Sinfonía Hidalgo* (1953), which deals with the feats of Mexican Independence led by the priest Miguel Hidalgo y Castilla, whose standard-bearer was the Virgin de Guadalupe; and the pastorela-ballet *Navidad en tierra azteca* (1955), based on one of the most important festivities of Catholic devotion.

In addition to being a champion of secular nationalism, Bernal Jiménez was a decisive individual who was influential in the origin of the new sacred music. Moreover, in what I call sacred nationalism, Bernal Jiménez was its major exponent. Among other works representative of this tendency was *Missa Aeternae Trinitatis* (1941), *Misa guadalupana Juandieguito* (1945), and *Maitines de la Asunción* (1949). Bernal Jiménez made the following comments on the *Misa guadalupana Juandieguito*:

> In Mexico we wanted to be Mexicans. There was already in Father Velázquez and Agustín González a nationalist abandon, as their exegetes have pointed out. Other more frank attempts have been made afterwards. Certainly not many, due to the scarcity of composers and intolerance of the medium. For want of better examples, let me cite the Misa Juan Dieguito . . . [and to underscore] the Mexican character that has resolved to imprint itself with the fundamental fact that its three themes [have] a frank indigenous flavor.[1]

The *Motu proprio* of Pius X in Mexico

The *Instrucción acerca de la música sagrada* (Instruction On Sacred Music), issued by Pius X and known as the *Motu proprio*, was conceived through the necessity of normalizing the musical practice of the church since the employment of "intrusive music," that is, opera arias and salon music, had been popularized in the Catholic world. The Vatican decided to quiet the operatic voices and to silence the piano inside the churches and, with that, the instruments traditionally foreign to the cult that were distorting the liturgical meaning of the music.

The *Motu propio* addressed the formation of *scholae cantorum* and higher educational schools of sacred music, the reestablishment of Gregorian chant and vocal polyphony in the liturgy, and the use of modern sacred music and the naming of specialized commissions in order to watch over the quality and good execution of music in churches. In this way, Catholic sacred music of the twentieth century evolved according to this change. After *Motu proprio* and up to the Second Vatican Council (1962–65) of popes John XXIII and Paul VI, the pontifical documents on this matter spoke of reform, recovery, restoration, and renovation. The Holy See and its diverse national bishopric commissions watched over the fulfillment of the papal standards profusely diffused throughout the Catholic world.

Of the redacted documents in the first half of the twentieth century that make special reference to sacred music, it is appropriate to also mention the apostolic statutes *Divini cultus sanctitatem* (1929) of Pius XI and the encyclicals *Mediator Dei* (1947) and *Musicae sacrae disciplina* (1955) of Pius XII.[2] Standing out in the second half of the century are *Instrucción sobre la música sagrada y la sagrada liturgia* (1958) of Pius XII,[3] the statutes *Sacro Sanctum Concilium* (1963) and the instruction *Musicam Sacram* (1967) of Paul VI.

In *Instrucción sobre la musica sagrada y la sagrada liturgia* of Pius XII, the fundamental ideas contained in the previous documents are recompiled. The *Instrucción* precisely states that sacred music comprises four genres of liturgical music: (1) Gregorian chant and vocal polyphony (without instrumental accompaniment); (2) modern sacred music (with various voices or without instrumental accompaniment); (3) sacred music for organ (without voice); and (4) two nonliturgical genres: popular religious song (which eventually was able to be used in some liturgical roles) and religious music (which expresses piety, but is not composed for adoration to God).[4]

In spite of the interest on the part of the Mexican episcopate to amply honor the content of the *Motu proprio*, this was not possible because of the political conflict between the state and church that existed in the first decades of the twentieth century.

The Fiftieth Anniversary of the Coronation of the Virgen of Guadalupe, 1945

In Mexico, the decade of the 1940s was generally characterized by good relations between state and church. This had been accomplished within the framework of the new modus vivendi, whose rise can be situated exactly in 1945. Among the concessions made by the state to maintain conciliation (the Constitution of 1917 had normalized the activities of the church) was included the authorization to hold public demonstrations of worship. The archbishop of Mexico was already saying that Mexican laws were like the English language—written one way and pronounced another. But in line with the current positive relationship, the Guadalupe festivities of 1945 occurred without incident.

On October 2, 1945, the archbishop of Mexico announced that the Guadalupan festivities would be celebrated that year with three meanings: one religious, another patriotic, and one more of American unity. Luis María Martínez remembered the occasion fifty years earlier when the Virgin of Guadalupe was proclaimed Queen of Mexico for having been the guardian of Mexicans during the apex of its historical changes. He pointed out that the country was not only a beautiful land, as were the generations that had inhabited it, but that it also constituted a set of traditions and hopes, of art and national culture. He said that the country was history, in its present and in the time to come. He concluded that in those moments of pain due to the war that had devastated the world, Catholics of the continent were entoning "a grand and sonorous hymn that was not only the canticle of Mexico, but the glorious symphony of America."[5]

One of the organizing committees of the festivities was the Committee of Sacred Music, presided over by the canon José María Villaseñor, director of the Escuela Superior de Música de Morelia; vice-president was Martín Villaseñor, choir master of the Basilica of Guadalupe; secretary was Miguel Bernal Jiménez; and prosecretary was Julián Zúñiga, titular organist of the Basilica of Guadalupe. Once appointed, the committee convoked the continent's composers of sacred music to compose works destined for the festivities; compositions were received from Canada, Colombia, Costa Rica, Cuba, the United States of North America, and, of course, Mexico. Likewise, the Committee of Sacred Music organized the Coro Nacional Guadalupano, integrated with three hundred voices of children and adults originating from the various dioceses. The choir, directed by Miguel Bernal Jiménez, commenced rehearsals on August 1, 1945.

As part of the commemoration of the fiftieth anniversary of the coronation of the Virgen de Guadalupe, morning and evening pilgrimages, pontifical masses and vespers, recitations of the rosary, and receptions and banquets were also organized, as was the Interamerican Marian Conference. Of the fourteen days that the festivities spanned, each was under the charge of a different national archdiocese and its supporting dioceses, as well as foreign representatives. September 30 was charged to the archdiocese of Yucatán, followed by Puebla (October 1), Durango (2), Oaxaca (3), Monterrey (4), Guadalajara (5), Morelia (6), Mexico City (7), the colony of Spaniards in Mexico (8), Canada (9), the United States of North America (10), the Latin American republics (11), and all of the communities of the continent and its islands (12). The festivities ended with a funeral mass in memory of the Marian prelates deceased since the apparitions of the Virgin to the present.

The October 6 program of Guadalupan festivities, organized by the ecclesiastic province of Morelia, was as follows:

7:30 a.m.—Pilgrimage of the Padres Josefinos del Espíritu Santo and other members of the religious.

8:30 a.m.—Solemn choral service.

10:00 a.m.—Welcoming of the pilgrims of the Province of Morelia, led by Archbishop Luís María Altamirano y Bulnes and prelates of the province. National Guadalupan Choir, directed on this occasion by Clifford A. Bennett, Director of the Gregorian Institute of America, and performing the Common parts of the *Misa Brevis* in Gregorian chant. From the pulpit, Bernal Jiménez directed the public. More than twenty archbishops and bishops were in attendance. Interpreted for the Proper parts of the mass were those of the Mass *Salve Sancta Parens* in Gregorian chant. During the Offertory, the choir and public sang *Tota pulchra* and the motet *Méxice* by Cesareo Munguía. Organist Guillermo Pinto Reyes, a disciple of Bernal Jiménez, performed music by Mendelssohn and Bernal Jiménez. After mass Luis Moreno sang *Salve Regina*.

4:00 p.m.—Solemn pontifical vespers. Gregorian chant was sung in addition to *fabordones* of Ludovico Grossi de Viadana, performed on organ by Guillermo Pinto Reyes.

5:30 p.m.—Pilgrimage from Peralvillo Station to the Basilica of Guadalupe. Marching were artists, philharmonic musicians, and employees of theaters and film—close to four thousand souls who carried small, illuminated lanterns. "Upon arriving at the atrium of the Basilica, they began to sing the Himno Nacional, accompanied by the monumental organ and the National Guadalupan Choir, composed of over 300 voices. The act was solemn and emotive. They then sang the Himno Guadalupano until arriving at the feet of the Virgin . . . The impressive ceremony ended with the Himno a Cristo Rey and Himno a la

Guadalupana . . . As people exited the Basilica, the monumental organ played the harmonious notes of the Himno Nacional."[6]

6:00 p.m.—Solemn rosary and sermon officiated by the canon Juan B. Buitron of Morelia. Sung were the *Cinco canciones sacras* of Felipe Aguilera.

October 11 was the day of the continental union. The program was published in the newspaper *El Universal* as follows:

7:30 a.m.—Pilgrimage led by the archbishop of Mexico. Mass celebrated with accompaniment of organ and singing.

8:30 a.m.—Solemn choral service.

10:00 a.m.—Welcoming of representatives from all of Latin America, led by the Latin American prelates. Premiered for the Common parts of the mass was *Misa guadalupana Juandieguito* for chorus, public, and organ, by Bernal Jiménez. For the offertory an Alelluia by the same composer was sung. Bernal Jiménez also interpreted the organ music of Bach in addition to his own compositions.

4:00 p.m.—Pontifical vespers.

5:30 p.m.—Pilgrimage from the Peralvillo Station to the Basilica. Procession includes workers and artisans.

6:00 p.m.—Solemn rosary. Performed is *Cinco Canciones* by Bernal Jiménez.

Each daily program was similar. Thanks to the sources that report the festivities, it is possible to perceive a mix of patriotic and religious fervor that demands attention, a fervor shared equally by the different social groups, from workers, artisans, and professionals to diplomats, laymen and religious, men, women, and children, coming from Mexico and other countries of the continent. This was the first time in the twentieth century that Mexico accomplished religious events of such magnitude and solemnity. The success of the project is not so strange if one takes into account the internal political situation and the necessity for social cohesion following World War II.

The culmination of the Guadalupan festivities took place on October 12, the day of America (Día de América). The city was splendorous: From balconies, trees, and windows hung flowers and chains of Chinese and crepe paper in blue and pink colors and lanterns, serpentines, banners of

Guadalupe, and the coat of arms of the festivities. The schedule of festivities on this day was as follows:

4:30 a.m.—*Mañanitas* to the Virgen, in the portico of the Basilica.

7:30 a.m.—Solemn choral service.

9:00 a.m.—Pontifical mass, officiated by Cardenal Rodrigo Villenueve. After the benediction of the roses, it was announced that the Proclamation of Our Lady of Guadalupe as Throne of Knowledge in America and Patroness of the Intellectual would be read. Soon after the reading, a radiophonic transmission from Rome began and everyone listened to the message and benediction of Pius XII, who finished by stating, "While she is being acknowledged, as queen and as mother, Mexico has been saved."[7]

Cardinal Villenueve blessed the crown and scepter that remained on the altar along with the different national flags, the mitres and staffs of the prelates. Then a procession began through the church and its atrium. The chimes of the bells and "vivas" to the Virgen de Guadalupe could be heard and, at one o'clock in the afternoon, according to a witness,

El arzobispo de México sube al altar y descorre el lienzo rojo que cubre la placa donada por la arquidiocesis de Oaxaca. En seguida desciende de nuevo para subir la corona y la coloca al centro, bajo el cuadro de la imágen . . . Vuelve abajo y recibe del Obispo de Tulancingo el cetro que dona la Acción Católica. Lo coloca en su sitio, sobre un cojín rojo. Se inclina y ora. La multitud canta el Himno Nacional . . . Se inicia el desfile de banderas, llevada la de México por el Sr. Arzobispo Martínez . . . Termina la función con el canto de los *Himnos Pontificio, Guadalupano y Nacional.*[8]

(The Archbishop of México climbs to the altar and removes the cloth that covers the plaque donated by the archdiocese of Oaxaca. He then descends to raise the crown and places it at center, under the frame of the image . . . He returns below and receives from the bishop of Tulancingo the scepter donated by Acción Católica. He sets it in its place, on a red cushion. He bows and prays. The multitude sings the National Anthem . . . The procession of flags begins, the Mexican flag being carried by Archbishop Martínez . . . The function closes with the singing of the Himno Pontificio, Himno Guadalupano, and Himno Nacional.)

Ecce Sacerdos by Agustín González was sung before the third part of the mass. For the Common parts of the mass, *Misa Salve Sancta Parens* was interpreted in Gregorian chant. For the Proper, the *Misa del Papa Marcelo* by Palestrina was interpreted. During the Offertory an *Ave Maria* by Tomás Luis de Victoria was sung, and after mass Julián Zúñiga performed the organ music of Gigout and Franck. The remainder of the day's schedule was as follows:

1:30 p.m.—Meal for the poor, organized by the festivities committee.

4:00 p.m.—Vespers. Singing of antiphons, psalms, and hymns in Gregorian chant.

6:00 p.m.—Rosary. *Cinco canciones* is interpreted by Paulino Paredes.

7:30 p.m.—Cloister of the Marian Congress and an evening of literature and music.

During the festivities the *Coro Nacional Guadalupano*, directed by Bernal Jiménez, premiered six of the ten masses of modern sacred music performed: *Eucarista* (October 1) by Pedro Alejandro Yon of the United States; *Solemnis Guadalupensis Jubilaei* (October 3) by Cirilo Conejo Roldán of Mexico; *Regina Coeli* (October 5) of Paulino Paredes of Mexico; *Ave Maris Stella* (October 9) by Julio Fonseca of Costa Rica; *Et in terra pax* (October 10) by Alejandro Gretchaninoff of the United States; and *Misa guadalupana Juandieguito* (October 11) by Bernal Jiménez. The choir also premiered eight of the fourteen vocal motets, among them were *O Gloriosa Virginum* by Felix Borowski of the United States; *Regina Coeli* by Salvador Herrera Fons of Cuba; *Regina Coeli* by Paul L. Callens of the United States; *Ave verum* by Roberto Pineda of Colombia; *Flores apparuerunt* by José Cedillo of Mexico, and *Cor Jesu* by Alfredo Bernier of Canada. Premiered in the final session of the Marian Congress was the oratorio *Tepeyac* by Julián Zúñiga, titular organist of the Basilica of Guadalupe.

On October 13, 1945, an article in the *Excelsior* entitled "Un México Nuevo" declared, "Un Nuevo espíritu que es necesario fortalecer, ha hecho su aparición benéfica en México. Los extremistas están siendo derrotados por la sensatez, la cordura y el patriotismo de las autoridades, tanto civiles como eclesiásticas" (A new spirit that must be strengthened has made a beneficial apparition in Mexico. The extremists are being defeated by good sense, prudence, and patriotism of both civil and ecclesiastic authorities). Luis María Martínez, Archbishop of México, reiterated, "Estamos descubriendo un México Nuevo, tolerante," and concluded, "El país de los altares ensangrentados va quedando atrás" (We are discovering a new, tolerant México . . . The country of the blood-stained altars has been left behind).

In effect, the city of Mexico had been a witness to the power of the convocation of the Catholic Church, of freedom of worship, of the importance that music had as part of the liturgy during this epoch, of the magnificent demonstration of faith, of a continental leadership in the church, of the necessity of unity in moments of crisis; in sum, of a magnificent demonstration of the political strength of the church in the country and in the continent. It would not be an exaggeration to affirm that neither during the coronation of the Virgen de Guadalupe in 1895, nor in the commemoration of the twenty-fifth anniversary celebrated in 1920, had there been as many musical works premiered as in 1945 during the fiftieth anniversary. This rise of sacred music declined between the death of Miguel Bernal Jiménez in 1956 and the celebration of the Second Vatican Council of 1962–65.

Notes

1. Miguel Bernal Jimenez, "Nacionalismo y música sagrada," *Schola Cantorum*, año XII, num. 3 (marzo de 1950): 36.
2. *La Santa Sede y la Música Sagrada: estudios y conclusiones del Segundo Congreso Nacional de Música Sacra, 1959* (Tulancingo: Escuela de Música Sagrada de Guadalajara, 1959), 122–25.
3. "Instrucción de la sagrada congregación de ritos sobre la música y la liturgia sagradas según las enciclicas Muscae Sacrae Disciplina y Mediator Dei del Papa XII," in *La Santa Sede*, 17–62.
4. The term "sacred" is employed here to refer to liturgical music, while the term "religious" is used here to refer to extraliturgical music.
5. Luis Ma. Martínez, "Tres sentidos de las fiestas guadalupanas," *Excelsior*, 2 de octubre de 1945.
6. "La provincia eclesiástica de Morelia en el Santuario Guadalupano," *El Universal*, 7 de octubre de 1945.
7. Lauro López Beltrán, *Album guadalupano* (Mexico, Jus, 1973), 305.
8. Ibid., 301–2.

Musical Witness to the Beautiful *Mestiza*

Art as Experience of the Sacred

SYLVIA TAN

⤢ EACH YEAR ON THE DAYS PRECEDING DECEMBER 12, THOUSANDS OF pilgrims make their way toward *La Villa de Guadalupe,* in the north part of Mexico City. They are of all walks of life. Some cycle, some drive, some slowly advance, inch by inch, on their knees. All approach the same subject of devotion: in a massive basilica, the painting of a woman surrounded by the sun, draped in turquoise and stars. The woman is known by many names: *Virgen de Guadalupe, Tonantzin,* or simply, *La Virgen.*

Outside on the plaza, indigenous dance troupes from various parts of Mexico perform in honor of La Virgen. Decked in traditional garb and accompanied by musicians, they dance as pilgrims watch. On December 11, the eve of the feast day of La Virgen, the sound of stomping feet accompanied by beating drums approaches a frenzy. Meanwhile, thousands of pilgrims stretch out on blankets throughout the plaza, keeping vigil beneath the stars. At the stroke of 11 p.m., the entire congregation sings *Las Mañanitas,* a happy-birthday song to the Virgin.

Inside the basilica, mass is celebrated continuously throughout the night and into the following morning. The apex of liturgies is at ten o'clock. The choir performs newly composed sacred hymns in the loft. Meanwhile, the stomping feet and indigenous drumming continue outside. The rhythmic drumming blends in with the melodic singing of the choir to produce a uniquely fascinating music.

Devotion to the Virgin of Guadalupe is transnational and has endured through the centuries. *Guadalupanismo,* as the cult of La Virgen is called, has been the subject of intense investigation and implicated in sociopolitical ideologies secretly enforcing traditional divisions of power (Limón 1986). However, in this essay I would like to address why La Virgen might retain significance for the people. Somehow, this image possesses the ability to transcend boundaries, be they social, cultural, or religious. The various artistic and musical forms of devotion give witness to this transcendence. Each song and dance, while performed within its individual tradition, is also performed for the same woman, viewed as personal Mother. I will reflect on the phenomenon of artistic and musical experience surrounding La Virgen that inspires the people and commands their respect. I ground this reflection in a little philosophy, a little ethnography, and a lot of love and admiration for La Virgen.

First, let's briefly discuss the phenomenon of artistic experience. How might works such as La Virgen de Guadalupe command the respect of millions across cultures? I suggest this is due to its status as art, which provides people an "access to the sacred" (Sierra 2001). Art mediates sacred experience through the work of symbol. A symbol references the intangible, that is, the "sacred," without fixing its meaning (Ricoeur 1967); the meaning of symbol is grounded first in the individual tradition of one who encounters it. Also, the meaning of symbol is dynamic in that it is reworked at each and every encounter, based on the current life experience one brings to it (Gadamer 1991). Thus, artworks such as La Virgen have the potential to mediate the sacred with everyday life experience because they work symbolically.

Aida Sierra, art historian at the Centro Nacional de Investigación, Documentación e Información de Artes Plásticas (CENIDIAP), gives witness to this phenomenon of La Virgen as more than a fixed belief: "Beliefs can explain this experience [of La Virgen], but the experience holds more than the discourse. *It's the renewed experience of the sacred.* It's not only [a 'religious' experience], it's an experience in your brain and your body, in everything. It's not only this image, or the story related to this image, or the goddess behind this image, but it's everything combined. *This figure brings the tradition into everyday life.*" (Sierra 2001, emphasis mine).

The artistic encounter of the sacred also inspires a renewed concept of self in relation to the sacred (Ricoeur 1978, 154). The icon of La Virgen itself configures a disparate array of Aztec and Spanish Catholic symbolisms making her at once accessible to different cultural groups. The ensuing tradition holds that all who approach this image, regardless of background, may turn to her as personal Mother who intercedes with the divine (Sierra 2001). This renewed encounter of La Virgen as mestiza Mother inspires a celebration in conceptual and cultural syncretism, the mestizaje identity.

And, finally, this renewed understanding of sacred and self itself inspires a creative, artistic response. In essence, these artistic responses reflect and even further promote the renewed world view. In the particular example of La Virgen, the artistic responses of devotion themselves transcend cultural boundaries. Mixed musical expressions of devotion to La Virgen give witness to this celebration of mestizaje, visible and aural evidence of the renewed encounter of the sacred.

Traveling to Mexico City in December 2001, I had the privilege of witnessing, firsthand, these mixed musical expressions of devotion to La Virgen. I was amazed, first, by the variety of expressions. I stood in the back of the Basilica during mass on December 12, pressed in on all sides by throngs of people. The choir performed Gregorian chant in the loft; at the same time, *conchero* dancers reenacted a prehispanic dance just outside the open doors. They wore large feathered headdresses and rattles strapped to their ankles, the forceful sounds of *hueheutl* drums accentuating their movements. Where I stood, the indigenous drumming outside combined with the solemn sounds of the chant inside, producing a unique music that seemed a fitting offering to the mestiza Virgin.

However, what truly impressed me was that the pilgrims on the plaza were not disturbed by the various sounds of regional groups performing within close proximity of each other. It was as if their ears were already accustomed to the mixing of music. It was as if, through these artistic expressions, the people understood mestizaje as "normal," as something to be celebrated. Pilgrims participate in a personal journey to access the sacred. With freedom and confidence, they approach *La Madrecita* and ask for whatever they may need. The December 12, 2001, edition of *La Jornada* contained an interview with Mateo Jiménez, who journeyed from Veracruz to the Basilica in Mexico City to ask the Virgin to lower the prices of coffee and corn. His confidence in his Madrecita exuded in expressions of music and dance, as he performed *La Danza de los Quetzales* (the dance of the quetzal birds) together with his family on the plaza. In his words, he dances for the Virgin, and he also dances in thanksgiving for the birds that "*bendicen las cosechas en nuestra tierra*" (bless the harvests in our land).

In my own interview of Ms. Sierra that same day, I expressed my amazement about these extremely personal expressions of devotion, such that traditional boundaries are blended or cease to exist. In the case of Mateo Jiménez, he dances simultaneously for the Virgin and for the birds that bless the harvests, breaking the boundaries of traditional Catholicism and indigenous belief. Sierra helped me reflect on how the phenomenon of La Virgen nurtures this renewed experience of the sacred.

A. S.: "With La Virgen, the people have the freedom to interpret, and the church cannot really impose; you can make up your own rules, in a way."

S. T.: "So, you have the freedom to interpret using your own imagination?"

A. S.: "Yes! And by using your own experience and I don't mean intellectual experience, but everyday life experience. That's how this image goes through classes."

S. T.: "It transcends boundaries?"

A. S.: "Yes! I was trying to say that! It transcends the boundaries you have in everyday life. It does not matter if you are middle class, a professor, a person who works at home, or a person who washes the clothes. When you talk to La Virgen, you are similar to everyone else."

As an example of the ability of the image to transcend boundaries, I present an anecdote from an interview I conducted with Lidia Guerberof Hahn (2001a). Ms. Hahn is a music archivist who took it upon herself to catalogue the hundreds of musical compositions recently discovered at the rear of the Old Basilica of Guadalupe. We initially spoke about the music and examined one of the scores. However, out of my own interest in art and music as sacred experience, I inquired after her impressions of Guadalupanismo. Thus, she revealed her story.

Born in Argentina and trained as a classical pianist, she arrived in Mexico City unfamiliar with the Virgin of Guadalupe. Even after the exciting discovery of the compositions in the Basilica, she did not feel any inclination toward the subject of devotion. She was only struck by the beauty of the music, which *"dice más que mil palabras"* (says more than a thousand words) (Guerberof Hahn 2001b).

One day, everything changed. She had been working in the archive for a year, watching pilgrims enter and exit the Basilica. She thought,

"I should go see what this is all about." So, she entered through the back, approached the picture of La Virgen, and then burst into tears. She was completely beside herself, and asked, "Now, Lidia, you are an educated woman. Why do you feel this way?" She had no rational explanation for it, but owed her experience to the presence of the Aztec goddess Tonantzin, who was worshipped "here" on Mount Tepeyac for centuries before the arrival of the Spaniards.

Today, Lidia keeps a small image of the Virgin in her home, as many Mexicans do, to which she brings all her needs. Middle class, educated, and Argentinian, Lidia took Tonantzin as her spiritual mother. She has faith that La Virgen will provide, in her words, "a resolution." We cannot positively explain what Lidia experienced there in the Basilica. We can only reflect on how the image of the Virgin, together with the surrounding traditions, projected a possibility that allows her to access the sacred, like a child.

I conclude with my own personal witness to the Virgin of Guadalupe as one who provides resolution. I am Chinese-Indonesian; my parents speak Dutch, and I've always lived in Los Angeles. In short, I am mestiza. I often meander among cultural traditions, searching for my own identity. I encountered the Virgin of Guadalupe for the first time as a child attending parochial school. However, at that time, she did not particularly impress me except as an image of Mary, the Mother of Jesus, who appeared five hundred years ago in Mexico.

Four years ago, while doing research as an ethnomusicology graduate student at UCLA, I learned of the different, mixed expressions of devotion to the Virgin. I approached Steve Loza about doing a study on musical practices devoted to the Virgin of Guadalupe. He replied, "That's strange, I just wrote a grant on that last year" (Loza 1999). To this day, I truly believe the Virgin facilitated this meeting of ours. With Steve's guidance, I began doing research, and I traveled to Mexico City to witness the musical practices firsthand.

I thought I would be studying just the music, but I realized that the greater significance of this project—the take-home message—was the personal manifestation of the sacred through art and music. Today, I give witness to the experience of La Virgen as mediating. I realized that as La Virgen projects a possibility for a resolution of competing cultures, she also projects a resolution for me through the experience of the fascinating traditions that surround her. I had only to interpret the symbols in the art and music and derive a resolution to my own mixed and confused experience. La Virgen is, at once, Aztec as Tonantzin and Catholic as the Virgin Mary. She is divine as she is as clothed by the sun, human as she holds her hands in an indigenous form of offering. I was moved to realize that I can turn to this Virgin of Guadalupe as my own mother, because she is in touch with the divine, and represents a mixed identity as something beautiful. My experience of her has helped me to understand that my own mixed identity is something to be celebrated.

I am both scientist and artist, and possess degrees in both fields. My own experience tells me that science can delineate reasons, but it cannot offer hope. Hope affords us glimpses into other possibilities, and this can be found only in the artistic, the imaginative, in the creative. It is in studying phenomena such as La Virgen de Guadalupe that we understand this better, and in philosophy that we can reflect upon it. She gives us personal access to the sacred, on which no rules can be imposed. I participate in a music group at a Catholic church in East Los Angeles, where the image of La Virgen is displayed prominently. Each Sunday, I play the piano in thanksgiving for this new-found resolution.

References

Gadamer, Hans-Georg. 1991. "Play as the Clue to Ontological Explanation." In *Truth and Method*. 2nd revised ed. Translated and revised by Joel Weinsheimer and Donald G. Marshall. New York: Crossroads.

Guerberof Hahn, Lidia. 2001a. *Interview*. Mexico City, December 7.

———. 2001b. Liner notes to *La Música de la Basílica de Santa María de Guadalupe Siglos XVIII y XIX, Vol. I*. Archivo de Música de la Basílica Santa María de Guadalupe.

Limón, José. 1986. "La Llorona, The Third Legend of Greater Mexico: Cultural Symbols, Women and the Political Unconscious." In *Renato Rosaldo Lecture Series Monograph*, ed. Ignacio M. García, Vol. 2, Series 1984–85 (spring).

Loza, Steven. 1999. *Religion as Art: The Aesthetics of Guadalupe*. Grant Proposal.

Ricoeur, Paul. 1967. *The Symbolism of Evil*. Boston: Beacon Press.

———. 1978. "The Metaphorical Process as Cognition, Imagination, and Feeling." *Critical Inquiry* 5, no. 1 (autumn): 143–59.

Sierra, Aída. 2001. Recorded interview, Centro Nacional de Investigación, Información e Documentación de Artes Plásticas (CENIDIAP), Centro Nacional de las Artes, Mexico City, December 12.

PART IV

Guadalupe and the
Native American Experience

Indigenous Mysticism

MARIA WILLIAMS

☞ THE THEME OF THIS VOLUME, RELIGION AS ART, BRIDGES A MAJOR chasm in Western thought. In this essay, I address the dilemma we face as scholars in mediating two worldviews—the Western worldview and the indigenous worldview.

Western perspective isolates an idea or thought and examines it almost as if it were within a vacuum. We are educated and trained to view the world in isolates. This is in contrast to an indigenous worldview, which is holistic and examines the physical world as an whole, interconnected with the spiritual world. Incorporated into this meta-matrix is the mystical realm. There is no separation between nature and people, between spirituality and everyday life, between religion and art. Generally speaking, worldwide indigenous or tribal people recognize spirituality as being an inseparable part of living energy.

I am Tlingit and was raised with an understanding of the world that integrates the spiritual world with the physical world. All of our clans are traced back to a founding animal-spirit ancestor, so the names of our clans—Raven, Eagle, Beaver, and Killer Whale—reflect our spiritual origin. More emphasis is placed on the spiritual than on the physical. Therefore the concept of indigenous spirituality incorporates an understanding of the mystical. Western positivist thinking denigrates the mystical because it cannot be measured and is difficult to define. Although bodies such as the Catholic Church and other Christian sects recognize mysticism, as with Juan Diego's vision and the apparition of the Virgin in Mexico, it is not recognized as fact in western thought because it cannot be scientifically proven, and therefore it is not viewed as reality or truth. I find this overarching view limiting in scope and feel it is this type of compartmentalized thinking that has separated people from nature, spirituality from everyday life, and has established a set of principles that examines the superficial and rarely the interconnected whole or meta-matrix.

What is mysticism? What does "mystical" mean? In the *Oxford English Dictionary* mystical is defined as: "mysterious, enigmatic, obscure, esoteric; of hidden meaning or nature; having an unknown or mysterious origin or influence." In the same dictionary, mysticism is defined as: "the opinions, mental tendencies, or habits of thought and feeling, characteristic of mystics; mystical doctrines or spirit; belief in the possibility of union with the Divine nature by means of ecstatic contemplation; reliance on spiritual intuition or exalted feeling as the means of acquiring knowledge of mysteries inaccessible to intellectual apprehension." It is clear from these classic dictionary definitions that mysticism is by its nature indefinable in the English language.

How do indigenous people define mysticism? There are many answers to this question because there are many ways in which mysticism exists in indigenous societies, and in many languages. The greater part of my knowledge is of the indigenous people of Alaska and North America, although there are certainly many characteristics shared among all indigenous peoples. I feel most comfortable speaking about what is known to me, as an indigenous person from Alaska.

One well-known example of mysticism is shamanism, which is an ancient yet powerful phenomenon that was a prominent part of the historical and cultural landscape of Alaska. I grew up hearing stories of *ixt!*, who could walk on water, turn into smoke and go into an enemy camp to obtain war strategies, cure people of illness, and fly to the moon. I believe these stories and view them as a historical record:

My father was quite ill as a young adolescent and was stricken with a terrible illness and could not walk. He was cured by an *ixt!*

My grandfather witnessed a female *ixt!* walk on water—in Lake Atlin, British Columbia. As she walked on the water the water indented under her feet slightly.

There was a Yup'ik shaman in the Bethel area that had a helping spir-it—it was in the figure of a small wooden bird. As his house burned down and the villagers attempted to put out the fire, they heard that bird calling out amid the smoking ruins.

An Inupiat shaman on King Island flew to the moon to gather moon rocks that would be used as a lure to bring the salmon back to their barren streams.

These are all incidents that took place within the last thirty to seventy years and there are many more stories about these mystics or shamans all over Alaska. Today, shamanism in Alaska no longer exists due to extreme colonial pressure and a strong Christian missionary presence in the nine-teenth and twentieth centuries. The reaction to shamanism by westerners was to destroy it, because it was contrary to the Christian understanding of the world, and shamans, because of their power, were deemed highly dangerous and a product of the devil.

In other areas of North America, shamanism does not exist in the same manner as it has in Alaska. There are a myriad of ways Native Americans experience a connection with the mystical or spiritual. Visions can come to any individual at anytime; in some instances, an individual can fast and participate in special ceremonials in order to commune with the spirit world; other times visions and apparitions can occur with no special context, as with Juan Diego's vision of La Virgen de Guadalupe. Virtually all North American indigenous peoples have histories that link them to visions. A prime example of this is the found-ing of what today is known as Mexico City: a holy man had a vision of a serpent and a cactus and this led to the founding of what became the Aztec empire. For indigenous peoples their mythic or legendary his-tory *is* their history, in contrast to Western thought that examines only recorded history or that which falls under what Western thinking rec-ognizes as fact.

Westerners viewed shamanism and other forms of indigenous mys-ticism as dangerous because they challenged their worldview; therefore great efforts were made to eradicate shamanism and other mystical prac-tices. Shamans were ostracized, had their hair cut; in Alaska, they were imprisoned and hanged. The Ghost Dance, a Native American nineteenth-century phenomenon, is associated with the massacre at Wounded Knee in 1897. So, much of this type of activity went underground and was hidden away from the outside nonindigenous world.

Despite the crushing blows and hegemonic pressure, indigenous mysticism has survived. What is disturbing to me is that it continues to be misunderstood and, although the brutality of the nineteenth and early twentieth centuries is no longer the norm, indigenous mysticism and especially shamanism have now been coopted by the so-called New Agers. The concept of shamanism or Native American spirituality fascinates Westerners; however, the examination rarely moves past the superficial. There is hyper-focus on the sensational; for example, in Santa Fe you can learn to become a shaman in a weekend workshop, a concept that is entirely offensive to me because it is shallow and devalues the spiritual skill and years of training needed to be able to commune with the spirit world. But even academic studies by Western scholars remove the cultural and spiritual context from the phenomenon of shamanism. In essence, they remove mysticism from the mystic (see figure 1).

FIGURE 1: Western Versus Indigenous Thought

WESTERN HEGEMONIC THOUGHT

- Oblivious to the power or spirit behind shamanism and other forms of indigenous mysticism
- Focus results in a superficial one-dimensional understanding
- Has no awareness of cultural or spiritual context
- Destroys what is not understood

INDIGENOUS THOUGHT

- Spirit World is the source of all power
- Holistic examination establishes a multidimensional understanding of the world
- Displays heightened awareness of culture and its spiritual roots
- Makes a path for the unknown

I make no attempt here to provide a comprehensive overview of indigenous mysticism or shamanism, because that would take volumes. What I would like to address is the dilemma of how academia and/or Western scholarship include indigenous perspectives, especially ones that focus on the spiritual or mystical. The essays in this volume make major contributions in this area.

Where do we go from here? How do we incorporate a more holistic approach that encompasses the spiritual or mystical in education, in learning, and in teaching? Is academia capable of incorporating non-Western thought and philosophy? Certainly one of the challenges we face is how to balance the Western hegemonic structure with the indigenous worldview; are they mutually exclusive? Steven Loza posed a brilliant question when putting together this volume when he asked, "How can spirituality and scholarship be bridged? Why do we continue to ignore or not adequately address the spiritual in theoretical frameworks?" In turn, I ask: "Can we move beyond the superficial understanding of images and history, and develop new models that incorporate the meta-matrix?"

In my own teaching and research I attempt to move in the direction taken by Steven Loza, Gregory Cajete, and others, who have refused to view the world in a compartmentalized manner and examine what I call the meta-matrix, and to include the spiritual and mystical, the ephemeral, in their work.

For example, I've been working on a project with an indigenous Inupiat group from Alaska. A small island community on the Bering Sea has been recording their entire music and dance repertoire. What surprised me was that they consider their most sacred repertoire their Polar Bear songs. To an outsider, hearing or watching a Polar Bear dance does not seem profound or particularly spiritual. Yet, upon learning more about the meaning of the polar bear hunt and the supplication of the polar bear spirit, of which the specially composed song forms are a large part, I learned that these strengthen their relationship with not only their physical world (which includes polar bears) but with that of the Polar Bear Spirit as well. In essence, it reaffirms their *spiritual* basis and center, their source of power and life.

How can one define this? In a Western academic setting, how can people understand the powerful spiritual relationship that indigenous people have with their environment, and how it is expressed? Where is that boundary between the mystical or spiritual and the environment—or the polar bear, in this example? Is there a boundary?

If we were all Inupiat people from King Island we would completely understand the profound meaning of a polar bear song. Can non-Inupiat understand this? Can we develop a dialectic that incorporates the spiritual and/or mystical so that we are able to understand this?

We live in a world with a strong undertow and, whether we are aware of it or not, it is full of powerful spirits. Although Western science and perspectives refuse to recognize this, it is so. We must continue to pose important questions, to interrogate the mainstream status quo: How do we counter the Western imperial hegemonic thought so that it includes recognition of the mystical or spiritual?

References

Chimegalrea, Vernon. 2002. Personal conversation, Bethel, Alaska (March).

Mayac, Ted. 2004. Personal conversation, Anchorage, Alaska (March).

Mayac, Ted, and Sylvester Ayec. 2000. Personal conversation, Nome, Alaska (June).

Oxford English Dictionary. 1993. 2 vols. (New York: Oxford University Press).

———. 1997. Vol. 3. (New York: Oxford University Press).

Williams, William M. 1988–89. Personal conversations, Anchorage, Alaska.

Guadalupe

An Indigenous Mythic Education Perspective

GREGORY A. CAJETE

Introduction

☞ THIS ESSAY IS ESSENTIALLY AN EXPLORATION OF INDIGENOUS education as viewed from the perspective of the mythic complex of Guadalupe as an Earth Mother symbol. It is not meant to represent an authoritative academic position but rather a creative, speculative exploration of the evolving myth of Guadalupe among indigenous peoples. Neither is it meant to be a retelling or historical analysis of the legend of Guadalupe, which is presented comprehensively by other authors in this anthology. This essay explores one possible aspect of the cultural psychology of indigenous mythic education, which may form a contextual backdrop for the evolution of the image of Guadalupe through time and cultural space. It presents a personal narrative based on personal experience and a culturally contexted conjecture of how and why the Guadalupe mythic complex is associated with Earth Mother symbolism by indigenous people themselves. It explores the mythic process of thinking behind the traditions and stories of Guadalupe wherein lie clues to her continued and expanding power as a religious symbol and highly creative subject of artistic rendering and interpretation. This essay also explores why the environmental-mythic construct of Earth Mother is important to explore in attempting to understand the mythic psychology of indigenous spirituality, adaptation to Christianity, and the overall role of the Earth Mother, in all her indigenous guises.

The current adoration of Guadalupe as Our Lady of the Americas continues a process of indigenous education or coming to know that combines history, myth, legend, tradition, emotion, religion, and artistic expression to metaphorically teach about relationship to spirit and the creative, feminine, fertile, nurturing, and care-taking qualities of Earth Mother mythologies. Using historical analysis, the Guadalupe legend provides an important foundation and necessary point of departure for understanding the multicontextual and multidimensional expressions of Guadalupe. However, to explore the deep mythic dimensions and cultural meaning of Guadalupe, it is necessary to extend ourselves beyond historical fact and into the realm of indigenous mythology and its epistemological dimensions. Exploring the mythic dimensions of a symbol requires using a lens that views myth through indigenous teaching, learning, story making and telling, history, tradition, politics, art, and spirituality to produce a composite view of what is essentially a dynamic field of symbolic relationships and interactive social and cultural psychologies. This mythic view tries to get at the meanings, understandings, and educative applications that surround a symbol such as Guadalupe among indigenous people.[1]

Guadalupe as An Integrative Sociopolitical, Mythic Symbol

As indigenous Mexican people tell the story, Guadalupe for indigenous peoples of the Americas is connected to Earth Mother symbolism. For the Aztec, she was associated with Tonantzin, Goddess of the Fertile Living Earth and Sister of the Moon. When introduced from Mexico into Pueblo country over three hundred years ago, Guadalupe also became associated with Earth Mother symbolism similar to that of the older symbolic complex of Corn Mother and Corn Maidens. In addition, she became a part of an evolving expression of Pueblo Catholicism as Pueblo people searched for ways to integrate the religion of Spanish conquerors with their own. For Pueblo people, then, Guadalupe was an introduced Catholic religious symbol and, while certainly not the same as the traditional Pueblo Corn Mother complex, the symbolic meanings associated with her paralleled those of traditional Pueblo belief. In a mythic-metaphoric way she has become another guise of Earth Mother.

As Jacqueline Dunnington states in her book, *Guadalupe: Our Lady of New Mexico*:

Her function as symbol of Mother; food, hope, health, life; supernatural salvation and salvation from oppression is ever expanding...Ultimately, The Virgin of Guadalupe derives stature as a primary vessel for the continuity of Catholic values and Mary's place in theology. Thus, she has an important symbolic function. The symbols of any culture often are drawn from historic sources and from the sacred realm, making religion, culture, and symbol interdependent. Guadalupe is one such master symbol. Her role as a religious symbol indicates a vitality and tenacity that have outlived historical eras, migrations, and cultural vicissitudes.[2]

Scholars continue to debate the question of whether Guadalupe was an invention of Spanish Catholic officials to further convert and enhance their dominion over the Aztec populace of 1531, or whether she was a new guise of the Aztec fertility goddess Tonantzin strategically created by the Aztecs themselves to outwardly appear to convert to Catholicism while holding onto older traditional spiritual thought, practices, and images. This essay presents thoughts on how this latter argument may have also figured as a part of the evolution of the mythic symbol of Guadalupe among indigenous peoples. Indeed, it is possible that Spanish Catholic authorities and the Aztecs may have embraced the symbolism of Guadalupe for their own separate reasons. When the legend and symbolism of Guadalupe migrated to New Mexico, it again underwent a transformation of meaning that served the sociopolitical and spiritual purposes of the Pueblo Indians and New Mexico Hispanics. Many mythic symbol complexes evolve and continue to have influence over time based on their mutual usefulness to many groups of people. Indeed, it might be said that Christianity itself, and its continuing influence as a world religion, is a direct result of this kind of integrative historical-social-mythic dynamic. The same might be said for the continuing viability of the Earth Mother symbolism, especially at this time of evolving awareness of ecological relationship and the rise of feminine consciousness.

There should no surprise in the fact that Guadalupe has had such a creative evolution among indigenous and Hispanic populations in the Southwest, Mexico, Central and South America, and now in Europe as well. The mythic meaning behind Guadalupe speaks to the psychology of many who feel oppressed, in need of spiritual nurturance and healing. She is a saint and protector of the common people, the poor, of women, children, and the Earth.

Our Lady of Guadalupe is symbolically at home with her devotees throughout the state: she dances with them, comforts them at funerals, walks with them on their pilgrimages, and lends her image to the arts—be they the painted praises and prayers of traditional folk art or popular likenesses of her image. As a symbol, she bridges the gap between the unseen spirit of the sacred and the material expressions of this mystery . . . she is . . . an agent for an epiphany, or manifestation, from the church to the classroom, from the studio to the barrio.[3]

A Personal Story

To remember is a way to re-know and reclaim a part of your life. The following personal recollections of my childhood growing up in my community of Santa Clara Pueblo, New Mexico, conveys my first exposure to the image, story, and symbolic reality of Our Lady of Guadalupe. Remembering these kinds of stories is a way of revitalizing the experience of indigenous education or ways of knowing in community.

When I was about five, I remember going with my grandmother to visit with her friends and relatives in the pueblo. I remember those days vividly because each visit was an adventure, a break from the usual routine. My grandmother was in every sense a matriarch—well known and respected in the pueblo as well as in the nearby Hispanic villages. She was of a generation born before the turn of the century. Her world and frame of reference were therefore of the "old" times of New Mexico, of a time when Pueblos reflected more complete expressions of symbiotic relationships with their respective environments.

I remember helping the old people prepare, plant, and hoe their gardens. I remember sitting with those old ones during the hot lazy afternoons eating Indian cookies and listening to their stories. I remember spending days in the foothills and mountains near the pueblo gathering plants my grandmother and other old ones directed me to collect. I remember playing with the other children who came with their grandmas and grandpas. I remember going to Santa Clara canyon and eating native trout baked in traditional fire pits with wild peppermint and watermelon and wild cherries with the old people and their grandchildren.

I remember always walking and visiting old people. I remember my grandmother telling me that all older people were my aunts and uncles and their children were my cousins and that I should call them such and treat them kindly. I remember that every one, young and old, shared with one another. When we went to visit older people we would take gifts, usually some sort of food, cloth, or meat. We would return with fruit, vegetables, and other gifts. It was a form of reciprocal giving, and that was how things got spread around. But that was not all: community news, prayers, shiny marbles, comics, toy soldiers, baseball cards, and a hundred other things got traded too.

When my grandmother and I attended a feast day at a neighboring pueblo, I remember the kindness with which we were received, especially by the other grandmas. In these visitations, I came to know the differences between Pueblos and other Indians, as well as the sense of oneness of the greater Pueblo world. I felt that, indeed, we were all related.

It is within this greater context of Pueblo life that I remember my first encounters with Our Lady of Guadalupe. Guadalupe had a special place in my grandmother's house and in all Pueblo communities. Our Lady of Guadalupe was many times referred to as the "Indian" saint because Juan Diego was an Indian and because the story of Guadalupe had a special resonance with Pueblo people.

I remember those times when I sat with my grandmother and other older women and men in what is called the "Saints' house," a small cottonwood leaf-lined shelter set up especially for pueblo feast days "so that the saints might also enjoy the dances." In the Saints' house the old ones sat with pictures, icons, and statues of Catholic saints praying the rosary, visiting and talking about the community news and, of course, the "old times." Guadalupe had a special place in the saint's house, too, and was especially attended to by women who would place special offerings of candles and prayers for healing at her feet. Guadalupe was, indeed, the patron of all the matriarchs of the pueblo. In this way, Pueblo people reaffirmed their faith in a Christian god while simultaneously reaffirming the traditional sense of Pueblo community, values, and way of life. Pueblo life has always revolved around tradition and age-old practices. Catholicism has been *adapted* to these ancient communal themes and thereby has been given a place in the Pueblo community, and this includes a very special place for Our Lady of Guadalupe.

I remember visiting people who were ill and my grandmother taking her small bags of herbs to give them with special instructions about their use and the proper prayers to say, including special prayers to Guadalupe. I remember my grandmother and other aunts baking bread in the special outdoor Pueblo ovens called *paan teh-ee* or *horno* in Spanish. I remember those special feasts when all my relatives would come to my grandmother's home or those times when she would go to help others prepare feasts for weddings, baptisms, and even funerals. In all of these contexts, some variation of the image of Guadalupe was prominently displayed, prayed to, and otherwise venerated.

There are many other memories of Guadalupe, many other events of communal life, in which Guadalupe was mentioned or her image displayed. These early memories still have the greatest vividness and remain with me even to this day as my "relational sense of community." Indeed, Pueblo people's sense of being, relationship, and education through community evolved through time. They adapt and transform over time in sync with the changes in our lives and, in this way, they form a foundation for personal and cultural history.

> Guadalupe is a fellow pilgrim, a family member far removed from theological, scientific, and historical arguments and proofs presented to disprove her 1531 apparitions and ensuing miracles. The core values that unite devotees of Guadalupe in her vast folk following are those very same elements that keep her veneration robust in New Mexico. Guadalupe as symbol links together family, heavenly order, colonial past, New World freedom, parish affiliations, and community bonds.[4]

Building on Earlier Realities

The legend of Guadalupe presents an excellent example of how indigenous peoples adapt mythic symbolism to their relational universe and to the important epistemological constructs that continue to guide their thoughts and traditions. The following example from Aztec thought and culture may help in understanding the educative and relational value of the mythic Earth Mother symbolism of Guadalupe.

The Aztec practice of building one pyramidal structure by encasing a previous one provides an appropriate metaphor for the developmental building process of indigenous ways of "coming to know" or what today may be called social, cultural, and spiritual education. This also may provide some insight into why indigenous people perceive Guadalupe as an expression of an earlier reality of the earth deity Tonantzin.

Following a common Mesoamerican dynastic practice, at the end of each Aztec dynasty the nobles of the reigning dynasty would commemorate their new order by erecting a symbolic new reality. In establishing this new reality, the nobles would engage in the building of a new ceremonial pyramid by encasing an older one, thereby metaphorically encasing an older reality by building a new one.

The new structure became the visible symbolic expression through which they espoused the new reality. As is evident from current excavations, these successive façades of "new reality" were actualized by recycling many of the materials used previously in the structures. A constant building upon earlier realities is a basic characteristic of an indigenous process of social and cultural adaptation. The newest reality may seem different from earlier ones, but its essential essence and foundation remain tied to the earlier realities that it encases. The Aztec pyramids were restructured, enlarged, and remolded, but their ancient foundations remained.

Building on the realities of past generations and expressing new realities with each dynasty, while remaining true to basic principles and orientations, are reflective of the kind of structuring process to which the evolution of indigenous mythic education is naturally tied. Extending the metaphor of the structuring of Aztec pyramids to the "building" of a contemporary expression of an indigenous Earth Mother figure in the guise of Our Lady of Guadalupe can be said to be plausible from the standpoint of the evolution of a mythic symbol, and we have several images of structuring, of engineering a new reality built upon earlier ones, while reflecting the needs and facing the "sun" of the times in which we now live.

Mythic education is always in process and essentially being built from the stones or foundations of prior structures. Indigenous mythic complexes have "prior structures," that is, metaphoric and symbolic stones and foundations from which new expressions may once again be built. Through the lens of this sort of mythic psychology, knowing whether the actual historic facts support the Guadalupe story is not as important to indigenous people as is the mythic meaning and purpose of her story.[5]

Education as Flower and Song: A Tribal Metaphor

In the tradition of the Náhuatl-speaking Aztec of the Valley of Mexico, the ideal purpose of education was to "find one's face, find one's heart" and search for a "foundation," a truth, a support, a way of life and work through which one could express one's life. To this end, the Aztec developed schools they called the "Calmécac," in which the "tlamatinimine," the philosopher poets of Aztec society, taught by using poetic chants that they called "flower and song." Through a variety of formal and informal methods including the use of mythic complexes, the tlamatinimine encouraged their students to "find their face" (develop and express their innate character and potential); to "find their heart" (to search out and express their inner passion); and to explore "foundations" of life and work (to find that vocation that allowed the student the fullest expression of self and truth). To this end the tlamatinimine led his students on many study paths including astronomy, architecture, religion, martial arts, medicine, philosophy, and various other cultural art forms.[6]

Through stories, the tlamatinimine explored with their students the mystery of life after death. They studied man as a creator of a way of life, man as creator of educational, ethical, legal, and aesthetic principles. They explored the nature of the social and personal ideals that gave rise to that divine spark in man's heart that transforms him into an artist, a poet, a sage.[7]

The Aztec quest for searching out and expressing the gift in each student in service to their community, which, in turn, made them capable of making divine things and being a complete man or woman, is an ancient and recurring theme of indigenous education whose variations occur in ancient cultures around the world.

Just as the Greek concept of *paideia* or educating for wholeness through teaching and learning of *arete* (enabling expressions of human life), the Aztecs sought to mold their young in accordance with an ideal. While this ideal was culturally defined by Aztec spirituality, thought, and tradition, it was a reflection of concepts and a way of educating held by indigenous people in the Americas. Other examples of tribal myth and metaphors exist that reflect a richness and depth of understanding of human learning. It is within this prior complex philosophical and mythic educative process that the symbolism of Guadalupe may be understood as a continuing expression of prior Earth Mother symbolism.

Tribal Myth as a Body of Knowledge

To gain a sense of this connection, it is necessary to explore tribal myths as bodies of prior tribal knowledge. Tribal myths contain tremendous psychological energy that illuminates and contexts the acts of both individual and community when it is appropriately accessed. Every body of tribal myth contains a variety of stories that are culturally important to a tribe and reflect their uniqueness. Tribal myths are filled with tribally significant metaphors, symbols, images, and creative linguistic/visual forms that are emotionally affective for members of a tribe. They are essentially interpreted accounts of the world experienced through the lives of the people of the tribe. As a whole, they are reflections of the role of people and their relationship to the spirits that affect a tribe's world. Collectively, tribal myths and legends form a body of explanation that, in turn, forms the "Story of the People" as they perceive it.[8]

Every tribe creates vehicles for skillfully and creatively accessing the inherent energy contained in their body of myth. Through the telling, performance, and artistic expression of myth, tribal teachers actively brought their tribal bodies of myth alive and made its lessons relevant to their audience's time and place. While keeping true to the core meanings of their myths, tribal teachers continually improvised, reorganized, and recreated the particular elements of a myth to fit their audience, the situation, and their own personal expression. In reality, every myth is renewed each time *and* in each place it is told. Myths live through each teller and through each audience that hears and actively engages them. Myths and their enactment in every form were the ways a tribe remembered to remember their shared experience as a people.

There are as many ways to tell a myth as there are myth tellers, and there are many ways to view myth as well. Western academic schools of mythic thought have ranged from evolutionist, to symbolic, to psychoanalytic, to functionalist, to structuralist, to folkloric orientations in their attempts to explain the human phenomenon of myth. Yet only recently have Western scholars turned to the keepers of myth for guidance and, only recently, have some Western scholars of myth begun to cultivate an appreciation for these keepers and reverence for the *power* of myths in shaping human learning and experience. Indeed, humans are story-telling animals. Story is a primary structure through which humans think, relate, and communicate. We make stories, tell stories, and live stories because it is such an integral part of being human. Myths, legends, and folk tales have been a cornerstone of teaching in every culture. These forms of story teach us about the nature of human life in all its dimensions and manifestations. They teach us how to live fully through reflection on or participation in the uniquely human cultural expressions of community, art, religion, *and* adaptation to a natural environment. The myths we live by actively shape and integrate our life experience. They inform us, as well as form us, through our interaction with their symbols and images.[9]

Myths explain what it means to live in community with one another. They explain human dependence on the natural world and essential relationships that must be maintained therein. They explore the life-and-death matters of human existence and relate such matters to basic origins, causes, or relationships. They reflect on the concerns that are basic *and* crucial to humans' understanding of themselves. Creation, survival, relationship, healing, wholeness, and death are the consistent themes of myth in every culture, place, and time. In short, myths are everything that the people and community that create them are.

The function of myth is as diverse and complex as human life and cultures. The myths we live by glue our communities together through shared metaphors of identity and purpose. Myths help to balance individual psychologies and connect them to the greater wholes of the tribe, natural environment, and global community. Myths resound the spiritual essence of religion and ritual in life-related terms. Myth mirrors the paradoxes of life and reflects the truth behind every paradox.

Myth, in both its expressions through narrative and performance, is a communicative art form that integrates other art forms such as song, dance, and visual arts in its expression. Indeed, myth is a primary contextual field for artistic expression and may have led to the development of art in the early stages of human culture. Art is one of the languages of myth!

Finally, myths live or die through people. Myths, as human creations, are messages—as well as a way of conscious reflection—that live through the people who share them, through the breath of their thoughts, words, and actions.

Living through myth means learning how to use the primal images and processes that myth presents in a creative process of learning and teaching that connects our past, present, and future. Living through myth also means learning to live a life of relationships to ourselves, other people and the world based on an appreciation, understanding, and guidance from our inner spirit and our wealth of ancestral/cultural traditions.

To seek such a life is a foundational metaphor of indigenous education that invites the empowerment and cultivation of a creative life of learning. And it is the images and symbols brought to life through myth at the personal and group levels that provide impetus for such a creative life of learning.

Mythic images are pictures that involve us both physiologically in our bodily reactions to them and spiritually in our higher thoughts about them. When a person is aware of living mythically, he or she is experiencing life intensively and reflectively.[10]

Tracking a Myth: The Concentric Rings of the Indigenous Education Process

The working of a metaphor is a creative way of exploring the teaching processes using myth in tribal societies, and this process can be used in an exploration of a symbol such as Guadalupe. Guadalupe symbolism began at a time of extreme upheaval in Mexico. The evolution of her symbolism among the indigenous people of Mexico and, later, New Mexico through five hundred years of colonization is reflective of one possible way mythological thinking can be used by a group of people under extreme sociocultural stress. Such a process reflects one possible dynamic of indigenous teaching and learning as an attempt to adapt to the dynamics of a rapidly changing world over which they seemingly have no control. This view of symbols and metaphors associated with Guadalupe might be said to be *a way of asking for knowledge about how to survive and sustain oneself* in the face of extreme social and spiritual stress. Yet even in this regard, the ways the legend of Guadalupe have been used and continue to be used by indigenous people as a connection to earlier Earth Mother symbolism is unique. While this sort of exploration would take a more extensive examination than this essay allows, some of the following operating understandings might be applied since earlier and contemporary indigenous stories related to Guadalupe resound with Earth Mother relationship and reflect the environmental connections of her stories.

Primal mythologies abound with examples of tracing and working the tracks of "the ancestors" through time and through a geographical landscape of mythology whose concentric rings radiate to the present time and place. A key to understanding mythological tracking is developing the ability to think in terms of concentric rings of relationship. For instance, within the contexts of Native American mythologies, certain geographical features personify ties between natural processes. Generally, such features are looked upon as sacred places. These natural features may be specific formations, springs, lakes, rivers, mountains, or other natural places. All these features physically, visually, and metaphysically represent concentric rings in nature. Many are symbols of life sustainers such as corn, deer, buffalo, fish, rain clouds, and forests. An understanding of the relationships inherent in these ties is essential to survival. Therefore, much attention is given to ways of knowing and learning about important natural phenomena.

Myths present a way of mapping a particular geographical landscape. Relating the stories associated with a particular geographic place is a way to begin to develop a cognitive map of that place and of its concentric rings of interrelationship. Migration myths, for instance, are tracking stories through a geographical landscape. In many Native American migration myths, it is implied that the ancestors left representations of themselves in various natural forms or phenomena to remind people how to act and how to relate to the natural world.[11]

Through the symbol of concentric rings, myth is able to give us a visual image of how one thing in reality is like something in myth and vice versa. Every myth has its concentric rings of meaning and is told and retold in this way. The telling of a myth begins with a simple version for children, and then moves to a slightly more complicated version for adolescents, to a deeper version for initiates, and to a still deeper version for the fully mature.

The symbol of concentric circles in its many manifestations throughout the cultures of the world universally seems to connote a process event. That is, the concentric ring, when it is used in primal myth, ritual, or art, denotes that something happened here or that something is happening here; it might be a waterhole, a ceremony, a distinct natural phenomenon, or an important life activity.

For instance, the concentric ring represents a major process symbol in the mythology, ritual, and art of the Australian aborigine. As represented in Aboriginal traditional art, the concentric ring is a place of an important event of sacred significance and great insight. The mandala and the medicine wheel are other symbolic exemplifications of significant process events. Since myth mirrors and analogizes natural process, it is no wonder that one of the simplest symbols represents one of the most complex processes of both nature and the human psyche—that of interrelationships.

The symbol of concentric rings also reveals that everything is unique and leaves its own signature track. Yet it also shows that all things share likenesses that are to be found in the overlap of rings. Knowledge grows and develops outward in concentric rings. Likewise, concentric rings can also form the basis of learning how to track ideas and intuitions, how to observe fields of knowledge, and how to see patterns and connections in thought and natural reality.

Indigenous education in "process" is basically following tracks in a particular field or level of natural, social, or spiritual reality. This tracking at any given dimension requires opening one's mind to the possibilities within each of the many concentric circles within that dimension. Learning how to blend the mythological, aesthetic, intuitive, and visual perspectives of nature with the scientific, rational, and verbal perspective is an integral part of indigenous education. Education, from this viewpoint, involves learning to see nature holistically. This requires a continual shifting and interplay between the two complementary perspectives mentioned. Facilitating the learning of how to orchestrate these two ways of viewing nature toward the greatest effect must become a major activity of contemporary Indian education.

In this indigenously modeled approach, a first track begins with a symbol. It is these symbols that are the connection or keys that access the myth, the relationships of concentric circles, and knowledge and perceptions of natural realities.

The Southwestern Indian symbol of the humpbacked flute player, sometimes called Kokopeli or ant man, provides a case in point: Kokopeli is a mythological symbol that represents the bringer of seeds, fertility, sexuality, abundance, and the spreading of art and culture. Kokopeli is a natural process symbol that is "pregnant" with meaning. As such, the symbol of Kokopeli is surrounded by many myths; these myths in turn abound with metaphors representing various dimensions of the procreative processes of nature. Each of these processes is encircled by a body of psychological, aesthetic, and cultural expressions. These expressions in turn are tied to realities that are observable and that form a basis for indigenous teaching through myth.

Kokopeli is a mythically contexted visual metaphor that acts as a kind of gatekeeper or master symbol. That is, through tracking its meaning at multiple levels of use and its various appearances in myths from Mexico to the Southwest United States, one reaches one of the foundational roots of an indigenous archetype and mythic tradition. There are other gatekeepers connected to other foundational Puebloan mythic roots. Thinking Woman, the Corn Maidens, and Spider Woman are some of the others.

Tribal-specific gatekeepers exist for the Aztec, Navajo, Lakota, Iroquois, Ojibway, Pima, Huichol, Inuit, and *every* other tribe from Alaska to the tip of South America. The complex of Raven myths in the Northwest, the Coyote/Trickster myths of the West and Southwest, the Inapi (Old Man) myths of the Northern Plains, the Sedna myths of the Far North, the Abiding Ston-Inyan and White Buffalo Calf Woman myths of the Central Plains, and the Tree of Peace and Great Turtle of the Northern Woodlands are only a few of the American tribal mythic bodies, each of which contains numbers of gatekeeper symbols whose tracking leads to the roots of a tribal tradition and its mythic knowledge base.

Tracking selected tribal gatekeepers through key myths illustrates a primary process of mythic education. This methodology is a form of creative analysis in which the logic for myth and its validation is internally consistent with the perspective of a tribe's understanding of an essential message reflected through the myth.

Those gatekeeper symbols widely used in a particular region that have a wide breadth of meaning can be explored within the context of myths from the same region. Behind each of these symbols is a major indigenous cultural or philosophical concept, and they provide ideal vehicles for ways of seeing, understanding, and relating considered important by a group of tribes in a region.

Elemental Points about Indigenous Education

Finally, there are a number of elements that characterize indigenous education and processes. These elements characterize some aspect of the expression of indigenous education wherever and however it has been expressed. A few of these characteristics are included here to provide landmarks to assist the reader. Aspects of the Guadalupe story certainly mirror these elemental points, qualifying it as a mythic teaching story.

The sacred view of Nature permeates and contexts the foundational process of teaching and learning.

It uses story and mythic complexes as ways to root a perspective that unfolds through the special use of language.

It recognizes the power of thought and language to create the worlds we live in.

It creates maps of the world that assist us through our life's journey.

It resonates and builds learning through the tribal structures of the home and community.

Integration and interconnectedness are universal traits.

Relationships between elements and knowledge bases radiate in concentric rings of process and structure.

Rites symbolize various elements of its processes and structures.

Its processes adhere to the principle of mutual reciprocity between humans and all other things.

It recognizes and incorporates the cycles within cycles, that is, there are always deeper levels of meaning to be found in every learning/teaching process.

It presents something to learn for everyone, at every stage of life.

It recognizes the levels of maturity and readiness to learn in the developmental process of both males and females. This recognition is incorporated into the designs and situations in which indigenous teaching takes place.

It recognizes language as a sacred expression of breath and incorporates this orientation in all its foundations.

It recognizes that each person and each culture contains the seeds of all that is essential to their well being and positive development.

Art is used as both a vehicle of utility and expression. Art is recognized as an expression of the soul.

It recognizes and applies ordering through ceremony, ritual, and community activity.

The ritual complex is used as both structure and process for teaching key principles and values.

It recognizes that the true sources of knowledge are to be found within the individual *and* entities of nature.

It recognizes that true learning occurs through participation and honoring relationships in both the human and natural communities.

It honors the ebb and flow of learning as it moves back and forth through individuals, community, nature, and the cosmos.

It recognizes that learning requires letting go, growing, and reintegration at successively higher levels of understanding.

Its purpose is to teach a way of life.

It occurs always within an authentic context of community and nature.[12]

These essential points are reflected in multiple ways through the contexts, methods, and expressions of indigenous mythic education presented by the evolving mythic complex of Guadalupe. They can provide the building stones for new structures, new foundations, and new realities in contemporary indigenous education.

In this essay, I have attempted to reflect on the mythic meaning of Guadalupe as viewed through my eyes as an indigenous scholar and educator. Guadalupe is a unique cultural/mythological hybrid born out of the historical, cultural, and spiritual dynamics that have characterized the history of the Americas for the last five hundred years. Indeed, the story of Guadalupe could not have been born anywhere else but in the Americas. Her story is, in and of itself, a story of the continuing survival of indigenous thought in the Americas and its integration of Western thought and spirituality while remaining true to an earlier relationship to the Earth Mother. The exploration of her story is important for all people of the Americas, but her story may have the greatest importance for indigenous people and their understanding of their own ways of teaching and learning. The key lies in indigenous people's own collective ability to create the contexts in which they may most appropriately be applied as they erect a new expression of indigenous life in the twenty-first century.

Notes

1. For an excellent and comprehensive history of the evolution of the symbol of Guadalupe in New Mexico, see Jacqueline Orsini Dunnington, *Guadalupe: Our Lady of New Mexico* (Santa Fe: Museum of New Mexico Press, 1999).
2. Dunnington, *Guadalupe*, xvi–xvii.
3. Ibid., xviii.
4. Ibid., 157.
5. Gregory Cajete, *Look to the Mountain: An Ecology of Indigenous Education* (Durango: Kivakí Press, 1994), 28–29.
6. Miguel León-Portilla, *Aztec Thought and Culture: A Study of the Ancient Nahuatl Mind*, trans. Jack Emory Davis (Norman: University of Oklahoma Press, 1963), 3–24.
7. Ibid.
8. Cajete, *Look to the Mountain*, 115–17.
9. Ibid.
10. Naomi Goldberg, *Changing the Gods: Feminism and the End of Traditional Religions* (Boston: Beacon Press, 1979), 47.
11. Cajete, *Look to the Mountain*, 121–23.
12. Ibid., 29–32.

The Pueblo Indian Experience

JOE SANDO

☞ THE U.S. CENSUS FIRST REPORTED IN 1980 THAT THE PUEBLO INDIANS of New Mexico were able to retain a greater amount of their culture than other groups. They have kept their native language and their native religion and cultural activities. There must be a reason for this report of existence and continuum. I have studied the situation and concluded that one has to review Indian history to arrive at a logical conclusion. As we are all aware, indigenous natives throughout the American continent have different histories and most have suffered in similar ways—invasions, strange wars, pressures on their cultures, loss of language, and, especially, the loss of aboriginal land base.

The first reason that came to my mind with respect to the retention of Pueblo culture was the Pueblo Revolt of 1680. Some writers today might call it ethnic cleansing. That revolt happened following years of struggle to retain spiritual harmony by practicing their native culture, which they did from the beginning of their existence. That was seriously threatened because the Pueblo people would not accept a new religion that was strange and not understood, but was being forced on them. This only compounded the injury, however, because there were other life-threatening policies that were menacing the people.

These were the policies of *encomienda* and *repartimiento*, which together took much of their food and forced them into doing unpaid labor. These were the main dissatisfactions, although there were cases of harassment by a few of the governor's men.

Through oral history the Pueblos had known of the initial invaders, Coronado's men, and how they killed a few Zunis at initial contact. A short battle took place at Zuni Pueblo when Coronado's troops innocently crossed or stepped over the sacred corn-meal line awaiting Zuni pilgrims returning home from a lake in Arizona. Then there was the killing of hundreds of Tiwa people in the Bernalillo area due to the misdeeds of one of the invaders. Many years later there was the episode at Acoma Pueblo with Juan de Oñate's nephew, which resulted in bad feelings for many years between the Acomas and the colonizers. Little did the Pueblos know of Columbus and the resulting deaths of millions of natives beginning in the Caribbean, or the much earlier killing and destruction campaign of Hernando de Soto through Creek and Chickasaw country. Many writers recounted activities north of Mexico only.

Mexico and south of Mexico were a different story, maybe worse. But out of this experience a hero appeared to the Pueblos. I say this because changes of policy took place in the Spanish mind, maybe created by Fray Bartolomé de las Casas. As a younger padre he had observed the cruelties of the Spanish invaders in Mexico and Peru. When he retired he began to write about his experience and what he had witnessed. He was thrown in jail for his writings and speeches. But it is thought that, in time, the Crown believed him and decided that if the Spaniards went to another new country they would be more apostolic and less militaristic. A padre was to be present with authority equal to that of the military leaders. Thus, I believe, the Franciscan missionaries who came to New Mexico helped the Pueblos in many ways, numerous times.

That said, the Spaniards were well schooled in the ways of war after battling the Moors in Spain for centuries and their experience in what we now call Latin America. Nevertheless, the Pueblos suffered from those actions I described earlier. The kind-hearted padres and civil leaders had to eat the food from Pueblo pro bono labor. It is rarely mentioned that most European invaders depended on native food and labor at the beginning of the colonies in America.

While suffering, the Pueblos were told that if they accepted the new religion they would be at peace. In 1581–82 Franciscan lay brother Augustin Rodriguez, military captain Francisco Sanchez Chamuscado, and a small party of Spaniards visited the pueblos and attempted to convert them to Catholicism, but their efforts failed. A decade later Captain Gaspar Castano de Sosa came and planted crosses at most pueblos. He supposedly also gave some Pueblos their patron saints. But he was taken back to Mexico in chains because he had come without permission from the viceroy. Much later, I believe, the Mexicans brought the story of Our Lady of Guadalupe. By that time the Pueblos were Catholics. Guadalupe was accepted immediately and given an honored place in the church circle and Pueblo calendar. She is the patron saint of Pojoaque and Zuni pueblos but many Pueblos celebrate her day on December 12. Many individuals named after her also celebrate by feasting and feeding friends.

Today celebrating their saint's day is a big day for each pueblo, and for the state of New Mexico, as it brings many tourists. For the Pueblos, it serves to preserve and continue their culture. These feast days remain more important to the Pueblos than U.S. holidays, especially the fourth of July. On feast days many individuals and families return home to renew their spiritual life. Traditional foods are prepared, people dress in traditional ways, and the native language is spoken. All these observations serve to maintain their ancestors' way of life and continue their culture.

Extended families also get together, and neighboring Spanish families come to assist, especially at mass and processions, by singing Spanish hymns. The Pueblo-Spanish union is probably the only native/European-based ancestry still living together, bonded originally by a common enemy their ancestors battled, the raiding tribes. Many of the two living styles are similar: food, religion, and language—language until recently. Today, the Pueblo's second language is English. The Spaniards brought not only Spanish ways of life, but also some traditions or ideas that the Moors had contributed to Spain. One of the Moorish contributions to the Pueblos is the Spanish *horno* (oven), which is found at nearly every Pueblo home today.

Another great act by our Spanish partners was the Spanish land grant of 1689 by Governor Domingo Cruzate. We cannot accept that he gave us the Indian land we already owned, but we do believe the act helped to guarantee that no one else might move onto the Indian land. The Spanish also had a law that said no colonists may locate near Indian land since their animals might damage Indian farm crops. But recently the land grants act has proved worthwhile, since the U.S. government has unilaterally taken much aboriginal Indian land throughout the country, but has not included the Pueblo land. Many other Indian tribes lost their lands when they were forced to relocate. Perhaps the Pueblos are the only Indian tribes that are still on their aboriginal lands as first seen by the Europeans. The U.S. Constitution does not help the American Indians, since in Article One, Section Eight, the Constitution says that the U.S. Congress shall deal in commerce with the foreign nations, the states, and the Indians, thus giving all equal status.

Some people try to say that the Bureau of Indian Affairs (BIA) exists to compensate for loss of land by the Indians. However, I don't buy that. The Indian bureau was created to protect American Indians from manifest destiny. The Pueblos were recognized or accepted as American Indians in 1912. When the Americans arrived in 1846 the Pueblos were equal citizens of the state. This occurred in 1820 when the Spanish governor in Santa Fe, Facundo Melgares, determined that the Treaty of Córdova qualified the Pueblos as equal citizens. The following year, the Mexican government took possession of New Mexico. Under the Plan of Iguala in 1821, Mexico also declared the Pueblos to be equal citizens. Because the Pueblos were equal citizens of the state when the Americans arrived in 1846, Indian land became the goal of many new citizens. After many years of complaining, in 1912 the Pueblos finally were recognized as Native Americans needing protection from the onslaught of the territory's new citizens.

In 1855 the territorial legislature took the right to vote from the Pueblos. We did not regain the right to vote until 1948, long after Pueblo men and women had served in the armed services during World War I and II. During those nonvoting years, the Pueblos existed at the mercy of the BIA, who supposedly did what they thought was good for us as helpless citizens. We could not speak or write to the congressional delegates in Washington or to the state government. One incident that took place at my home will tell you what I am trying to say. In 1880 my village council leased land to the Presbyterian Church for the purpose of operating a school and to offer medical help. According to the contract agreement the lease was to terminate when there were no more students. In 1924 there were only three students so the council wanted to close the school. But the BIA advised it was not the time. Since that date two more governors have asked the BIA about returning the land to the tribe. Each time the BIA has refused to approve a court hearing. Learning about it in 1984, I spoke to the right people, and got the papers for the land in question. Today this piece of land contains offices for the Pueblo programs, and the land was returned without attorney fees as a result of my research.

In conclusion, I wish to state that the Pueblo Indians were fortunate that they met the Spaniards first. The Spaniards did not let the Pueblos have horses and guns, which might have changed their history. I say this because history tells us that the English and French sold guns to the Indians in the East. Once they had guns their European friends encouraged the Indians to kill their European competitors, the French or English. They both used Indian allies in their wars and in the end the Indians lost out. An example is the French-Indian wars, between the English and the French. In this confrontation the French lost; many of them, along with their Indian allies, went to Canada, where their descendents reside today. The use of Indians as allies was repeated during the American Revolution and again in the Civil War.

The year 1694 was a fateful year, as many unexpected disasters took place in Pueblo Indian country. The genesis of the troubles may be the expedition by Governor Domingo Cruzate in 1689, when he attacked and destroyed Zia Pueblo. During this battle a Zia man by the name of Bartolomé de Ojeda was seriously wounded. The ever-thoughtful Spaniards convinced the wounded man to return with them and be healed. This Ojeda did. While in El Paso del Norte healing, Ojeda learned to speak and write Spanish. Thus he was prepared to be a valuable ladino friend for the Spanish. Consequently, on the second trip by Governor don Diego de Vargas with the settlers, Ojeda and his Keresan followers led the way. So it was a safe return in October 1693 and the people in Santa Fe called it a bloodless reconquest.

But where Ojeda really contributed to the Spaniards was when he and his Keresan followers, Zia, Santa Ana, and San Felipe, helped DeVargas and his troops attack three Keresan villages—Santo Domingo, Cochiti and La Cienega—in April 1694. Eventually many from Santo Domingo and Cochiti and most from La Cienega fled to Acoma. The Acomas placed them at Cocima, north of Acoma proper. In August 1694 DeVargas and Ojeda tried to make them return to their Rio Grande homes but they refused. When DeVargas was replaced by Governor Pedro R. Cubero, he and Joseph Naranjo of Santa Clara were able to persuade the refugees to get off the high rock. They traveled north until they reached a beaver pond to rest. The people liked the area so they petitioned the governor to stay there and build their homes and church. Their request was approved and, on July 2, 1698, the refugees became the Laguna tribe or pueblo.

Following the April attack on the Keresan villages, DeVargas and Ojeda and their troops attacked Jemez people on San Diego mesa in July

1664. The story is commonly repeated that during this battle the likeness of San Diego appeared on the east side of the mesa on the sandstone cliff visible on the way to Jemez Springs. Following this battle the Jemez people were split into three groups. One group, the prisoners, was taken to Santa Fe. The second group fled to Hopi country and did not return to the land until 1718 under the rule of Governor Felipe Martínez. The third group fled northwest to Boulder Canyon in Rio Arriba County, today just north of Counselor. Anthropologists call the Jemez refugee home Navajo pueblitos, which is wrong. Eventually, many married Navajos, becoming Navajos of the Coyote and Young Corn clans from Jemez. These people acculturated many Jemez values. The Navajo language has many Jemez words, and I noticed that the code talkers' word for "P" is a Jemez word.

PART V

Comparative Concepts in the Praxis of Religion as Art

The Virgins of Guadalupe (Tonantzin) and La Caridad del Cobre (Ochún)

Two Marian Devotions as Fluid Symbols
of Collective and Individual Cultural Identities

FRANCISCO J. CRESPO

☞ DEVOTION TO THE VIRGIN MARY HAS OCCUPIED AN IMPORTANT ROLE in Christian life and theology since its emergence in the fifth century. With the conquest and colonization of what was called America, the cult of the Virgin Mary took root, gained an extensive following, expanded into new regions, and her sanctuaries have become important spiritual centers for millions of people. Today, under many representations and names, in every Latin American country, she is the patroness, protector, and mediator before God for the oppressed, exploited, and afflicted (Wheeler 1998, 7). In Latin America she is referred to as Our Lady of Mercy, Our Lady of the Rosary, Our Lady of Remedies, Our Lady of the Immaculate Conception, Our Lady of the Annunciation, and Our Lady of Sorrows, among others (Taylor 1987, 1).

This essay focuses on two such representations: La Virgen de Guadalupe/Tonantzin from Mexico and La Virgen de La Caridad del Cobre/Ochún from Cuba. These two devotions to the Virgin Mary are of miraculous origins and have played a major role in the histories of their respective countries. It would be difficult to convey, or even fully appreciate, the inner experiences and motivations underlying the devotion in Mexico and Cuba to these two Madonnas, and I do not attempt to do so here. Instead, this paper provides a comparative overview of these multivalent and multivocal national and religious symbols and their various representations through time.

Over several centuries, La Virgen de Guadalupe/Tonantzin and La Caridad del Cobre/Ochún not only have been attributed with miraculous cures and rescues, but have served as amalgamating forces that have brought together people of different social classes, creeds, genders, professions, cultures, and ethnicities. Their images evoke a powerful symbolism. National identity, rebellion, health, salvation, nourishment, motherhood, and motherly love are some of the common symbolic attributes of these Marian images.

The Growth of Our Lady of Guadalupe as a Powerful Symbol of Religious, Regional, and National Identity

Today considered the empress, goddess, and mother of the Mexicans, the Virgin of Guadalupe earlier was referred to as Tonantzin, the "mother of the gods," or simply "our mother," by the Nahua-speaking people from the valley of Mexico. Renowned Franciscan missionary Fray Bernardino de Sahagún provided one of the earliest accounts of the veneration of the Virgin of Guadalupe by the indigenous people of Mexico in the early colonial period (Taylor 1987, 14). Father Fray Bernardino de Sahagún suspected and denounced in 1576 the cult of the Virgin of Guadalupe practiced on a small hill known as the Tepeyacac (on the nose of the mountain) in northeastern Mexico City. According to Sahagún, a new form of ritual dedicated to the Virgin of Guadalupe had been superimposed on practices formerly dedicated in honor of Tonantzin, a prehispanic supreme female deity (León-Portilla 2002, 112–13). He complained that the cult of Guadalupe provided the Indians with an excuse to commit idolatry (Brading 2001, 2). Sahagún also criticized the Spanish Catholic Church's preachers for calling the Virgin by the name of Tonantzin. He blamed those clerics' use of the Aztec name for the Virgin for sparking and masking the idolatry of the indigenous entity (Gruzinski 2001, 190). Father Sahagún wrote that:

> It appears a satanic invention to palliate idolatry under the equivocation of this name Tonantzin. And now they come to visit this Tonantzin from afar, as distant as before. This devotion is suspicious, because in all parts there are many churches of Our Lady and they do not go to them; and they come from distant lands to this Tonantzin, as they did a long time ago. (Brading 2001, 215)

No known evidence has survived of the existence of any prehispanic image of Tonantzin (Brading 2001, 12). However, some historians have established a relationship between Tonantzin and other female Aztec deities, such as *Cihuacóatl, Cinteotl, Teteoinnan,* and/or *Coatlicue* (Zires 1994, 283).

The absence of such evidence is not surprising. Religious institutions in New Spain (colonial Mexico) have been dominated by the Roman Catholic Church ever since Cortés arrived, accompanied by priests, in 1519. The Spanish conquerors pressed their spiritual values on the peoples of Mesoamerica and had no tolerance for native religions. The conquerors systematically sought to eliminate written, oral, visual, and ritual representations of indigenous Mesoamerican worldviews with the cross in one hand and a sword in the other. Cortés's military campaign banner carried an image of the Virgin Mary, and Cortés himself placed images and statues of the Virgin Mary, of which he brought a generous supply, on the altars of the peoples he defeated (Taylor 1987, 10). When the archbishopric of the kingdom of New Spain was established at Mexico City in 1546, the Catholic cathedral was intentionally constructed over the ruins of the Great Temple of Tenochtitlan, the physical and symbolic center of the Aztec empire.

Sahagún's attempts to cast out the then new cult to the Virgin of Guadalupe had little effect over the growing ardent faith of the native population (Gruzinski 2001, 197). Today some people still refer to her as Guadalupe-Tonantzin. This phenomenon is consistent with the view of anthropologist Nestor García Canclini, who introduced the notion of hybrid culture. García Canclini challenged the dominant notion of culture as homogeneous; instead, he argued, all cultures are more or less hybrid. García Canclini (1990) views the hybridization of the Latin American cultures as the product of indigenous traditions and colonial Spanish Catholicism. For García Canclini, hybridization is a continuous process in which the hegemonic and subordinate classes interact and appropriate the cultural expressions of the other with the sole purpose of building a consensus. García Canclini argues that his hybridization idea not only avoids the static and exclusive dimensions of the identities but favors the integration and the act of living together of heterogeneous groups within a shared society. Culture is defined by García Canclini as "the production of phenomena that contribute, through symbolic representation or re-elaboration of material structures, to the understanding, reproduction, transformation of the social system, in other words, all practices and institutions involved in the administration, renewal, and restructuring of meaning" (García Canclini 1993, 10).

Much has been written and made of the legend and protagonists of the apparition of the Virgin of Guadalupe. The origin and the author of the legend are unknown. Is the story of the Virgin of Guadalupe truth or fiction? This question has proven difficult for scholars and enthusiasts alike to answer, although many have attempted with essays that range from scholarly to the intensely personal. But whether the story is "true" is beside the point. What we see throughout history is a steady incremental presence of the Virgin of Guadalupe in the devotional life of Mexico.

The controversy regarding the historical basis of the legend has not affected the faith and devotion of Guadalupe's followers and, in fact, her following continues to grow. Since 1648, the year the story of the 1531 apparition was first published in Spanish, devotion to Guadalupe has been on the rapid rise. The development of the cult honoring the Virgin of Guadalupe occupied a key place in colonial society, especially because church leaders and clergy promoted and intensified the veneration of the image of the Mexican Guadalupe even in rural areas of central Mexico (Taylor 1987, 14). By the end of the seventeenth century, the Virgin had emerged as the key symbol of Mexican identity. As a consequence of her rising popularity between 1695 and 1709, the Catholic Church decided to build a majestic new church for her at Tepeyac (also known historically as "Tepeyacac"), replacing the modest chapel built by orders of Archbishop Montúfar (Brading 2001, 5). In 1746, the Virgin was acclaimed the patron saint and protector of all the kingdom of New Spain, an action confirmed later in 1754 by Pope Benedict IV (Wheeler 1998, 7; Brading 2001, 6).

Devotion to Guadalupe continued to flourish in Mexico, despite repeated reports that her legend had no basis in fact. For example, toward the end of the eighteenth century, chief cosmographer of the Indies, Juan Bautista Muñoz, presented a document to the Royal Academy of History in Madrid in which he concluded that the apparition narrative had no reliable historical foundations (Brading 2001, 7). Nevertheless, when Napoleon invaded Spain and captured Ferdinand VII at the beginning of the nineteenth century, father Miguel Hidalgo y Costilla launched a revolt against Spain. It is widely known that when Hidalgo gathered his army of local Indian and mestizo forces, the Virgin of Guadalupe became the insurgents' banner. This banner's inscription read: "Long live religion.

Long live our most holy mother Guadalupe. Long live Ferdinand VII. Long live America and death to bad government." With the banner of Our Lady of Guadalupe as their standard, the insurrection marched toward Mexico City with a cry, "Long live the Virgin of Guadalupe and death to the *gachupines!*"[1] (Alamán 2002, 173).

After Hidalgo's death, the Virgin of Guadalupe continued to be invoked as a symbol of Mexican identity and an icon of Mexico's war of independence from Spain. For example, José María Morelos y Pavón, another prominent military leader of the independence movement, convoked a Constitutional Congress in 1813 where he requested that "the Constitution shall establish that the 12th of December be celebrated in all villages in honor of the patroness of our liberty, the Most Holy Mary of Guadalupe. All villages shall be required to pay her monthly devotion" (Morelos 2002, 190). Eight years later, in 1821, the Virgin became the patron of the Mexican Empire when Mexico's Congress declared the 12th of December as the greatest day because of her apparitions. Sometime during the War of Independence, Manuel Féliz Fernández (who became Mexico's first constitutional president in 1824) changed his name to Guadalupe Victoria (Taylor 1987, 24). Soon after Mexico obtained its freedom in 1821, preachers loyal to the new Agustín Iturbide's empire thanked the Virgin of Guadalupe for uniting the Mexicans in pursuit of independence (Brading 2001, 6).

The end of the official relationship between the state and the Roman Catholic Church came in 1858, during the radical government of Benito Juárez. The Liberal Reform of the Juárez administration expropriated all church property, stripped the clergy of their legal privileges, dissolved the monasteries, and secularized education, imposing a separation of church and state. As a result, ties between the Guadalupe Virgin and the political arena slipped away. However, in 1859, President Juárez retained the Guadalupe Virgin's feast as a national holiday (Gruzinski 2001, 215–16). President Juárez was careful not to challenge the fundamental role of the Virgin, by then the most powerful and sacred Mexican Catholic religious symbol. Thus the political conflict between the church and state ultimately did not affect Our Lady of Guadalupe's popularity among the general population.

The evolution of the cult of the Virgin of Guadalupe continued well into the twentieth century. Between 1876 and 1911, the years of the *Porfiriato* (the dictatorship of Porfirio Díaz), the church reestablished its public influence and recognized the Virgin as the founder of the new mestizo nation.

It was argued that she had reconciled and united Indians and Spaniards (Brading 2001, 9). During the 1910 Mexican Revolution, anticlericalism was prevalent, but the devotion to the Virgin of Guadalupe only grew in strength. A fervent shout was heard during battles: "Long Live the Virgin of Guadalupe! Long Live Francisco I. Madero!" (Lewis 2002, 377), and her image was carried by Zapatista and Villista antigovernment revolutionary soldiers on their hats for inspiration and protection.

Between 1926 and 1929, during the *Cristero* rebellion, hundreds of Catholic peasants who fought the federal army escaped government persecution, fleeing to the United States, taking with them the cult of the Guadalupe Virgin to East Los Angeles and other urban centers in the Southwest. This is not to say that the cult to Guadalupe was not already present in that region, given that what is now the southwestern United States was part of New Spain and Mexico until about 1848. It is likely that the devotion to Guadalupe first came from colonial Mexico with Mexican colonists who settled in the frontier of "El Norte" at the end of the sixteenth century.

In the 1960s and 1970s, the Chicano civil rights movement and the United Farm Workers took the Virgin de Guadalupe as a revolutionary symbol of Chicano resistance and of La Raza empowerment. Banners that pictured the Virgin of Guadalupe with an inscription that read "Don't Eat the Grapes" was a common sight on picket lines and at political marches and rallies (Wolfteich 2005, 158).

Today, the image of Guadalupe can be found everywhere in Mexico and the United States: painted on murals; tattooed on backs, chests, or arms; embroidered on clothing and hats; photographed in magazines; sculpted on jewelry; and on countless numbers of other commercial products. The commercialization of the image of the Virgin has reached such an alarming level that a small sign placed on the Basilica in Mexico City reads: "*Esta es mi casa, por favor no comercies con mi imagen*" (This is my house; please don't sell my image). Moreover, the technological developments of the late twentieth century, combined with the various forces of globalization, have taken the cult of the Virgin of Guadalupe to new levels. Her various representations, along with the beliefs of her devotees, can now be found all over the World Wide Web.

The Virgin of Guadalupe has been an important presence in the history of Mexico for Spaniards, Indians, Creoles, Mestizos, and Chicanos alike. Almost five-and-a-half decades ago, Mexican Nobel Prize winner Octavio

Paz pointed out that, "It is no secret to anyone that Mexican Catholicism was centered about the cult of the Virgin of Guadalupe" (Paz 2002, 24). The Mexican poet remarked that Indians simply transformed the beliefs and practices of the Catholic Church to conform with and support their own prehispanic religion and world outlook, according to their historical situation. Thus, according to Paz's analysis, the worship of Guadalupe-Tonantzin originally had a direct relationship to fertility and fecundity rituals. As the Spanish colonized Mexico, the Virgin came to be regarded among indigenous and mestizo Mexicans as the protector of the Indians (the weak, the poor, the oppressed) because of their social conditions (25).

Our Lady of Guadalupe is a richly multivalent religious symbol that has been invoked to represent both dispossessed indigenous people as well as the political aspirations of the elite (Burkhart 2001, 1). Anthropologist Eric Wolf, in his now classic examination of a master symbol, explains how symbols such as the Virgin of Guadalupe can become exceptionally powerful when they draw on both deep psychological and social dimensions. Wolf suggests that the Guadalupe symbol links psychological sources with the social struggle for class, dignity, and national identity (Wolf 1958).

However it is viewed, the image of the Virgin of Guadalupe has become an integral part of everyday life—a source of inspiration, creativity, and hope for millions of people. As Mexico moves into the twenty-first century, many people continue to make pilgrimages to the Basilica of Guadalupe during the week of December 12. Each year in mid-December, hundreds of thousands of pilgrims invade the Tepeyac hill, continuing an ancestral tradition. Approximately fifteen million people—from Mexico and abroad—visit the Basilica to pay homage to Guadalupe every year, and an estimated seven to ten million of those people make the trip during the week of December 12.

The Expansion of the Cult of La Caridad del Cobre/Ochún in Cuba

Although the devotion to Our Lady of Charity at El Cobre emerged more than a century after that of the Virgin of Guadalupe, the development, diffusion, and symbolism of her devotion in Cuba bear certain similarities to those of the Virgin of Guadalupe. Just like the *"morenita"* (the little dark-skinned one) of the Tepeyac, the virgin *"morena"* (the dark-skinned one) of El Cobre has been associated with a variety of social ideas, such as creolization, meztizaje, hybridization, nationhood, and independence (Díaz 2000, 1). And just as for the Virgin of Guadalupe, the powerful story of the apparition of the Virgin of El Cobre, the historical and mythical place where her image is venerated, and the ethnic identity and social status of the protagonists of the myth are all important elements in the development of the cult of La Caridad del Cobre.

According to the legend of the apparition of the Virgen de La Caridad, the original statue was discovered in the Bay of Nipe near Santiago de Cuba at the beginning of the seventeenth century by men of different ethnic background—all named Juan (Juan Blanco, Juan el Negro, and Juan el Mulatto or Indio). As a curious note, it is interesting to mention that the legend of Guadalupe of Tepeyacac had also three main protagonists named Juan (Juan Diego, Juan de Zumárraga, and Juan Bernardino). Cuban scholar Fernando Ortiz argued that the three men represent an araucoafrohispanic trilogy in the Caridad del Cobre legend, which symbolizes Cuba as a nation, since they represented the entire ethnic makeup of the island at the time (Portuondo Zúñiga 1995, 29). According to María Elena Díaz (2000, 4), the Virgin symbolically enforced the new relations between the church, state, and the other sectors of seventeenth-century Cuban society.

The official foundational story of Our Lady of Charity was propagated by an old royal slave (Juan Moreno) of El Cobre, who claimed as a child to have been a witness and protagonist in the miraculous apparition (Díaz 2000, 20). Juan Moreno's narrative of the miraculous finding of the Virgin's effigy was documented when he was an elder, but has been changed many times. According to Cuban historian Olga Portuondo Zúñiga, the "standard" legend has changed over time due to historical circumstances and spiritual necessities of each generation of Cubans (Portuondo Zúñiga 1995, 149). Portuondo Zúñiga has documented that in some versions of the legend, the protagonists include one Indian, one black, and one Spaniard; in other versions, there are two blacks and two Indians. In any case, the archetype story, according to Portuondo Zúñiga, includes the image of La Caridad, Juan Moreno (actor/eye witness), and a population of indigenous people (170–73). Unlike Guadalupe's story, the ethnic identities of the eye witnesses to La Caridad's apparition have changed over time, reflecting changes in the ethnic composition of the population and socioeconomic factors.

Cuban scholars interested in Afrocuban traditions have observed that

Ochún and the Virgin of La Caridad del Cobre were evoked interchangeably by the people of Yoruban descent who practice Santería (Yoruba-based religious system). Ochún, according to Yoruba mythology, is commonly known as the owner and ruler of the sweet waters, love, gold, coral, and amber.[2] She is represented as a happy seductress who loves the color yellow and the element of copper (Cabrera 1974, 54). In Cuba she is popularly imagined as a mulatto woman (Murphy 2001, 90). This identification of a prehispanic deity with a Christian icon is another parallel between the Guadalupe-Tonantzin in Mexico and La Virgen de la Caridad in Cuba; indeed, the practice of associating prehispanic deities with Christian icons—particularly saints—is common in other parts of Latin America.

The identification of Yoruba (Lucumí, as they were known in Cuba) orishas with Catholic saints did not start until the end of the nineteenth century for historical and cultural reasons. Enslaved Yoruba began to be shipped to Cuba in considerable numbers to work in the growing sugar cane plantations of the Havana and Matanzas regions, the Western part of the island. According to Santería scholar Joseph M. Murphy, "The Yoruba chose La Caridad del Cobre to stand for Osun [Ochún] and also to stand for themselves in the mosaic of Cuban history and society" (Murphy 2001, 88). Murphy also observes that "The Lucumí found in the image of La Caridad del Cobre a crowned female divinity who miraculously appeared from the waters to save humble people of color from the storm" (91).

The first church, La Ermita de la Caridad del Cobre, was constructed in honor of the Virgin near the village of El Cobre. Founded in 1598, sixteen kilometers west of Santiago de Cuba, El Cobre was one of the oldest settlements on the island, and was populated almost exclusively by royal slaves owned by King Felipe III and free people of color (Díaz 2000, 9). According to Father Onofre Fonseca, a slave girl named Apolonia witnessed a miraculous light at the top of a hill near El Cobre that indicated where the Virgin wanted her temple built (Díaz 2000, 112). This orthodox version of the story was produced by the Catholic Church and shares many similarities with the story of Our Lady of Guadalupe, in which the Virgin requested the place where she wanted to be venerated.

Like Guadalupe-Tonantzin in Mexico, over time, Our Lady of Charity at El Cobre became the official patroness of the new republic, the "queen" of Cuba, and the mother of all Cubans, regardless of ethnic background and social status (Díaz 2000, 329). Like the Virgin of Guadalupe, Our Lady of Charity accompanied the Cubans who fought for slavery's abolition in

1886, and in Cuba's two wars of independence of 1868 and 1895. Cuban-born whites, blacks, and mestizos who fought these armed conflicts adopted her as their spiritual leader. "*Virgen de la Caridad, Patrona de Cuba, con el machete en la mano pedimos la libertad*" (Virgin of Charity, Patroness of Cuba, with machete in hand we ask for freedom) was the forces' cry of the anti-Spanish independence movement (Portuondo Zúñiga 1995, 226–29). It was also during this historical period that she was referred to as "La Virgen Mambisa," a name that means powerful and fierce (Murphy 2001, 90).

Just like the heroes of the Cuban independence movement, the forces of the revolution of Fidel Castro fought battles entrusting themselves to the Virgin "cachita." For aid and inspiration against the dictatorship of Fulgencio Batista, members of the rebel army carried images of the Virgin on medallions and rosaries and celebrated masses in her honor (Portuondo Zúñiga 1995, 271).

Soon after the triumph of revolution that brought Fidel Castro to power, Cuban exiles in Miami arranged for a replica of the Our Lady of Charity statue to be sent from Cuba. On September 8, 1961, the image of the Virgin, which had been smuggled out of Cuba, arrived at Miami International Airport from the archdiocese of Havana. Since then, Cuban exiles gather in Miami every eighth of September to celebrate the feast day of Our Lady of Charity. In 1972, a chapel (Ermita de la Virgen de la Caridad) built by Cuban exiles to house the imported image of the Virgin was inaugurated and consecrated, and on September 8, 2000, the United States Bishops' Conference pronounced the chapel a national sanctuary of the United States (https://thefloridacatholic.org/mia/mia2007/miaarticles/20070928_la_virgen.php).

Conclusion

Whether there is truth or not about the historicity of the apparition of the Virgin of Guadalupe-Tonantzin and Our Lady of Charity-Ochún, it is evident that their symbolic meanings were subject to various appropriations, interpretations, reinterpretations, and transformations that transcended ethnic and cultural boundaries. The histories of Cuba and Mexico make evident this dynamic and complex process of appropriation, transformation, interpretation, and reinterpretation. In both Mexico and Cuba, the symbol of the Virgins helped claim and reclaim the homeland; fostered the construction of nationhood distinct from Spanish (peninsular) citizenry; helped liberate people from oppression; united peoples of different ethnic and cultural background; provided a source of precepts and social values fundamental to society's well being; and was invoked to protect and defend the most vulnerable sectors of those societies.

What becomes clear in the histories of these two Madonna icons is that their legacies have endured—indeed flourished—as they repeatedly have been called into service by the poor, disadvantaged, and oppressed. Because our global community is still a long way from addressing the social, political, and economic inequities that continue to pervade most countries—including Mexico and Cuba—one thing seems certain: these dark-skinned Virgins will continue to have a role to play in the spiritual and political lives of their devotees for many years to come.

Notes

1. Gachupines was the derogatory name given to the peninsular Spanish by the Spanish born in Mexico.
2. Ochún has many representations in the Lucumí/Yoruba pantheon of gods.

References

Alamán, Lucas. 2002. "The Siege of Guanajuato." In *The Mexico Reader: History, Culture, Politics*, ed. Gilbert M. Joseph and Timothy J. Henderson, 171–88. Durham and London: Duke University Press.

Brading, D. A. 2001. *Mexican Phoenix Our Lady of Guadalupe: Image and Tradition Across Five Centuries*. Cambridge: Cambridge University Press.

Burkhart, Louise M. 2001. *Before Guadalupe: The Virgin Mary in Early Colonial Nahuatl Literature*. Albany, New York: Institute for Mesoamerican Studies, University at Albany (Distributed by University of Texas Press).

Cabrera, Lydia. 1974. *Yemayá y Ochún: Kariocha, Iyalorichas y olorichas*. Madrid: Ediciones C. R.

Díaz, María Elena. 2000. *The Virgin, the King, and the Royal Slaves of El Cobre: Negotiating Freedom in Colonial Cuba, 1670–1780*. Stanford: Stanford University Press.

Florescano, Enrique. 1987. "Guadalupe de todos." *Nexos* 109:29–35.

García Canclini, Néstor. 1990. *Culturas híbridas. Estrategias para entrar y salir de la modernidad*. México: Grijalbo.

————. 1993. *Transforming Modernity: Pop Culture in Mexico*. Austin: University of Texas.

Garza-Valdés, Leoncio A. 2002. *Tepeyac: Cinco siglos de engaño*. Mexico City: Plaza y Janés Editores, S. A.

Gruzinski, Serge. 2001. *Images at War: Mexico from Columbus to Blade Runner (1492–2019)*. Translated by Heather Maclean. Durham and London: Duke University Press.

León-Portilla, Miguel. 2002. *Bernardino de Sahagún*. Translated by Mauricio J. Mixco. Norman: University of Oklahoma Press.

Lewis, Oscar. 2002. "Pedro Martínez." In *The Mexico Reader: History, Culture, Politics*, ed. Gilbert M. Joseph and Timothy J. Henderson, 375–86. Durham and London: Duke University Press.

Morelos, José María. 2002. "Sentiments of the Nation, or Points Outlined by Morelos for the Constitution." In *The Mexico Reader: History, Culture, Politics*, ed. Gilbert M. Joseph and Timothy J. Henderson, 189–91. Durham and London: Duke University Press.

Murphy, Joseph M. 2001. "*Yéyé Cachita: Ochún* in a Cuban Mirror." In *Osun Across the Waters: A Yoruba Goddess in Africa and the Americas*, ed. Joseph M. Murphy and Mei-Mei Sanford, 87–101. Bloomington: Indiana University Press.

Paz, Octavio. 2002. "The Sons of *La Malinche*." In *The Mexico Reader: History, Culture, Politics*, ed. Gilbert M. Joseph and Timothy J. Henderson, 20–27. Durham and London: Duke University Press.

Portuondo Zúñiga, Olga. 1995. *La Virgen de la Caridad del Cobre: Símbolo de cubanía*. Santiago de Cuba: Editorial Oriente.

Taylor, William B. 1987. "The Virgin of Guadalupe in New Spain: An Inquiry into the Social History of Marian Devotion." *American Ethnologist* 14, no. 1:9–33.

Wheeler, Marion. 1998. *Mary: Images of the Virgin in Art*. New York: BCL Press.

Wolf, Eric R. 1958. "The Virgin of Guadalupe: A Mexican National Symbol." *Journal of American Folklore* 71:34–39.

Wolfteich, Claire. 2005. "Devotion and the Struggle for Justice in the Farm Worker Movement: A Practical Theological Approach to Research and Teaching in Spirituality." *Spiritus: A Journal of Christian Spirituality* 5, no. 2:158–75.

Zires, Margarita. 1994. "Los mitos de la Virgen de Guadalupe: su proceso de construcción y reinterpretación en el México pasado y contemporáneo." *Mexican Studies/Estudios Mexicanos* 10, no. 2:281–313.

Guadalupe, Yemanjá, and the Orixás of Candomblé

An Embodiment of Religion, Art, and Music

CLARENCE BERNARD HENRY

☞ THIS ESSAY EXAMINES SOME OF THE WAYS THAT GUADALUPE AND THE *orixás* of Candomblé religion embody and influence the national character, religion, art, and musical expressions in Latin America. Guadalupe has been described and referred to as a symbol of Mexican independence, defender of dignity, celestial mestiza, and mother of the Americas. From generation to generation, Guadalupe tells Mexican Americans who they are as a people and to whom they belong (Rodríguez 1996, 121). The orixás of Candomblé, revered and celebrated in the city of Salvador, Bahia, Brazil, are referred to as intercessors, ancestral spirits, *senhoras* and *senhores dos cosmos* (ladies and gentlemen of the cosmos) and *donas do mundo* (mistresses of the world) (Montes 2002, 335–37). In Brazil, the *orixás* keep the African spirit vibrant. They symbolically link nature with mankind and are personified as water, wind, storm, rainbow, and rain. They are also conceptualized as living beings—wives, mothers, husbands, fathers, sea creatures, warriors, hunters, and martyrs.

Religion

In Mexico, the equation of Tonantzin, the indigenous Aztec mother-goddess, with the Christianized Mary and realized as Guadalupe is similar to the experience of Candomblé religion where the orixá Yemanjá, the ruler of the ocean, is equated with the Christianized Mary. The realization of Guadalupe in essence is a cultural mestizaje that has changed Mexico since the early part of the sixteenth century. As is the case in Brazil, in the early part of the sixteenth century there was also a cultural change and synthesis as Africans were transported into the area as slaves from ethnically diverse cultures—Yoruba, Ewe, Fon, Gêge, Ijexá, and Ketu. This synthesis greatly influenced music and culture not only in Brazil, but also in other areas that scholars describe as the African Diaspora. Music scholar Samuel Floyd emphasizes that African influence in regions such as Brazil is part of what can be described as the "circum-Caribbean," where African religion, music, and culture were merged with European religion, musical forms, structures, and genres through processes known variously as syncretism, creolization, *creolité*, and cultural *metissage*, all of which signify the hybrid character of the cultural products of the region (Floyd 1999, 1–37).

As early as the sixteenth century, Africans in Brazil began to combine elements of African spirituality with Roman Catholicism as a way of secretly paying homage to their ancestral guardians. They linked their ancestors with many of the saints of the Catholic Church. In this synthesis of the ancestral spirits with Roman Catholicism, Yemanjá, the great mother and ruler, began to take on the divine characteristics of the Virgin Mary, the orixá Oxalá as Jesus Christ, and so forth. The religion for worshiping these spiritual beings became known as Candomblé.

The emergence of Candomblé religion is not as straightforward and detailed as the experience surrounding Juan Diego's apparition of Our Lady of Guadalupe on the hill of Tepeyac. In Candomblé there was no apparition to one man, but the religion came into existence as the result of Africans trying to adjust within a new society, understanding their need to continue their cultural heritage by reconnecting with their spiritual and ancestral world. A substantial amount of Candomblé religious practices stem from the Yoruba religious tradition of West Africa, where religion and art are highly integrated as a way of communicating with ancestral spirits, and the creation of various types of artifacts and shrines are incorporated for prayer and sacrifice. These types of rituals and practices are evident in Candomblé religion and can be experienced in special ceremonies that celebrate ancestral spirits making use of visual depictions of the orixás, elaborate costumes worn by initiates that communicate with the spiritual world through music, dance, and spirit possession, and elaborate houses of worship where the ceremonies are held.

Although Candomblé religion has its roots in the marginalization of displaced Africans, for many people in Brazil the religion often determines the details of daily existence. Each day of the week is associated with a specific orixá, whose colors are apparent in the clothes people wear or the foods they eat or certain types of altars that they may construct in honor of the orixás. The association of days with particular orixás may even determine whether people have intimate relations, in that individuals must abstain from sex on the day their guardian orixá is celebrated so as not to provoke the orixá's wrath. In essence, individual behaviors and social relations are understood in terms of the orixás' myths and their interrelationships with other deities.

Reasons as to why and how the vibrancy of religious traditions surrounding Guadalupe and Candomblé religion continues to be debated in postmodernity. One such theory suggests that religious devotion for Guadalupe is part of popular religion or religiosity for Hispanic cultural communities. As part of the popular religion complex of Hispanic culture, Guadalupe stems from the *sensus fidelium* (sense of the faithful) that continues to be expressed in the symbols, language, and culture of the faithful (Espín 1995, 148–51). Another theory suggests that admiration and devotion for Guadalupe is continued through cultural memory that is passed on generationally. In this way Guadalupe is remembered through the tilma (the cloak bearing the image), construction of the Basilica of Guadalupe in Mexico City, images, stories, celebrations, and the *Nican Mopohua*, a historical source that documents the apparition to Juan Diego. As a major iconic figure, the cultural memory of Guadalupe evokes a feeling of reverence, aspiration, devotion, and hope. From my experience, I believe that there is a great amount of cultural memory or the passing on of tradition in Candomblé religion that informs practitioners and devotees in the so-called era of postmodernity. Older Candomblé members often begin training their children to become leaders, musicians, or initiates that serve the spiritual world. In this way Candomblé continues to be invigorated and revitalized as an important religious tradition in Brazil. Myths, images, annual celebrations in public spaces, governmental support for historical preservation of Candomblé houses, the city museum that houses some of the artifacts of Candomblé religion, and the Rosários dos Pretos, a Catholic Church that was constructed by African slaves, all contribute to the vitality of Candomblé.

African-influenced religions such as Candomblé are also theorized as being part of what Molefi Kete Asante describes as part of the African cultural system that is manifested in diverse Afro-diasporic communities with different versions of African aestheticism and cultural memories. Thus, the legacy is that people of African descent respond to the same rhythms of the universe, cosmological sensibilities, and general historical reality. Asante goes on to state that although the African cultural system is modified according to specific histories and regions, the spirits of ethnic groups such as the Yoruba, Ewe, and Fon are alive and vibrant. In this way the orixás such as Yemanjá, Xangô, and Oxum continue to be meaningful as great symbols (Asante 1988, 2).

Guadalupe, Yemanjá and the Orixás Compared

In comparing Guadalupe and Yemanjá as iconic figures and as equations with the Virgin Mary, there are some similarities. As a Marian figure, Guadalupe has always been perceived as a tender mother, always compassionate, accepting, supportive, and forgiving. Guadalupe emerges as a symbol of justice and mediates the promise of new life. Each generation of Mexicans has been able to see mirrored in the tilma the reflections of its sufferings, struggles, life, and ideas (Elizondo 1980, 69). Guadalupe also affirms the liberating power of the cross as the place of resurrection. By participating in the Guadalupe story we affirm our dignity as persons in the face of crucifixion and dehumanization (Goizueta 1996, 285). Thus, the name Guadalupe is synonymous with strength and endurance. The name Guadalupe is not only bestowed by parents on their children, both girls and boys, but also given to parishes and churches, streets and towns, rivers and mountains.

As a Mary, or Our Lady of the Immaculate Conception in Brazil, Yemanjá is also a great mother and, as ruler of the ocean, she is also reinvented as Our Lady of Navigators, a female patron saint of fishermen and businessmen (Omari 1984, 28–29). If given a suitable celebration and offerings she brings good fishing and prosperity. Yemanjá is often imagined with open hands tossing pearls of good fortune into the ocean. Furthermore, because of her association with water, Yemanjá is often depicted as a mermaid with large breasts, fair skin, blue eyes, and long brown hair. She is also imagined as a queen who controls the moon and the stars.

Amos Niven Wilder, in his paradigm of "theopoetics," suggested that faith and confession of human beings are highly motivated by images

(Wilder 1976, 1–2). Daphne Patai believes that in Brazil there is a strong linkage between the images of the Virgin Mary and Yemanjá. Furthermore, this linkage may possibly explain why many women in Brazil are named Maria, after the Virgin Mary. Maria is ever present in the streets, houses, and in songs. The Roman Catholic Church brought the European image of Mary as holy, entranced, blue-eyed, obedient, and asexual. For centuries in Brazil, the church continued to use this image of "ideal womanhood" to foster a subordinate role for women. However, as Catholicism and Candomblé came together, the image changed to incorporate the traditions of women in the Afro-Brazilian community. The fusion of Catholicism and Candomblé religion produced a "multi-faced" Mary (Patai 1988, 68–70). Females in the Afro-Brazilian community identified with the image of Mary as poor: her husband was a craftsman, they had no home in which to bear her child, and they migrated from place to place (68–70). Eventually this image was replaced with Yemanjá, who became the culmination of these experiences.

Art and Music Expression

Jeanette Rodríguez (1996) posits that religion often becomes art through visual depictions of divine beings. Jacques Soustelle contends that in Mesoamerican culture artistic renditions are a way of conjuring up the sacred world by providing the iconography and the ritual framework that rituals demand and making visible the symbols that constitute the esoteric language of religion (Soustelle 1984). Scholars such as John Dewey (1934) and Suzanne Langer (1953) posit that expressions such as art and music are based on experience that stimulates certain types of emotions. In addition to the religiosity of specific beliefs and practices surrounding Guadalupe and Candomblé religion, experiences are invigorated through various forms of artistic expressions. Art, both visual and musical, creatively presents an image or performance that seems to provide a sense of beauty and the divine for the devotees of Guadalupe and Candomblé religion. With a visual depiction of such images as Guadalupe's praying hands one seems to be transcended to the divine. In Candomblé, practitioners attempt to somehow merge the artistic renditions of the beautiful with the divine with a visual display of their orixás, such as Tempo, an Angolan deity who holds a grill that is representative of the burning at the stake of his Christian counterpart, Saint Lawrence. Also, many of the

Candomblé houses are in themselves works of art and graphic depictions of the orixás' spiritual domain.

The image of Guadalupe pervades many neighborhoods of people of Mexican descent: a statue or painting in a sacred corner of the home or as an image on T-shirts, on the sides of buildings, and even as business logos (Rodriguez 1996, 123). Similarly, in Salvador, Bahia, Brazil, there are many buildings that bear the images of symbols from Candomblé such as mirrors, amulets, and bows and arrows of the orixás. Many buildings and streets are named after the orixás. Furthermore, local businesses often profit commercially from selling images of the orixás on T-shirts, candles, and dolls, and many Candomblé houses profit by allowing tourists to attend special ceremonies.

The divining quality of music is very prominent in the experiences of Guadalupe and Candomblé religion. The apparition of Guadalupe to Juan Diego on the hill of Tepeyac was shrouded with music. In the description of the apparition, flower and song together manifested the presence of the divine. Virgilio Elizondo, a noted scholar on mestizaje, describes Juan Diego's experience with music as follows:

> The first striking thing upon reading the legend is that Juan Diego heard beautiful music so beautiful that he thought he was in paradise. Music alone was capable of communicating truth. It was the medium of divine communication. In some way he was in the presence of the gods. The lady did not have to explain to him that she was appearing and speaking in the midst of the most beautiful music he had ever heard. The music itself was sufficient to establish the veracity and importance of the Lady. The beautiful flowers that appeared in the cold December morning on the desert hilltop of Tepeyac were the sign chosen by the Lady. This will complete the divine revelation begun with the sign of music. (Elizondo 1980, 87)

In Candomblé religion various forms of artistic expressions culminate with musical performance. The spiritual world of Candomblé is enlivened with mythological and poetic recitations spoken or sung in Yoruba and Kimbundu (Angolan languages), and Portuguese, with choreographic movements and ecstatic states of spirit possession. Music serves as a form of mediation between the world of the orixás and the human world. People believe that through singing and dancing to special drum rhythms they come into the presence of powerful and divine beings. The musicians always have a special seating area within the Candomblé house and are important because the music that they perform can summon an orixá from the spiritual realm that is then manifested in the bodies of special devotees who are able to portray the moods, personalities, and movements of the orixá they are serving. Depending on the particular orixá, devotees, while in spirit possession, portray a wide range of moods and personalities, from joy to sorrow. Devotees also mimic movements of the orixás that are similar to running, jumping, galloping, and holding sacred objects such as amulets or mirrors. These movements are assisted by the characteristic quality of Candomblé music.

Outside of religion proper, the musical influence of Guadalupe and Candomblé is often heard in public spaces in the form of hymns, symphonic works, and folkloric dances. For example, during special days for Yemanjá, people offer flowers, perfume, dolls, and cosmetics as gifts to this orixá. Thousands of people wait in line for hours to lay flowers at special altars constructed in her honor and to anoint themselves with water from the ocean. While this is occurring, Candomblé music can be heard in makeshift Candomblé houses and on the beach, where people often go to experience spirit possession.

Brazilian artists such as Dorival Caymmi, Gilberto Gil, Caetano Veloso, Gal Costa, and Maria Bethaniâ have all produced albums that feature songs about the orixás such as the laments that describe the sword of Ogun, the Blessing of Olorum, and the Lightning Bolts of Yansã. Other songs give a sense of inspiration of good fortune, prosperity, and freedom (Dunn 2001, 81). There are also folkloric dance troupes such as Balé Folclórico da Bahia that present choreographic programs based on the musical repertoire of Candomblé. Other examples of how Candomblé has influenced musical production in Brazil are through the performances of Filhos de Gandhi (Sons of Gandhi), one of the most famous groups in the city of Salvador, Bahia. Filhos de Gandhi was founded in 1949 in homage to Gandhi of India, and members of this group dress in white in homage to the orixá Oxalá, the father of all orixás, who is associated with peace. They use an assortment of musical instruments: drums, *shekeres* (gourd rattles), whistles, and *agogôs* (bells). Most of their song repertoire is drawn from the traditional repertoire of Candomblé. In addition, during many of the celebrations Filhos de Gandhi also participate in and make special food offerings to the orixás of Candomblé.

Since the 1970s, groups such as Filhos de Gandhi have also used Candomblé music in performances and thematic displays centering on black pride. Another group that emerged in 1979 was Olodum, a name derived from the Candomblé supreme being, Olódùmarè. The major emphasis of Olodum is to attract young blacks by giving them opportunities to develop as proficient drummers. The group combines the rhythms of Candomblé with *salsa, merengue, reggae,* and many other styles. Olodum has now become a corporation, selling memorabilia, tapes, and CDs of their music.[1]

Conclusion

The theme of this volume is "Toward a Theory for Religion as Art." With Guadalupe and the orixás, religion and art are integrated. Guadalupe and the orixás both inspire generations of devotees. These spiritual beings also continue to influence religion, art, and musical tradition in Latin America and in other areas of the world. Understanding the many facets of Guadalupe and the orixás is complex and is not solely a topic for religious studies. Thus, an interdisciplinary approach in this area of research is very appropriate, and my own research can be greatly enhanced by art historians, linguists, among many other interdisciplinary scholars. Our future work can only be of greater significance as we develop more dialogue and interaction.

Notes

1. For a complete discussion of popular culture in Bahia see Piers Armstrong, *Cultura Popular na Bahia & Estilística Cultural Pragmática* (Bahia, Universidade Estadual de Feira de Santana, 2001). Also see discussion on Filhos de Gandi and Olodum in the following sources: Clarence Bernard Henry, "Celebrating the Orixás: The Influence of African Religion and Music in Salvador, Bahia, Brazil," in *Musical Cultures of Latin America: Global Effects, Past and Present, Selected Reports in Ethnomusicology, Vol. XI,* ed. Steven Loza (Los Angeles: University of California Press, 2003), 175–86; Ari Lima, "Black or *Brau*: Music and Subjectivity in a Global Context," in *Brazilian Popular Music and Globalization,* ed. Charles Perrone and Christopher Dunn (Gainesville: University Press of Florida, 2001); Larry N. Crook, "Black Consciousness, Samba-Reggae, and the Re-Africanization of Bahian Carnival Music in Brazil,"

World of Music 35, no. 2 (1993): 90–108; Charles Perrone, "Axé, Ijexá, Olodum: The Rise of Afro and African Currents in Brazilian Popular Music," *Afro-Hispanic Review* 11, no. 1–3 (1992): 42–50.

References

Armstrong, Piers. 2001. *Cultura popular na Bahia e estilística cultural pragmática.* Bahia: Universidade Estadual de Feira de Santana.

Asante, Molefi Kete. 1988. *Afrocentricity.* Trenton, N.J.: Africa World Press.

Crook, Larry N. 1993. "Black Consciousness, Samba-Reggae, and the Re-Africanization of Bahian Carnival Music in Brazil." *World of Music* 35, no. 2:90–108.

Dewey, John. 1934. *Art as Experience.* New York: Putnam.

Dunn, Christopher. 2001. "Tropicália, Counterculture, and the Diasporic Imagination in Brazil." In *Brazilian Popular Music and Globalization,* ed. Charles Perrone and Christopher Dunn, 72–95. Gainesville: University Press of Florida.

Elizondo, Virgilio. 1980. *La Morenita: Evangelizer of the Americas.* San Antonio: Mexican American Cultural Center.

Espín, Orlando O. 1995. "Tradition and Popular Religion: An Understanding of the *Sensus Fidelium.*" In *Mestizo Christianity Theology from the Latino Perspective,* ed. Arturo J. Bañuelas, 146–74. Maryknoll, N.Y.: Orbis Books.

Floyd, Jr., Samuel A. 1999. "Black Music in the Circum-Caribbean." *American Music* 17, no. 1:1–37.

Goizueta, Roberto S. 1996. "U.S. Hispanic Catholicism as Theopoetics." In *Hispanic/Latino Theology: Challenge and Promise,* ed. Ada María Isasi-Díaz and Fernando F. Segovia, 261–88. Minneapolis: Fortress Press.

Henry, Clarence Bernard. 2003. "Celebrating the *Orixás*: The Influence of African Religion and Music in Salvador, Bahia, Brazil." In *Musical Cultures of Latin America: Global Effects, Past and Present, Selected Reports in Ethnomusicology, Vol. XI,* ed. Steven Loza, 175–86. Los Angeles: University of California Press.

Langer, Susanne. 1953. *Feeling and Form: A Theory of Art.* New York: Scribner.

Lima, Ari. 2001. "Black or *Brau*: Music and Subjectivity in a Global Context." In *Brazilian Popular Music and Globalization,* ed. Charles Perrone and Christopher Dunn, 220–32. Gainesville: University Press of Florida.

Montes, Maria Lucia. 2002. "African Cosmologies in Brazilian Culture and Society." In *Brazil: Body and Soul,* ed. Edward J. Sullivan, 334–45. New York: Guggenheim Museum Publications.

Omari, Mikelle Smith. 1984. *From the Inside to the Outside: The Art of Bahian Candomblé.* Museum of Cultural History, Monograph Series No. 24. Los Angeles: University of California Press.

Patai, Daphne. 1988. *Brazilian Women Speak: Contemporary Life Stories.* New Brunswick and London: Rutgers University Press.

Perrone, Charles. 1992. "Axé, Ijexá, Olodum: The Rise of Afro and African Currents in Brazilian Popular Music." *Afro-Hispanic Review* 11, no. 1–3:42–50.

Rodríguez, Jeanette. 1996. "Sangre llama a sangre: Cultural Memory as a Source of Theological Insight." In *Hispanic/Latino Theology: Challenge and Promise*, ed. Ada María Isasi-Díaz and Fernando F. Segovia, 117–33. Minneapolis: Fortress Press.

Soustelle, Jacques. 1984. "The Sacred and the Profane: Two Faces of Meso-American Art." *UNESCO Courier* 5:4.

Wilder, Amos Niven. 1976. *Theopoetic: Theology and the Religious Imagination.* Philadelphia: Fortress Press.

Afro-Cuban Danced Religious Practices as Everyday Art

Confluence in Motion

TERESA MARRERO

A Dedication and Prayer

Respeto a la tradición religiosa:

Elegguá usted es el dueño de los caminos, ábranos uno bueno, líbrenos de los arayé, de onilú, de maledicencia, envidia. No suceda nada malo en el camino, haya sosiego en el camino, tranquilidad en el camino, fresco, que no haya muerto, ni enfermedad ni sangre [un rezo de aperture].

Respect to Religious Tradition:

Elegguá you are the master of the roads, open us a good one, free us from arayé, onilú, curses and envy. May nothing bad occur on the way, may the way be peaceful, tranquility in the path, freshness, let there be no death, or sickness nor blood. (Cabrera 1980, 257, *translation mine, a prayer of beginnings*)

Admiration for Beauty and the Aesthetics of the Body

Through dance training and practice an individual marshals power to discipline the instinctive and culturally patterned everyday movements of the body. As a result, the dancer gains control over the body and freedom to use it in particular ways ... dancers shape the rhythms of life and make the difficult look simple in testament to human competency and potential. (Hanna 1988, 4–5)

Introduction

⁙ IN THIS ESSAY I SPOTLIGHT THE IMPORTANCE OF DANCE AS AN integral psychophysical, cultural, and religious expression within the Cuban tradition of danced religions, which include *Santería, Palo Monte,* and *Abakuá*. I begin by demarcating symbolic and ontological differences between the Catholic ritual practices and the ones of Yoruba/Congo/Dahomenian origin, which I will call Africanist or Afro-Cuban. These include notions of the body as a medium not only of religious expression, but also of social, secular expression. The movements executed by dancers in the Afro-Cuban tradition integrate movements related to the pelvic area and hip gyrations as well as spinal undulations. These lower body movements suggest a repertory usually absent from the Western, classical tradition. Some scholars have called this the sexualized body, a body not divorced from its potentiality to suggest erotic as well as sacred ideas (Sloat 2002, 6).

I begin by establishing a dichotomous overview of ritual differences between Catholic and the African-based, danced religions. However, I immediately shift into what dance professor Brenda Dixon Gottschild has coined the Africanist principle of "and" (i.e., the sexual and spiritual, body and soul), which alludes to the notion of integration and acceptance of polarity. Rather than using the Eurocentric "spirit possession" to denote part of what occurs in these danced religions, I will appropriate dance anthropologist Yvonne Daniel's term of "embodied wisdom" to denote the transference of the Orisha's *aché* or energy onto its initiates during a *toque de santo* or *bembé*. I will describe the basic body movements for the four main groups of danced religions (of differing origins) in Cuba—the Congo, the Arará, the Carabalí, and the Yoruba—as they pertain both to religious dance ceremonies and to folkloric performance representations. A differentiation will demarcate the boundaries between sacred dancing and profane dancing in performance. The stylization of ceremonial dance movements is investigated through the groundbreaking work of dancer/choreographer Ramiro Guerra, creator of *la técnica cubana* (the Cuban technique) of modern dance. I will end with a look at the difference between devotional dancing as ritual and its folkloric version as theatrical performance.

Scarce Studies on Ethnic Cuban Traditional Dance and Its Contemporary Secular Offspring

Almost anyone familiar with Cuban, Haitian, or Brazilian cultures can utter the words Santería, Voudou or Candomblé and invoke exotic notions of wildly possessed bodies dancing (sometimes indecently) to wild drum beats, as represented in Hollywood films. In terms of Afro-Cuban ethnic dance forms, little has been published in the United States. Much has been written about traditional Afro-Cuban religious practices (see, for example, Ortiz 1917, 1940; Cabrera 1980; Castellanos 1992; Cros Sandoval 1975; González-Whipler 1994). And as much or more has been the subject of study by anthropologists and ethnomusicologists (e.g., Béhague 1992; Bascom 1972; Boggs 1992; Dixon Gottschild 2002; and Stoat 2002) regarding Afro-Cuban and Hispanic Afro-Caribbean music and their modern offspring, such as the hybrid Afro-Cuban jazz and Latin jazz, the more autochthonous *son*, the *danzón*, the *rumba* (which includes the *guaguancó*, the *columbia*, and the *yambú*), the *cha cha chá*, the *mambo*, the *merengue*, the *bachata*, and modern *salsa* (this last danced in three variations in the United States—Casino, Los Angeles, and New York style). Cuban (commonly known in the United States as Casino) style is danced on the one beat, but with a tap on the fourth; the flamboyant and swing-influenced Los Angeles style is danced on the first beat; and New York style (commonly known as mambo but with little stylistic similarities to the type danced in the New York Palladium in the 1960s and 1970s) on the second beat.

While many of the contemporary dance publications in the United States focus on professional dance techniques related to modern, jazz, ballet, and musical theater, some will include references to the Argentinean *tango*. Little reference is made to Afro-Cuban dance forms, ritual or secular. Ivonne Daniel has a seminal (and the only) study called *Rumba, Dance, and Social Change in Contemporary Cuba* (1995), and Susan Cashion (1989a) has also published a number of shorter studies on ethnic Cuban dances (1989b). Practically nothing has been written in the United States about salsa dancing here or worldwide, while debates on the origins of salsa, listening to salsa, and salsa in various parts of Latin America as musical forms abound. There is an obvious silence when it comes to this musical style as a dance form. This is an amazing fact, given that dance movement has been an integral and vital part of the religious, cultural, and musical expression of African diasporic peoples in the Americas and also influenced U.S. and world dance traditions. Many Afro-Cuban forms are danced globally in social, professional, and competitive contexts. In spite of the depth and breadth of the Afro-Cuban and Afro-Caribbean dance influences, amazingly few scholarly studies are available on the dance itself.

Dancing Believers

The appearance of the wonderful and rare anthology *Caribbean Dance from Abakuá to Zouk: How Movement Shapes Identity* (2002), edited by Susanna Sloat, is an oasis in the desert. In the first chapter of the book Brenda Dixon Gottschild asserts that:

> Whether spoken, sung, sculpted, sketched, written, or danced, the Africanist aesthetic values process. How a thing is done is as important as getting it done—the journey is as important as the destination. Language, sculpture, and visual arts are conceived as living, vital, motional concepts—moving movers, so to speak . . . A stellar example of this premise is that deities of African and African diasporic practice are dancing spirits that come to life through the dancing bodies of the faithful . . . these danced religions exhibit the principle of "embodied wisdom." (Dixon Gottschild 2002, 4)

Thus Africanist aesthetic values action and movement as an ontological tool toward expression of the spiritual and the material. While Santería and other Afro-Caribbean religions have been called syncretic, mixing iconography with that of the dominant Catholic Church, there are basic differences that separate the two worldviews. I have created here a dichotomous system of comparison between Africanist religious contexts and Catholicism as a liturgical, exclusively word-based religion, in order to draw some basic conclusions:

Catholic liturgical non-danced system:	Africanist liturgical danced system:
Centrally and hierarchically structured, symbolic through realistic representational signs (statues of saints, Christ on the cross).	Decentralized, structured communally through a series of *fundamentos*, or patakies (sacred stories of the Yoruba), naturistic and abstract. Use of rocks, herbs, drawings.
The mass: a symbolic sacrifice represented through wine and bread.	Bembés or toque de santos: Symbolic yet concrete sacrifice of animals to extract their energy or aché.
Spoken or silent prayer as sole means of instruction and conveyance of meaning.	Orality, music, and physicality integrated as means of instruction and conveyance.

Catholic liturgical non-danced system:	Africanist liturgical danced system:
Repetitive choreography of priest's movements, not open to improvisation.	Ritualized movement open and subject to improvisation.
Music is an adornment of praise, not integral to the process itself.	Movements to rhythmic music are essential and integral to the liturgy.
Quotidian movements easily legible. No virtuosity or stamina necessary. Static.	Movements require strenuous physicality and stamina. Legible to initiates.
Monotheistic God as Supreme, above and beyond the pitfalls of human foible. A savior died for all of our sins once and for all.	Pantheistic deities or orishas who have gender identities and narrative stories of human-like conflict (loves/hates). They mirror the human condition.
God in a remote heaven. Passive believer participation. Believer literally consumes the body and blood of Christ (opens mouth and swallows). No visible physical transformation takes place.	Gods among us. Orishas embody their adepts and increase energy (aché). A visible physical transformation takes place. Active devotee participation.
Liminality reserved for ecstatic, mystical experiences, usually reserved for special beings called saints.	Liminality occurs as a matter of course in the toque de santo. The community establishes it. Reverie is available to all believers.
Ritual spaces are architectural buildings called churches. Proscenium stage with its invisible fourth wall separates believers from the ritual.	Liminal spaces are demarcated anywhere by the believers though rituals. No fourth wall to separate believers from ritual.
Ceremonial garments are worn only by the priests and his helpers.	All believers wear ceremonial garments.

Unlike non-danced religions, danced religions appropriate the physical body to express spiritual and religious beliefs. Energy is consumed to experience and demonstrate the visible connection between ordinary persons and supernatural powers. Believers gain energy by expending it. In fact, dichotomous distinctions between the sacred and the profane are blurred. Dixon Gottschild asserts that: "Voudou and all Africanist danced religions are examples of [Yvonne] Daniel's concept of embodied wisdom and embrace the contradictory, conflicting ethos of spirit world and body/ material world" (Dixon Gottschild 2002, 5). Further on in her article, she proposes the Africanist principle of "and": "we are sexual *and* spiritual, body *and* soul, human *and* supernatural, good *and* bad" (6). Thus the corporeality of danced Africanist religions does not attempt to erase the sexuality inherent in certain body movements such as gyrating hips or pelvic thrusts. These movements may allude to forceful aché or energy of certain orishas.

These movements incorporate an aesthetic that contrasts with that of Western European classical traditions. The importance of hip movement kinesthetically occurs in a bent-knee posture, relaxed, undulating back; therefore, Africanist postures will be lower to the ground. The European aesthetic calls for a straight-backed posture and an elongated, straight-legged attitude. In fact, in Cuban popular dances, the "whitening" process can be seen in the body posture. In a *guaguancó* (or any rumba) the body will be relaxed, low, with hips loose and arms relaxed, as polyrhythmic movement can initiate from any part of the body and often involves the upper torso and the lower body executing syncopated, independent dance actions. As anyone who has seen an international Latin ballroom "rhumba" competition will attest, the transformation of the African aesthetic to a Western one involves the straightening of the legs with the back upright and the tightening of the hips. The whitened version is almost unrecognizable to its original counterpart.

Various African Origins

Yvonne Daniel has made an in-depth study of Cuban dance, distinguishing between African traditions in Cuba. African-based danced religions include: the Congo, the Arará, the Calabarí, and the Yoruba, and each contributes specific body movements, instruments, and ritual expressions to the rich repertory of Cuban dance and religion. For instance, the Congo, or Bantú, Central African religious tradition in Cuba is called Palo Monte. Congo culture contributes characteristic hip rolls and the all-important instrument the conga drums, which are barrel shaped and played by the hands. The Arará or the people of Dahomey, West Africa, which includes the Ewe and the Fon peoples of the former kingdom of Benin, do not use barrel drums but the cylindrical drums accompanied by a metal bell or *ogan*. These drums are played with sticks and the drummers often stand.

The characteristic Arará body movement is the rising and falling of the shoulders (Daniel 2002, 36).

Daniel calls the Carabalí the most distinctive African music/dance tradition in Cuba. Hailing from the Carabal River region that is now Cameroon and Nigeria, the Carabalí in Cuba are known as Abakuá. The Abakuá form secret societies and they offer the only masked dance tradition that has survived in Cuba. The masked spirit dancers are called Ñáñigos, and they perform characteristic smooth and sustained lunging stances that alternate with standing positions, high on the toes. Another Abakuá distinctive characteristic involves the pointed, cone-shaped head of the mask and tiny drums (*enkríkamo*) (Daniel 2002).

The last wave of Africans to arrive in Cuba during the *travesía* (crossing) was the West African Yoruba. In Cuba they are known as Lucumí. The Cuban adaptation of beliefs is called Santería or *La Regla de Ochá*, and its pantheon of male and female divinities called orishas characterizes it. Orishas represent natural elements and their energies through a variety of male and female deities. Each orisha has a characteristic dance and drum rhythm that the initiates use to call spirits to embody them during a toque de santo. Orishas are often seen represented in their syncretic form as Catholic saints. In Brazil, Candomblé of the northeastern region most resembles Cuban Santería, as it shares the same Yoruba origins, although some of the orishas may be syncretized with different Catholic saints. Candomblé closely resembles Santería as a danced, Africanist religion.

In the popular or street musical tradition, there are four main complexes of Cuban music—el son, la rumba, el danzón and *el punto guajiro o campesino*. All have dance counterparts. These refer to dance and popular musical styles developed during the nineteenth and twentieth centuries. The rumba, for example, is the most Africanist in movement. The guaguancó rumba is danced by a man and a woman, while only men dance the columbia rumba. The footwork of the rumba is an amazing syncretic amalgamation of Africanist dance and the Spanish *zapateo*. Many of the steps are taken from Santería ritual dance. For instance, the dance of "el cojo" (the lame man) conveys a man whose body is shaky and unstable, yet when the music enters his body, his steps become strong, intricate, and full of virtuosity. You can see this dance in the second of a three-part video documentary entitled *Routes of Rhythm*, narrated by Harry Belafonte on the history of Cuban music and dance (Dratch and Rosow 1990). The dancer is symbolically cured through the music. In Santería, the curing of the sick is the province of the orisha Babalú-Ayé, represented by Saint Lazarus.

National Cuban Identity in Contemporary Dance

While Cuban religious dance music has always influenced popular street-dance forms, with the advent of the Cuban Revolution in 1959, the Cuban government created new opportunities for the development of the arts. A key figure in the area of the performing arts is Ramiro Guerra, the creator of la técnica cubana. Guerra was appointed director of the Department of Modern Dance within the Teatro Nacional in Havana and was charged with the creation of an indigenous Cuban modern dance form (John 2002, 73). He created the company Danza Contemporánea. What is most interesting about the Cuban technique in modern dance is that it sprang from what Guerra has called the Cuban way of moving, which, of course, is influenced by Cuban religious dance forms.

Dancer and choreographer Suki John describes it thus:

> Many exercises are repeated in different rhythms, emphasizing contrasting dynamics . . . several drummers, a singer and a flute player always accompany company classes at Danza Contemporánea. The music ranges from country melodies to the orisha songs of Santería. This attention to musical detail marries the dancing to its Cuban roots. It transforms the movement both rhythmically and kinesthetically. (John 2002, 76)

John later goes on to describe modern dance techniques that, when adapted by la técnica cubana,

> take on a sensuous richness that invites embellishment in the head, pelvis, and torso . . . The floor work has a distinct [Martha] Graham[1] base, but includes rippling flexibility in the spine and folkloric pecking and twisting motions of the head. . . . Company class in the técnica cubana usually ends with a low traveling step that is a variation on several orisha images, including that of the freshwater goddess Oshún observing herself in the mirror. (2002, 77)

Dancers in the Escuela Nacional de Arte, where la técnica cubana is taught, are trained for an average of ten years in all three dance forms: modern dance, ballet, and Cuban folklore. Thus dancers who represent theatrical-ized versions of the folkloric Santería, Congo, Arará, or Calabarí religious dances are all trained within the Cuban aesthetic of ritual Africanist music and body movements. As incorporated dancers of la técnica cubana, they perform a secularized version of the religious dance. Their bodies become a locus where secular and profane distinctions disappear.

Religious vs. Theatrical Performance

Yet, even if the religious dance forms' influence, in fact, shape Cuban sec-ular, street, and performance dancing, is there a distinction between the religious experience and the secular one? From all accounts, there is. In Voudou, for instance, it is said that it is through the *nommo* or power of the word (the incantations and prayers) that one type of experience is called ritual and another social, while the actual body movements, steps, and postures may be the same. In Cuba, the artists of the Conjunto Folklórico Nacional are clear about making the distinction. Most of those inter-viewed in the documentary *Everyday Art: Jazz, Salsa, Traditional Music and Dance by Some of Cuba's Greatest Performers* (1995), a film by María Luisa Mendoça, acknowledge being *religiosos* (that is, practitioners of Santería, Palo Monte, or the Abakuá religions). They repeatedly make the distinc-tion between the religious and the artistic.

Amelia Pedrozo, a woman batá player from the Conjunto Folklórico Nacional, states clearly: "I teach the art, the dance, the artistic aspect of the religious. The religion in itself I do not teach. I teach that which can be taken as artistic; in a sense, it is the superficial" (Mendoça 1995). Many of the musicians and dancers reiterate the authenticity of their art by claiming to have learned it not in a schooled environment but at home, in the neigh-borhood, from family and friends since early childhood. The fact that they are now part of a professional group of artists that stylizes the movements becomes an extension of a way of life that began outside of a formal context and that originated in the everyday practice of popular religious beliefs.

In a personal interview with Afro-Cuban dancer Teresita Domé Pérez[2] from the group AfroCuba de Mantanzas (who trained with Juan García, now the director of the Conjunto Folklórico Nacional de Cuba), she reit-erates the differences between dancing for the orisha in a ceremony and dancing as theatrical entertainment. She maintains that the purpose is significant, as well as the space in which the event takes place.

In a performance, there is a dialectic purpose to the dancing, that is, to demonstrate to the public the prototype of an orisha's dance (for instance the dance for Oshún will have certain characteristic movements that distinguish it from that of Yemayá or Changó or Obatalá). In a religious ceremony one calls the saint or orisha, and certain prayers or words are repeated in the toque. This chanting can have the effect of putting a devotee in a trance-like state. He or she may even lose consciousness.

I asked her why, then, does a devotee who may also be a professional ethnic dancer not get mounted (the common word used for possession) by an orisha. Her reply was straightforward: "Because during a performance, dancers are thinking about other things such as the count, the placement, the choreography. The religious intention is not present. Neither is it a sacred space made sacred by those who are offering the ceremony." Teresita did remember having a personal experience of dancing professionally at a church courtyard during the feast of La Virgen de la Caridad del Cobre (Oshún, to whom Teresita is devoted) when she felt a strong presence and almost lost consciousness. She admits, however, that she did not fall into a full trance (interview in Los Angeles, California, June 2004). In this circumstance the church courtyard was considered a sacred space (even though it lies outside the church walls). While the dancer's intention began as professional, it potentially became more than that. In the Santería worldview, orishas have the right to mount or embody anyone they choose, whether the person knows him or herself to be a devotee of that orisha or not. Orishas make their preference known by mounting that person.

By Way of Conclusion

Afro-Cuban danced religions and secular dance forms demonstrate the ontological worldview mentioned at the beginning of this article as the principle of the "and." Integration becomes part of a process between aesthetic and religious experience in the body of the dancer. The physical body as creative site gives way to endless possibilities for the continued creation of meaning in motion. The definition of "dancer" is democratized in as far as everyone who is physically disposed to movement is a dancer, whether it be in a religious ceremony of embodiment of sacred energies or in the exchange of energies with oneself (in a solo) or with others (ensemble or partner dancing). Many of the musicians and dancers interviewed in the video *Everyday Art*, as well as my informant Teresita Domé Pérez, began their musical lives with the daily sounds and steps of their families' religious practices. They began at home, in their neighborhoods, and later became professional folkloric musicians and dancers. Those who study Afro-Cuban music and dance know that the origin of this music is sacred, but cradled in the homes and solares of urban and rural Cuban barrios. Dancing religions thus offer a rich field of study for the articulation of the religious as a daily practice of both credence and aesthetic values. ¡Aché!

Notes

My warmest thanks to Steve Loza for offering me the opportunity to participate in a memorable and unique conference, from which this essay originated. I have been a street dancer and avid fan of Afro-Cuban music as well as a specialist in Latin American theater and performance studies, but this was my first participation in a conference as musically interdisciplinary as this one.

1. Martha Graham is arguably the most influential and innovative creative artist in the area of contemporary dance worldwide. She revolutionized dance by incorporating movements until then not considered appropriate to dance into her experimental choreography.

2. Thanks to my colleague Francisco Javier Crespo for providing me the contact that led me to meet and take a dance workshop with Teresita Domé Pérez. At the time of this writing, she teaches Afro-Cuban dance with the traditional batá drummers (of which Mr. Crespo is often part) at the MacArthur Park Community Center in Los Angeles, California, on the first and last Saturdays of the month.

References and Selected Bibliography

Aparicio, Frances R. 1998. *Listening to Salsa: Gender, Latin Popular Music, and Puerto Rican Cultures*. Hanover, N.H.: University Press of New England.

Aparicio, Frances R., and Cándida F. Jáquez, eds. 2003. *Musical Migrations, Transnationalism and Cultural Hybridity in Latin/o America*. New York: Palgrave/Macmillan.

Bascom, William. 1972. *Shangó in the New World*. Austin: University of Texas, Afro and Afro-American Research Institute.

Bastide, Roger. 1978. *The African Religions of Brazil: Towards a Sociology of the Interpretation of Civilizations*. Translated by Helen Sebba. Baltimore and London: Johns Hopkins University Press.

Béhague, Gerard, ed. 1992. *Music and Black Ethnicity: Caribbean and South America*. Miami: North-South Center, University of Miami.

Boggs, Vernon. 1992. *Salsiology: Afro-Cuban Music and the Evolution of Salsa in New York City*. New York: Greenwood Press.

Cabrera, Lydia. 1940. *Cuentos negros de Cuba*. La Habana, Imprenta La Verónica.

———. 1954. *El monte: igbo finda, ewe orisha, vititinfinda (Notas sobre las religiones, la magia, las supersticiones y el folklore de los negros criollos y del pueblo de Cuba)*. La Habana, Ediciones C.R.

———. 1957. *Anagó: vocabulario lucumí (El yoruba que se habla en Cuba)*. La Habana, Ediciones C.R.

———. 1958. *La sociedad secreta Abakuá, narrada por viejos adeptos*. La Habana, Ediciones C.R.

———. 1974. *Yemayá y Ochún: Kariocha, Iyalorichas y Olorichas*. Madrid, Ediciones C.R.

———. 1975. *Anaforuana: ritual y símbolos de la iniciación en la sociedad secreta Abakuá*. Madrid, Ediciones C.R.

———. 1977. *La Regla Kimbisa del Santo Cristo del Buen Viaje*. Miami: Peninsular Printing, Col. del Chicherekú en el exilio.

———. 1979. *Reglas de Congo: Palo Monte Mayombe*. Miami, Peninsular Printing, Col. del Chicherekú en el exilio.

———. 1980. *Yemayá y Ochún, Kariocha, Iyalorichas y Olorichas*. New York: Colección del Chicherukú en el exilio.

———. 1984. *Vocabulario congo: el Bantú que se habla en Cuba*. Miami, Ediciones C.R., Col. del Chicherekú en el exilio.

———. 1988. *La lengua sagrada de los ñáñigos*. Miami, Ediciones Universal.

Calvo Ospina, Hernando. 1992. *¡Salsa! Havana Beat: Bronx Beat*. Translated by Nick Caistor. London: Latin American Bureau.

Carpentier, Alejo. 1946. *La música en Cuba*. México: Fondo de Cultura Económica.

Cashion, Susan. 1989a. "Educating the Dancer." In *Cuba in Dance: Current Selected Research*, Vol. 1, ed. Lynnette Y. Overby and James H. Humphrey, 165–85. New York: AMS Press.

———. 1989b. "A Taxonomy of Cuban Dances." Unpublished chart.

Castellanos, Isabel y Jorge Castellanos. 1992. *Cultura afrocubana, Vol. 3, Las religiones y las lenguas*. Miami: Ediciones Universal.

Cros Sandoval, Mercedes. 1975. *La religión afrocubana*. Madrid: Playor.

Cuervo Hewitt, Julia. 1983. "Ifá: Oráculo Yoruba y Lucumí." *Cuban Studies/Estudios cubanos* 13, no. 1 (winter): 25–40.

Cuervo Hewitt, Julia, and William Luis. 1987. "Santos y santería: conversación con Arcadio, santero de Guanabacoa." *Afro-Hispanic Review* 6, no. 1 (January): 9–17.

Daniel, Yvonne. 1995. *Rumba, Dance and Social Change in Contemporary Cuba*. Bloomington and Indianapolis: Indiana University Press.

————. 2002. "Cuban Dance: An Orchard of Caribbean Creativity." In *Caribbean Dance from Abakuá to Zouk: How Movement Shapes Identity*, ed. Susanna Sloat, 23–55. Gainesville: University Press of Florida.

Díaz-Díaz, Eduardo. 1998. "Salsa, género y etnicidad: el baile como arena social." *Revista de Estudios Sociales* 4 (Enero): 80–101.

Dixon Gottschild, Brenda. 2002. "Crossroads, Continuities, and Contradictions: The Afro-Euro-Caribbean Triangle." In *Caribbean Dance from Abakuá to Zouk: How Movement Shapes Identity*, ed. Susanna Sloat, 3–10. Gainesville: University Press of Florida.

Fuentes, Leonardo Podera. 2003. *Faces of Salsa: A Spoken History*. Translated by Stephen Clark. Washington and London: Smithsonian.

Fraser Delgado, Celeste, and José Esteban Muñoz, eds. 1997. *Everynight Life, Culture and Dance in Latin/o America*. Durham and London: Duke University Press.

Hanna, Judith Lynn. 1988. *Dance, Sex and Gender*. Chicago and London: University of Chicago Press.

Hamilton Crowell Jr., Nathaniel. 2002. "What is Congolese in Caribbean Dance." In *Caribbean Dance from Abakuá to Zouk: How Movement Shapes Identity*, ed. Susanna Sloat, 11–22. Gainesville: University Press of Florida.

John, Suki. 2002. "The Técnica Cubana." In *Caribbean Dance from Abakuá to Zouk: How Movement Shapes Identity*, ed. Susanna Sloat, 73–80. Gainesville: University Press of Florida.

Leymarie, Isabelle. 2002. *Cuban Fire: The Story of Salsa and Latin Jazz*. New York and London: Continuum.

Marrero, María Teresa. 1997. "Historical and Literary Santería: Unveiling Gender and Identity in U.S. Cuban Literature." In *Tropicalizations: Transcultural Representations of Latinidad*, ed. Frances R. Aparicio and Susana Chávez-Silverman, 139–59. Hanover and London: University Press of New England.

Mousouris, Melinda. 2002. "The Dance World of Ramiro Guerra: Solemnity, Voluptuousness, Humor, Chance." In *Caribbean Dance from Abakuá to Zouk: How Movement Shapes Identity*, ed. Susanna Sloat, 56–72. Gainesville: University Press of Florida.

Murphy, Joseph. 1988. *Santería, An African Religion in the Americas*. Boston: Beacon Press.

Ortíz, Fernando. 1917. *Hampa afro-cubana, los negros brujos*. Madrid: Editorial América.

————. 1940. *Contrapunteo cubano del tabaco y el azúcar*. La Habana: Casa Editora Jesús Montero.

Sloat, Susanna, ed. 2002. *Caribbean Dance from Abakuá to Zouk: How Movement Shapes Identity*. Gainesville: University Press of Florida.

Steward, Sue. 1999. *¡Música! The Rhythm of Latin America, Salsa, Rumba, Merengue and More*. San Francisco: Chronicle Books.

Verger, Pierre Fatundi. 1981. *Orixás. Deuses Iorubás na África e no Novo Mundo*. Salvador, Brazil: Editôra Corrupio Comércio Ltd. and Círculo do Livro S.A.

Waxer, Lise, ed. 2002. *Situating Salsa: Global Markets and Local Meaning in Latin Popular Music*. New York: Routledge.

Selected Videography

Mendoça, María Luisa. 1995. *Everyday Art: Jazz, Salsa, Traditional Music and Dance by Some of Cuba's Greatest Performers*. The Cinema Guild, www.cinemaguild.com

Dratch, Howard, and Eugene Rosow. 1990. *Routes of Rhythm*, Vols. 1, 2, and 3, narrated by Harry Belafonte. The Cinema Guild, www.cinemaguild.com

Observing the Unobservable

CHARLES E. MOORE

A Posteriori: First-Order Lived Experiences

☞ THIS ESSAY ADDRESSES CREATIVE AND SPIRITUAL PRAXIS SOLELY through the African Yoruba Orisha. To begin, it is necessary to understand how religion and art are thought of in the African native or natural first-order, lived context.

African People: Beliefs and Creative Praxis

The African a posteriori is the time where the oldest first-order, lived empirical and continuing experiential praxis of the idea and form of religion occurs. According to Professor John Mbiti (1991, 11–19), the eminent theological scholar of the affairs of religion in Africa whose work is studied in ethnomusicology, there are five parts to any religion or spiritual praxis in Africa. In his book *Introduction to African Religion*, Mbiti lists the five parts and their meanings as:

1. Beliefs. The essential part of an ontology showing the way the people think about the universe and their attitude towards life itself.
2. Practices, Festivals and Ceremonies. Group activities or praxis that show how people express their beliefs in practical terms (praying, making sacrifices and offering, performing ceremonies and observing customs). These are joyous occasions when people sing, dance,

eat and celebrate at particular events such as harvest time, childbirth, rainy season, victory over enemies, etc.

3. Spiritual Objects and Places. Things and places seen in metaphysics as expressions in materials which people have set apart as being holy or sacred. Some materials are made by hand while others are taken in their natural form and set apart for spiritual purposes (shrines, groves, sacred hills or mountains or objects such as rivers, charms, masks, etc.).

4. Spiritual Officials and Leaders. These are people who conduct religious matters such as ceremonies, sacrifices, formal prayers and divination. They are trained men and women who hold offices such as priests, rain-makers, ritual leaders, medicine men, kings and rulers. They are the keepers of the spiritual heritage and those who are to be considered as specialists and experts in all spiritual matters.

5. Values and Morals. Ideas in value theory that safeguard or uphold the life of people in their relationship with one another and the world around them. Topics such as truth, justice, love, right and wrong, good and evil, beauty, decency, respect for people and property, keeping promises and agreements, praise and blame, crime and punishment, the rights and responsibilities of both the individual and the community, character, integrity, etc., are found under the activities of these ideas. (Mbiti 1991, 11–19)

As an ontological essence, African religion belongs to the people where it has evolved. It would mean absolutely nothing to try to transplant or change it theoretically without its peoples' will to be there with it. No single person, for example as in the case of Jesus, Muhammad, and Buddha, started any African religion. The practice of spiritual beliefs evolved slowly over many centuries as African people led their lives and reflected on their living experiences. The spiritual practices are a part of an African heritage whose origins are many hundreds and thousands of years old.

The heritage of spiritual practices is a product of the thinking and experiences of the practitioners' forefathers, mothers, and children, for generations. These are the people who have formed spiritual ideas and formulated beliefs while observing ceremonies and rituals. There can be no understanding their heritage without understanding the part about the spiritual praxis. Each distinct people is informed and influenced by their practice of religion in their first-order lived traditions and customs.

Early historical records show that the traditional Africans continue to be a very spiritual people. An overall view of African culture reveals the idea that different cultures and people all have their spiritual practices. This is still an unabated historical part of African culture from the time of ancient Kemet to the present. Their spiritual practice is thought to be the normal way of viewing the world and experiencing life. All of this was and is found to be true even though there is no single word for religion among the approximate two thousand languages and dialects existing on the continent. However, there are words for spiritual ideas, practices, objects, and places.

When Africans migrate from one part of the continent to another or from one continent to another, the practice of their native religions is taken with them. Even if they have converted to Islam, Buddhism, or Christianity, Africans do not completely abandon their spiritual traditions. The traditions remain with them for several generations or centuries. For example, for the purpose of this essay, the native spiritual practices of the African Americans and the African Caribbeans have been suppressed and bombarded by other cultures as a means of controlling the people as slaves. This lasted until the nineteenth century. However, despite this brutality, many elements of their original native spiritual practice survive, even today.

The Yoruba Orisha

Regarding a theory for religion as art, African people have always expressed their spiritual views and values in the materiality of spiritual objects and places. Specifically, the Yoruba traditional civilization is, historically, one of the most urbane on the African continent. This quality of first-order living suggests living in a city or town removed from rural character. The urbanity, courtesy, polished manners, and refinement in behavior have their origins in the Middle Ages in Ile-Ife, the Yoruba holy city, where the culture bearers believe that their world began. According to Robert Farris Thompson's *Flash of the Spirit* (1984, 5–18), during the period of the tenth to the twelfth centuries, before anything of comparable quality was produced in Europe, the Yoruba, from their religion, were adept at sculpting and shaping art. Yorubaland, the traditional homeland, consists of self-sufficient city-states where life is characterized by artistic and poetic fervor and richness. Among the Yoruba people, everything is assessed aesthetically. This would include taste, color, human deportment, height, freshness, improvisation, and so forth. They are known to have a rich and vast collection of works of religion as art celebrating the Yoruba religion.

In the Yoruba religion, the worship of spirits under Olorun, the spiritual force or God, the supreme deity, has an infinite panorama of vibrant mortals. The various animal forms of Olorun are the supreme quintessence of *Ashe*, the force that is both generous and intimidating. All of the animal forms are messengers and embodiments of ashe, the spiritual command in the forms of a python, a viper, a white snail, and a woodpecker. In these animals is the spiritual power to make things happen, moral and neutral power, giving power, taking away power, and life or death power. Further still are found the avatars of ashe with semiotic elements and displayed on items such as ritual ceramic bowls with the image of Shango, the thunder god, within zigzag patterns of lightening. Other art pieces include iconography crafted upon or in the form of trees, iron staffs, iron sculptures, long-beaked birds, or snails. Most importantly, certain works for religion as art are created that transcend questions regarding makeup and confinements. These are inherent with ashe, the divine force incarnate. Those persons who are considered the most merited in Yorubaland, such as the master priestesses, diviners, kings, and paramount chiefs all have ashe. Their very spoken words are spirit invoking and predictive experiences for ashe.

An important consideration for Yoruba religion as art is *iwa* or character. *Iwa rere* is, in essence, a coolness with gentle generosity of character (*iwa pele*). Seen as originating from Olorun, this coolness attains proximity to ashe, the divine spirit. Signs that signify the coolness of character are considered a noble quality, and their artistic expressions are often white in color. Signs of white cloths are draped over sculptures honoring expression in the case of the cult of Obatala, the God of creativity. Qualities in sculpture such as purity of presentation, symmetry, custom, the traditional way of life, postures and gestures of spiritual alertness, the giving to an elder, good character, and the image of the descent of the bird of mind coming from ashe are creative expressions and examples of qualities supporting the idea for religion as art.

Another important character among the Yoruba is *itutu*, the character of mystic coolness, and the sense of certainty in which ashe and iwa confer. It is thought that much Yoruba art is informed by itutu. The character is manifest in the calm faces carved in thunderstone, on a divination tray, in the curves of the calabash used for holding sacred things, and idealized action. Itutu is not semantically separated; rather, it is shaded and blurred into the ashe and iwa qualities. It is said that constant smiling is not a Yoruba characteristic. Sealed lips are a sign of seriousness and this would also imply that coolness of image is a merit of high praise. Two forms of spiritual coolness arise:

1. *ebo*—direct sacrifice, and
2. *irele*—propitiation, the utterance of conciliatory words and acts to hardened and angered deities as an entreatment toward them to become more generous and concerned, especially in times of crisis.

Itutu, a part of mystical coolness of character and the objectification of proper custom, is exhibited when the Yoruba live generously but discreetly and exhibit grace under pressure. All appearance and acts become a virtual form of royal power. It is at that point that the Yoruba become a noble, fully realized flame of creative goodness endowed by Olorun. Thus the notion of coolness in Yoruba art extends beyond representations of the act of sacrifice and acts of propitiation.

Itutu is a highly developed concept of ideas regarding beauty and correctness that one finds in a carnelian or a passage of drumming. Thus, along with ashe and iwa, itutu brings forth the idea for Yoruba religion as art. The three qualities come directly from the all-powerful Olorun as the power of commands in service of their expression in and of spiritual worship. As a complete force, they cannot be separated from one another, either in action or verbally. Rather, they are shades of creative qualities blended into each other and signifying the existence of God for the Yoruba people.

African Art

According to V. Y. Mudimbe, in his book *The Invention of Africa* (1988, 5), from the middle of the sixteenth century the objective in European art was to assimilate bodies or forms into painting methodology, reducing and neutralizing all differences into the sameness signified by the white norm. This was more of a spiritual history than a simple cultural tradition. This means that a "biblical solution to the problem of cultural differences was regarded by most European men as the best that reason and faith could propose" (5). Thus it was believed that the Bible stipulated an African could only be the slave of his brethren. Furthermore, on another level, signs of an epistemological order or content, silently and imperatively, indicated the process of integrating and differentiating figures within the normative sameness by their accumulation of accidental differences, such as nakedness, blackness, curly hair, bracelets, and strings and pearls. It was to be the beginning of an epistemological foundation of art in the West, including theories of the diversification of beings, and classificatory tables that attempted to explain the origins of constructing taxonomies and their objectives. As such, Michel Foucault (1973) believes that the "discovery" of African art led to African Studies and the invention of Africanisms as a scientific discipline illustrating the differentiating efficiency of classifying devices of patterns of reality, designation, arrangement, structure, and character: a new epistemological ordering. Essentially, this becomes a theory of understanding and looking at signs or semiotics in terms of "the arrangement of identities and differences into ordered tables" (72).

Professor Mudimbe, however, believes that during the fifteenth century African art was first brought to Europe by the Portuguese as fetishes (1988). These objects, supposedly having mysterious powers, were considered by the Europeans to be signs of a state of barbarism; however, on the whole, they were culturally neutral. It was not until the eighteenth century that these same objects, considered by some to be strange and ugly, entered the domain of African art. Along with the increase in the slave trade, the fetishes became symbols of African art. The objects were still being viewed as primitive, simple, childish, and nonsensical.

A Priori: Second-Order Reflections on the African Lived Experience

The African a priori concept views theory as contrasted with the condition of an a posteriori empirical experience. As a coherent group, the a priori reflections are used to distinguish between two ways a concept, form, or idea may be acquired (Moore 2002, 330). Nevertheless, before beginning the discussion regarding references to the second-order reflections on the lived experiences of the Yoruba people, language should be mentioned concerning this essay's delimitations surrounding how the discourse was presented by all of the distinguished conference scholars.

One concern is the idea of a "theory" for religion as art. In Greek philosophy, Plato established the concept of the empirical, observable world as an imperfect image of a realm of theoretical and unobservable and unchanging forms, and the concept of the best life as one centered on the love of these divine objects. In his treatise *Phaedo*, Plato argues the existence of abstract objects that he called "forms" or "ideas" (the term "ideas" should be used cautiously, since these objects are not creations of a mind, but exist independently of thought). Plato established the idea that these forms are eternal, changeless, and incorporeal; since they are imperceptible, we can come to have knowledge of them only through thought.

Plato established and insisted, for example, on the error of the identity of two equal sticks with what equality itself is, or what beautiful bodies with what beauty itself is, or what pious acts with what piety itself is. Thus equal, pious acts and beauty are implicitly appealing to a standard of equality, piety, or beauty; they are all forms. Forms, according to Plato, are what many of our words refer to, even though they are different objects from the ones revealed by our senses. Thus, forms are not unusual items; rather, they are a source of moral and spiritual inspiration.

Observing the Unobservable

Theoretical Considerations

Since there are many theories covering such diverse topics as philosophy, aesthetics, mathematics, science, statistics, social science, critical issues, and so forth, how then does one choose or create a "theory" for religion to support the aesthetic considerations within the creative and intuitive processes and the production of expression? To that end, several more questions arise: who is the person endeavoring to establish such a theory, why is it necessary, and for what purpose is this theory for religion as art being established? Is it being established for socioeconomic and political reasons? Or is it for reasons that are to be found in the area of creative and aesthetic activities? These questions and possible answers are thought-provoking issues surrounding the determined boundaries that may well exist in the title of this anthology.

The African Aesthetic

According to Kariamu Asante (1994, 72–74), the beauty of African aesthetics is in its complexity. Only knowledge by word of mouth or oral narratives can inform persons who are interested in the deeper knowledge of such things. There are no permanent stamps of the creators, only changing designs, rhythms, and movements that change with the performers.

What a creative work represents is guarded and revered. The mark of the artist is in his or her creativity as its permanence or signature deals with the work itself and the culture it represents. Thus, the signature of the artist is inherent in the creation and the spiritual or divine deserves and is given credit. The African artist is regarded as a conduit and is not responsible for the greatness of the work of art. This does not mean that the artist is irresponsible; rather, he or she must accept responsibility as conduit, where appreciation is acknowledgment.

The ontology of African aesthetics is memory. All permanence of creative work is based on harmony with nature, the people, and their God. Ontology, concerned with the nature, constitution, and structure of reality, simply put, allows African aesthetics to provoke collectiveness in terms of spirit and individuality for the artist. The religion of the African aesthetic, although not spiritual by definition, can involve ritual and a conscious and subconscious call to the ancestors, gods, and mind, to permit the flow of energy for the artist to create.

Marimba Ani (1994, 199–200) believes there are two uses for the term "aesthetic." First, she identifies it as a European scientific or philosophical value concept of beauty, in the sense of forms, images, and experiences that provoke positive emotional responses for enculturated persons within their traditions, and, second, that there is an added "objectification" of the experience. According to the experience of objectification, within the cultural logos of Europe various aspects cohere. The aspects are the development germ or seed, its ideological core or matrix that is identified as the sense of its collective creations.

Conclusions

Taking a closer view of the notion of a theory for religion as art, one finds and can argue that there are several philosophical positions and ideas to be considered. First, the philosophy of religion is thought by many to be a complex system of theory and empiricism, including both myths and rituals. It therefore includes the possibility of examining "truth claims" whereby there is a concern for the importance of the existence, nature, and activities of God. Second, as an aesthetic, from the Greek word *aisthanomai*, all religion and spiritual objects need to be perceived and considered as embodying the existence, nature, and activities of God. From the spiritual objects, there must also be an examination of their truth claims as to the nature of art and the character of the human experience of art and the natural environment. A philosophy of art deals with the nature of taste, beauty, imagination, creativity, representation, expression, and expressiveness. These ideas must be blended with ideas regarding the philosophy of religion as an understanding of God to be something like a creative person who is disembodied, eternal, free, all powerful, all knowing, and the proper object of human obedience and worship.

The blending of such theories encompassing religion and aesthetics provides for the possibility of a third discourse that purports to the making of a reference to an observation of an unobservable entity, property, or relation. It thus stands to reason that a theory for religion as art could be a theoretical concept referring to an unobservable entity that must be expressed by terms in any of the foregoing senses. Since all theories for religion as art must be expressed in distinct terms, there are some who might argue that all observations are theory laden, either because human perception of the world is colored by perceptual, linguistic, and cultural differences, or because no attempt to distinguish sharply between observation and theory, the unobservable, has been successful.

Nevertheless, such issues regarding aesthetics have been discussed as recently in western history as during the period of Alexander Gottleib Baumgarten, a German philosopher of the seventeenth century, who wrote textbooks in metaphysics and ethics on the lectures of Emmanuel Kant. Baumgarten's principal contribution to western philosophy was his introduction of the term "aesthetics" as well as the discipline of aesthetics into German philosophy. From the Gottfried Wilhelm Leibniz concept of metaphysics and the explanations of pleasure by Christen Wolff, Baumgarten introduced the discipline and term called aesthetics as a departure from the idea of pleasure as a response to the perception of perfection by means of the senses. To Baumgarten, the human response to beauty was pleasure in the perfection of sensory perception. This idea is to be found in his inaugural dissertation *Philosophical Meditations on Some Matters Pertaining to Poetry* (1954 [1735]). The term "aesthetics" was used to define a poem as a perfect sensate discourse, meaning a discussion of the consciousness of perceiving or seeming to perceive some state or affection of one's body or its parts or senses or of one's mind or its emotions (38–39, 77–78).

From the aforementioned ideas, Benedetto Croce, the literary and historical scholar, joined his great interest in these fields to philosophy.

One of Croce's most circulated works in the English-speaking world is *Aesthetics as Science of Expression and General Linguistics* (1992 [1902]). Because Croce regarded the aesthetic experience as a primitive (first) type of cognition, he believed that intuition involves the awareness of a particular image, which constitutes a nonconceptual form of knowledge. Further still, Croce believed that art is the expression of emotion that can produce cognitive awareness in the sense that the particular intuited as an image can have a cosmic aspect, so that in it the human spirit is perceived.

Croce's work appears to stand in sharp contrast to the work of Karl Marx, who viewed religion as a form of subjugation for workers at the hands of the powerful and designed to comfort while it simultaneously justified privilege. In *Deutsch-Französisch Jahrbucher*, a single-issue journal published in Paris in 1844 by Karl Marx and Arnold Ruge, Marx discussed his ideas further. Believing that the state and society produced religion, he viewed it as a general theory of this world with its encyclopedic compendium, its logic in popular form, its spiritual *point d'honneur*, its enthusiasm, its moral sanction, its solemn complement, and its universal basis of consolation and justification. Finally, Marx saw the struggle against religion as an indirect struggle against that world whose spiritual aroma is religion.

Croce and Marx provide us with a dichotomy of thought and choice, or a third dimension of dismissal of both their views. Marx dismissed religion in addition to the metaphysical while Croce embraced them. But dismissing either point of view would be contrary to the spirit (the unobservable and abstract) and theory (the unobservable and abstract) that constitute my basic thesis in this essay. The Yoruba orisha tradition is only one of hundreds of religious concepts in Africa, representing a grand diversity and unity of African belief systems. The polarity of Croce to Marx, or of any religious or ideological position to another, cannot annihilate any form of spiritual being or its artistic representation or embodiment. This point we find in Yoruba orisha is the central thesis I present here as a basic, theoretical alternative to our understanding of the relationship of religion as art, or what we may refer to as the first-order lived context, in Africa.

References

Ani, Marimba. 1994. *Yurugu.* Trenton: African World Press.

Asante, Kariamu. 1994. *The African Aesthetic.* Westport: Praeger.

Baumgarten, Alexander. 1954 [1735]. "Philosophical Meditations on Some Matters Pertaining to Poetry." In *Reflections on Poetry*, translated from the original Latin by Karl Aschenbrenner and William B. Holther, 38–39 and 77–78. Berkeley: University of California Press.

Croce, Benedetto. 1992 [1902]. *Aesthetic as Science of Expression and General Linguistic.* Trans. Colin Lyas. Cambridge: Cambridge University Press.

Foucault, M. 1973. *The Order of Things.* New York: Pantheon.

Mbiti, John. 1991. *Introduction to African Religion.* New York: Heinemann Educational Books.

Moore, Charles E. 2000. "William Christopher Handy and Uraeus Mi: A Bantu-Centered Philosophical and Intracultural Assessment." Ph.D. Diss., University of California, Los Angeles.

Mudimbe, V. Y. 1988. *The Invention of Africa.* Bloomington: Indiana University Press.

Thompson, Robert Farris. 1984. *Flash of the Spirit.* New York: Vintage Books.

Path to the Divine

Music in the Sufi Experience

ALI JIHAD RACY

⌣ MYSTICISM IS DEFINED AS AN APPROACH TO KNOWING THE DIVINE through direct experience, through intuition, rather than mere doctrine. It is regarded as a quest that stems from within, rather than as a dictum that exists on the outside. Mysticism has been viewed as the innate propensity for the soul to reach out toward the otherworldly, the sublime, the all embracing. Existing in Judaic, Christian, Islamic, Hindu, and other world traditions, the mystical quest has over the centuries assumed different social configurations, ritualistic practices, and ideologies.

In the world of Islam, mysticism is represented by the Sufi movement, which began as asceticism that turned away from worldly attractions during the early centuries of Islam, but by the thirteenth century had already developed into myriads of sects (or *turuq*, singular *tariqah*, literally "path" or "way"). Each of these sects paid homage to and venerated the teachings and life experiences of a founding saint, whose legacy was upheld by subsequent generations of *shaykhs*, or sect leaders, and followers.

The impact of Sufism upon Islamic culture has been profound. To begin with, Sufi groups exist practically throughout the Muslim world, from Mauritania to Iraq, from Turkey to Pakistan and India, from Yugoslavia to South East Asia. Over the centuries, Sufism has been a driving force in the domains of poetry, storytelling, calligraphy, architecture, and certainly music and dance. For example, the Mevlevi order, which was founded by Mevlana Jalal al-Din Rumi in Turkey in the thirteenth century, and which included numerous outstanding performers and composers among its members, has been viewed as the musical conservatory of the Ottoman Empire. We may ask: Why did the Sufis in general have so much interest in the arts, to the extent of making music and dance an integral part of their rituals, all this against a backdrop of Islamic conservatism that frowned upon such expressions and at times even declared them antithetical to religious piety?

Sufis have traditionally followed the basic sacraments of Islam and adhered to the teachings of the *Qur'an*, the holy book revealed through Prophet Muhammad. However, they added to the prescribed principles of the faith an all-encompassing worldview that integrated such presumably disparate realms as the secular and the sacred, this world and that world, the obvious and the hidden, the human and the rest of the cosmos. Their vision as such was expressed through a rich repertoire of images, concepts, and symbols.

Two principles were fundamental to Sufism: one is Divine Love (*al-Hubb al-Ilahi*), known to have originated with one of the early Islamic mystics, a woman by the name Rabi'ah al-'Adawiyyah (d. 801 AD), who lived in Basra, now in Iraq. Rabi'ah spoke of love for God, not for fear of hell, or ambition for paradise, but rather as a natural affinity for the beauty of God. The idea of Divine Love is linked to the desire for *wasl*, or the urge for reunion with the beloved, a symbolic motif ubiquitous in Sufi love poetry.

The other closely related principle is the Unity of Being (*Wahdat al-Wujud*), according to which the universe exists in the form of emanation from the Divine, or the One. Rooted in Neoplatonic philosophy, the concept of cosmic unity implies that (1) the divine substance is omnipresent either in a manifest or hidden form, and that (2) the human soul, which similarly derives from the Divine Source, may yearn to return to, or to relive, prior experiences of its place of origin. This happens when music is said to soften the soul and cause it to remember. In the writings of eleventh-century Abu Hamid al-Ghazali (n.d.), remembrance, which leads to a state of transcendental ecstasy, is a combination of pain (because of separation) and pleasure (because of the rekindled hope to merge into the broader realm of consciousness). It may also lead to what has been explained as *fana'* (literally, annihilation), metaphorically speaking, the withering away of ordinary consciousness or sense of being in favor of a subsuming realm of existence or, in paradoxical terms, a wholesome void or totalizing nothingness.

Meanwhile, the themes of separation and longing for reunion are quite often expressed through symbolic allusions and double meanings. In Sufi poetry, the beloved could be a human being or the Divine (the two considered interlinked). Such symbolism also underlies Rumi's celebrated poem about the *nay*, the reed flute, an instrument that the Mevlevi dervishes (sect members) venerate and use in their ritual. Here, the basic themes of separation, remembrance, and longing for reunion are illustrated:

> Hearken to the reed-flute, how it complains,
> Lamenting its banishment from its home:—
>   "Ever since they tore me from my osier bed,
> My plaintive notes have moved men and women to tears. . . .
> He who abides far away from his home
> Is ever longing for the day he shall return.
> My wailing is heard in every throng,
> In concert with them that rejoice and them that weep.
> Each interprets my notes in harmony with his own feelings,
> But not one fathoms the secrets of my heart.
> My secrets are not alien from my plaintive notes,
> Yet they are not manifest to the sensual eye and ear.
> Body is not veiled from soul, neither soul from body,
> Yet no man hath ever seen a soul." . . .
> 'Tis the fire of love that inspires the flute,
> 'Tis the ferment of love that possesses the wine. (Whinfield 1975, 1)

In Sufi rituals, the music—buttressed by spiritually uplifting lyrics—and the dance serve as catalysts for the occurrence of *wajd*, namely the ecstasy associated with spiritual yearning. French ethnomusicologist Gilbert Rouget, who in his *Music and Trance* (1985) examines the music-trance relationship cross-culturally in spirit possession, shamanic, mystical, and secular contexts, speaks of three models related to Sufi practice. The first model fits the early mystical concert, or *sama'*, as described by al-Ghazali and others, and continues to apply in contemporary spiritual and secular concerts. Here, those who perform the music for others who go into trance do not go into trance themselves. Instead, they are mere "musicators," as he calls them. In other words, (1) the trancees' experiences are instigated by someone other than themselves, and similarly their own trances are passively received, and (2) the trance is caused directly by the music, which Rouget, in this case, calls "pure message." In today's Sufi music, this is perhaps illustrated by the *qawwali* concert, which uses Sufi lyrics and often features highly celebrated singers from India and Pakistan, or the performances of Sufi vocalist Shaykh Hamzah Shakkur of Syria.

The second of Rouget's models is equated with the Sufi *dhikr* ritual, in which the participants themselves dance, as they sway their torsos, breathe rhythmically to the accompaniment of some percussion instruments, and reiterate certain mantra-like religious formulas, such as *Allah* (God) or *la Ilaha ila l-Lah* (There is no deity but God, or Allah). Accordingly, the group here is self-musicated, as the participants induce their own trance state.

The third of these models is associated with the Whirling Dervishes, namely the Mevlevis, or followers of Mevlana Jalal al-Din Rumi. Here we find elements from the other two models. On the one hand, the participants are essentially musicated by others, since the musicians produce within them a mood conducive for dancing. On the other hand, their own subsequent dancing (in this case whirling) generates ecstasy within them. They are both musicated and self-musicated.

To conclude, music and dance are basic to the Sufi experience for a number of reasons. Essentially, they propel the desired state of spiritual transcendence, the sense of losing oneself into the bliss of Divine Oneness. This happens as a result of three types of mergers or dualities. First, as explained in the writings of Sufi Inayat Khan (1976), Seyyed Hossein Nasr (1987), and others, music is worldly, as it appeals to our human senses, and at the same time otherworldly, as it symbolizes the perfect harmony of the higher cosmos. Second, the musical idiom links its innate ecstatic message with pertinent lyrics that imbue it with distinct spiritual directionality. The poetical themes of devotion, yearning, reunion, and being intoxicated by the beauty of the beloved all direct the Sufi seeker toward the higher state of consciousness. Third, music, as a ritual practice, creates an appropriate synergy for the various participants who listen as they perform. In this regard, I believe that Rouget's rather mutually exclusive models need to be qualified. For one thing, I believe that, in real practice, his constructs overlap considerably. The listening and the performing dynamics can, and most often do, occur simultaneously. This takes place, for example, when members of the congregation reiterate certain religious formulas while the lead soloist chants highly ornate and aesthetically engaging melodies over their reiteration. Furthermore, the idea of passive listening does not always apply. For example, in Arab countries, the audience engages in a dynamic feedback process that inspires the performers to excel (see Racy 2003). Active listening is extremely desirable in both Sufi and secular contexts.

In any case, music remains at the heart of the ecstatic religious experience. By observing the different Sufi approaches to mystical transformation, we become more cognizant of the intimate relationship between art and spirituality and, in a related sense, of music's own transformative powers.

References

al-Ghazali, Abu Hamid. n.d. *Ihya' 'Ulum al-Din*, Vol. 2. Damascus: Maktabat 'Abd al-Wakil al-Durubi.

Khan, Hazrat Inayat. 1976 [1962]. "The Mysticism of Sound," "Music," and "The Power of the Word." In *The Sufi Message of Hazrat Inayat Khan, Vol. 2.* Wassenaar, Netherlands: Service for the International Headquarters of the Sufi Movement, Geneva [originial ed., London: Barrie and Rockliff].

Nasr, Seyyed Hossein. 1987. *Islamic Art and Spirituality*. Albany, N.Y.: State University of New York Press.

Racy, A. J. 2003. *Making Music in the Arab World: The Culture and Artistry of Tarab.* Cambridge, UK: Cambridge University Press.

Rouget, Gilbert. 1985. *Music and Trance: A Theory of Relations Between Music and Possession*. Chicago: Chicago University Press.

Whinfield, E. H., ed. and trans. 1975. *Teachings of Rumi: The Masnavi*. New York: E.P. Dutton.

Yoruba Religious Arts, Secularization, and Modern Music Theater

AKIN EUBA

☞ AMONG THE YORUBA OF SOUTHWESTERN NIGERIA, RELIGION IS AN important aspect of traditional life and is also one of the principal contexts for the display of traditional arts. The status of a divinity as perceived by members of Yoruba society is directly related to the artistic quality of the rituals performed for that divinity by his or her devotees. In major celebrations for the divinities, several different arts are combined within the same context, including poetry, music, dance, mime, drama, together with the plastic arts. The effect of such a combination is akin to total theater, and Yoruba religious ceremonies are a prime example of theater as it existed in Africa before the coming of Europeans.

In modern Yorubaland, things are not what they used to be and, in the space of twenty years, between the early 1970s when I was doing doctoral research and 1991, when I again did some fieldwork, there was a sharp decline in the celebration of the divinities. My observation of a decline was confirmed by Chief Muraina Oyelami, Eesa of Iragbiji, some twenty kilometers from Osogbo, whom I interviewed during my 1991 visit to Yorubaland. One might ask: "Have the Yoruba become less religious, or have they transferred their allegiance to other religions?" The answer to that question is that most Yoruba are today fairly equally divided between Islam and Christianity and the devotees of traditional divinities are in the minority.

In the course of my doctoral research in Yorubaland between 1967 and

1974, I became fascinated by the traditional religious arts for their purely artistic value, and was, therefore, very much concerned later to discover that religious ceremonies were in decline. I wondered what would happen to the religious arts if the ceremonies that they embellish should die out. It was this concern that led me to a serious engagement with the concept of secularization of religious arts. It seems to me that one way of ensuring the survival of the arts is to secularize them. I was so excited about this concept that I briefly (around 1993) toyed with the idea of founding a new journal that would be devoted to discourse on secularization, not only in the music arts, but in African religious and ritual arts in general, because the secularization theory applies to all of them. In the course of my attempt to theorize the secularization of religious arts, it occurred to me that secularization is not a new phenomenon and had already existed in Yorubaland for at least three hundred years.

My purpose in this essay is to look at historical and modern processes in the secularization of the religious arts of the Yoruba and consider what implications such secularization has for modern music theater. I will also raise the issue of whether secularization can ever dissociate the arts from their original spirituality. In other words, is secularization a process of creating art for art's sake, or another way of celebrating the divinities?

I would first like to discuss the Yoruba masked theater (*egungun*) and show how a secularized form of the theater grew out of an old ritual form. Yoruba ritual masks celebrate the ancestors and have been in existence for many centuries. Whenever these masks appear in public, they are believed to be a reincarnation of dead ancestors, and they symbolize the idea that the dead continue to maintain contact with the living.

According to J. A. Adedeji (1981, 221–24), the secular form of egungun emerged at Oyo in central Yorubaland between 1610 and 1650 and was based on the dramatic roots of the old ancestral masked theater. The new type was nonritualistic and was designed for entertainment. It was at first restricted to the king's palace at Oyo but eventually moved out to become the *alarinjo* (traveling) theater.

The entertainment masquerade theater has survived until today and is variously referred to as *oje*, egungun *apidan*, *agbegijo*, or egungun *akewi*. The term apidan refers to specialization in magical displays while akewi refers to the performance of poetical chants. The performance of vocal music by entertainment masquerades distinguishes them from ritual masquerades, whose vocal music is performed by unmasked singers and not by the masks themselves.

The egungun apidan is, as far as I know, the first documented example of the secularization of ritual arts in Yorubaland, and it is noteworthy that this process was generated through internal forces of change and not by European intervention. Some three hundred years after the development of the traveling theater, another innovation in music theater began to emerge in Yorubaland, popularly known as the Yoruba folk opera. According to Biodun Jeyifo, the alarinjo masquerade theater "provided a structural and methodological paradigm for the Yoruba folk opera and other types of modern Yoruba popular traveling theater" (1984, 39). A play titled *King Elejigbo*, written by D. A. Oloyede in 1903 (Jeyifo 1984, 47), may have been the first example of the Yoruba folk opera, which culminated in the 1960s in Duro Ladipo's masterpiece, *Oba Koso*. This work is based on the traditions of Sango, a fifteenth-century king of Oyo, who later became the Yoruba god of thunder and lightning; *Oba Koso* is an important model for the secularization of Yoruba ritual arts. In composing the opera, Ladipo drew extensively from the artistic resources used by current devotees of Sango when performing ceremonies for him, including the music of bata drums (Sango's special instruments), praise poetry, and dance. Although featuring substantial material normally found in religious ceremonies for Sango, the objective of *Oba Koso* is not religious worship but theatrical entertainment.

The idea of extracting Yoruba performing arts from religious and secular ceremonies for presentation as entertainment is something that became increasingly common during the twentieth century and may have a lot to do with the reaction against Western-derived types of entertainment introduced to Yorubaland during the second half of the nineteenth century by returnees from Sierra Leone, Brazil, and Cuba; the returnees were former slaves and their descendants who settled mainly at Lagos and comprised the neo-African elite. The Western-derived types of entertainment they cultivated were not well received by everybody in Lagos and some members of the church, including African priests, advocated the indigenization of theatrical entertainment by drawing on local cultural and artistic resources, such as dance and drumming (Jeyifo 1984, 42–44).

In the course of the twentieth century, various opportunities existed for the transformation of religious and ritual arts (and other arts that normally accompanied social ceremonies) into media devoted solely to entertainment. There were, for example, periodic government-sponsored festivals of the arts that featured groups from various parts of Yorubaland who specialized in indigenous idioms. Moreover, Nigerian secondary schools often organized extracurricular activities in which students from various parts of the country were encouraged to learn one another's dances.

I would like to supplement the examples of secularization outlined above by discussing my own activities in this area. My first attempt at secularizing the religious arts goes back to 1972 when I composed *Dirges*, a piece of music theater that was performed by the University of Ife Theatre at the Cultural Olympics in Munich. The work is scored for three speakers, three singers (who also dance), four drummers, and two tape recorders. The text consists of twenty-four modern poems by African authors (spoken in English) and, in the finale, which is a setting of Birago Diop's *Viaticum*, the reading of the poem is accompanied by a chant (in Yoruba) from the Ifa literary corpus, traditionally performed by the priests of Orunmila. After the reading of Diop's poem, I conclude the finale by introducing traditions of Obatala, the Yoruba god of creation, including drumming, singing, dance, and a traditional reenactment ceremony portraying an incident from Obatala's life (when he lived on earth), which I observed in Ede.

I should point out that in my secularization of religious arts in *Viaticum*, I took a lot of artistic license, first by integrating the traditions of Orunmila and Obatala into one single continuum and, second, by using materials derived from different performance contexts and at different periods of time.

My most comprehensive effort in the secularization of Yoruba religious arts is in the composition of *Orunmila's Voices: Songs from the Beginning of Time* (2002). The work is a music and dance drama consisting of a fusion of Yoruba traditions with Western symphonic and performance idioms. In other words, secularization in this case involves the transformation of Yoruba religious arts into a performance medium that is accessible to performers and audiences on the international concert circuit. The performance resources are soprano, mezzo-soprano, and baritone, together with chorus, dancers, and symphony orchestra.

My original intention in writing the work was to base it exclusively on poems used by Ifa priests when performing divination and, in preparing for the composition, I studied the book of Ifa poems collected by Professor Wande Abimbola (1977), the leading scholar of Ifa. In the end, although there are six movements in *Orunmila's Voices*, I made use of poems selected from Abimbola's book in the last three movements only; I did other things in the first three movements, but all six movements are based on rituals and customs associated with Yoruba divinities.

In their traditional contexts, the Ifa poems used in *Orunmila's Voices* would normally be chanted in free rhythm by an unaccompanied solo voice. Furthermore, the poems are not customarily meant for public performance and are most often chanted by priests when holding private consultations with their clients. I should note, however, that these poems may also be heard during the annual festivals for Orunmila, which are public occasions. The main point is that in transforming the poems from ritual to secular contexts in my composition, I moved many degrees away from traditional practice.

The first three movements of *Orunmila's Voices*, though excluding Ifa poems, are nevertheless an important preparation for the last three movements in which the poems are actually used. For example, the second movement, titled "My Name is Orunmila" and scored for baritone solo, chorus, dancers, and orchestra, is especially designed to introduce persons unfamiliar with Yoruba culture to the traditions of the divinities. I should explain that Orunmila is the god of divination and keeper of the Ifa oracle; in fact, Ifa is often used synonymously with Orunmila. The baritone soloist sings the role of Orunmila and begins by introducing himself, after which he describes the principal divinities, namely Esu (the trickster, god of fate), Ogun (god of war and all things made of metal), Obatala (god of creation), Sango (god of thunder and lightning), and Osun (wife of Orunmila and goddess of the river that passes through the historically important town of Osogbo). In each case, Orunmila first sings in English about the divinity, followed by the chorus singing (in Yoruba) texts performed vocally or on the talking drum during actual ceremonies for the divinity.

Here are some samples of traditional religious texts that I used in the second movement of *Orunmila's Voices*. In each case, the title is the name of the divinity with whom the text is associated.

Orunmila

1. Eni ti n foju ekuro wo Orunmila / Those who perceive Orunmila as if he were no better than palmnuts (his favorite sacrificial offerings), Ifa o pa 'luwa re / Will be destroyed by Ifa.

2. Ifa temi ni o ba mi se / Ifa help me to promote my interests
Balabosi soro fun o lehin, ma ma gba / If my opponents say things
behind my back, do not listen to them
Temi ni o ba mi se / Help me to promote my interests.

Obatala

Obatala gbobi je / Obatala, accept our (sacrificial) offerings of cola nuts
Orisa gbo je / O divinity, accept our offerings of cola nuts.
Obatala omo n mo wa gba n o gba ke / Obatala, I have come to
receive a child from you, not a hump,
Omo n mo wa gba / I have come to receive a child.

Esu

Eni o m'Esu to pekee mi je / He who knows which Esu killed my
eke (Esu's dog)
Odara moo boluwee rele / May Odara (a praise name for Esu) go
home with that person
Bi n looko sa si moo tele / When that person goes to the farm may
Odara continue to abide by him or her
Bi n loodo sa si moo tele / When that person goes to the river,
Odara should continue to follow him or her
Baba Esu / Supreme Esu
Latopa Esu gongo / Esu, man of prestige who walks with a stick
and wears an elongated cap.

Sango

1. Afeniti kogila kolu / Only persons attacked by madness
Afeni Esu nse / Or persons afflicted by Esu
Lo le ko l'Esu / Would dare to provoke Esu
Lo le kolu Sango / Would dare to provoke Sango
Afeniti Sango o pa / Only persons that Sango would destroy.
2. Afi to ba ni ba / There must be a good reason
Sango o ni ponimogba / (Otherwise) Sango would not destroy an
offending priest
Ko tun ponibata o / And also destroy the priest's bata drummer
Afi to ba ni ba / There must be a good reason.

Ogun

Ogun se ree mi fun mi / Ogun, grant me the good fortune that is
due to me
Orisa seree mi fun mi / O divinity, grant me the good fortune that
is due to me.

I would now like to briefly describe the contents of the three Ifa poems
used in *Orunmila's Voices*, all of which have to do with Orunmila's suprem-
acy over Death (in its human personification). The first poem is about
Agbigboniwonran, the strong man who carves coffins and who may
be seen as an ally of Death. After making a coffin, it was his custom to
place it in front of a person's house, a sign that the person's death was
imminent. On this occasion, Orunmila was the intended victim. When
Agbigbo arrived at Orunmila's house carrying a coffin, he found Esu at
the entrance. Esu asked what Agbigbo intended to place in the coffin and
Agbigbo replied that it was Orunmila. Esu then asked what Agbigbo would
accept (as offering) in order to desist from causing Orunmila's death, and
Agbigbo replied that he would accept a rat, a bird, and an animal. Esu
replied that all had been provided and promptly brought them out for
Agbigbo, who grabbed them and immediately proceeded to deposit his
coffin elsewhere.

In the second poem, Orunmila sought to seduce Ojontarigi, the wife
of Death. The Ifa oracle advised Orunmila to perform a sacrifice and, after
doing so, he took Ojontarigi away from Death. Death, angered, picked
up his club and headed for Orunmila's house. When he arrived there, he
found Esu at the entrance and Esu asked where Death was going and why.
Death answered that Orunmila had taken his wife and that he intended
to kill him. Esu invited Death to sit down, after which he gave Death food
and drink. When he had had his fill, Death got up, picked up his club
and started to go. Esu again asked where he was going and Death replied
that he was going to Orunmila's house. Esu then asked, "How can you
eat a man's food and turn round to kill him? Don't you know that the
food you have just eaten belonged to Orunmila?" Baffled, Death said, "Tell
Orunmila that he can keep the woman" (The quoted statements are from
Abimbola 1977, 101.)

In the third poem, Orunmila was driven back home from his farm
because something at the farm had frightened him. He consulted Ifa and

was advised to perform a sacrifice. After doing so, he was given three arrows (by his Ifa priest, according to Abimbola 1977, 107) and told to shoot them around the farm. One of the arrows hit Death, who fell and promptly left the earth. Orunmila returned all the way home from the farm with music and dancing, saying that things happened precisely as the oracle had predicted.

In Yoruba traditional culture, the concepts of Orunmila and Esu are closely juxtaposed and Esu's symbol always appears next to Orunmila's. Esu's role in the first and second poems manifests this idea. Furthermore, Orunmila is the knower of destiny while Esu controls destiny.

A clear message from the three Ifa poems is that Orunmila and Esu are highly intelligent divinities while Death (personified in Yoruba mythology as a wielder of clubs) relies mainly on physical strength and is otherwise dense. I tried to portray this dichotomy in my settings of the Ifa poems.

The idea of secularizing the Yoruba religious arts poses some interesting questions. What I describe as secularization may also be described as recontextualization and the question arises: Can religious arts be disconnected from their spirituality simply because they are presented in nonreligious contexts? This question is pertinent because in African traditional culture there are strict restrictions on the presentation of ritual and religious arts out of context. For example, among the Tutsi of Rwanda, the drums of the king (which are ritually dedicated to him) are only sounded at his coronation; thereafter they are kept in a special enclosure and a replica of the ritual drums are used on occasions when drums have to be sounded for the king. Among the Akan of Ghana, all talking drums belong to the king and whenever these drums are used in contexts outside of kingship, they are not allowed to talk (Nketia 1963, 119, n. 3). Moreover, it is well known that research scholars working in African studies are denied access to certain rituals, in or out of context. On those occasions when permission is given for ritual and religious arts to be performed or presented out of context, it is often necessary to make special sacrifices in order to avoid offending the divinities. This suggests that religious arts are perceived to retain their spirituality even when presented out of context.

I would like to cite examples of the reactions of people to some events in which I was personally involved. In February 2002 when we were rehearsing for the premiere of *Orunmila's Voices* in New Orleans, one knowledgeable Yoruba woman, a senior citizen, watched the rehearsals and said to me: "If I had known what your performance was about, I would have brought some kola nuts in order to say prayers for the appeasement of the divinities." Another incident occurred at Ile-Ife, one of the main centers of Yoruba culture. Following a highly successful production of Wale Ogunyemi's folk opera, *Obaluaye*, which I directed, I was convinced that a recording of the opera would be equally successful. We therefore produced one featuring the University of Ife Theatre, the same group that gave the earlier performance. We were surprised to find that it was poorly received and reports came back to me from Ile-Ife town that people were afraid to buy it because of the powerful maledictions pronounced by Obaluaye, also known as Sonponna, the dreaded god of smallpox, in the opening scene of the opera. People's perception was that these maledictions carried force even in the context of a recording that was produced on the basis of art for art's sake.

This same opera, *Obaluaye*, elicited another type of reaction when we staged an excerpt from it at the National Theatre in Lagos. I invited a friend who was a born-again Christian to the event and afterwards she said to me: "I enjoyed your performance, but why did you have to keep calling the divinities? Don't you know that they were listening and would be happy to hear you calling them?" I was baffled by this remark and thought to myself: "If I am happy, why should they not be happy?" Nevertheless, her comment struck a chord. Hitherto, I had freely used resources derived from traditional religious arts in my creative work without engaging any thought about the consequences. Now I began to wonder whether such usage might be a compromise of my Christian faith. For example, between 1986 and 1991 when I lived in Germany, I contemplated writing a set of pieces for the piano under the general title *Duru Orisa: Keyboard Music of Yoruba Divinities*, based on resources derived from religious arts. For the first time, it crossed my mind that such a composition could amount to a celebration of the divinities, which, in view of my Christian faith, is unacceptable. I agonized over the matter for some time but finally resolved it; although I have not yet written the piano pieces, I am ready to do so whenever time permits. In any case, I have in the meantime composed *Orunmila's Voices* without having any qualms!

Incidentally, comments made by another born-again Christian friend of mine about *Orunmila's Voices* are revealing. When I first told her about the composition, she was disturbed and, in the ensuing discussion, I pointed out that, since I believe in God (from a Christian's perspective), everything that I do is done in praise of God. Later, I was surprised when she announced to me that she perfectly agreed with me—in other words, she fully approved of *Orunmila's Voices* in the belief that the work celebrates God rather than Yoruba divinities. Her statement goes a long way to assure me that it is all right to compose the piano pieces, *Duru Orisa*.

In conclusion, it is arguable that the most important artistic forms in Yoruba culture are those pertaining to religious ceremonies. There is reason to believe that these ceremonies are declining and it is a matter for concern that, if the ceremonies die out, the arts that embellish them may not survive. One way of ensuring the survival of the arts is to give them a new context by secularizing them. Such a process has been in existence in Yorubaland since at least the seventeenth century and may well be typical of Yoruba culture. The question remains, however, whether it is possible to disconnect religious arts from their inherent spirituality simply by recontextualizing them.

References

Abimbola, Wande. 1977. *Ifa Divination Poetry*. New York: Nok Publishers.

Adedeji, J. A. 1981. "Alarinjo: The Traditional Yoruba Travelling Theatre." In *Drama and Theatre in Nigeria: A Critical Source Book*, ed. Yemi Ogunbiyi, 221–47. Lagos: *Nigeria* magazine.

Euba, Akin. 2000. *Orunmila's Voices: Songs from the Beginning of Time*. Unpublished orchestral score.

Jeyifo, Biodun. 1984. *The Yoruba Popular Travelling Theatre of Nigeria*. Lagos: *Nigeria* magazine.

Nketia, J. H. 1963. *Drumming in Akan Communities of Ghana*. Edinburgh: Thomas Nelson.

PART VI

The Spirit of Guadalupe

Immigration, Human Rights,
and Spiritual Conflict

Tlecuauhtlazupeuth

Belief and Resonance: El contradecir
de Guadalupe-Tonantzin

JUAN GÓMEZ-QUIÑONES

Introduction

☞ CONTENT, PERCEPTIONS, AND USES OF THE MEXICAN GUADALUPE-
Tonantzin have evolved for nearly five hundred years. In this essay, I comment on some quite recent occurrences and some of a hundred years
ago. As a participant in the early Chicano movement, I witnessed the
political deployment of Guadalupe from the sixties to the present. For
Mexican believers, the power of the historical Guadalupe-Tonantzin myth
is revealed as recently as the 1966 march on Sacramento, exemplified in
the 1966 Plan de Delano as well as in the sharp debate centered on a contemporary artist's rendition of her lover as Guadalupe in Sante Fe, New
Mexico, in 2001. To capture Guadalupe's power in the first example, the
march, a quote from the plan could minimally suffice: "At the head of the
Pilgrimage we carry La Virgen de Guadalupe because she is ours, all ours,
Patroness of the Mexican People."[1] The plan consists of organized farmworkers' voices, the words of Luis Valdez and probably one of the Chávez
brothers directed to a base constituency and opponents of workers. In the
New Mexico incident of 2001, you have the artist's words as well as the
later remarks of one of her academic interlocutors, Margaret Montoya
in May 2004 at the Albuquerque conference.[2] The debate over the work
of art centered on its intended representations of sexuality rather than
being a challenge to a singular iconic voice. In this controversy there were
numerous voices and odd alliances; for instance, Catholic Guadalupe

devotees and Mexicans on one side and, on the other, the artist and various academic feminist allies and cultural institutional representatives. When I was growing up in East Los Angeles, I do not recall such allies for the *pintos* (felons), who wore Guadalupe designs on their backs for protection or for those who built Guadalupe shrines in their barrio yards, shrines intended to safeguard the family.[3] Preceded by several earlier phases, the current postmodern phase of Guadalupanismo ironically represents a convergence of the institutional Guadalupe and the ultra-secular Guadalupe: Guadalupe means anything or nothing.

Always the Story

But first let us return to the basic story and its consequences. Let us examine the historical context underscoring certain aspects often overlooked, just a few among many. The story is there; in its invocation the myth contains powerful ethics and aesthetics, in a word, spirituality. Here the artful story is real, regardless of what else may be questioned. The central figure, the woman, is the actor, the Indian is the narrator. There is nothing passive. Guadalupe names herself in Nahua: Tlecuauhtlazupeuth (she who soars among the highest peaks). She uses languages, celestial and earthly, with elaborate communicative ceremonies. She is a pregnant active young woman who speaks and commands. She offers protection because she has the power; the Indians understood who they needed protection from. Her audience is Indians who also speak and show their amazement and their will. There is trust, quite obviously, and interactive concern. The story is family and group centered and locality grounded, but there is no father, visible or audible. Seemingly the story is for Indians, maybe from Indians.

An enduring artwork of remarkable attractions, the full portrait of Guadalupe in textile or fiber weave, which itself is as contested as it is palpable, is central. This art is also a cosmological, epistemological representation, a science. Tlecuauhtlazupeuth, like an immigrant child, goes through a name change in her first encounter with authorities, but more telling is that from the first she is associated with Tonantzin, a very specific association. There are two consequential aspects, preceding and following the story. The first is the pre-Christian Indian spiritual and cosmological aspect, which shades and shapes the story. Clearly the story is not accidental or happenstance; it is contingent; it is an expression of specific historicity. It is arguable that an original story may have preceded the written versions, one in Castilian, the other in Nahua. Some reputable scholars reject this possibility. Even so the question remains: did the story circulate originally in Nahua or in Castilian? Is the story an Indian assertion or a European appropriation continually contested? Is it both?

In the European and Church's telling of the story, the initial narrator and his behind-the-scenes uncle are stereotypically portrayed as *indios humildes* (humble Indians). One Indian version or tradition depicts them and identifies them differently—the uncle is a knowledgeable elder, Juan Diego an adult. They, too, are representations. Guadalupe, both as story and in its aesthetic representation, is the first hymn post-1521 that is not a poem of loss. Guadalupe's portrait is basic art and consequently all the arts are impacted thereafter. The homage offered by Indians, as indicated by all reports, consisted of art, expressions, paintings, effigies, dance, music, poetry, narrative, and so forth. Today the fact that some scholars doubt the widespread and enthusiastic acceptance of Christianity by native peoples opens doors for a modern critique of the historical evolution of Guadalupe and critical historiography underscores its phases and multiple residences.

Content

The Guadalupe story and its uses unfolded in the social aftermath of 1521 during an initial phase of the European occupation of Mesoamerica whose main characteristics were violence and exploitation.[4] This colonialism desperately depended on religion, ideologically, socially, and politically. An economist might consider that the construction of the European colonial economy—its plantations, mines, factories, roads, aqueducts, and cities—represented development, but, actually, poverty increased. As the Hapsburg colonial regime evolved, social differentiation separated the indigenous from the European *peninsular*, and the criollo, American-born Spaniards from the mestizo-mulatto majority, and the Africans are separated from all other groups. In the story of Guadalupe, however, there are only Indians and Europeans. Quite soon there would be other sectors involved, and one that sought leadership.

Quickly certain criollos sought to appropriate Guadalupe's story and, up to a point, succeeded, in that the Indian component is glossed over. Rather than the peninsulares, the criollos appropriated Guadalupe on their way to appropriating the country, as a part of their European and American heritage. The colonial process patently, religiously, involved a manifest pride on the part of the criollo in criollo character, with some attention to indigenous heritage, but more attention to the manners, customs, and styles of the Mexican-born Europeans. A major source of appropriative exultation was the environment and its wealth—Mexico was on the verge of a great future. Criollos took pride in their creative achievements—in the cities, the education, and in the literature to be found in New Spain. There was a tenuous sense of confidence about the New World versus the Old World. Between the 1500s and the 1700s, gradual changes occurred among some residing in colonial Mexico; they lost the use of their indigenous group names. In self-denotation they progressed from indio, español, criollo, americano to, finally, mexicano. Religiosity stamped criollo and ultimately mestizo pride.

All Christian sites in the world had their venerations, and Mexico surely had many also, including one in particular, Guadalupe Tonantzin at Tepeyac. The first church notice dates from 1556 where it is described as a cult among Indians and the redoubtable Bernardino de Sahagún, the European priest most informed about the Nahuas, asserted the cult was Indian derived, as would the studious Lorenzo Botturini Benaduci. But, in fact, not all Indians accepted Guadalupe, either then or for that matter today.

Among the civically conscious, after the decades of initial occupation and perhaps because the indio-criollo-mestizo-mulatto world was so permeated with religion, or perhaps because of rationalization and a growing sense of identity and group pride, from early on people focused on a powerful religious symbol, La Virgen de Guadalupe.[5] At this time the most compelling question about the phenomenon of guadalupanismo was what motivating factors explained its incremental acceptance by so many diverse peoples of New Spain? Graphic representations and medals of her likeness spread, indeed the wearing of Guadalupe medals today continues a four-hundred-year-old tradition. Guadalupe devotions and shrines appeared from northernmost New Mexico to southernmost Chiapas, including a noteworthy one at San Antonio, Texas. As a local defining devotion, Guadalupe quickly became an indigenous Mexican symbol of the native-born Indians, mestizos, criollos, and mulattos. Though the apparitions reportedly date from the sixteenth century, Guadalupe's popular magnetism began to flourish in the mid-seventeenth century, precisely when New Spain was crystallizing into something neither European-Spanish nor Indian-American, but a unique combination of both. The church hierarchy, always leery of nationalist sentiments attached to religious symbols among colonials, saw these identifications as problematic. Of course, the church sees no equivalent problems among Europeans. Moreover, devotees did not need a priest to pay homage to Guadalupe Tonantzin. The church has never accepted a radical, populist, ethnicist Guadalupe.

Perhaps concurrently with oral transmissions, in the seventeenth century, after more than a hundred years, literature on Guadalupe, written by creole clerical and mestizo nativist intellectuals, appeared in Spanish (1648) and Nahua (1649).[6] In these writings there was more or at least as much nativist self-assertion and pride as Christian advocation. Eventually by the late eighteenth century, as today, guadalupanismo was a conglomeration of values and sentiments and even ideas that intertwined the secular with the theological, as even the most cursory knowledge of modern Mexicans would attest. Clearly the populist cult of Guadalupe was a notable contributor to the forging of a sense of community among many in diverse classes during the colonial period and, maintaining its overwhelming populist weight, the devotion spread. The prominence of intellectuals in giving narrative meaning and conceptual substance to Guadalupe presaged their contributions to a sense of community in other areas and times. Their participation was a seminal adjunct to the specific populist dynamism that occurred.

Among the savants of the colonial period in the seventeenth century were several who are noticeable for their sense of regional pride and attention to Guadalupe. Three are of particular note—one a native, one a creole, and the third a woman.[7] The writings of Fernando de Alba Ixtlilxochitl (1580–1648) represent the work of the indio-mestizo, driven by the urge to let the world know of ancient Mexico's legacies, with which he identifies. Yet in these writings there is an apologetic tone as well as a schizophrenic perspective: he is a militant "new" Catholic describing a richly religious world that, though he criticizes it as pagan, he also admires. But he was further at war with himself, for as he empathizes with the Indian past, he associates with the conquest by highlighting Indian contributions to it. If he could have, he would have overlooked that the conquest felled the Indian sovereignty. Another writer of transition was the criollo-mestizo Carlos de Sigüenza y Góngora (1645–1700). In his work the concern for things Mexican does not have the driving anxiety of Ixtlilxochitl. He does not have to prove the worth of his heritage, he is extending his heritage.

Thus, Sigüenza's writings heralded what was American and defended the Indian past by extolling the political values he identified in his supposed Aztec past. Sor Juana Inés de la Cruz (1648–90) actually probed and extolled Guadalupe more subversively in poetry and plays: "Protectora Americana/que a ser se pasa Rosa Mexicana/apareciendo Rosa de Castilla" (Protectress of the Americas/Who makes herself a Mexican Rose/while appearing to be a Castilian Rose). She did not write civic advocations, but she affirmed: "el águila Mexicana el imperial vuelo tienda" (the Mexican eagle soars in imperial flight).[8]

Sigüenza and Ixtlilxochitl are followed by more national-minded writers, the so-called Mexican Jesuits. In 1754 Guadalupe is declared, somewhat redundantly, the patroness of Mexico by an office of the Vatican. One can also point out the continuing flare-ups of discontent, riots, and rebellions in the late eighteenth century, including the conspiracy of the "Gualupanos" in the 1790s.

Midhistory

A hundred years after Carlos de Sigüenza's death, the crisis of independence unfolded, representing yet another Guadalupe phase.[9] Guadalupe nevertheless figured in many ways among the insurgents on both sides, including the Guadalupanos' conspiracies (1810–16), the Miguel Hidalgo y Costilla campaigns (1810–12), and the José Morelos Pavón stratagems of 1813–14. Hidalgo and Morelos insistently underscored Guadalupe. Two consequences unfolded for the next hundred years. During the ten-year-long pro-independence struggle, many of the liberal clerics who endorsed populism suffered casualties and the loss of parishes. The church hierarchy weakened despite the mischief its hierarchical monarchist members caused. In contrast, for once there was space for the repudiation of antipatriotic clerics and even anticlerical actions and, for over a decade between the 1850s and 1870s, the state could do without religion. These are the precedents for more modern developments of the late-nineteenth and early-twentieth centuries, during which Guadalupe fervor rose but anticlericalism did also. In an uncertain world, the people sought strength in Guadalupe, and the church and the elite needed Guadalupe.

To exemplify my observations about modern circumstances, I recall a polemical partisan debate one hundred years ago. Catholic conservatives of the times spoke in terms that resonated with ideas of the independence era, but that also represented a new phase that preceded the ten years of violence between 1911 and 1921.[10] For many devout rural and working-class Mexicans, Guadalupe inspired the arts festival of the people, their moments of contemplation, their inspiration to speculate on a world without degradation, brutality, and exploitations. In contrast, Guadalupe also could be a mirror for a privileged few of their parasitism, how they lived well at the expense of others. These elite were strong on traditional "morality." Many upper class persons were absolute parasites. They were quite religious. For some, religion rationalized their privilege; for some, Guadalupe sanctioned dissent. Given the times and the scienticism current in educated circles, Guadalupe's stature drew the attention of some pseudo-scientists who sought to materially explain the portrait provided by Juan Diego. There is science here, but the pseudo-scientists could not explain it as they could not understand the epistemology of the portrait, that is, representations made on cloth, paper or wood.

In the years preceding the Mexican revolution (between 1890 and 1910) Guadalupanismo, the devotion to Guadalupe, co-existed with *patriotismo*, that is, loyalty to the nation, among most Mexicans. The availability of more effective communications contrasted with earlier times. Both Guadalupanismo and patriotismo were frequent and explicit topics in the Mexico City newspapers from 1890 to 1911. Speakers are editorial writers, who invoked devotion to both concepts on the occasion of major national events, especially on national holidays. The extant printed verbiage was voluminous, the ephemeral material may have been equally large, and oral testimony and music presentations were surely common. On patriotism and also on devotion to Guadalupe, there were several disputing parties—liberals and conservatives foremost, the then-reigning Porfirio Díaz administration (1884–1911), and some dissidents. Two major political partisan facts undergirded the discourse. The first was that much of the nineteenth-century political struggle represented contentions between two loosely identified poles—liberals and conservatives. These elements were affinities rather than cohesive parties—one seen as more democratically inclined, the other as more authoritarian; one as insisting on secularism, the other on church recognition. The second major characteristic of the alliances was the role played by the Porfirio Díaz administration, identified as pro–foreign capital, pro–exploitive elite, and pro–authoritarian government. The church hierarchy should have been explicitly part of this scenario, but it was not. Due to political turpitude, some of the leaders were too far to the right, having been associated with the wealthy and foreign interests; to be sure, there were important Catholic Church representatives among the elite. Nevertheless, neat bipolarities do not hold in these times. Díaz claimed liberal antecedents, but some liberals were his strongest critics. Rising in his youth as a liberal, Díaz was in practice a conservative, though some conservatives saw his administration as too liberal. In this political arena, Guadalupe became contested: Is Guadalupe with the people or with state and clerical institutions? This era's capitalism needed religion just as desperately as colonialism had and, as in the colonial era, signs flourished of economic changes and crass profiteering. The statistical signs of economic growth underscored the poverty of the people. But this regime held religion at bay while an undertow of turbulence pulled it down.

Discoursing

Certainly patriotism was a premise and a rationale for interested parties to advance views on issues. In debate, allied concepts such as nation, nationality, and national dignity were interspersed and, toward the first decade of the twentieth century, concern for self-determination became more evident and insistent. References to Guadalupe often bracketed these allusions, which shifted from left to right. Around these subjects, explicitly less often than implicitly, the attributes and functions of the state drew comment from the left and the right. Although the evolution of this supposed pairing is uneven, it is certainly evident over the years. Patriotism became something more than love of country and its symbols; consequently, what writers meant had become more complex by 1911 than in 1890.

Religious convictions hovered over ideological differences, and both religion and partisanship exerted strong influence on views concerning patriotism. Keeping in mind the heterogeneity of peoples across the Mexican republic and also those north of the recently established border, militant Catholics believed "el primer elemento de nuestra unidad nacional es el elemento religioso" (the first element of our national unity is the religious element).[11] For them, religious loyalty coincided with loyalty to the nation. This attachment reactivated conservative Catholic opposition to Protestant activity. To be sure, even some who were critics of the church would not tolerate Protestant propagandizing or foreign immigrants because they felt that this would undermine "nacionalidad," or be a source of disrespect for popular beliefs such as Guadalupe. Even among liberals, there was identification of religion with nationality and respect for the people's devotions.

The Virgen de Guadalupe was a major symbol advanced by active Catholics to associate and stress nationality and religion. This icon was identified as a uniquely Mexican Catholic veneration up to a point and, to some, of course, a manifestation of the cosmopolitan Mary. To the Catholic press, religion, fatherland, and nationality were inseparable. Church spokespersons argued that to advance the interests of the church was to advance those of the nation, as was expressed in the saying: "En religión Católico, en política Mexicano" (In religion Catholic, in politics Mexican).[12] Guadalupe co-joined these in an ideological climate of differentiation between conservatives and Catholics. In the early 1890s, notions on political affiliation distinguishing between liberals and conservatives influenced the idea of what was patriotic in history.

The liberals stressed the heroism of Miguel Hidalgo, José Morelos, Vicente Guerrero, and Guadalupe Victoria (Manuel Féliz Fernández), viewing them as the initiators of the independence movement and as co-founders of liberalism among Mexicans.[13] Though often insistently secular, stressing not only a separation but a divide between themselves and the clericals, liberals embraced the populist content and symbology of Guadalupe. They also made some references to particular outstanding women figures, such as those who had been prominent in the movement for independence and resistance to the French (1862–67). The promotion of the reform, the struggle against the oppressive military, elite, and church, as a heroic movement widely perceived as anticlerical, underscored favorably the measures and styles of the Benito Juárez and Lerdo de Tejada liberal administrations. Liberals particularly claimed resistance to French intervention and support for Benito Juárez, who liberals claimed as particularly their own. Liberals saw the period of 1857–72 as years of strongly expressed patriotism in which they alone kept alive the glow of national democracy. Gradually among a few liberals, the Native American heritage was underscored, as parallel to that of "Spanish" culture. The Aztecs and Cuauhtémoc were seen positively in the liberals' view, while the social and economic imports of the Spanish occupation and colonial period were increasingly questioned. Liberals considered their party to be the truly patriotic one; they defended the nation and promoted public welfare. The liberal view at this time came to be the one generally espoused by most of the press in the nationalism project.

An almost opposite notion of national history was held by the clerical-conservative element.[14] Conservatives highlighted Catholic faith, Spanish language, and European culture. Though endorsing independence, the contribution of Spain and the colonial experience as a whole were seen as valuable and fundamental to Mexico's modern development. To the conservatives, Hernán Cortés was the father of Mexican nationality, Malinche was symbolic of Indian predisposition to European culture, and Augustín Iturbide (1783–1824), the conservative militarist, was the true harbinger of independence. A mythified Malinche counterpointed the real liberal heroines. To the conservatives, *La Reforma* (1855–67?) was a dark hour, a step back, a crisis perpetrated upon the Mexican people presumably because of its anticlerical, pro-republic stances. Conservatives were most sensitive about being associated with the regime of Antonio López de Santa Ana (1833–55), held responsible for the loss of Texas and who had been accused of providing support for the French intervention. The conservative-clerical coalition stigmatized liberals as possibly traitors and held them responsible for the worst modern historical mishaps—the U.S. war and the defeat of 1848 and the French-led invasion of 1862.

Liberals and conservatives had some things in common; for one, they both suffered the past in the sense that it was to be argued about. They shared a romantic view of the heroic Indian past, though stress on contemporary continuity with it varied. Both agreed on the subject of the Mexican-American War, regarding it with bitterness and resentment, and both were proud of the resistance of the Mexicans. On holidays, especially, all newspapers devoted much space to historical accounts. Events related to Guadalupe received notable coverage. As a preeminently populist icon, Guadalupe could not remain centered in the colonial. This myth is what many liberals and conservatives had in common most overtly, though interpreted with somewhat different emphases.

National holidays, commentators noted, were enthusiastically celebrated, and yearly more people participated.[15] Full front-page spreads appeared in the newspapers with detailed accounts of the festivities in Mexico City and, in some cases, the provinces. The favorite secular days were clearly established as September 16, Independence Day, and May 5. The latter, honoring the repulsion of the French forces at Puebla in 1863, was very popular, as was at this time September 8, commemorating the battle of Chapultepec during the Mexican-American War in 1847. More disputed, the anniversary of the Iturbide independence, September 27, 1822, was celebrated by the conservatives. They argued that this date was the authentic holiday, because on this date independence was secured. With time the insistence on this particular holiday lessened. These celebrations particularly stressed patriotism, and this increased as the period progressed. In the foreground of these secular holidays, December 12, the feast of the Virgen de Guadalupe, the Guadalupe commemoration, ostensibly wholly religious, survived, spread, and strengthened by sheer popular participation.

Guadalupe's feast day, December 12, was more than a religious celebration; it was a national commemoration, in practice *the* national holiday. This day commemorated the coming into being of Mexicanos, recognized through Guadalupe as a nation in the modern era.

Particular liberal anniversaries, especially for the public that differed with the regime, were February 5, Constitution Day; March 21, the birthday of Benito Juárez, a preeminent liberal hero; and January 20, the birthday of Miguel Lerdo de Tejada, also a liberal hero. Each provided occasion for heralding the accomplishments of the reform and for oblique criticism of conservatism or conservative policies. As an individual hero, Juárez acquired the greatest popularity, noticeably during those years after the mid-1890s. Importantly, Morelos and Cuauhtémoc, as militant resistance figures, received increasing attention. One newspaper, on the occasion of a national holiday, stated: "Consideramos que las fiestas de hoy tienen una alta significación, ellas arraigan el ánimo del pueblo, la vida de lo grande, de lo inestimable, de lo augusto que es la autonomía de una nación" (We believe that the fiestas of today have a great significance; they nurture the soul of the people, the life of grandeur, of the invaluable, of the majestic that is the autonomy of a nation).[16] As mentioned, December 12 remained the major commemoration and, tellingly, liberal intentions of eliminating state-church commingling stopped short of prohibiting public celebrations on this date.

Whose People

In popular caricatures, liberal figures and symbols were nearly always depicted heroically and at the side of the people. The poor, the worker, and the Indian were depicted in the caricatures as heroic, wise, and beautiful. They were associated with the symbolic figure of the nation and, of course, seen positively in caricature art, especially after 1900. Guadalupe was preeminently associated with the poor.

Guadalupe, a populist referent, was also antistatist, if you will, from the first, given her arguable identification with the poor, but the elite controlled the government and the church and thus, from the first, could manipulate the image. Editorially, one newspaper identified two types of patriotism, that espoused by the government spokesmen, the other espoused by the opposition.[17] These two kinds of patriotism were placed in juxtaposition—one critical, the other benign. The newspaper agreed with the former. The editorial granted that both exalted the nation, but one did not give cause for censure to the government. Even at the risk of understating national welfare, the rhetoric of adherents was placid and voiced no major grievance, and its audience was a tranquil, prosperous, unreal citizenry.

The voices of the other patriotism were critical of any action or event that might be negative to the nation, regardless of who was annoyed. They were vehement and supposedly addressed to the "real" nation, the middle and working classes. This point of view rejected explicitly the notion that the government should be above the nation or that it was truly identifiable with the nation, and argued that criticism of current ills, rather than the hiding of the existing malaise, was the true expression of patriotism.

As can be seen, the matter of who was or was not patriotic, who was or was not correct, was often polemical. Guadalupe became part of this debate, given her popularity and significance. One prime accusation used for discrediting conservative confessional spokesmen was that they had, as their first allegiance, religion and its institutions. In fact, they were charged with greater loyalty to the papacy than to the nation. Turning the argument, conservatives charged that liberals and Masons, seen as one and the same, were antipatriotic, since by definition espousing republicanism, they were pro-United States civically and antitraditional culturally. Significantly, both the opposition liberals and independent conservatives questioned the regime's loyalty to the nation by implication when dwelling upon the blatant pro-foreignism within Mexico and the regime's catering to the United States. Guadalupe straddled this divide in a sense as a pan-nationalist referent.

Everyone's Guadalupe

Major Guadalupe events took place during these years; for example, these were times that were to see some significant clerical or religiously premised questioning of Guadalupe.[18] For example, in 1888 Joaquín García Icazbalceta, a respected scholar of colonial history, and, during the following years, a popular liberal cleric, Eduardo Sánchez Camacho, the bishop of Tamaulipas, raised well-reasoned, research-grounded questions pertinent to the myth. If you add the respected missionary ethnographer Bernardino de Sahagún's questioning, you have a compelling trilogy of respected Catholic doubters concerning Guadalupe as the Virgin Mary. Actually, several church scholars over the centuries since 1556 had raised critical questions. The church authorities were not about to engage in public debate on Guadalupe or to lose her.[19] On October 12, 1895, a "coronation" of Guadalupe took place underscoring her importance, perhaps more to the worldwide Catholic Church than to the people who saw her as Indian and Mexican. Moreover, she was institutionally recognized as important to all the Americas by Pope Pius X, one among several popes to appeal to her charisma, declaring her patroness of the Americas. As "Reina de México-Emperatriz de las Américas," her mythic powers were invoked for the church.

The pope now came into the picture. The conservatives, never keen on the interpretation of Guadalupe as Indian, would have their royalty in two senses—Mary and the papacy. The church hierarchy was consolidating its position around Guadalupe through especially designated rituals and ceremonies, by important churches dedicated to her, through the establishment of a teaching order under her rubric, and publicly by religious music and poetry, which were quite popular. A historical relic of immense public interest, the standard of Guadalupe invoked by Hidalgo headed the festive monumental parade commemorating independence in 1910. This was the major civic commemorative event and one, of course, sponsored by the government, though ostensibly by nonpartisan commissions. The major feature of the event, as visual imagery communicates, was Guadalupe. For her the crowds cheered.

After 1900, and certainly after 1906, the liberal/conservative diatribe over who was indeed more patriotic lessened somewhat, as speakers for both groups focused their attention on the reigning regime and on social issues rather than on each other. Defenders of the regime were quick to indict critics as unpatriotic, whether they were liberals or conservatives. They maintained that criticism encouraged disharmony, which made difficult the patriotic work of the government geared toward national development. As can be shown, the opposition to the government replied that the Díaz regime through its repressiveness, coupled with largess to the foreigner, was endangering national unity and development. References to Guadalupe undergirded public commentary. Descriptions of ideal patriotism were common throughout the period 1890–1911. It was seen to have various heroic qualities: enthusiasm, sacrifice, courage, consciousness, abnegation, responsibility, idealism, and faith.

Nationalist Synthesis

After 1900, definitions of patriotism became more militant. Now patriotism was defined as the struggle for the national future. The phrase "Mexico para los Mexicanos" was used. Nationalist tempo quickened visibly after the incidents at Cananea in 1906, involving conflict between Mexican workers and foreign-company others. Dismissing the upper classes and, perhaps by implication, the government as irrelevant, the call was made for a popular crusade:

> la lucha por la reconquista de la soberanía nacional no perdida aún pero humillada. Mexicanizemos al pueblo, allí está la base del edificio social . . . Pero al pueblo . . . ése es el que soporta el edificio social, a ese hay que enseñar a ser Mexicano! (the struggle for the reconquest of national sovereignty not lost as yet but humiliated. We will Mexicanize the people, that is the base of the social edifice . . . But for the people . . . that is what supports the social structure, that is, what must be taught to be Mexican!)[20]

In this discourse the ideal civic good represented national greatness by Mexicans striving for improvement. In the journal *Revista Positiva*, and in the anticlerical *Diario del Hogar*, an article appeared calling love of country the noblest sentiment of man, and exhorting further progress to obtain national greatness. Patriotism came to be associated with plural participation for populist goals: "La consolidación de la nacionalidad Mexicana sólo podrá conseguirse por medio de la participación del pueblo." (The consolidation of the Mexican Nationality can only be achieved through the participation of the people).[21] Though this thought may be voiced by a liberal anticlericalist or a pro-church conservative, "participation" would entail spiritual and religious sentiments and referents.

Among Mexicans in their civic discourses, patria is arguably masculine;

its feminine pairing is Guadalupe. The fatherland was defined to include the territory, past generations, religion, culture, language, customs, civilization, and spirit. The consolidation of the patria was the ideal of the past, is that of the present, and shall be that of the future, for this means an independent Mexican state, prosperous Mexicans, and a culturally united citizenry. From proud romantic reminiscences, often nostalgic, patriotism was becoming an exhortation to action and the postulation of a goal. To increase the moral and material greatness of the fatherland was the just duty of the patriot. After 1911 it was admitted that there had come into existence a sizable *movimiento nacionalista,* justified or not, sincere or superficial, and the government had best take the fact into account. The point was, however, that though certain agreements were defined as to major national symbols, goals, problems, and duties, there were divergent views on how national greatness was to be attained. Political statements and actions delineated how particular groups identified goals and means for national greatness, not simply as points of discussions but as inducements for the politically conscious to mobilize. The Zapatistas wore imprints of Guadalupe on their hats in 1910, as Independistas or Guadalupanos had worn her image on their lapels in 1810. However, unlike during the movement for independence, when religious devotees participated on both sides, major figures such as Ricardo Flores Magón, Francisco Villa, and Emiliano Zapata criticized the church and the clergy, and Francisco Madero, though not radically anticlerical, practiced "spiritualism," heavily censured by the church. Even as popular expression of Guadalupe devotion flared, many civic activists insisted that devotion to the nation must be secular and the church must be further curtailed even beyond the Juárez-Lerdo measures.

Prior to 1910, Latin American as well as Hispanic cooperation was advocated on pragmatic and idealistic grounds; that is, mutual protection and cultural affinity.[22] The general consensus in the press was for strong political and economic ties among Latin American nations. As public literate consciousness of foreign relations and foreign dependency sharpened, and the need for social reform percolated, consciousness of the devotion owed the nation broadened. At its most sharply critical, say in the speech of Jose Martí, what was being grasped went beyond the statism of Simón Bolivar as a response to influence. There was realization that a new colonialism, born of social and economic influence, had to be repudiated throughout the Americas. Conservatives and church leaders had a rejoinder to this seemingly liberal-inspired pan–Latin Americanism.

Specific Speech

In Mexico references to Guadalupe increased as crisis intensified. Rather than liberal articulators, conservative ones struck notes. In the midst of this "national" debate, a particular forging took place. One particular articulator of the above advocations and fervent Guadalupano was the writer and activist Trinidad Sánchez Santos. Icons only metaphorically speak; persons do the talking for them. Sánchez Santos was almost too representative to be representative. He was a particularly strong articulator and an exceptionally respected conservative. "Por la religión y por la Patria" (For Religion and for Country) was his chosen motto, and it synthesized his guiding ethos as the foremost Catholic publicist during the years 1890–1911.[23] Though not often remembered today, in his day he was a man of wide public influence because of his well-received writings, his gifts as an orator, his newspaper, and the respect his reputed integrity and well-known independence commanded, both from sympathizers and antagonists. Sánchez Santos saw himself as a lay apostle, a crusader dedicated to the greatness of Mexico achieved through the country's re-Catholization. In effect, Sánchez Santos represented Catholic social and political criticism of the society and the regime. He apparently did not see these as contradictory, even though supposedly religion and the nation both claim complete loyalty. Actually he was a fervent Catholic *and* an adamant patriot. For him, the well-being and greatness of the nation and the cause of religion were intertwined. This was how he avoided the contradiction of two ostensibly supreme loyalties. Luís Islas García wrote:

> Sánchez Santos representa la parte de los católicos en la revolución, en la oposición a los errores del régimen liberal de don Porfirio; representa la lucha de las escencias nacionales contra la deformación de la dictadura. Sánchez Santos representa la defensa de los derechos de los humildes en una sociedad en que éstos carecían de voces que los defendieran (Sánchez Santos represents the part of Catholics in the revolution, in the opposition to the errors of the liberal regime of don Porfirio; it represents the struggle of national essence against the deformation of the dictatorship. Sánchez Santos represents the defense of the rights of the poor in a society in which those that lack voice should be defended).[24]

This period of journalistic maturity and apogee (1899–1912) began with the publishing of *El País*, his own newspaper in Mexico City, and closed with his death. This was the period of direct and explicit forward-looking social and political criticism linked to pro-church values and hierarchies.

Modernizing

More often than not the issues of Sánchez Santos were triple—social, moral and religious. He strongly emphasized the significance of the family, and he wrote historical, defensive essays upholding the Catholic-conservative side on past events. But he did more: he socialized and modernized histori-cal Catholic social speech by including issues of social justice and civic par-ticipation. In his later years he espoused Catholic reformist social views, added social criticism to his political commentary, and proposed reforms to enable a better future. In 1896 he said, "El ataque a los errores sociales es un deber de la conciencia, un apostolado al patriotismo" (The attack against social errors is a duty of conscience, a discipleship to patriotism).[25] And, one may add, timely for the church, as would be the case in the twentieth century. The change Sánchez Santos underwent is parallel to the noticeable alteration of the milieu in Mexico at the time. Effectively he communicated his views through his newspaper, *El País*, based in Mexico City but with a national circulation. Importantly, Sánchez Santos, seeing echoes of his own social views, endorsed the more benign socially concerned Catholics as they participated in several so-called Catholic congresses. These assem-blies endorsed certain social and educational rights for workers, women, and the indigenous. The speech of Guadalupe devotees such as Sánchez Santos now voiced relatively liberal social messages.

El País, a Catholic voice, became a major newspaper rivaling *El Imparcial*, a secular pro-regime voice, and went from a circulation of a few thousand to the remarkable figure of over 200,000 in its last two years, 1910–12.[26] It was a professional newspaper, with an attractive layout presenting excel-lent national and international news coverage, utilizing regular reporters and correspondents and providing an excellent feature section. *El País* was, indeed, among the best newspapers of the times and a high point in Mexican journalism of the day. In addition to his work as a publisher, Sánchez Santos was one of the best orators in his day, much in demand as a public speaker.

Sánchez Santos was an idealist, yet something of a moral sociologist; that is, he was concerned with spiritual reality, which for him should be the focus of man's endeavor. Sánchez Santos believed that the malaise of man was primarily spiritual and ideological. From defects in these stem the injustice and imperfection apparent in society. A fervent Catholic and patriot, the question of religion and fatherland were integral to his actions and ideas. His own obsession with charity and justice, because they were Christian imperatives, propelled his earnest desire for the reinvigoration and eventual greatness of Mexico. The times in which he lived determined that he would become more specific and more progressive in what he advocated.

Sánchez Santos held an apocalyptic vision of his times. It was an era of crisis, in which he saw impending doom for his country and religion. The view was couched in moral terms, though in the final decade it was extended to include economic and political perspectives. Much of the fervor and anxiety in his writings, and especially in his speeches, stemmed from this belief. For him, the contest was between the forces of evil and social degeneration, and those of salvation. Mexico was a major battleground and Mexicans had a special stake in the battle—their future. The major issue was morals. Hence vice and virtue are constants in his writings. Individuals and families must be moral. This was both civic and religious. He had principally three major themes: religious polemic, social-political criticism, and patriotic exhortation. His ideal was the realization of justice for the salvation and greatness of his country, both spiritually and materially.

The church was seen by Sánchez Santos as the preeminent social institution, a view shared by some but not all clergy.[27] For him ideally, in a society universally and consciously Catholic and Christian, morals and values would determine a benign operation of the state; the state would be a reflection of that society; there would be no church-state conflict. The form of government mattered little. However, Sánchez Santos was a confirmed electoral democrat and social reformer.

On history, heroes, and symbols, Sánchez Santos shared conservative bias except in his view of past Indian civilizations.[28] He had no patience with commentators who degraded the pre-Columbian Indian civilization, though he admitted that there were those who exaggerated Indian historical virtues and accomplishments. In his judgment, to deny their merits was an indulgence in "anti-mejicanismo." Understandably perhaps, what he found attractive in Indian civilization was the religiosity in all aspects of life and the high sense of morals, coupled with austere discipline and intense energy. Mexicans could do well to emulate the virtues of the native civilizations, he felt. This Catholic moderate conservative repeatedly encouraged a proud appreciation of Indian cultures.[29] This led him to believe that the greatest debt was owed to the Indian in terms of heritage and labor contribution from time immemorial to the present. He argued that the colonial period was the formative one in the social molding of the modern Mexican nation. In this, however, he argued that the church played a major and beneficent role. It mitigated the harshness of the Conquest and brought Catholicism to Mexico, which in turn led to the basis for future unity. Without the work of the church, the amalgamation of Indian and European would have been longer and more subject to animosity. The incorporation also included the amalgamation of previously divided Indian peoples. This positive view of the colonial period did not make Sánchez Santos a fervent Hispanophile as was the case, for the most part, with conservative writers.

Heroism

The national symbols Sánchez Santos preferred were the *Virgen de Guadalupe* and the national anthem. In heightened rhetorical prose he eulogized the virtues of each. What he stressed most in both was that they were symbols, both meaningful and accessible, uniting all. The *Virgen* was of prime importance to him as *the* Catholic, nationalistic, and continuing preeminent symbol to Mexicans over the years: "Guadalupe: tu nombre y tu historia son como el silabario de nuestro patriotismo" (Guadalupe: your name and your history are like the grammar book of our patriotism).[30] For Sánchez Santos, the Virgin, God given and uniquely Mexican, was the figurative expression of religion and patria. It was an Indian-Mexican symbol that evoked the past, while offering, he believed, the promise for a great future, as summarized in the phrase "*non omni taller nacioni*" (Such has not been done to all nations).

On the speaker's forum or in articles, his efforts were toward disseminating a view of the past in which Guadalupe is the central figure. This included defending the church's role, especially in regard to the Indian and in vindicating conservative heroes and actions during the nineteenth century. For him, the reforms of Bourbon Spain's Charles III truncated Mexico's historical evolution.[31] From the point of these reforms, Mexicans had been alienated from their "natural" development as it had been unfolding since 1520. The alienation stemmed, in his view, from the proto-liberal reforms that weakened the church, the monarchy, the state, the bulwark of society, and the constituent fiber of the nation. Nevertheless, Sánchez Santos endorsed independence, believing the church could work well with a sensible government. The compromise of Agustín de Iturbide with Guadalupe Victoria and the three guarantees (church, state, and equality) was a sound attempt at avoiding anarchy, and he insisted Iturbide was the father of the country. In Sánchez Santos' historical analysis, liberalism and its adherents had done incalculable harm to Mexico by forcing adoption of political forms, particularly republicanism, which it could not effectively fulfill, thereby endangering its future. Naturally he rejected the charge that the conservatives had been traitorous during the U.S. invasion and French Empire intervention wars, though he did not endorse the Empire, and certainly not the U.S. aggression. He was a critic of the Porfirio Díaz regime for its lack of a social policy and its negation of democracy. Through the 1880s and 1890s he was much concerned with polemics on history, though visibly less so in the last decade of his life, when contemporary problems absorbed most of his attention.

Clearly stated by Sánchez Santos in 1889 was that the fundamental task in politics for him was the "constituting" of the nation, by which he meant that the preeminent civic-political duty was to make law effective, a view shared by some liberals: "Venimos, por tanto, a luchar porque el país se constituya. Obra lenta y enorme que formará el objeto de nuestras labores en la política fundamental" (Thus we come to struggle so that the nation may constitute itself, a slow and enormous task that will forge the object of our efforts in fundamental politics).[32] He believed the constitutional principles and the legal precepts should become reality.[33] Sánchez Santos was for the rule of law, not specific men; in this he was consistent if not necessarily realistic given judicial practices under any circumstances. Actually, he again meant morals. For him, Mexico was yet to be constituted into a state. A strong state could be constituted, however, through a firm, moral religious base, ethnic unity, education, propitious laws and government, and respect for the church and for the family. Currently the spirit and the letter of the law did not determine the functioning of government authority, a fault that, in turn, was related to the lack of a moral base. The state and its laws ought to protect and advance social Christian interests.[34] He firmly endorsed democracy as the correct form of government and felt that Catholic religious beliefs would strengthen its practice, though he allowed that for the church there was no *one* form of government, since it asked of government only liberty to function and imperative morals.

Over the years he was a consistent, though not a fulsome, critic of the regime. Sánchez Santos viewed Díaz as politically able and administratively capable; but in the social sphere he believed his regime was a disaster. In his view, Díaz had impoverished the people economically and civically. As early as 1903 Sánchez Santos warned that serious consequences were bound to follow the Díaz social policies or lack of them.[35] Sánchez Santos was a severe critic and exposer of *caciquismo*, authoritarianism, whether national or local, and was relentlessly courageous in his criticism. From caciquismo flowed national disunity, corruption, and injustice, and these factors were to be found at national, state, and local levels. In addition to caciquismo, the denial of electoral democracy and limits on the freedom of the press were his most vigorous complaints against the Díaz regime. Now Sánchez Santos advocated that criticism of the government was, for the journalist, the preeminent patriotic obligation. He in effect aligned his politics, social views, and religiosity in ways that had broad acceptance. He buttressed Catholic conservative discourse on the public and the personal.

A Heartless World Conclusion: Theses

Cued by Ludwig Feuerbach, Karl Marx's comment on the purposes of religion for the laboring people is not as cynical as often read.[36] Indeed religion may be a sedative, but also an inciter. From their religiosity, laboring people may draw strength, in a sacred space, for facing real secular oppressors. Looking at Mexico on the eve of its revolution, two questions can be posed: How have Guadalupe and her audiences changed? How are the changes related to shifts among the people and the needs of the clerical authorizations?

As 1911 approached, the view of the contrasting patriotisms was argued again by a newspaper, but the terms were much harsher and the views on Guadalupe more encompassing than in earlier years. One form of patriotism was seen as hypocritical and compromising, identifiable with the regime and the elite; the other form was seen as insurgent, that of the people and the workers. Guadalupe could not easily be fitted into the former. Even icons have their vulnerabilities. Populist patriotism represented the tradition of the emancipatory national heroes and was the continuation of their ideals. Concurrently Guadalupe was now both national and international. Mexicans were required to see themselves as part of the worldwide Catholic domain. In effect, two divergent discourses about Guadalupe emerged: one in opposition to the antinational, false patriotism, and indulgent self-interest—in other words, all things antithetical to the community at large. At the same time, Guadalupe increasingly became allied to the church's worldwide struggle against secular nationalists and godless Bolsheviks.

As the twentieth century unfolded, further phases of Guadalupe's influence became evident. For us, the time between the Sacramento of 1966 and the Albuquerque of 2004 seems much longer than the distance between 1810 and 1911. In the history of this icon, I see nine basic theses on Guadalupe, and these constitute a rudimentary Guadalupe paradigm.

1. Guadalupe from the first is constructed as a populist resolution, which is to say there is a human purpose and use to Guadalupe.
2. Guadalupe involves the contest between the multivaried populist publics and the multilayered institutional interests.
3. Within the Guadalupe phenomenon, the church and its religiosity versus a nonchurch devotion to Guadalupe has been a recurring tension throughout the course of Mexican modern evolution.
4. The deployment of the Guadalupe myth politically by radicals and proto-nationalist elements may have appeared early in postindependence Mexico, but is certainly present by the nineteenth century.
5. The appropriation of the myth by conservative/proto-reactionary political elements has also occurred, a process abetted by secular and church authorities.
6. Guadalupe is an interactive myth, a Native American Delphic oracle who listens to the people and speaks to them. Hers is a voice of the people who are both speakers and listeners.
7. The appropriation and the eventual internationalization or globalization of Guadalupe, suspending an enduring us-vs.-them argument, is a more contemporary feature, which has led to a political neutralization of the powerful myth.
8. Guadalupe is among the few images and discourses both integral to and consistent throughout the precolonial, the colonial, and the postcolonial eras.

9. Guadalupe is a feminine-centered interactive myth, synthesizing religion and art, spirituality and science, and a Native American Delphic oracle who listens to the people and speaks to them. Here Guadalupe is a voice of the people for the people, who paradoxically are both speakers and listeners.

Without overly intending a paradox, to theorize on the Mexican Guadalupe requires us to historicize and particularize the myth, the story, and its uses. As a specific national devotion, Guadalupe encourages us to look at spirituality and myth in critical social relations in order for us to better appreciate social change.

For some Mexicans Guadalupe is imagination and belief, which involves identity, religion, and politics—in two words, philosophy and aesthetics. Personal dreams, fears, and beliefs—our very own myths—at one level are expressions of identity. Such is Guadalupe. More than simply *illusions*, myths are invoked ideals or potent appeals to ourselves and those immediately around us. At one colloquial level myth is a description for a counterfeit or counter factual statement. Here in this examination of Guadalupe, myth is used in the oppositional, the radical sense of what ought to be, inspired in part by what is or was. Whether positive or negative symbolic messages, myths explain, they rationalize. In practice they may be the individual standard for judging self and the group. They are a statement of ethics. Myths are maps and depictions of social relations that reside in the mind's eye of an individual, private yet intended to be shared.

Some myths are inherited from elders, some are devised in some historical present, some are wholly invention, and some weave historic facts and imaginings. Although myths may vary in density, many relate to social needs in both a personal and a public sense. Publicly voiced reasons of groups endorsing specific popular expressions, or group-promoting histories, have myths as part of their content. Group myths are conventional validations, justified by rationalization of selected memories usually in the name of survival, ethics, and progress. In contrast, personal myths are specific to individual aspirations in specific contexts.

Diverse, even contradictory, Mexican myths are personal and public references to ourselves in relation to others—and to others in relation to ourselves. As shared beliefs, myths provide identity and order; myths are expressed by individuals in word and action. They are internalized designs that code the parameters of social relations evaluated and performed in a particular time and space. Mexican cultural expressions are continually transforming themselves. The transformation is nourished by historical memories and impelled by social conditions and needs, but is not limited to these. Through renovation and innovation, cultural practice redefines what one is and what one believes. Although certain cultural practices subsume both existential being and historical myth, much altruistic cultural practice is dependent on them. Interactive transformation is voiced in longings and actions: Who am I? What do I want? These in turn may lead to the questions: Who are we? What do we want? In other words, group identification by an individual is preceded by an individual or personal (I am) existential affirmation.

Guadalupe's politics entail certain conceptualizations related to ideology and aesthetics. This spirituality is contemplation of beauty and harmony. Here art facilitates awareness of beauty. This Mexican myth is a story that explains the amazement, the awe, of our contemplation. Hence, this myth is a form of art requiring imagination, where art is our ability to visualize an image or an understanding and to give these form and expression. Perhaps the amazement at perceiving the universe, and the awe of perceiving ourselves as able to perceive, encourage human explanations. Humans are thinking beings that both imagine explanations and critique explanations. Like art, science is also an explanation for awe and wonder at the universe and often arises from metaphor and always involves imagination. Science can also prompt aesthetic pleasure. All of the above are grounded in the thinking of real persons about the material world around them. Religion, belief in supernatural forces, if principally and firmly rooted in altruistic ethics, may be a preliminary step to spirituality; however, religious practices are quite obviously an ideology, a rationalization for authority, status, and wealth of some over others. Guadalupe has been a contradiction in that both affirmation and denial are present within her.

Notes

1. See "Plan de Delano," in *Aztlán: An Anthology of Mexican American Literature*, ed. Luis Valdez and Stan Steiner (New York: Vintage, 1972), 197–201.
2. "Cyber-Arte: Tradition Meets Technology," Museum of International Folk Art, Sante Fe, NM. February 25, 2001. For the curator's point of view, see Tey Mariana Nunn, "The Cyber-Arte Exhibition: A Curators Journey Through

Community and Controversy," Smithsonian Center for Latino Initiatives, Washington DC: 2003. For the artist's point of view, see Alma López, "Tradition Clashes with Technology," *Albuquerque Journal*, Viewpoint, April 16, 2001. For a discussion of Alma López's art, see Laura E. Pérez, *Chicana Art: The Politics of Spiritual and Aesthetic Altarities* (Durham, NC: Duke University Press, 2007), 169–77 and 264–80.

3. Allan Warnick, *Our Lady Lupe*, privately produced documentary, Los Angeles, California, 2003.

4. Basic historical works on Guadalupe include: Francisco Miranda Godínez, *Dos cultos fundantes: Los Remedios y Guadalupe (1521–1649)* (Zamora: El Colegio de Michoacán, 1998); and Jacques Lafaye, *Quetzalcóatl and Guadalupe: The Formation of Mexican National Consciousness*, trans. Benjamin Keen (Chicago: University of Chicago Press, 1976). For the story see *The Story of Guadalupe: Luis Laso de la Vega's Huei tlamahuiçoltica of 1649*, ed. and transl. Lisa Sousa, Stafford Poole, and James Lockhart (Stanford: Stanford University Press/ UCLA Latin American Center Publications, 1998).

5. For the colonial period, see a recent analysis by William O. Taylor, "The Virgin of Guadalupe in New Spain: An Inquiry into the Social History of Marian Devotion," *American Ethnologist* 14, no. 1 (February, 1987): 9–33.

6. On early Guadalupe literature see Francisco de la Maza, *El Guadalupanismo Mexicano* (Mexico City: Fondo de Cultura Económica, 1992 [1953]).

7. For Fernando de Alba Ixtlilxochitl see *Obras históricas de don Fernando de Alva Ixtlilxochitl*, 2 vols., edited and annotated by Alfredo Chavero (México D.F.: Editoria Nacional, 1965).

8. On Carlos de Sigüenza y Góngora, see *Obras, con una biografía*, ed. Francisco Pérez Salazar (México D.F.: Sociedad de Bibliófilos Mexicanos, 1928); and on Sor Juana, see: *Obras completas* (Mexico City: Porrua, 1975), 164.

9. On the independence crisis, see Luis Villoro, *El proceso ideológico de la revolución de independencia*, 2nd ed. (Mexico City: CONACULTA, 1999 [1967]).

10. For the broader context see my *Porfirio Díaz, los intelectuales y la Revolución* (Mexico City: Ediciones El Caballito, S.A., 1981).

11. *El Tiempo*, April 2, 1980, and *El Partido Liberal*, January 2, 1896.

12. *El Tiempo*, January 19, 1892.

13. *Diario del Hogar*, September 8, 1891.

14. *El Tiempo*, September 16, 1890, and September 16, 1891.

15. *El Monitor Republicano*, September 16, 1891; *Diario del Hogar*, September 18, 1896; and *El Tiempo*, January 18, 1910.

16. *El Monitor Republicano*, September 16, 1891.

17. *El Monitor Republicano*, September 16, 1891.

18. Francisco Aguilera et al., *Album conmemorativo del 450 aniversario de las apariciones de Nuestra Señora de Guadalupe* (Mexico City: Ediciones Buena Nueva, 1981).

19. See Ernesto de la Torre Villar and Ramiro Navarro de Anda, eds., *Testimonios históricos guadalupanos* (Mexico City: Fondo de Cultura Económica, 1982).

20. *Diario del Hogar*, July 21, 1906.

21. *Diario del Hogar*, May 25, 1909, and *Revista Positiva*, October 8, 1906.

22. *Diario del Hogar*, September 29, 1900.

23. This was the motto for the newspaper *El País*, 1899–1912.
24. Luis Islas García, ed., *Trinidad Sánchez Santos* (Mexico City: Editorial Jus, 1945), 89–90.
25. Trinidad Sánchez Santos, *Obras selectas de Don Trinidad Sánchez Santos*, 2nd ed. (Mexico City: Editorial Jus, 1962), I:177.
26. *El País*, passim, and Sánchez Santos, *Obras*, II:46–47.
27. Sánchez Santos's views on church are critical as well as endorsing. See *Obras*, passim.
28. *Obras*, II:269–71.
29. *Obras*, I:276–99.
30. *Obras*, II:259.
31. *Obras*, I:270–75.
32. *Obras*, II:318–19.
33. *Obras*, II:103–4.
34. Ibid.
35. *El País*, January 1, 1903.
36. Karl Marx, "Toward the Critique of Hegels, Philosophy of Right," in *Basic Writings on Politics and Philosophy*, ed. Lewis S. Feur (New York: Anchor Books, 1989). Marx said: "Religious distress is at the same time the expression of real distress, and the protest against real distress. Religion is the sigh of the oppressed creature, the heart of a heartless world, just as it is the spirit of an unspiritual situation. It is the opium of the people" (263).

References

Aguilera, Francisco M. *Album conmemorativo del 450 aniversario de las aparicones de Nuestra Señora de Guadalupe*. México D.F.: Ediciones Buena Nueva, 1981.

Alva Ixtlilxochitl, Fernando de. *Obras históricas de don Fernando de Alva Ixtlilxochitl*. 2 vols. Edited and annotated by Alfredo Chavero. México D.F.: Editorial Nacional, 1965.

Carrasco, David. *Quetzalcóatl and the Irony of Empire*. University of Chicago Press, 1982.

Islas García, Luis, ed. *Trinidad Sánchez Santos*. México D.F.: Editorial Jus, 1945.

Lafaye, Jacques. *Quetzalcóatl and Guadalupe, the Formation of Mexican National Consciousness*. University of Chicago Press, 1976.

Maza, Francisco de la. *El Guadalupanismo Mexicano*. México D.F.: Fondo de Cultura Económica, 1992 [1953].

———. "Los evangelistas de Guadalupe y el nacionalismo Mexicano." *Cuadernos Americanos* 48 (November–December, 1949): 163–88.

Miranda Godínez, Francisco. *Dos Cultos fundantes: Los Remedios y Guadalupe (1521–1649)*. Zamora: El Colegio de Michoacán, 1998.

Sánchez Santos, Trinidad. *Obras selectas de Don Trinidad Sánchez Santos*. 2 vols. 2nd ed. México D.F.: Editorial Jus, 1962.

Sigüenza y Góngora, Carlos. *Obras, con una biografía.* Edited by Francisco Pérez Salazar. México D.F.: Sociedad de Bibliófilos Mexicanos, 1928.

Sousa, Lisa, Stafford Poole, C. M., and James Lockhart, eds. *The Story of Guadalupe: Luis Laso de la Vega's* Huei Tlamahuiçolitca *of 1649.* Stanford: Stanford University Press/UCLA Latin America Center, 1998.

Taylor, William. "The Virgin of Guadalupe in New Spain: An Inquiry into the Social History of Marian Devotion." *American Ethnologist* 14, no. 1 (February, 1987): 9–33.

Torre Villar, Ernesto de la, and Ramiro Navarro de Anda, eds. *Testimonios históricos Guadalupanos.* México D.F.: Fondo de Cultura Económica, 1982.

Warnick, Allan. *Our Lady Lupe.* Privately produced documentary, Los Angeles, 2003.

Can Hispanic Immigration
Change Fundamental Attitudes
in United States Foreign Policy?

LUIS ANTONIO PAYAN

Introduction

⮑ IN *WESTERN POLITICAL QUARTERLY* IN 1980, RODOLFO DE LA GARZA
wrote that there were several reasons why the power of Hispanics was
beginning to be recognized as having a potentially important political
influence on U.S. domestic and foreign policy.[1] That was over a quarter
of a century ago. Yet Hispanics have remained the untapped force in U.S.
politics. With very few exceptions, Hispanics have yet to make important
inroads in U.S. domestic politics, and they are nearly absent from foreign
policymaking structures. Most Hispanics in the middle-to-upper echelons
of government are generally quota appointments chosen by politicians
to appeal to the Hispanic community in general. The potential that de
la Garza spoke about has not been actualized. The lack of coincidence
between the political power of Hispanics and their numbers is obviated
by the statistics themselves. The number of Hispanics in the country is
growing at a fast pace, constituting now 16 percent of the total population
of the United States by 2010, according to the U.S. Census Bureau.[2] Yet in
2004, the Congressional Hispanic Caucus in Washington, DC, contained
only twenty members or 3.7 percent of Congress members—and not one
single member in the Senate. Less than 3 percent of the U.S. Foreign
Service was of Hispanic origin. And so on. This kind of underrepresentation is widespread in all the power structures in the United States.

This lack of political power commensurate with population percentages could be attributed to forces beyond Hispanic control, but before exploring any potential variables that contribute to this Hispanic underrepresentation in government, blame must also be duly apportioned to Hispanics and Hispanic leaders as well. And although it is not the task of this essay to seek groups responsible for the current state of affairs, one example is illustrative of the responsibility that Hispanics and Hispanic leaders themselves bear for their own political disenfranchisement. In the state of Texas, Hispanics, in alliance with African Americans, could have turned out in sufficient numbers to insure the elections of Ron Kirk, an African American to the U.S. Senate, and Tony Sánchez, a Mexican American, to the Texas Executive. Yet, both groups failed to come out to the polls and, as a result, Hispanic representation in the Texas structures of power remained well below that of their numbers in the state. This was clearly a failure of the Hispanic population and their leadership given that, in Texas, Hispanics now constitute 33 percent of the state's population.

That Hispanics have remained weak and ineffective in influencing domestic and foreign policy processes and outcomes is quite different than their growing influence on the *cultural* landscape of the United States. In fact, the cultural influence of Hispanics in the United States far surpasses their political effectiveness in either domestic or foreign policy. Hispanics now constitute an important percentage of Catholics in the United States and growing numbers in public schools across the nation. Latin beats populate the music charts in the entertainment industry, and Latin faces have become increasingly part of the cultural landscape of the United States. It is as if suddenly being Latin is "in."

The discrepancy between (1) the growth in the Hispanic population and Hispanic advances in shaping the cultural landscape of the United States and (2) their political ineffectiveness is a puzzle to be sorted out. Ideally, one would expect both to rise simultaneously. Yet this has not been the case. Before this conundrum, the question becomes, what explains the *differential* between Hispanic advances in the cultural landscape and their rapidly increasing numbers on the one hand and their ineffectiveness in the political arena on the other? There are probably many factors that can explain why Hispanic political effectiveness is not as extensive as Hispanic cultural influences and why Hispanic political influence over U.S. domestic and foreign policy processes does not reflect the numbers. But even so, there is already a sober debate over what the future of the country will be when Hispanics become a significant percentage of the total population of the United States. While some welcome the "Latinization" of the United States, others are quite concerned that the country's very character might change. And not everyone agrees that such a change would be for the better. This debate rages on, often polarizing politicians, academics, and members of the media, although the general public's opinion on the matter is not as well articulated as that of U.S. elites.

For the sake of parsimony, this essay will separate and explore the two factors—values and interests—most often cited in the national debate on the role of Hispanics in U.S. society and assess whether these have the potential to balkanize the United States, as some doomsayers would argue. At the heart of the debate lies the matter of values or culture and whether Hispanic values and culture are compatible with U.S. values and culture; on the other hand lies the matter of power and interests and whether Hispanics threaten to divide the United States by bringing its power structures under renewed stress not seen since the Civil Rights movement. Some recent publications point to both of these factors as important. One of these is the article "The Hispanic Challenge" by Samuel P. Huntington, that serves as the springboard for our examination in this essay because Huntington's argument illustrates both of these issues—values and interests.[3] Although Huntington's article conflates the issue of values and the issue of interests, these are quite different in nature and deserve separate, more nuanced treatment. This essay will argue that values do not really matter in the presumed challenge that Hispanics pose to the future of the nation, and perhaps not even the issue of interests is that crucial because democratic political accommodation can help diffuse tensions that might endanger the U.S. way of life. Values and interests are less important in understanding whether Hispanics represent a negative or a positive challenge within the United States. The Hispanic historical experience instead is a much more powerful factor in understanding why Hispanics hold somewhat different views than mainstream United States on foreign and domestic policy issues. Furthermore, I argue that Hispanic public opinion on policy issues does not represent a threat to the unity of the United States or its future, but that it adds to, rather than subtracts from, the national debate on the role of government in society.

The Question of Values

With regard to values, the public debate is often hijacked by a point of view known as nativism. The "nativist" point of view has been expressed by Peter Brimelow[4] and Arthur M. Schlesinger Jr.[5] in the 1990s, and by Samuel P. Huntington more recently.[6] The alarmist stand, manifest in the form of rabid anti-immigration positions, that these nativists take is, of course, not new. Nativists join others in the past of U.S. history in doubting that the values of the United States can survive a new wave of immigration. The most recent focus of these nativists is the wave of immigration from Latin America that began at the end of the twentieth century and continues today. Nativists argue that multilingualism and diversity threaten the mainstream values of the nation. Samuel P. Huntington goes as far as advocating that the United States should stop all immigration from Latin America immediately, particularly from Mexico, because these immigrant groups threaten to bifurcate U.S. culture, values, politics, and territory. He even argues that immigration from Latin America and Mexico could eventually balkanize the United States and polarize U.S. society. Focusing on Latin Americans, much the same way nativists of other times had focused on Italian, Polish, Irish, Catholic, and other waves of immigrants, nativists argue today that the values of Latin Americans are incompatible with "U.S. values." Huntington writes that,

Most Americans see the creed as the crucial element of their national identity. The creed, however, was the product of distinct Anglo-Protestant culture of the founding settlers. Key elements of that culture include the English language; Christianity; religious commitment; English concepts of the rule of law, including the responsibility of rulers and the rights of individuals; and dissenting protestant values of individualism, the work ethic, and the belief that humans have the ability and duty to try to create heaven on earth, a "city on a hill."[7]

Without going into the factual errors or the fallacies of Huntington's statement, or the prejudices that it might contain, suffice it to say that his idea that there are some specific traditional U.S. values that can be accurately defined and pegged to a specific ethnic or linguistic group is common among nativists. In turn, they conclude that multiculturalism and diversity endanger national unity in the United States because they threaten to "fragment" the United States and smash the dream of "one people." The *unum* becomes much more important than the *e pluribus*, so to speak, a position ominously and unfortunately reminiscent of movements that found their extreme manifestation in German and Italian fascism. The argument nativists make is that Hispanic values do not belong in the processes that determine U.S. foreign or domestic policy. According to nativists, Hispanic values are not only not relevant but outright dangerous to U.S. foreign policy interests and domestically Hispanics are a threat to a hypothetical consensus based on Anglo-Protestant values. Hispanics have no place in determining or influencing the kinds of values that underlie the making of U.S. foreign or domestic policy. Racial, ethnic, and linguistic diversity do not have a place in the symbolic assessment of motives behind action abroad or in shaping national priorities at home. Hispanics are perceived as less patriotic than Jews, blacks, Asians, southern whites, and whites in general.[8] For these reasons, Hispanics, according to nativists, are to be largely kept from becoming part of the policy decisionmaking establishment, and their migration flow to the United States should be ended immediately.

Indeed, when the rhetoric turns to labeling "unpatriotic" that which is critical of United States foreign policy, Hispanics give some thought to elites in charge of decisionmaking in that area.[9] This concern, however, stems not from the fact that Hispanics are fundamentally less patriotic than the mainstream population but from the fact that Hispanics have different policy preferences from other national groups. There are two recent sources, for example, that reveal the gap between U.S. leaders' choices in foreign policy and Hispanics' preferences on the subject. The Pew Hispanic Center conducted two surveys of Hispanic attitudes toward the 2003 war with Iraq. The first survey, conducted February 13–16, 2003, before the invasion of Iraq, showed that support for military action in Iraq was weaker among the Hispanic population and was even less among foreign-born Hispanics. The second survey was conducted April 3–6, 2003, following the invasion of Iraq. In this survey, the Hispanic population showed itself to be largely divided over the war. Hispanics born in the United States expressed strong support and optimism over the course, while foreign-born Hispanics expressed much more concern over the same issues. Both of these results, even if the second survey revealed greater support for the war than the first, show why Hispanics are sometimes seen as uncertain about their loyalties to the United States.[10]

These are the differences that lead nativists to draw conclusions regarding the patriotism of Hispanics, though the logical leap is questionable because disagreement or criticism is defined as being unpatriotic, an unsustainable position in a democracy. Moreover, in regard to domestic policy, clearly Hispanics exhibit certain preferences that are somewhat different from those of the mainstream. Hispanics, for example, are very concerned with education and health care. Most agree that the government should provide health care to those who cannot afford it and are even willing to pay higher taxes for it. Most Hispanics also favor an immigration amnesty to resolve the current impasse on that matter.[11] Such positions differ from mainstream U.S. stands on these subjects but cannot be ascertained to threaten a presumed domestic consensus because Hispanic stands are often in line with a more liberal segment of the U.S. public itself. Nativists, of course, would argue that Hispanic stands on domestic issues are contrary to the values of the United States. But again, Hispanic stands are not necessarily unpatriotic, given that many U.S. whites hold the same views as Hispanics regarding the role of government in society. This is a historical debate in the U.S. democracy. Hispanics only add to the diversity of arguments in this quintessential national debate.

Nativists, however, are mistaken, because they conflate the issue of Hispanic public opinion regarding foreign and domestic policies with their ability to adapt culturally to the values of the United States and become members of the mainstream. In spite of the gap between Hispanic and mainstream public opinion, integration is not a fundamental problem. Hispanic cultures are not only amenable to Western culture but they are part of the vast richness of what is considered Western culture. Asking whether the traditional Anglo-Protestant values can remain the same before the tide of immigration is asking the wrong question. Clearly, the answer is no. There is a dialectic in which Anglo-Protestant values and Hispanic-Catholic values will shape each other. Thus nativists are not asking the right question, but the right answer to the wrong question in any case would be that perhaps they should not remain the same; that both sets of values should indeed merge into a single set of values drawing the best from each. The reality is that Anglo-Protestant values and Hispanic-Catholic values are not irreconcilably different. Let us take a hard look at the purported values of Anglo-Protestants and Hispanic-Catholics in the United States (see table 1).

TABLE 1: Comparing Values

Values	Anglo-Protestant Values	Hispanic-Catholic Values
Religion	Christian/individualistic	Christian/collectivist
Religious commitment	Varied	Varied
Rule of law	Developed	Developing/not absent
Individualism	High	Low to moderate with a considerable increase as Latin America develops
Work ethic	High	Medium/high
Shape of the future	Optimistic	Mixed, wavering between optimistic and pessimistic
Unit of focus	Individual/nuclear family	Collective/extended family, but increasingly nuclear as migration and mobility increase

Although there are some fundamental differences, the reality is that the orientation for each of these values Huntington lists in his article is only a matter of degrees and, even then, there is variation among the different nations of Latin America. Mexico, for example, is increasingly a country of values that tend to look like Anglo-Protestant values without capitulating on important Hispanic-Catholic values. This is certainly the case among the many young urban professionals and young families that can be found in nearly all major urban centers. As Weintraub argued, the North American Free Trade Agreement (NAFTA) seems to have resulted in some degree of cultural convergence between Mexico, the United States, and Canada that seems attributable to the economic integration of North America.[12] Clearly, Mexico is a good example of the manifestation of what appears to be historic convergence between Anglo-Protestant values and Hispanic-Catholic values. Mexico, along with Chile, Argentina, Brazil, and other specific urban enclaves within the major countries of Latin America, is but a few examples of this historical value-convergence. These four countries are found to more closely reflect the values Huntington attributed to a white Anglo-Protestant culture than the values of other

Latin American nations, although one could expect that a blend of the two types of values is a more likely result. Economic development and its contingent globalization values are increasingly the driving value-setting forces in Latin America, over religious and other value-setting factors.[13] The effect of the processes of globalization cannot be underestimated. As Berger put it,

> All sectors of the emerging global culture enhance the independence of the individual over against tradition and collectivity. Individuation must be seen as a social and psychological process, manifested empirically in the behavior of consciousness of people regardless of the ideas they may hold about this.[14]

In effect, the issue of convergence of values is not trivial. As globalization proceeds and countries are required to compete for investment with other countries, the general push is for greater individualism, a higher work ethic, a stronger rule of law, and a stronger belief that policies are what shape the future in the minds of Latin Americans and not an otherworldly fateful force as was presumed to be the case. And as capitalism and democracy make enormous strides in Latin America, the traditional forms of familial relations are quickly eroded. The nuclear family and a more self-centered approach to life begin to be the dominant values. This is clearly evident in most Latin American urban centers and among Latin Americans moving to the United States; even when they build enclaves in large areas like Los Angeles, Chicago, or Houston, they tend to adapt quickly to the so-called Anglo-Protestant values, at a minimum in the workplace, where one sees nothing but hard work and long hours by immigrant workers. Stereotypes of Latin Americans, particularly Mexicans, having to take a siesta in the afternoon and having a lackadaisical work ethic are easily shattered when one observes the habits of immigrants working in the agricultural fields of California, the construction industry in Texas, or the restaurant kitchens in New York or Washington, DC. Studies based on the World Values Surveys increasingly demonstrate this value convergence.

Clearly when it comes to values, the reality is that nativists err, because they mistakenly equate the differing policy preferences by Hispanics in the United States with being unpatriotic, un-American, or unable to adapt to the values of the country, and thereby with threatening to collapse

America. Framing the issue in this fashion frankly creates a storm in a teacup and reveals the prejudices of nativist thinking, rather than being a careful study regarding the compatibility of Anglo-Protestant and Hispanic-Catholic values in the context of globalization and economic integration. Later in this essay I argue that the policy preferences of Hispanics in the United States stem not from their values so much as from their historical experience.

Interests

The second explanatory factor that can help us understand the "Hispanic challenge," as seen by many nativists in the United States, is the matter of interests. As already pointed out, nativists conflate the issue of values and interests and attribute what is fundamentally a matter of interests to cultural values. Separating culture from interests, whether group or individual interests, however, is fundamental to understanding the actual or imagined friction among groups within a given social context. In this essay, I make the argument that the cleavages that Huntington points to between Hispanic America and mainstream America are not more "cultural" or value-driven than they are interest-based.

The fundamental issue of interests can be examined through an analysis of social power structures and dominance networks. This issue is as ancient as human beings. Jesus broke several of the rules imposed by the religious and political powers-that-be in his time to expose the interests beneath influence distribution and, by doing so, the abuse of authority by which priests maintained control of society. Thus even in the old biblical texts, one can see the importance of understanding power structures and dominance networks in any given society because this understanding can reveal the degree to which those occupying the upper echelons can interpret new arrivals as a threat to the distribution of influence. The most vital factor in such conditions is, of course, the numbers. At some point, the Israelites became a serious threat to the Egyptians because their numbers became considerably large within Egyptian society. (Witness how Huntington perceives the "fertility rates of these immigrants" as a threat to the United States).[15] As the new arrivals, Hispanics have had to adjust and adapt to their new social context, including the prevailing distribution of power and dominance, but as their numbers increase they are more and more perceived as a group that will likely compete for positions of power and influence. Because power and influence are often perceived as a zero-sum game, groups already enjoying these in U.S. society may see Hispanics as a challenge to their own share. Hence Huntington, like other nativists, uses the term "Hispanic challenge" in a negative rather than a positive sense. He correctly perceives that there is potential for some friction between the growing up-and-coming Hispanic groups and the traditional power elites generally associated with the white Anglo-Protestant culture of the United States. What is perverse in Huntington's argument is that it pits the new immigrants not against the power structures and dominance networks—where the real danger of social unrest lies—but against the lower echelons of U.S. society. He explicitly states that this new wave of immigration is a threat to "low wage earners," suggesting in a veritable logical somersault that it is new immigrants who threaten to undo the United States rather than representing a potential struggle for political spaces among various segments of society.

Besides the concern with the scale of the current wave of immigration, another major concern that Huntington expresses is that Hispanics have created enclaves in the United States, which he labels "regional concentration." Huntington, of course, contradicts himself by arguing that Hispanics have created enclaves or "beachheads," on the one hand, and that they are everywhere in the United States, on the other hand. But regardless of this contradiction, the reality is that Hispanics created enclaves for several practical, rather than malevolent, reasons. And their reasons are no different from the reasons that have led other immigrant groups in the past to create such enclaves—witness the Irish, the Italians or the Polish in various U.S. cities and states. Immigrant groups create enclaves to receive and welcome new immigrants, including their family members. These immigrant communities serve as the places where the new arrivals feel at once at home and begin to learn U.S. ways. These communities, rather than conspiring against the United States, serve as the first stepping stone to the later integration of many of their members into the mainstream. Indeed, these centers serve as a point of transition from the old culture to the new. They ease the new arrivals into a new life.

The second reason why Hispanics create enclaves, like any other immigrant group in the past, is that they generally experience an initial, even if not malicious, rejection as members of the mainstream culture of the United States. They simply do not fit in it. Initially, and consistent with the economic motives behind their decision to migrate, new arrivals are mostly welcome in the context of cheap labor for U.S. businesses. This "alien" or, better put, purely economic treatment of first generation Hispanics in many U.S. areas has forced Hispanics to create their own institutions, processes, and networks to enjoy the benefits of belonging to a community even as they begin to experience the greater context of U.S. culture and society. In effect, Hispanics have created support structures that both welcome them and help them make a successful transition into the U.S. cultural, economic, and, hopefully, soon political landscape. Enclaves, therefore, facilitate assimilation rather than impede it, an argument that counters, with no less legitimacy, the conclusions that Huntington draws from the same empirical observations.

But even when new immigrants create enclaves, generations of Hispanics have already shown that they can integrate well into the mainstream United States. California and New Mexico are two good examples of ongoing and even consolidated integration, just as Texas and Arizona are two examples of the kind of potential friction that Huntington believes can stem from the clash between the interests of the Anglo-Protestant and the Hispanic-Catholic newly arrived. Many studies have established that by the second and third generation, Hispanics are largely assimilated into mainstream U.S. culture. Hence, the discomfort that nativists feel toward the Hispanic challenge is not a matter of cultural or value assimilation—to attribute the challenge to Hispanic incompatibility with U.S. culture appears to be a red herring—but rather a matter of encroaching on the political power of traditional elites.[16] This is made evident by the fact that generally, while Hispanics remain in their enclaves contributing to U.S. economic power without any social or political demands, they constitute no real threat to the powers-that-be in society and they are largely tolerated. The intimidated young man preparing meals or washing dishes in the kitchen of a restaurant in Washington, DC, or Chicago is not a threat to anyone. It is when that young man makes social justice and political demands that he is pitted against the power and influence of structures of society. Hispanics have indeed begun to demand larger and higher spaces in the social and political landscape of the United States and some centers of political power can begin to feel under stress. State elites in Phoenix and Austin are beginning to read the writing on the wall and realize that Hispanics are becoming a force that, though still unrealized, will likely offer a future challenge to the prevailing political power structures in those states.[17] Because much of the power in Texas and Arizona, as well as in other states with substantial Hispanic minorities, is in the hands of mostly white Anglo-Protestant males, it is that group that feels under stress, as Huntington himself suggests. Consequently, it is that group that may be expected to react by attempting to reverse its losses in power and status. To Huntington, this is the gravest danger to the United States, that the Anglo-Protestant elites may react so as to balkanize the country. Unfortunately, Huntington, like many other nativists, confuses his own logic again. He blames Hispanics for causing this reaction and thereby the supposed balkanization of America, rather than assigning responsibility to these same Anglo-Protestant elites for reacting somewhat virulently and in exclusionary ways to the Hispanic challenge and thereby contributing to his hypothesized crumbling of the country.

If the danger is the balkanization of the United States, and the cause is the Hispanic challenge to the prevailing interests—and we add to this that the "challenge" is now historically inevitable—then the fundamental mistake, the mistake that would most split the United States asunder, would be *not* to involve Hispanics in the relevant debates on the future of the nation and the definition of U.S. national priorities and interests, both domestically and abroad. An excluded group (Hispanics and their underrepresentation in U.S. power structures) will naturally be a group that will never be able to identify with the priorities of the society in which it resides because it had nothing to do with creating and shaping those interests. Hispanics must develop a stake in the future of the United States. To have a higher stake in the future of the United States, and to avoid the type of balkanization that nativists fear, it is necessary to involve Hispanics in the decisionmaking processes that determine national policy, whether domestic or foreign. Otherwise, the very techniques used to maintain control of policy decisionmaking—exclusionary politics by federal, state, and local elites—may lead to the very problem that Huntington is trying to point out: the fragmentation of U.S. society.

Explaining Hispanic Values: History Not Culture

Having defined some of the reasons why cultural or value-based arguments are not sufficient to speculate on a presumed balkanization stemming from a clash between Anglo-Protestant and Hispanic-Catholic values, and having explained why an interest-based account is more likely to explicate any such balkanization and, even so, only under certain conditions, it is now pertinent to explain where Hispanic attitudes in both domestic and foreign policy come from and why they differ from mainstream U.S. attitudes. If it is Hispanic attitudes that disturb nativists, then their source must be understood if fears are to be put to rest and alarmist stands viewed in perspective.

This essay makes the argument that Hispanic attitudes stem from the Hispanic historical experience rather than from their values. The explanation of the difference between Hispanic public opinion and mainstream opinion is to be found in historical variables, rather than in values or cultural differences. To examine the origin of Hispanic attitudes on foreign and domestic policy requires us to divide Hispanic public opinion attitudes into those on foreign policy and those on domestic policy, and analyze them separately. The historical experience of the United States and the Latin American nations is abysmally different. Throughout the country's history, the foreign policy discourse of U.S. elites has been largely hegemonic. In 1832, when Alexis De Tocqueville wrote *Democracy in America*, he observed that Americans were truly convinced that their mission went well beyond their borders, that they strongly believed that their responsibility transcended the boundaries of the United States, that they possessed a civilizing mission.[18] U.S. elites were already determined to have a global reach, even as many of them preached moderation in national ambitions. In spite of some initial difficulties, the twentieth century saw the rise of the United States as a great power, which cemented the hegemonic discourse already present among the historic elites of the country.

The foreign policy discourse of the Latin American peoples, on the contrary, has never been hegemonic. No nation of Latin America, perhaps with the exception of some very short historical moments in Argentina or Brazil, has ever had a sense of hegemony, be it regional or global. Where U.S. elites spoke of conquest, expansion, manifest destinies, civilizing missions, and global reaches, the discourse of Hispanic American elites has always been defensive, guarded, limited in its reach. Where U.S. diplomats have conceived grand doctrines, like the Monroe Doctrine with its corollaries or the Containment Doctrine with its consequence of global reach, Latin American diplomats have conceived doctrines such as the Estrada and the Tobar doctrines of international relations. Latin American diplomatic and political doctrines embody mostly concepts such as nonintervention, mutual respect for domestic policies regardless of their nature, and self-determination of the peoples. Latin American governments have continuously preached the virtues of showing absolute respect for national sovereignty and preventing governments from interfering in each other's affairs.

These attitudes originating in the history of Latin America are the same attitudes that many Hispanics bring with them when they come to the United States. Most education systems in Latin America are replete with such doctrines and socialize their generations in the language of oppression and invasion. From this historical experience come, I argue, the fundamental attitudes that Hispanics express on U.S. public opinion polls. The historical experience of Hispanics is one of oppression, not one of conquest; it is one of submission, not one of victory; it is one of being intervened, not one of intervening. In fact, the Hispanic experience often included incursions by the United States itself, as well as by other great European powers. Faced with the inability to fend off many great power interventions and military incursions, the Hispanic nations of the Americas largely adopted a policy of laissez-faire designed to oblige great powers to stay away from their affairs and from threatening their national survival. A "live and let live" foreign policy—or attitude—is generally one chosen by those who are weakest and cannot defend themselves head-to-head from the stronger.

It should not surprise anyone, therefore, that Hispanics, particularly first generation Hispanics in the United States, would prefer a different approach by U.S. foreign policy, a "come home, America" approach, rather than an actively interventionist approach. The Hispanic historical experience could not but evolve into a laissez-faire preference in policy because that is the position of the weak vis-à-vis the strong. This explains, to a large extent, why Hispanics are more reluctant to support U.S. intervention abroad, regardless of its nature, as the Pew Hispanic Center polls on Hispanic support for the Iraqi War show.

Hispanics also exhibit different attitudes on domestic issues from mainstream United States. Hispanics prefer greater government intervention in the economy and on social issues than the general public. Hispanics prefer that the government guarantee some form of universal health care. They also believe that the government should guarantee basic quality education for all. They also have more liberal attitudes on immigration.[19] And so forth. This is particularly true of first generation Hispanic immigrants, although it is a position that is modified gradually by the second and third generation. But even in these later generations, Hispanic policy preferences are considerably more liberal than mainstream public opinion. So, what are the hypothesized historical causes of Latino attitudes in the United States? I argue that Hispanic preferences, even on domestic policies, stem from the historical experience of the Latin American peoples. For decades, Latin Americans were socialized in political and policy environments where governments were often unstable and generally quite incompetent in satisfying the needs and demands of their publics. Much of the middle class of Latin America, and large segments of the lower classes, have long desired more effective governments to guarantee a type of society where economic opportunity and progress are available and where political stability is a fact. Yet most Latin Americans have not counted on competent states to bring this about. Many immigrants, in fact, come to the United States fleeing these very economic and political conditions in their own countries. It is therefore not surprising that Latin Americans, upon arriving in the United States, encountering a strong state with the ability to create and implement strong, long-desired social and economic policies, prefer governmental action to create them.

Latin Americans, long deprived of state competence and effective policies to guarantee a minimal standard, should then be expected to want to make use of state effectiveness to establish a more even social field. Thus, the historical experience of Latin Americans, with their own states' ineffectiveness in providing for the basic public good, makes them place greater faith in the ability of the U.S. government to accomplish this. They are therefore expected to put greater emphasis on the obligation of the government to provide everyone with a minimal standard of living. This does not mean, however, that Hispanics threaten to divide the United States. It simply means that they contribute to the historical debate over the role of government in society. Incidentally, for anyone traveling through Latin America and talking to people in the streets, it is easy to see the desire of most Latin Americans to have effective government and governing structures in their own nations. Latin Americans admire the ability of the U.S. government to do things, not its ability to restrain itself from doing things, as the more conservative forces of the United States would like it.

Conclusion

In general, Hispanics should be expected to make their preferences felt once they acquire the critical mass to pressure federal, state, and local governments to respond to their policy preferences. But pressuring a government to accommodate policy preferences does not indicate lack of patriotism or the possibility of a divided United States. Similarly, because values are a dud in trying to explain the attitudinal gap between Hispanics and mainstream Americans, we must appeal to the issue of power, influence, and interests if we are to find reasonable explanations for this gap. Indeed, the fragmentation of the United States is more likely to occur under circumstances where Hispanics continue to be largely excluded from participating in determining the foreign and domestic policy agenda of the U.S. future. At some point, Hispanic elites will become aware of the discrepancy between their numbers and their political clout. Under such conditions, a second civil rights movement would be necessary. And this is what could potentially threaten to fragment the United States. A gradual opening of the power structures is likely to diffuse most of the concerns of nativists regarding the ability of the United States to absorb and "Americanize" the new immigrants. Resistance by Anglo-Protestant elites, whom Huntington believes to be the "real" Americans, would only create the very conditions that he sees as dangerous for the nation.

Finally, it is important to understand that Hispanic attitudes do not pertain to who they are, what they believe, or even what positions they take in regard to any policy issues, domestic or foreign. It is important to understand, rather, that it is the Hispanic historical experience that makes them more inclined to demand a lesser role by the U.S. government in foreign affairs and to expect U.S. government intervention in the domestic economy and in society in general with greater effectiveness. But not even in this regard are Hispanics a threat to the United States. Their attitudes are simply somewhat different from the attitudes of mainstream America and likely to be beneficial to the ongoing dialogue on what democracy should be, what government should do, and the type of democracy we should build.

Notes

1. Rodolfo de la Garza, "Chicanos and U.S. Foreign Policy: The Future of Chicano-Mexican Relations," Western Political Quarterly 33, no. 4 (December, 1980): 571–82.
2. See http://www.census.gov/population/www/projections/summarytables.html.
3. Samuel P. Huntington, "The Hispanic Challenge," Foreign Policy (March/April 2004): 30–45.

4. Peter Brimelow, *Alien Nation* (New York: Harper Perennial, 1996).

5. Arthur M. Schlesinger, Jr., *The Disuniting of America: Reflections on a Multicultural Society* (New York: Norton, 1992).

6. Huntington, "The Hispanic Challenge."

7. Ibid., 31–32.

8. Tom Smith. "Ethnic Survey," in *GSS Topical Report No. 19* (Chicago, National Opinion Research Center of the University of Chicago, 1990).

9. There is, of course, a whole debate over whether criticism of foreign policy-making (more so than domestic policymaking) is unpatriotic. Gore Vidal has argued in several of his writings that being critical is not only patriotic but a duty of all citizens.

10. "Summary Findings: Survey of Latino Attitudes on the War with Iraq Conducted February 13 to 16, 2003, Before the Invasion of Iraq," and "Summary Findings: Survey of Latino Attitudes on the War with Iraq Conducted April 3 to 6, 2003, Following the Invasion of Iraq," *Surveys by the Pew Hispanic Center: A Project of the University of Southern California Annenberg School for Communication.* See the Pew Hispanic Center website: www.pewhispanic.org.

11. "Key Issues for Hispanic Voters Include Education, Economy and Health Care," Survey by the Pew Hispanic Center conducted between April 21, 2004, and June 9, 2004. See www.pewhispanic.org.

12. Sidney Weintraub, "NAFTA Evaluation," *Issues in International Political Economy* 8 (August 2000), Two Page Report for the Center for International and Strategic Studies.

13. See Paul Lamy, André Tremblay, and Victor Armony, "Values, Culture and the Economic Integration of Latin America and North America: An Empirical Perspective on Culturalist Approaches," paper presented at the XXIV International Congress of the Latin American Studies Association, Dallas, Texas (March 2003).

14. Peter L. Berger, "The Cultural Dynamics of Globalization," in *Many Globalizations: Cultural Diversity in the Contemporary World*, ed. Peter L. Berger and Samuel P. Huntington (Oxford, UK: Oxford University Press, 2002), 1–16.

15. Huntington, "The Hispanic Challenge."

16. For another set of statistics showing the remarkable ability of Hispanics to adapt to mainstream United States, see "Changing Channels and Crisscrossing Cultures: A Survey of Latinos on the News Media," conducted by the Pew Hispanic Center between February 11, 2004, and March 11, 2004. See www.pewhispanic.org.

17. See Rodolfo O. de la Garza and Louis DeSipio, eds., *Muted Voices: Latinos and the 2000 Elections* (Lanham, MD: Rowman & Littlefield, 2005). The authors make the argument that the influence and power of Latinos has to be measured state by state. Of the states they analyze, Texas and Arizona are perhaps the two with the most conservative political structures where the Hispanic challenge is likely to draw the most resistance.

18. Alexis De Tocqueville, *Democracy in America*, translated by Henry Reeve (New York: Colonial Press, 1900).

19. "The 2004 National Survey of Latinos: Politics and Civic Participation," conducted by the Pew Hispanic Center and the Kaiser Family Foundation between April 21, 2004, and June 9, 2004. See www.pewhispanic.org.

Religion and Art

The Santa Fe Art Controversy
About the Imprint of Our Lady of Guadalupe

JANICE SCHUETZ

☞ IN LATE FEBRUARY OF 2001, THE INTERNATIONAL FOLK ART MUSEUM of Santa Fe, New Mexico, opened an exhibit entitled, "Cyber *Arte*: Tradition Meets Technology." Alma Lopez, a Los Angeles artist, created a computer-generated image of a dark-haired woman wearing undergarments of roses and a blue cape. Underneath her feet was a crescent moon held up by a bare-breasted woman. A bright aura of sunshine radiated from the woman's body. The visual depiction carried the rhetorical imprint of Our Lady of Guadalupe. According to Roman Catholic tradition, this image originally appeared on the cloak of Indian Juan Diego during an apparition of the Virgin Mother in Mexico City at the shrine of Tepeyac in 1531. The religious icon has served as a cultural inspiration for the Catholic faithful of Mexico for centuries. It is also a powerful image for Catholics in the United States and Central and South America.

The opening of the Santa Fe exhibit of four cyber artists generally met with little controversy. The exception was Alma Lopez's feminist representation titled *Our Lady*. Her digital art created a furor, especially among Hispanic Catholics, who lashed out at the museum in general and Lopez in particular for what they called "blasphemy" of a sacred icon (Constable 2001a). Opponents asked for the resignation of the director of the Museum of New Mexico, a public apology from its board of directors, and demanded the museum close the exhibit. The conflict about the sacred image and Lopez's secular, feminist depiction raged on for eight months. In an effort to reach a compromise between protestors and the artist, museum officials eventually closed the exhibit in October of 2001.

Controversial depictions of the Virgin Mary are not new. Lopez previously had exhibited several feminist depictions of the Virgin in Los Angeles galleries with little negative public response. But several months before the Lopez controversy, a New Mexico artist was forced to take down a portrayal of a golden-haired Barbie doll virgin and remove it from an exhibit at Our Lady of Guadalupe Church in Santa Fe, and an artist at the Brooklyn Museum of Art smeared a depiction of the Virgin Mary with elephant dung (Constable 2001c).

The controversy about *Our Lady* at the International Folk Art Museum played out in public demonstrations that created a media drama in which religious leaders and church members butted heads with the Board of Regents of the Museum of New Mexico and civic leaders. The archbishop of Santa Fe, Michael Sheehan, as well as priests and lay leaders of the diocese, asserted religious rights to protect the sacred image. These protestors characterized Lopez's depiction as "insensitive," "lesbian," and "blasphemous." In an attempt to respond to dissenters and the resulting unfavorable press coverage, Lopez defended herself on Internet websites. She claimed she had a personal right to "relate to her [the Virgin of Guadalupe] in my own way." A conservative religious group based in Pennsylvania, the American Society for the Defense of Tradition, Family, and Property, added their support to protestors by writing thousands of letters in support of closing the exhibit. Artistic allies supported Lopez through her Internet messages (Lopez 2001a). This media spectacle of the conflict became the number one news story of 2001; at first, it dominated the front pages of state newspapers, and later made headlines in the *New York Times* and *Los Angeles Times*. The controversy also resulted in local television programs, extensive Internet communication, public meetings, political lobbying, and numerous demonstrations near the Santa Fe Museum where the work was on exhibit. The dissidents included thousands of religious devotees to Guadalupe, and the defenders of Lopez included advocates for artistic freedom and Chicana feminist artists.

This essay investigates the media's portrayal of the controversy by (1) showing how this controversy challenged a traditional artistic imprint, (2) explaining the strategies of the disputants, and (3) identifying the way the civic leaders managed the conflict.

Art Imprints

Divergent sacred and secular rhetorical imprints of Our Lady of Guadalupe created this controversy. Carl R. Burgchardt (1985) developed the construct of rhetorical imprints to explain how patterns of discourse develop through the legacy of a public spokesperson. Burgchardt's construct of an imprint can be expanded to include the artistic images and stories of Our Lady of Guadalupe that have been transmitted by religious leaders through the centuries. An imprint contains a surface structure of visual characteristics accompanied by a deep story structure that interprets the meaning of the visual image. In ways similar to the rhetorical imprints found in other public persuasion, the Guadalupe image and story are a prototype that informs the subsequent production and reception of this iconic image (441). The imprint functions as "an indelible stamp" that manifests itself in each depiction of the image. The manifestation of the imprint has "psychological, persuasive, and social significance" for the creators and interpreters of the image (441). The artistic imprint of Guadalupe has a recognizable "rhetorical personality" that unifies the image and connects it to a sacred story recognizable to those in the religious community (453). This artistic imprint is an iconic representation of a sacred personage that contains recurring features that can be reproduced or appropriated for both sacred and secular purposes.

The imprint of Guadalupe serves a variety of functions for interpreters. For millions of Catholics, the image is a source of veneration, pilgrimage, and prayer. Others view the image as a goddess symbol of feminine power (Cisneros 1998). Some claim Guadalupe is an emblem of hope, protection, and liberation for Hispanic people. For political revolutionaries in Mexico and the United Farm Workers in California, Guadalupe symbolized political power. For some Hispanic feminist writers, the imprint symbolizes the power and strength of Hispanic women (Rodriguez 1994).

The Theological Imprint

The origin and history of the Guadalupe image and story inform contemporary interpretations and suggest the essential motifs of the religious imprint. The religious tradition of Guadalupe claims that in 1531 the Virgin Mary appeared to a young peasant Indian named Juan Diego at Tepeyac, the location of an ancient shrine to Aztec goddesses located near present-day Mexico City. The story has a four-part structure: First, Diego hears beautiful singing and a bright cloud appears to him atop Tepeyac hill. Then a voice summons Diego to come near. A young woman, whom he later recognizes as the Virgin Mary, identifies herself to Diego and promises to help his native people if the bishop builds a temple on the hill there. Part one then features the motifs of apparition and promise. Next, the Virgin asks Diego to go to the bishop and request that he build a church in honor of the Virgin Mary. Diego relays her message to the bishop, but the church leader does not believe Diego's story. Diego returns to the Virgin and reports that his mission has failed. The Virgin asks Diego to try again, even though he claims that a messenger with more importance and nobility would be more persuasive than he is. Part two emphasizes the motifs of the church-native people relationship. Third, even though Diego's second encounter produced no response from the bishop, the Virgin told him to return. But Diego was unable to return, since his uncle was very ill and he had to find a priest to minister to him. On his way to find a priest, the Virgin appeared a third time and told Diego that his uncle was cured and that he should go to the top of the hill at Tepeyac to find a rose bush, pick the roses, and put them inside his cape as a sign of the spiritual favors granted him. Part three features the motifs of roses as an expression of miracles performed by the Virgin for the native people of Mexico. In the final part of the story, Diego found and picked the roses, placed them inside his cape, and took them to the bishop. When he loosened his cape to drop the roses, the image of the Virgin appeared on his cape. Part four emphasizes the fulfillment of the Virgin's promise and the religious devotion of Juan Diego and his people. A church was built on the site of the apparition and religious authorities believe the image was the reason many native people converted to Catholicism and gave up their Náhuatl beliefs. The original apparitional image on Diego's cape, according to tradition, has not decayed even though its imprint is on fragile material. The image hangs in the Basílica de Nuestra Señora de Guadalupe in Mexico City, the third church constructed on the site of the apparition. Despite the well-chronicled story of the apparition, this sacred imprint has been the source of theological and political dispute for centuries (Brading 2001).

The symbols and the color of the image are significant to the imprint. The image is of a single olive-skinned young woman with her face bowed and her hands folded and pointed upward as in prayer. She wears a red gown covered by a blue turquoise cloak adorned with gold stars. Her reddish colored gown is rolled up at the bottom to reveal a crescent moon held up by a winged, boyish angel. Sunlight radiates from her body and sometimes a crown appears on her head.

Miguel Sánchez published the first major theological interpretation of the Guadalupe story and image in 1648 (Brading 2001, 359–79), using a method of biblical interpretation called "topology" to provide a detailed explanation of the Guadalupe image. Topology systematically compares the Guadalupe image and story to verses and images found in the Old and New Testaments. Sánchez explained that Guadalupe was an image of the Virgin Mother of Scripture in the form of the apocalypse, that is, "a woman clothed with the sun and the moon at her feet, and on her head a crown of twelve stars, a young woman radiant with life" (Revelations 12:1). He claimed further that Juan Diego was the new Moses and Tepeyac referred to a new Mount Sinai in Mexico. For him, Guadalupe was the new Eve, as well as the symbol of the Christian and political presence in Mexican culture. Sánchez supported the Spanish conquest of Mexico by claiming that the Guadalupe apparition was a divine sign that Mexico was blessed by God and destined to be governed by Spain. He noted that the moon at the Virgin's feet symbolized pre-Christian Mexico, the stars on her cloak represented the Spanish conquerors, and therefore Guadalupe showed the Aztec religion was to be replaced by Christianity and the rule of Spain. Specifically, Lafaye (1976) claims that Sánchez is responsible for "the 'invention' of the Mexican Guadalupan tradition" (244).

Sánchez's interpretation underwent a variety of modifications. Brading (2001, 11) notes, "The changes in the way the Virgin has been presented and interpreted reflect the equally profound changes wrought in Mexican society across the centuries." Some subsequent interpretations focused on numerology and the meaning of the number of stars and the number of points on her crown. Others concluded the cloak imprint was not a miracle but a baroque painting by an Indian artist of the imprint of Our Lady from Estremadura, Spain (Lafaye 1976, 238–40). Still others tried to prove the image by scientific means and to disprove the historical existence of Juan Diego and the apparition. Despite challenges by many scholars to this religious tradition, millions of contemporary Catholics still accept the theological interpretation offered by Sánchez. The participation of so many people in the Santa Fe protests in 2001 demonstrates the importance of the image and the apparition story to contemporary New Mexico Hispanic Catholics.

The Goddess Imprint

Even though Sánchez's interpretation remains the dominant sacred interpretation, goddess connections to the apparitions of Guadalupe surfaced centuries before in accounts of Mexican scholars in the late eighteenth century (Gonzales 1980; Castillo 1996; Brading 2001). Goddess interpretations in scholarship in the United States achieved prominence in the 1960s when anthropologists and historians provided explicit analysis of the prehispanic era in Mexico (León-Portilla 1962, 1963, 1969). Feminists applied further interpretations to Guadalupe as an image of womanly strength and power (Gonzales 1979, 1980; Rodriguez, 1994, 1997).

Goddess interpretations of Guadalupe emphasize the Aztec motifs of the visual imprint. Patricia Harrington (1988) provides a typical explanation of the goddess imprint of Guadalupe. She claims that the Spaniards replaced the "terrible devouring goddess" of the Aztecs with "a benevolent, nurturing and inspiring" image of the Virgin Mother (27). Guadalupe is both a religious and a secular image that justified the Spanish conquest and the "destruction of Aztec temples and statues" and then enforced the slavery and then the conversion of the native people to Christianity. In this interpretation, the Guadalupe visual imprint combined the symbols of the fertility goddess Tonantzin with the benevolent Virgin Mary of Christian tradition. The Guadalupe icon combined the goddess of the Aztecs with the new Eve, mother of Jesus of Scripture. Harrington says, "the symbols of sun and moon that appear in the painting, and even the colors used, are universal elements of religious symbolism that had special significance for the Aztecs." Moreover, Harrington claims that the symbol of a goddess was the moon, the sun represented by the "solar cult in Aztecs," and the flowers symbolized divinity for the Aztecs (34). She agrees with the interpretations of Bernal Díaz del Castillo and Fray Francisco de Bustamante that an Indian painted the religious image on the cloak in the late sixteenth century in order to combine Christian teachings with Aztec cosmogony symbols (Lafaye 1976, 240–41). Because the Guadalupe imprint syncretized the Aztec and Christian female religious images, this made it easier for Catholic clergy to convert the native people to Christian beliefs and practices (León Portillo 1962; Lafaye 1976; Brading 2001).

Strategies of Disputants

At the center of the controversy over Lopez's cyber-art depiction at the International Folk Art Museum was the meaning of the Guadalupe image. Does the imprint provide sacred and secular evidence? Do the motifs suggest a religious icon, or an appropriation of the meaning for personal or political purposes? Is the authority of religious or feminist interpretation more credible? The disputants opposing and supporting Lopez grounded their evidence in Guadalupe motifs, justified their positions by divergent authorities and appeals to rights, and promoted a heated public debate about the relationship among religion, culture, and art.

Evidence

The evidence for both the protestors and Alma Lopez and her allies resides in the image motifs of the Guadalupe imprint. Evidence refers to the information on which the conclusions are drawn. The press published the Lopez image many times as part of their extensive coverage of the controversy. Table 1 shows that Lopez's depiction has similarities to the image in the Basilica in Mexico City.

TABLE 1: Image-Story Imprint

Basilica Image	Lopez Image
Blue cloak	Blue cloak
Crescent moon	Crescent moon
Angelic figure holding a moon	Angelic figure holding a moon
Solitary brown-skinned woman	Solitary brown-skinned woman
Rose image motif	Rose image motif
Title, "Our Lady"	Title, *Our Lady*
Storied interpretation of motifs	Storied interpretation of motifs

The Basilica imprint depends on Sánchez's biblical interpretation, and Lopez's image contains several recognizable features of the visual imprint. Her appropriation of the surface structure of the "sacred" imprint without the deep structure of the religious story is the main reason that religious protestors charged Lopez with blasphemy. They believed that Lopez desecrated Guadalupe's sacred image by imposing a secular and sexualized image. Lopez's conversions of the evidence (or perhaps "perversions") of the evidence of the visual imprint appear in table 2.

TABLE 2: Differences in Image and Story

Basilica Image	Lopez Image
Face downturned, humility	Face upturned, defiance
Hands folded in prayer	Hands on hips, assertive
Feet concealed	Feet exposed
Boyish cherub	Bare-breasted female
Yellow moon	Black moon
Stars on cloak	Aztec architecture on cloak
No roses on Virgin's body	Roses present in undergarments
Fully covered body	Exposed body
Covered head	Exposed long black hair
Apocalyptic motifs	Aztec goddess motifs
Miracle motif	Doubting motif
Promise motif	Challenge motif
Devotion motif	Assertion motif

The imprint of Guadalupe appears in the surface structure of both the Basilica image and story. Lopez mimics this image but replaces the apparition with her personal story. She converts the humble, passive virgin into a defiant, assertive, sexualized female constructed from pictures of Lopez's personal friends. Lopez replaces the apocalyptic motifs of Scripture with the physical features of what she considers to be empowered bodies of contemporary Hispanic women. While observers have sufficient visual clues to recognize the imprint of Guadalupe in the surface structure of Lopez's cyber art, they also find feminist, lesbian, and political motifs in the deep structure of the imprint. According to the press coverage, Lopez's conversion of the imprint for some produces a blasphemous interpretation of a sacred, devotional imprint and, for others, a strong Hispanic woman (Lee 2001d, March 24, A1; 2001d).

Methods of Arguing

The differences in the evidence of the image also contribute to divergent methods of arguing. Many of the arguments reported in the media were taken from the Internet debate between protestors and Lopez. One of the main spokespersons for the Santa Fe protesters, Juan Villegas, justifies the image as a sacred icon because its meaning derives from church traditions and centuries of religious devotion and veneration toward the image. Alma Lopez justifies her digital art by explaining that her work is her personal interpretation and that it extends the feminist interpretations of Guadalupe by Sandra Cisneros. The Internet debate between community activist Juan Villegas and artist Alma Lopez emphasized the divide between sacred and secular interpretations of Our Lady in the Santa Fe controversy. Villegas explains his interpretation in this way:

> How can you transformed [sic] a fifteenth century "sacred" image of our blessed mother into a millennium [sic] century man-made object? What you consider "devotion" in this type of art is not what my generation was taught by our parents, grandparents, and ancestors. . . . Our Indio-Chicano-Mexican religious beliefs, customs, traditions, principles, and value system is part of an entire Nuestra Señora de Guadalupe story. Our sacred images and religious symbols is [sic] the foundation of our faith and belief systems in place and should not be taken advantage of. (Lopez 2001b)

Villegas justifies his argument based on the authority of the traditional interpretation (similar to that given by Sánchez) and its expansion by church and political proclamations, the historicity of the divine apparition and the Basilica tradition, and the religious rights of New Mexico Catholics to religious interpretation of the imprint. Lopez's response to Villegas presents her justifications of the meaning of the Guadalupe imprint. She says,

> *Our Lady* image is based on an essay titled "Guadalupe the Sex Goddess" by Sandra Cisneros . . . I feel that essay, as well as my image, are attempts by Chicanas to find personal connections with the image that we grew up with. I portray Our Lady as a strong Indígena/Chicana/Latina/Mexicana, and not as the young passive (head bowed with clasped hands) image that I grew up seeing in my home and in my community. The reason for this is because all the women I have known in my family and in community are very strong mujeres who struggle to nurture and provide for families. I wanted to honor and respect their strength . . . I portray the angel carrying her on the half moon nude because men and women are beautiful children of our creator . . . When I see women's breasts I think of how beautiful they are . . . My two friends who collaborated with me on this image are strong and beautiful women whom I respect and admire. (Lopez 2001b)

Lopez claims her deep structure interpretation comes from feminist writer Cisneros rather than from a theological source. The argumentation for both the protesters and Lopez starts with the evidence of the imprint. However, the justifications of the disputants reside in a deep structure from different stories and authorities who provide radically different meanings for Guadalupe.

Issues

Several secondary issues about culture, gender, and rights influenced the media portrayal of the controversy. The cultural issue generally centered on the differences between traditional religious Hispanic culture and contemporary feminist interpretations of personal cultural experience. The gender issue focused on the male-dominated church and its attitudes toward women's bodies, and the rights issue stressed the legitimate but incompatible rights of both the religious and artistic communities.

CULTURE AND COMMUNITY STANDARDS

According to the press accounts, the public expects that their tax-supported artistic displays will reflect the local culture and community standards. One of the disputed issues was: What is Hispanic culture and to what extent is ethnic culture connected with traditional religious belief? According to press accounts, many of the protestors brought together cultural and religious beliefs in their reactions to Lopez's digital image. Richard Medina claimed, "Our culture is under attack." "Catholics, especially Hispanics, regard the Virgin Mary as their own mother," added Anthony Trujillo, and therefore "a picture (of the Virgin) dressed in a bikini is therefore offensive" (McKee 2001b). Other protesters echoed this cultural sentiment. For example, Richard Cordova noted, "I don't like to see my mother trampled on, I am insulted" (Lee 2001c, March 24, A1).

News reports claimed that those who supported the exhibit viewed the conflict as a reflection of the strong religious commitments of New Mexico Hispanics. For example, a volunteer at the Folk Art Museum said "We want to see that the sentiments the artist had in mind are presented. The people involved (in the protest) are very traditional, and I can appreciate that. I think they also need to understand that everyone does not have the same approach" (Lee 2001b, March 24, A1). But Frank Ortiz, a former U.S. ambassador and a member of the Folk Art Museum's Board of Regents, as well as a Catholic, concluded that the people of Northern

New Mexico are primarily traditional Catholics so the museum should have anticipated the conflict. He noted, "There is a school of thought that Catholic icons are fair game for far-out interpretation." The decision to include this work is insensitive "for a public museum in a community of deeply held beliefs" (Constable 2001a). The press reports stressed that the controversy had two legitimate but opposing positions. The Santa Fe art community has a stake in artistic freedom, and the religious beliefs of the majority of citizens also play a role in the culture and traditions of the community.

One approach to community standards is to look at opposing viewpoints as the press accounts did. When audiences have a high degree of ego involvement with a subject anchored in strongly held reference group values, their propensity to accept messages that deviate from these values is low (Sherif, Sherif, and Nebergall 1965). On the other hand, audiences with low degrees of ego involvement and weak anchors in reference groups can be easily persuaded. Both the religious dissenters and supporters of Lopez had strong reference group values that created divergent interpretations of Lopez's representation of Guadalupe. Press reports recognized that these opposing but strongly anchored reference group values led to a polarized conflict in which both sides were unwilling to accept each other's values.

Another press interpretation of the art-religion controversy recognized that marginalized groups find voice in public arenas through their artistic works. McKerrow (1993) claims traditional art (including religious images) emphasizes "social realism," abstains "from social comment," and thereby fails to acknowledge the forces of social change at work in society (356). Artists dissatisfied with society use their artistic work to challenge the normative standards of a community. The media reports concluded that she failed to convince most of the Hispanic religious community that her contemporary representation was a legitimate reconstruction of a traditional and highly valued imprint. Lopez simply underestimated the commitments and beliefs of the Santa Fe religious community and overestimated her own reputation. In her Internet messages, Lopez explained that art accepted by the religious community is a symbol of the domination and control of the church and that her new art represented a voice from oppressed Hispanic women (Spohn 2001). Re-imprinting and re-storying of a cherished image can be a vehicle for social change or at least an indication that artists seek participation in social reform. This goal is not achieved when a majority of the community resists the work of an artist as many protestors did in Santa Fe (Constable 2001g).

The question of whose reference groups and beliefs would prevail fueled the press coverage of the controversy. Some parties to the dispute believed that traditional religious values were only a smokescreen for the real issue, which was deep resentment in the Hispanic community about being trampled on by outsiders from the art community who took over their cultural celebrations and sought control over the community even though they had no sense of local history or tradition. Because Alma Lopez was an outsider from Los Angeles, to some extent she was a scapegoat for some of the negative feelings of New Mexico Catholics. According to press reports, the controversy was not only about religion but about cultural preservation (Gurza 2001). Some artists found the effort to dismiss religious values as offensive. For example, artist Pedro Romero claimed the entire exhibit was a mockery of the New Mexico Hispanic tradition of home altars. He explained that the museum's exhibit was set up as a devotion to technology. He led a group of protestors who desecrated the exhibit in which Lopez's depiction resided by placing tires, toilets, and sanitary napkins in the exhibit hall. His guerrilla act of ridicule, he said, was "a postmodern cultural intervention" that would challenge the museum's attempt to "thrust its ideological wedge into Hispanic cultural identity" and to "resist the museum's imperialist agenda to confuse and ideologically divide and conquer this (religious) identity." The museum quickly removed the distasteful objects and publicly labeled the actions of Romero and his followers as "an act of intimidation" (Constable 2001e). The issue about which community standards and whose values should prevail promoted rather than resolved the conflict.

GENDER

Is the Virgin of Guadalupe a religious or a goddess icon? According to some press accounts this question was at the center of the debate (Lee 2001c, March 24, A1; Lee 2001c). Lopez's depiction was entitled *Our Lady*. The name itself achieves what Kenneth Burke calls entitlement; that is, communicators (like artist Lopez) decide which words they wish to feature. By entitling their art, they reveal the motives that underlie the meaning of their work. Lopez clearly wanted to emphasize "Our" and "Lady." "Our" referred to Lopez's personal feminist perspective. "Lady" referred to contemporary Hispanic women with feminist values similar to her own.

Lopez says, "She is everyone's virgin . . . This is an image I have grown up with. She is everywhere in my home and my community. The idea for me was to relate to her in a way that was empowering . . . There are so many women like me. I'm not the only one who has seen her this way" (Constable 2001c). In subsequent justifications of her depiction of Guadalupe, Lopez claimed, "I have a right to relate to her in my own way. After all, doesn't she belong to everyone? Isn't everyone's relationship with their creator/god/virgin, a personal relationship?" (Lopez 2001b). But the exhibit did not mean the same to many Hispanic women in Santa Fe as it did to Lopez. For example, in a letter to the editor of the *Santa Fe New Mexican*, Juliana Sánchez wrote, "The digital photograph of Our Lady in a bikini is not exactly an interpretation of strong woman . . . It is a mockery. It is the insult of insults to the very depth of her dignity" (2001, "Letters"). To the protestors, the traditional religious meaning entitled the "Virgin of Guadalupe" as an object of devotion and Christian meaning was not for the personal and political meaning of the artist.

Another element of the deep structure of the digital imprint was Lopez's emphasis on the importance of women's bodies. According to the press accounts, Lopez's digital depiction sought to venerate women's bodies. Lopez explained, "I see this woman's legs and her belly and the angel's breast, and I don't see anything wrong" (Gurza 2001). She also criticized church leaders for not focusing on a woman's body in the same way she does. Lopez noted the importance and value of pictures of nurturing bodies and beautiful breasts and wondered how church representatives "see bodies of women." Lopez inquired further by saying, "I wonder why they (churchmen) think our bodies are so ugly and perverted that they cannot be seen in an art piece in a museum" (Constable 2001a). Lopez clearly understood that her entitlement of the body and of her subjective experience was very different from the entitlement the Santa Fe religious community had given to "the Virgin of Guadalupe" as a spiritual figure, the mother of God, the apocalyptic virgin of Scripture, and an iconic image for devotion. According to media reports, the more the religious protestors understood Lopez's perspective, the more they challenged her right to re-imprint the traditional image for her own personal goals (Constable 2001d).

RIGHTS

Who has the right to interpret Guadalupe? Should a state-funded museum feature artistic representations that offend community standards? Clearly,

both the protestors and the artist have the right to make personal interpretations, and the museum has a right to show the controversial depictions.
As the controversy progressed, Lopez used the press to respond to the protestors. She voiced her opinions about the embodiment of women in the
imprint and later explained that the imprint was made from nude photos of
two women friends, Raquel Salinas and Raquel Gutiérrez (Constable 2001c).
The more Lopez elaborated the secular nature of her artistic re-imprinting
and her personal motivations, the more she offended the religious community. The press reported the extent of this offense by publishing many letters
from religious protesters (2001, "Letters").

During the controversy, the press featured the views of the religious
dissenters more than they did the supporters of Lopez. For example, the
Santa Fe newspaper featured Archbishop Michael Sheehan, the religious
figurehead of the Archdiocese of Santa Fe, who claimed Lopez's depiction
of Guadalupe was "insulting, even sacrilegious, to the many thousands
of New Mexicans who have deep religious devotion . . . I wish those who
want to paint controversial art would find their own symbols to trash and
leave the Catholic ones alone" (Constable 2001b). Other members of the
Hispanic Catholic community were also covered. For example, Henry J.
Casso stressed, "We have a right to stand up for what we believe . . . Artists
may have the right to express their opinions, but they do not have a right
to publicly offend those who have brought this devotion to us since 1531"
(Constable 2001a). Others also felt that the issue involved respect for the
theological meaning of imprint. Ana Consuelo Matiella claimed, "The traditional Hispanic Catholic community also has a right to express its out-
rage, grief, and feelings of disrespect [toward the Virgin of Guadalupe]"
(2001). The picture of posters containing phases such as "blasphemy is
not art" accompanied many front-page stories. Pictures of this type summarized the viewpoint of the religious protestors and gave a justification
for their demand that the museum remove Lopez's representation of Our
Lady of Guadalupe.

Although the press gave more attention to the religious than to the artist's viewpoint, several articles acknowledged the rights of the museum.
For example, one story quoted Executive Director of the Civil Liberties
Union Peter Simonson who concluded, "The museum has every right to
display provocative and controversial art, even if some see it as an insult
to their religious beliefs." This story also noted that Joyce Ice, Director of
the Museum of International Folk Art, claimed that "a lot of people are

interested in coming to their own conclusions about the piece and don't want people to tell them what they should see or not see" (Barol 2001b).

Sorting out the issues helped the press to explain the nature of the controversy and show why it would not abate until Lopez's image was removed from the museum. According to the press, neither the protestors' nor Lopez's argumentation resolved the problem of deep-seated and divergent interpretations of the Guadalupe imprint. Instead of creating understanding between the adversaries, the task of resolving the conflict was turned over to a Sensitive Materials Committee appointed by the director of the Museum of New Mexico. This committee issued a formal statement that gave the impression that the conflict over the imprint was being successfully resolved in May of 2001. After the museum issued its statement, however, the protests continued, and protestors and artists remained divided about the imprint and its meaning for the community (McKee 2001a; Navrot 2001).

Managing the Controversy

How should a community manage conflict between hundreds of protestors, one artist and her allies, and officials of the Museum of New Mexico? According to media accounts, continuous protests exacerbated the problem for public officials. The conflict could not be resolved in a political forum, although some state legislators threatened to cut off funding of the museum if the entire exhibit was not removed, and the governor of New Mexico proffered that the exhibit should remain open (Barol 2001c). The conflict was not a matter to be decided legitimately by the courts, even though Juan Villegas and other protesters tried to get a court order to open the meetings of the museum's Sensitive Materials Committee to the public. After this exhibit had closed, Judge James Hall issued a statement that the museum had violated the Open Meetings Act by not holding hearings prior to the displaying of Lopez's version of Guadalupe. He recommended that in the future culturally sensitive works of art must be reviewed prior to the time they are placed on exhibit in a state-funded museum. Although a museum review committee for Native American art had been in place for many years, the decision to create a new one for Hispanic art infuriated some members of the Santa Fe art community (Eller 2002). This wasn't a matter for church leaders to decide either, since the exhibit was funded by public money and presented in a public museum. Nor was this a matter for the artistic community to decide, since Hispanic artists were divided on the appropriateness of Lopez's depiction of Guadalupe.

The press claimed that the director of the museum should take responsibility for dealing with the conflict. The obvious strategy, according to the media, was that museum officials had to address the public about their efforts to resolve the conflict, express regret, and appease angry legislators so they would not follow through with their threatened cuts of public funding for state museums. The press reports emphasized that the director of the museum, Tom Wilson, recognized the political, cultural, and economic implications of the conflict. He took immediate action, including hiring a professional mediator, conducting five public meetings, giving reaction to the press about the protestors' rallies and desecration of the exhibit with images of waste. He promoted the Sensitive Materials Committee and eventually sanctioned the release of a report by that committee about how the International Folk Art Museum would deal with the Guadalupe conflict and other conflicts between art and religion in the future (Constable 2001e; Wilson 2001). Whether or not these strategies led to a mutually agreeable resolution to the dispute is questionable. Parties involved in the controversy did not seem to know who the mediator was or what the outcomes of the mediation were. The public meetings provided opportunities for disputants to air grievances and express opinions, but those attending the public meetings and the reports of the newspapers agree that most of the speakers and the audiences opposed Lopez's depiction. Giving people an opportunity to give voice to grievances leaves the impression that public officials cared about the conflict. The Sensitive Materials Committee decided to continue showing Lopez's depiction of Guadalupe even though they promised to close the exhibit four months early (Constable 2001f).

In the end, the Sensitive Materials Committee held eleven closed meetings and issued a final report in an effort to resolve the controversy about Guadalupe. Although the press did not publish the report in its entirety, it did present large segments of the report and refer readers to the complete report on the museum website. The findings of the report justified and defended the policies of the museum. According to the final report, the committee reviewed all policy and mission statements, the codes of ethics for U.S. museums, and hundreds of statements given at public meetings (Wilson 2001, 3). The report predictably concluded that the museum dealt "in good faith and compliance" with their mission, acknowledged the "depth of feeling and emotion" on the issues, and made clear that the museum "meant no disrespect in exhibiting nondevotional or secular art that presents ideas derived from religious imagery"(5). The report also developed new policy claiming that, in the future, the museums of New Mexico would "encourage greater responsiveness to cultural and religious sensitivities"(5).

In a rather patronizing statement, the report then concluded that the conflict had been very productive for the religious protestors because "the image has come to symbolize all challenges to faith in the secular work, and as such, the image has become a focus for passionate dedication of religious faith through protest." This statement acknowledged the religious values that contributed to the conflict and at the same time tried to put a positive spin on the conflict by claiming it had helped the faithful understand their own values. Finally, the director made a public apology, concluding that the museum had "presented the art of one segment of the community that has offended another." The final statement of the report was a public criticism of the protestors, who have created a "climate of intimidation," and the report blamed both the religious community and the free speech advocates while absolving the museum's personnel of any blame (Constable 2001f; Baker 2001; Wilson 2001).

The press reported that the Sensitive Materials Committee listed positive actions that the museum had taken to try to resolve the conflict. This public relations maneuver was an attempt to validate the practices of the museum and its curators and appease politicians. It attempted to show the good faith effort that the museum officials had used to resolve the conflict and, by implication, showed the public that the museum deserved future tax dollars for their public sensitivity and effort on behalf of the local community. The source of these arguments of self-defense and self-promotion was Joyce Ice, the director of the Folk Art Museum where Lopez's cyber art hung. Ice noted that the following steps had been taken to resolve the conflict: (1) Panel discussions were held on the opening day of the exhibit; (2) after the controversy started, the museum placed a warning that some objects might disturb viewers at the front of the exhibit; and (3) the museum curators wrote explanations of selections of art and invited a church person to write a statement to be placed with the artwork. By highlighting certain parts of the report, the press emphasized that the museum officials were not avoiding the conflict, but were committed to their original position that controversial art must remain in public museums (Constable 2001f; Baker 2001; Facteau 2001; Wilson 2001).

Conclusion

The press represented the controversy about Our Lady of Guadalupe as rooted in deep-seated differences between the religious and artistic communities about their respective interpretations of sacred and secular art. This essay concludes that it is common for artists to appropriate the surface structure of a common visual imprint. The artist incurs a significant risk, however, if he or she alters the imprint in ways that appear to ridicule the dominant cultural beliefs and religious authority as Lopez did. Although the press reported the controversy over Our Lady of Guadalupe as a conflict between religion and art, these reports did not explain why the appropriation of some of the surface visual structure without the theological deep structure was the source of the conflict. The press did report that Lopez appropriated familiar visual aspects and gave personal and sexual interpretations to Our Lady of Guadalupe. She challenged the deep theological structure, the story of the apparition that gave religious meaning to the image for thousands of New Mexico Catholic taxpayers and patrons of the International Folk Art Museum.

Artists create controversy when their work questions the religious values of the majority of the population it is supposed to serve. In controversies about religion and public art, disputants take positions that reflect their own deeply held values and beliefs. As a result, the community often is unable to deal effectively with these controversies through standard political, legal, and religious forums. Just as in the Santa Fe controversy, a public figure or agency has to assume responsibility so the museum will not become a scapegoat for the inability of the religious and artistic community to resolve its deep-seated differences about who has a right to interpret a religious imprint, what the imprint means, and what constitutes a legitimate artistic appropriation of the imprint. The majority of artists, including the other women whose art shared the exhibit with Lopez, re-imprinted the Guadalupe image icons in creative ways using unusual media that reinforced the religious visual and storied imprint of Guadalupe. Lopez, however, overtly appropriated the religious images for personal goals anchored in feminist values. By using the traditional title for a radically new image, Lopez offended many New Mexico Hispanic Catholics.

Other conflicts about religion and art likely should follow similar patterns of resolution in cases when the evidence of the religious visual imprint and story are used by artists to serve personal and secular purposes at odds with the values of the majority of patrons and taxpayers who support museums. The press thrives on reporting stories about difficult-to-manage conflicts, and their coverage of Guadalupe was no exception. The press created an eight-month-long serial drama that attracted the interest of readers, making it the top story of the year with more coverage by the New Mexico press than the 9/11 terrorist attacks. The extensive coverage of the protestors helped this part of the religious community draw public attention to their beliefs and, at the same time, gave free publicity to Alma Lopez, the museum exhibit, and her feminist agenda. In this way the press presented the religion-art conflict as a win-win situation. The press also concluded that the New Mexico museum established reasonable new policies to prevent offense or establish an official channel for dissent. Although dissenters representing the traditional religious position continued to challenge the new policy and challenge Lopez's digital image, the press concluded its coverage of the controversy by reporting that the museum had done its best to appease the protestors and reduce the potential for future conflicts between public art and the religious beliefs of the community. In doing so, the press tried to assure the public that conflicts of this magnitude would not occur in the future. When the museum closed the exhibit, four months early, the press ceased its eight-month serial drama about the controversy.

References

Baker, D. 2001. "Committee Recommends Controversial Work Remain on Exhibit," *Associated Press*, May 22, BC cycle.

Barol, J. M. 2001a. "'Our Lady' Art Unrobes Icon and Unleashes Parish Protest," *Albuquerque Tribune*, March 22, A1.

———. 2001b. "'Our Lady' Protest Has Raised Exhibits' Profile, Officials Say," *Albuquerque Tribune*, March 28, A5.

———. 2001c. "'Our Lady' Forum Sharp, Emotional," *Albuquerque Tribune*, April 2, A1.

———. 2001d. "Vehement Feelings Flow from Orderly Gathering," *Albuquerque Tribune*, April 17, A1.

———. 2001e. "Parish to Appeal Decision to Keep 'Our Lady' Displayed," *Albuquerque Tribune*, June 15, A3.

Brading, D. 2001. *Mexican Phoenix: Our Lady of Guadalupe: Image and Tradition across Five Centuries.* London: Cambridge University Press.

Burgchardt, C. R. 1985. "Discovering Rhetorical Imprints: La Follette, 'Iago,' and the Melodramatic Scenario." *Quarterly Journal of Speech* 71:441–46.

Castillo, A. 1994. *Massacre of the Dreamers: Essays on Zincanisma*. Albuquerque: University of New Mexico Press.

———. 1996. *Goddess of the Americas: La Diosa de las Américas, Writings on the Virgin of Guadalupe*. New York: Riverhead Books.

Cisneros, S. M. 1998. "A Woman of No Consequence: Una mujer cualquiera." In *Living Chicana Theory*, ed. C. Trujillo, 78–86. Berkeley, CA: Third Woman Press.

Constable, A. 2001a. "Catholics Protest Depiction of Virgin Mary," *Santa Fe New Mexican*, March 24, A1.

———. 2001b. "Artist Lopez Speaks on Virgin Controversy," *Santa Fe New Mexican*, March 27, B1.

———. 2001c. "'Our Lady' Only Latest in String of Art Controversies," *Santa Fe New Mexican*, April 1, A3.

———. 2001d. "The Debate Rages On," *Santa Fe New Mexican*, April 17, A1.

———. 2001e. "Committee Nears 'Our Lady' Decision," *Santa Fe New Mexican*, May 15, B1.

———. 2001f. "Museum Shortens Stay for 'Our Lady,'" *Santa Fe New Mexican*, May 25, A1, A2.

———. 2001g. "Other Cyber Artists Discuss Opposition to Bikini-Clad Virgin," *Santa Fe New Mexican*, October 25, B1.

"Critics Slam Collage of Virgin in Bikini." 2001. *Los Angeles Times*, Times Wire Service, April 17, A1, A14.

Eller, P. 2002. "'Our Lady' Court Order Hogties Art Museums," *Albuquerque Journal*, February 17, B3.

Facteau, L. 2001. "Gov.: Art Should Remain," *Albuquerque Journal*, April 7, E3.

Gonzales, S. 1979. "La Chicana: Malinche or Virgin." *Nuestro* 3:41, 42, 45.

———. 1980. "La Chicana: Guadalupe or Malinche." In *Comparative Perspectives of Third World Women: The Impact of Race, Sex and Class*, ed. Beverly Lindsay, 229–50. New York: Praeger.

Gurza, A. 2001. "Our Lady of Controversy," *Los Angeles Times*, May 27, E6.

Harrington, P. 1988. "Mother of Death, Mother of Rebirth: The Mexican Virgin of Guadalupe." *Journal of the American Academy of Religion* 56:25–50.

"Hearings Required on Controversial Art, Judge Rules." 2002. *Santa Fe New Mexican*, January 6, B3.

Janofsky, M. 2001. "Uproar over Virgin Mary in a Two-Piece Swimsuit," *New York Times*, March 31, A11.

Lafaye, J. 1976. *Quetzalcóatl and Guadalupe: The Formation of Mexican National Consciousness, 1531–1813*. Trans. B. Keen. Chicago: University of Chicago Press.

Lee, M. 2001a. "'Lady' Debate Continues," *Albuquerque Journal*, March 24, A1.

———. 2001b. "Museum to Hear 'Lady' Debate," *Albuquerque Journal*, March 24, A1.

———. 2001c. "From Lady to Lightning Rod," *Albuquerque Journal*, April 5, A1.

———. 2001d. "Decrying, Defending 'Lady,'" *Albuquerque Journal*, April 17, A1.

———. 2001e. "Museum Asks Patience of 'Our Lady' Critics," *Albuquerque Journal*, May 18, A1.

———. 2001f. "'Our Lady' Protests Planned," *Albuquerque Journal*, May 25, A1.

León-Portilla, M. 1962. *The Broken Spears: The Aztec Account of the Conquest of Mexico.* Trans. L. Kemp. Boston: Beacon Press.

———. 1963. *Aztec Thought and Culture.* Trans. J. E. Davis. Norman: University of Oklahoma Press.

———. 1969. *Pre-Columbian Literature in Mexico.* Trans. G. Boanov and M. León-Portilla. Norman: University of Oklahoma Press.

"Letters to the Editor." 2001. *Santa Fe New Mexican*, April 4, A7.

Lopez, A. 2001a. "The Artist of 'Our Lady.' Latino Culture USA." Commentary available at www.almalopez.com/ORemail/emo41401.

———. 2001b. "L.A. Artist Alma Lopez Fights for Chicana Creativity." www.chicanas.com/alma.html.

Martinez, C. 2001. "Letter to Editor," *Santa Fe New Mexican*, April 4, A7.

Matiella, A. C. 2001. "Ignorance and Lack of Intention No Excuse," *Santa Fe New Mexican*, April 15, F1.

Matovina, T. M. 1997. "New Frontiers of Guadalupanismo." *Journal of Hispanic/Latino Theology* 5:20–36.

McKee, J. 2001a. "Protestors Say They Will Continue to Fight Until Museum Takes Down 'Our Lady,'" *Albuquerque Journal*, May 27, A1.

———. 2001b. "Persevering Against Picture," *Albuquerque Journal*, May 27, B1, B5.

McKerrow, R. E. 1993. "Visions of Society in Discourse and Art: The Failed Rhetoric of Social Realism." *Communication Quarterly* 42:355–56.

Navrot, M. 2001. "500 Protest 'Our Lady' Art," *Albuquerque Journal*, July 1, A1, A8.

Rodriguez, J. 1994. *Our Lady of Guadalupe: Faith and Empowerment among Mexican-American Women.* Austin: University of Texas Press.

———. 1997. "Contemporary Encounters with Guadalupe." *Journal of Hispanic-Latino Theology* 5:48–60.

Sánchez, J. 2001. "Letter to the Editor," *Santa Fe New Mexican*, April 4, A6.

Sherif, C. W., M. Sherif, and R. E. Nebergall. 1965. *Attitude and Attitude Change: The Social Judgment Approach.* Philadelphia: Addison Wesley.

Spohn, L. 2001. "Whose Lady Is She?" *Albuquerque Tribune*, April 20, D1.

Steele, T. J. 1982 [1974]. *Santos and Saints: The Religious Folk Art of Hispanic New Mexico.* Santa Fe: Ancient City Press.

Wilson, T. 2001. "Recommendations from M.N.M.'s Committee on Sensitive Materials," May 22, press packet in author's possession.

Unbraiding Stories About Law, Sexuality, and Morality

MARGARET MONTOYA

⮑ IN MARCH 2002, I WAS HONORED TO BE INVITED TO BE A MEMBER of the Chicana Caucus Plenary at the annual meeting of the National Association of Chicana/Chicano Studies (NACCS) held in Chicago, Illinois. The panel, entitled "*Destejiendo Pasiones*: Speaking Desires," also included Alma López, the Los Angeles artist. The panelists were asked to talk about sexual identity and sexuality.

The following is an essay based on the talk I presented, and it is inspired by the controversy that embroiled the exhibition of Alma López's painting *Our Lady*, Nuestra Señora de Guadalupe. *Our Lady* is shown wearing undergarments of roses and is held up by an angel with prominent bare breasts. The exhibit at the Museum of International Folk Art in Santa Fe, New Mexico, was called "Cyber *Arte*: Tradition Meets Technology." It opened on February 25, 2001, and was curated by Tey Mariana Nunn, one of the few Chicana museum curators in the country and included the artwork of four Chicana artists.

A vocal portion of the local Catholic community in Santa Fe called the painting "an abomination" and "a sacrilege." Virtually all of the protesters identified themselves in the media as Chicanos/as or as *hispanos/as*. Alma López was excoriated by the local archbishop, who claimed that the Virgin Mary was depicted as a "tart" and described her garment as a "bikini." Backed by the archbishop, the local people organized large protests against the decision to include Alma's painting in the exhibit, sought the resignation of the museum director, asked for a public apology, and initiated legal and political challenges to the exhibition. Eventually, several state legislators made statements threatening the funding of the museum.

Three named plaintiffs, all men, sued under the state Open Meetings Act demanding an injunction to force the museum to remove the exhibit. The Open Meetings Act allows citizens to have access to the decisionmaking processes of government agencies and requires government entities, such as boards and committees, to provide notice to the public about meetings and about the agenda items that are to be taken up at the meeting. The plaintiffs alleged that "both the decision to display the exhibit by the curator and the decision not to remove the exhibit by the Sensitive Materials Committee were in violation of the [Act]." Specifically, the plaintiffs were alleging that the decisions were made without notice to the public and an opportunity to be heard. Judge James A. Hall of the First Judicial District Court in New Mexico concluded that the curator's decision is not a policy decision covered by the Open Meetings Act but the Sensitive Materials Committee is a "delegated authority" and therefore must comply with it. However, the relief requested—the injunction—was not available under the act and so the lawsuit was eventually dismissed.

As is often the case in this country in the twenty-first century, public controversies can end up in the courts. I want to use Alma Lopez's images of Our Lady of Guadalupe to think critically about what's moral or immoral and what's good or evil. I want to focus on the effect that sexuality has on our ability to link art with religion. I want to reflect on how to connect art with the moral lives of women. I am examining our ability to use imagery to give expression to a complex notion of spirituality, specifically, a spirituality that is expressed through art and uses both religious and sexual symbols.

Alma's courageous art has caused an impassioned but truncated debate among Catholics in New Mexico and, more importantly, her work has sparked important conversations within our *familias, entre nuestras tías y las comadres* (families, among our aunts and godmothers). Chicano Catholics in Santa Fe vilified Alma and Tey Mariana Nunn, the curator of the museum exhibit, for including Alma's painting in an exhibition at the Museum of International Folk Art in Santa Fe, New Mexico. Some members of the Chicano community claimed that those of us Chicanas who are educated and those of us who defend Alma's art have broken our ties with the community. They assert that we don't speak for the Chicano community. I think we need to confront this charge.

The debate becomes one about ownership: Who can lay claim to Nuestra Señora de Guadalupe? Whose icon is she and who can control how she is represented? The institutionalized church says we Chicanas can't have her, and we certainly can't have her if we dare envision her as fully woman. We must submit to the idea that she is not anatomically correct; she has no breasts, no nipples, no pubic hair, no vagina, and no erogenous zones. Under that *túnico* she wears, some would have us believe that she has the body of a Raggedy Ann.

Alma's work insists upon a spirituality that is animated by transgression. Her work makes us come to terms with different forms of repression. Here is the representation of a Guadalupana who, having emerged out of colonialism, offers us a clear choice: she has been and is, for the patriarchal, colonizing church, a figure of docile and silent submission. Or she can be, for us, a survivor, a woman of experience who understands and values autonomy, agency, and desire because these values are hard won. Alma's art is an act of resistance, an envisioning of an icon consistent with Alma's life experiences. We, too, must resist the church's attempt to re-colonize this iconic figure.

I have learned important lessons through sexuality, lessons about good and evil, about passion and compassion, about humanity and divinity, about the secular and the sacred. My most important moral dilemmas often centered on my sexuality. Many of us have had to learn painstaking lessons about loyalty, secrets, boundaries, health and sickness, fertility, life and death through our sexuality and desire. Many of us have faced sexual assault or sexual abuse, unwanted pregnancies, abortions, miscarriages, sexually transmitted diseases, sexual harassment and every form of dysfunctional relationship, whether heterosexual or same sex. Those of us who are older admit to a wisdom that has been won, to a significant extent, through sexual experience. My self-esteem, always fragile, has been paid for by hard lessons of the heart and of the soul and of the body.

Alma's representation of a Guadalupana with a woman's body allows for a spirituality and a religiosity that integrates our sexuality with our morality. A mature sexuality is not one-dimensional, regardless of our orientation. Our lives are not a continuum from child *vírgenes* to chaste mothers to de-sexed *abuelas*. For me, Alma's art confronts and challenges this myth maintained by the organized church.

Theorizing a coherent code of mature and moral sexuality is an urgent concern for us as Chicanas. Many, if not most of us, have been raised in families with ties to Catholic beliefs, especially those teachings about what it means to be a good girl and a good woman. From my experience, the educational and professional success of Chicanas, whether straight or queer, depends on coming to terms with our sexuality. Many Chicanas decide to leave school all along the pipeline from middle school to doctoral programs because we as a community have failed to deal in a mature way with sexuality. Chicanas are left to their own devices to deal with unplanned pregnancies, abortions, contraception, STDs, and, for our lesbian sisters, all of the pitfalls of coming out to families and friends. How many of us who are now professors have listened to the stories and wiped the tears of our Chicana students whose graduate studies are complicated or interrupted or disrupted because of issues of sexuality. Mostly, we all deal with these issues with heavy silences and whispered solutions.

We must break this silence. We should initiate an ad campaign that identifies those of us who have had abortions, those of us who have survived sexual abuse or sexual assaults, those of us who love other women. This ad campaign should emphasize that our responses to sexuality are moral ones. Good and moral women have abortions, good and moral women experience and sometimes overcome sexual exploitation, good and moral women use contraception, good and moral women enjoy sex with other women. In the past, we have surrendered this debate about good and evil to the organized church, and we must reclaim it. That is the power of Alma's art.

Coming to terms with my sexuality has been a difficult struggle for me personally. It's been a collective struggle for LatCrit and for NACCS as academic communities and it continues to be an issue as well for the society in which we live. How sexuality is negotiated is an important measure of an individual's, a community's, and a society's maturity. The Catholic Church has some growing up to do with respect to sexuality and the current scandals over the widespread child abuse in the church are evidence of that.

Concientización. There is no adequate translation for this concept. For me it has meant developing a consciousness about the inequalities of power, whether racialized, gendered, or monetized. Today I am calling on us to develop *una concientización sexual*, a mature morality that integrates our sexuality.

Traditional doctrine insists that we tame sexual desire by pretending that goodness and Godliness are defined by celibacy and abstinence. But the church is simply wrong to insist that we accept a theology that negates and silences and suppresses a central part of our lives. To the extent that we believe in a life after death, many of us have won a chance at Heaven not by denying and suppressing our sexuality but by struggling to develop our capacity to experience joy through sexual desire and to honor the responsibility of not generating misery for ourselves and others through that capacity.

The genius of Alma's art is that it suggests that we can be saved through our sexuality, not in spite of it. That is at the heart of the controversy. Thank you, Alma, for vindicating our struggles and for representing la Guadalupana in a way that links our sexuality with beauty and joy here on earth and with redemption in the Hereafter.

Conclusion

The Mystical Roots of American Political Democracy: Social Justice and Religious Belief in a Newer World

TIMOTHY A. CANOVA

☞ THE SPIRIT OF GUADALUPE IS A MYSTICAL SPIRIT AND, LIKE ALL mystical spirits, needs no cleric or religious authority to mediate between mortal and Divine.[1] It is said that in December of 1531, some fourteen years after the arrival of Cortez, an Aztec Indian named Juan Diego first saw the apparition of the Virgin of Guadalupe.[2] Historians may debate whether Juan Diego even existed, but all agree that news of his Guadalupe sightings swept Mexico and transformed its religion and its politics. Within a few years, millions had converted to the Cross and centuries later peasants in Hidalgo's uprising and soldiers in Zapata's army carried the banner of the Virgin of Guadalupe with them into battle.[3]

The Guadalupe is not the only Christian or Catholic mystical spirit. Other apparitions of the Madonna have been reported around the world, perhaps most notably in Fatima, Portugal.[4] These and other such myths held close by millions of believers suggest a power within to transcend earthly limitations, observe the unobservable, and experience union with God,[5] central tenets of all mysticisms, from the Orishas of Africa to the Sufi mystics of Islam and the Kabbalah of Judaism.[6]

As one Sufi scholar has written, mysticism is at the heart of all religions: "Just as a river that passes through many countries and is claimed by each as its own is still only one river, all mysticism has the same goal: the direct experience of the Divine."[7] There are times when the mystic river runs weak, when it is kept alive by a relatively few seekers and believers. At other times it is a mighty river that sweeps through history and through the lives and beliefs of countless men and women, it transforms our arts and institutions.

As this volume well demonstrates, religious mysticism has served for centuries as powerful inspiration for human creativity. Perhaps the ebb and flow of the mystic river correlate with currents in our arts, sciences, and politics as well. In some of the arts—the graphic, visual, performance, and literary arts—a theory of mysticism as art is rich in shared experience. More difficult to see, yet no less important, is the development of a theory of mysticism as motive force in our arts of statecraft.

This essay suggests a view of mysticism as nonsectarian, nondogmatic, inspired belief in political and social equality. It is contrasted with the exclusivist, intolerant, and ego-driven thought systems of religious and secular fundamentalisms. By seeing all men and women as capable of achieving enlightenment through direct experience of union with the Divine, mysticism more easily embraces a politics of tolerance and social justice.[8]

Realists are fond of saying that politics is an art, the "art of the possible."[9] The range of what's possible is often constrained by elite consensus and ideological dogmas, all that casts doubt on democratic capabilities.[10] If so, then expanding the boundaries of the possible may await a renewed mystical faith in shared common interests that transcend the aggregation of our private interests, a whole that's greater than the sum of our parts.

In recent years, the pendulum has swung far from the mystical. Instead, a pernicious kind of fundamentalism has held sway: the idle worship of the free market.[11] As with any religious orthodoxy, today's market fundamentalism demands that narrow doctrine be accepted as truth and that its rites be practiced by others.[12] Perhaps its first commandment is that there be no leading role for the state in mobilizing and redistributing society's resources.[13] Market fundamentalism thereby limits the range of the possible. Public discourse is narrowed, debate is limited, and mystical narratives and values are atrophied by neglect. Our ideas of what's possible and of what's necessary are never fully influenced by wider currents of thought, feeling, and shared experiences.[14] As a result, ordinary people fail to aggregate their political preferences, let alone see the range of shared possibilities. The flow of popular political action is damned.

If the art of politics is a kind of performance art writ large, practiced mostly by those with influence and resources, then perhaps our social progress and political renewal will demand a wider, more inclusive participation in politics in the future. Perhaps there is room for mystical belief to motivate people to assume their political roles in the drama of shaping the future.

The mystical spirit—whether Catholic, Gnostic, Sufi, or other—promises to sanctify the individual's soul.[15] But in a time when the sacred is increasingly marginalized by the profane, it is uncertain whether any mystical spirit can purify the body politic by mobilizing ordinary people in the cause of freedom and the hope of social justice. Perhaps the answer depends in part on our collective memory and belief in a mystical heritage, and in our imagination and belief in a mystical future.

The Mystical Roots of American Political History

All religions seem to share common purposes and core attributes.[16] September 11th and its aftermath forced us to focus on the outward differences between religions. Around the world, we have witnessed the clashing of major religions—Islam, Christianity, Judaism, Hinduism, and others.[17] Yet the more compelling differences may be those that cut across all the major religions—namely, the divide between mysticism and fundamentalism.[18]

The mystical tradition in each religion is characterized by the search inward for God, and therefore a liberal respect for the religious paths of others.[19] This tolerance stems from a supremely mystical faith in the sanctity of each individual's search for God unfettered by the dogmas or dictates of clerics. Whereas the fundamentalist preaches exclusivity and literal adherence to rites and ancient texts, the mystic values the peace and freedom to meander on his or her own path to the Divine. Perhaps it is the individuality of the mystic's spiritual quest that leads to tolerance and curiosity about the paths of others.[20] Or maybe it's the mystical view of man created in God's image and therefore endowed with natural rights and unlimited potential.[21] Whatever the complex of causes, mysticism is generally seen as less dogmatic and more tolerant than fundamentalist modes of belief.[22]

This mystic tolerance should not be confused with a hands-off, laissez-faire, libertarian political philosophy.[23] Mysticism should be seen as compatible with an activist philosophy that seeks to redress injustices and contemplates discipline and balance within the self, as well as within the community.[24] Within all mysticisms—whether it be Sufi mysticism, traditional Hawaiian mysticism, Judeo-Christian mysticism, or the mysticism within musical subcultures—that balance within the community is suggested by a deep concern for the well being of one's neighbors and ideals of social justice.[25]

The Gnostics were the egalitarian mystics of early Christianity. In the fourth century, they were suppressed by the church orthodoxy so severely that all traces of their gospels were eradicated for fifteen hundred years.[26] The Gnostics found expression in dance, which they promoted as a kind of active governance of the self, a disciplined transcendence and spiritual exercise that brought the mystic closer to God and God to the mystic.[27] The "whirling dervish" is perhaps the most visible example of the Sufi seeking union with the Divine through the ecstasy of peak experience.[28] But for the dervish to feel the freedom to whirl presupposes a sense of security in the surrounding environment, a sense that those around him mean him no harm.[29] That kind of balance in the community and security in the individual necessarily rests on the material preconditions of social justice and mutual tolerance.

American political history was born in a time of religious ferment and enlightened skepticism.[30] The founders elevated the ideals of religious tolerance and separation of church and state into political and constitutional tradition.[31] The revolutionary period was a time when the mystic river was cresting in American society. According to the historian Gordon Wood, in *The Radicalism of the American Revolution*, the institution that best embodied the egalitarian ideals of the American Revolution was freemasonry, a fraternal religious order with mystical beliefs and rituals.[32]

Freemasons were anticlerical and antimonarchy. The most significant segment of American society excluded from freemasonry was the Tories, the colonial allies of the British monarchy. But the door was open to most other propertied white males. Membership in Masonic lodges grew suddenly in the mid-eighteenth century, swept through the colonies, and included many revolutionary leaders.[33] Freemasonry encouraged a globalization of spiritual sensibilities by carrying the republican banner against monarchy and religious orthodoxy. It crossed borders, provided a space for alliances to form, and by calling for a new order resting on "brotherly affection and sincerity," it served as the "surrogate religion for an Enlightenment suspicious of traditional Christianity."[34]

Freemasonry was imbued with Enlightenment values. By way of example, the words and symbols of the National Civic Association, a Masonic-inspired, post–World War Two community association, attest to such idealistic beliefs. Along with the image of an anchor, a mystical symbol of hope, and the words "Liberty, Fraternity, Equality, Humanity," its letterhead includes the spiritual command of Isaiah and the hope of any participatory democracy: "Come, let us reason together."[35]

The importance of freemasonry in the radicalism and egalitarianism of the American Revolution cannot be overstated.[36] Although the revolution itself was disruptive to the organizing of Masonic lodges, it also revitalized the movement. In the decades that followed, freemasonry "exploded in numbers, fed by hosts of new recruits from deeper levels of society": it brought together men from divergent occupations, social ranks, and even religions, and united them around a common belief in a social equality based on merit, rather than inherited privilege. As Wood concluded, "Masonry transformed the social landscape of the early Republic."[37]

In such a milieu of mystical ferment, it is not surprising that many in the revolutionary generation believed in a Divine Justice and egalitarian principles grounded in natural law.[38] The Declaration of Independence reflected this mystic and humanistic sentiment in grandly pronouncing that "all men are created equal" and endowed with natural rights to "life, liberty and the pursuit of happiness."[39] Even the British historian Norman Cohn, critical of "revolutionary millenarianism and mystical anarchism," traces such mystical and egalitarian "fantasies" to "the ancient-world idea of an ideal state of nature, in which all men are genuinely equal and none is persecuted."[40]

In contrast, every fundamentalism claims exclusivity, that its path to salvation is the one and only path. Such intolerance is not compatible with notions of universal equality and justice. And without a natural right to justice or freedom, those who stray from the fundamentalist path are seen to be less deserving of each.

Fundamentalist thinking, whether religious or secular, may for some time avoid the dangers of anarchy and revolution that some claim are implicit in mystical commitments to universal justice, but it also leads to the ossification of social institutions and classes, the reproduction of orthodox hierarchies, and the entrenchment of illegitimate privilege.[41]

The American Revolution represented a giant step forward for political freedom and social justice.[42] Wood suggests the mystical and spiritual contagion of the revolution when he claims that extension of the voting franchise to most adult white male citizens regardless of wealth or property qualifications "planted a germ which has gradually evolved, and has spread actual and practical democracy and political equality over the whole union."[43]

The mystical pull of freemasonry, along with an anti-Masonic backlash, would animate politics in America for another half century, at least through the age of Andrew Jackson.[44] Although Jackson is remembered by many for his extreme brutality to Native American Indians, his broad populist appeal among the voting white male population may have found traction in a society that was remarkably egalitarian compared with the old European order.[45] When freemasonry began to wane, a newer and less organized mysticism, the Transcendentalist movement, arose to capture the American imagination and stoke the fires of Abolition in the prelude to Civil War.[46]

Lincoln is perhaps foremost in the pantheon of American political mystics. The economic causes of the Civil War have been well researched by historians.[47] What is much harder to analyze are the qualities of faith and mystical belief that inspired Lincoln through the war's darkest days and held the Union together. Perhaps no other American president was so divinely inspired. Lincoln's farewell address to Springfield to assume the presidency reflects a faith in the mystic:

> I now leave, not knowing when or whether ever I may return, with
> a task before me greater than that which rested upon Washington.
> Without the assistance of that Divine Being who ever attended him, I
> cannot succeed. With that assistance, I cannot fail.[48]

Lincoln's view of democracy was based on mystical ideas of equality and freedom.[49] His abiding popularity among Union soldiers and his improbable landslide reelection during America's bloodiest war, suggest that Lincoln's mystic faith was contagious.[50]

Many dictators and tyrants have believed in their own divine inspiration.[51] What separates their false mysticism from the genuine mysticism of the democrat is ultimately political action and the values embodied in it. Lincoln's greatest acts embodied the ethics of the mystic. For all his flaws as a leader, and for all the criticisms that he moved too slowly, when seen from the vantage point of history, Lincoln was a bolt of lightning. In one presidential term, he issued an Emancipation Proclamation and pushed through Congress the Thirteenth Amendment that would finally open the door of freedom to a long-suffering slave population. No one can seriously doubt that enormous sacrifices—ultimate sacrifices—were made for the great mystic causes of freedom and justice and to restore the American political community's sense of balance.[52]

The economic historian Eliot Janeway argued that Lincoln "never organized the Union for victory; he was too practical to try. Instead, he inspired and provoked it to mobilize the momentum for victory. The result was inefficient but irresistible. A victory small enough to be organized is too small to be decisive."[53] Nothing less than the mass participation of the people was needed if the Union and perhaps democracy itself was to be saved for the future.[54]

Particularly in a democracy, such mass participation depends in large part on countless, invisible mystical relationships connecting ordinary citizens with each other and their elected leaders. As Janeway concluded, "During the war, people looked at the politician in the White House and they saw a person. They lived with the person and created an epic. The Lincoln epic produced a mystic force which disciplined democracy and generated the momentum for victory."[55]

Lincoln, like few leaders before or since, was able through the power of his words to inspire others to seek divine inspiration. Lincoln's first inaugural address was a call to action, to participate in the art and drama of the political moment, precisely because it was an appeal to the better angels, the mystic, in each American: "The mystic chords of memory," he said, "stretching from every battlefield and patriot grave to every living heart and hearth-stone all over this broad land, will yet swell the chorus of the Union when again touched, as surely they will be, by the better angels of our nature."[56]

The mystic chords of which Lincoln spoke were not between the living and any divine commander, but between past and present generations. Perhaps we experience union with the Divine when we discover the divine inspiration of our forefathers. Franklin Roosevelt spoke of the "mysterious cycle in human events."[57] Those generational cycles are the ebb and flow of the mystic river itself.

American history has also been marked by recurring periods of fundamentalist thinking, intolerance of other belief systems, and terrible and deep social injustices. We have been living for too long in such a fundamentalist moment in which mystical commitments to social justice have been routinely rejected as inviting anarchy, upsetting property rights, and otherwise undermining the rule of law.[58] This is the fundamentalism of the free market. The dominant ethos has been laissez-faire, individual gratification, and materialism alongside a doctrinaire intolerance for other economic belief systems.[59] While we can point to times of great social progress as mystical periods, the inverse may be easier to recognize. Times of intolerance and arbitrary power are often fundamentalist periods.[60]

Perhaps, to paraphrase Emerson, the mystical tradition awakens in times of terror.[61] When the fundamentalist momentum goes too far, religious faith is tested and the human spirit demands correction.[62] The terrors faced by the generation that lived through the Great Depression and World War Two certainly tested the religious and political faith of millions of Americans.[63] The country was ready once again for mystical leadership. Early in the twentieth century, a great influx of immigrants from Eastern and Southern Europe contributed to a strange resurgence in freemasonry.[64] Perhaps it's not surprising that Franklin Roosevelt's New Deal was all about relief and reconstruction. The basic tenets of freemasonry are "brotherly love, relief, and truth," "to make good men better" and thereby empower them to "create, build, and sustain" their communities.[65]

A great leader follows, though a step ahead. Franklin Roosevelt seemed to understand his role from the beginning. The historic 1929 collapse of the stock market, a global economic depression, and one out of four Americans without work, without unemployment compensation, and the poor, the sick, and the aged without support. Prior to Roosevelt, relief and reform were prevented by the free-market fundamentalist dogmas of his own day. But the American people longed for spiritual and moral leadership, and Roosevelt recognized that the presidency was "preeminently a place of moral leadership."[66] As Supreme Court Justice Felix Frankfurter concluded at the time, Roosevelt had led Americans "out of a period of deepening economic and moral deterioration by invigorating the forces of democracy."[67]

Franklin Roosevelt's New Deal was based in large measure on mystical values and beliefs.[68] When Roosevelt spoke for "the forgotten man," he articulated mystical principles of equality, social justice, and balance within the community:

> What do the American people want more than anything else? To my mind they want two things: work, with all the moral and spiritual values that go with it; and with work, a reasonable measure of security

. . . Work and security . . . These are the spiritual values, the true goal toward which our efforts of reconstruction should lead.[69]

In his first term, Roosevelt called for a "broader definition of liberty" to provide "greater security for the average man."[70] Social Security and a host of other New Deal relief programs did just that. The New Deal employed millions of Americans in building schools, hospitals, post offices, libraries, public parks, infrastructure projects, flood control, reforestation, and other conservation programs. In addition, the federal government provided work for struggling actors, artists, and musicians, and created part-time jobs in colleges and universities that helped students complete their education.[71] Full employment of human resources and fulfillment of human potentials were the goals, if not yet the universal reality.

Two presidential terms later, Roosevelt called for a new world order based on "four essential human freedoms—freedom of speech and expression, freedom of worship, freedom from want, freedom from fear."[72] The Four Freedoms completed Roosevelt's mystical redefinition of liberty by balancing the concept of liberty with social justice.

Roosevelt's approach—"bold, persistent experimentation"—was suggestive of the eclecticism of the mystic.[73] He liberated policy from the ideological dogmas of a pre-Keynesian free-market fundamentalism,[74] and borrowed instead from sometimes divergent economic theories and philosophical traditions.[75] Roosevelt's trial and error approach may have lacked intellectual consistency, but people saw action and, as a result, their confidence was restored.[76]

Under Roosevelt's leadership, instead of a narrow free-market rationalism that justified the pursuit of self-interest, there was a more mystical rationalism that understood the common enemies and common needs of the American people.[77] Relief and Social Security were rationalist responses to the suffering and dislocations of modern society. They also reflected a mystical belief in man, a humanistic ethic that Hemingway captured in *For Whom the Bell Tolls*, his 1940 novel of the Spanish Civil War that took its title from lines written by John Donne in 1623: "No man is an island, entire of itself; every man is a piece of the continent, a part of the main . . . any man's death diminishes me, because I am involved in mankind, and therefore never send to know for whom the bell tolls; it tolls for thee."[78]

According to Janeway, Roosevelt followed the war president epic of Lincoln. Whether by design or by accident, this cycle of history was completed. Perhaps both Roosevelt and Lincoln were divinely inspired during a time of great national crisis and yearning. Roosevelt too understood that the war his generation faced would be won on the home front and that the participation of the American people would push it forward faster than he could lead it. Throughout the war, Roosevelt "looked to democracy and not to leaders, to democracy's reservoir of mass energy and faith and not to the custodians of specialized wisdom."[79]

This religious faith in man, an ageless optimism that it is never too late "to seek a newer world,"[80] was perhaps best articulated by Roosevelt when as a candidate on the eve of his first election to the presidency he spoke of the unity arising out of people's many and diverse hardships and suffering:

> Out of this unity that I have seen we may build the strongest strand to lift ourselves out of this depression. . . . To be the means through which the ideals and hopes of the American people may find a greater realization calls for the best in any man; I seek to be only the humble emblem of this restoration.[81]

This restoration in every man became more urgent, more compelling, and politically possible with America's entry into war. Mobilization would provide the means. Roosevelt, like Lincoln, was too practical to micro-manage a wartime mobilization. What Janeway said of Lincoln also held true for Roosevelt: "A victory small enough to be organized is too small to be decisive."[82] The American war effort was decisive because it was anything but small; it was simply the greatest economic and military mobilization in human history.[83] Approximately 16 million Americans served in the Armed forces during World War Two, and about 12 million were in uniform at the war's peak.[84] For the first and perhaps only time in American history, full employment was a reality. There was no involuntary joblessness; anyone who wanted work could find work quickly.[85] The U.S. civilian unemployment rate fell to 1.2 percent, factories worked in double and triple shifts, and steel mills operated at 120 percent of what had been their estimated capacity.[86] The success of the American mobilization suggests that it is social democracies, not liberal democracies, that are most effective in waging war and maintaining the peace.[87]

At the height of the war effort, the federal government was training millions of Americans, not just for combat, but for support roles, including in such strategically important languages as German, Russian, Chinese, and Japanese.[88] America's immigrant populations contributed to these efforts. Americans of German, Italian, and Japanese descent proved their loyalty by giving of themselves and often their lives to the U.S. war effort. On the land, on the sea, and in the air, the war literally turned on the ability to crack enemy codes.[89] With massive armies of translators and cryptographers monitoring German, Japanese, and Italian codes and large volumes of communication traffic, America's foreign language and intelligence capabilities proved decisive in winning the war in only four years; and then winning the peace with highly effective occupations and reconstructions of Germany and Japan, unfortunately in stark contrast to the present long war and perhaps "perpetual war" efforts in Iraq and Afghanistan.[90]

Lincoln and Roosevelt did more, of course, than provide inspiring words. Each used politics to expand the art of the possible, to mobilize people into action, provide them with the financial resources they needed to play their democratic roles in the dramatic moment and participate in shaping history. For both mystic leaders, these were mobilizations "of the people, by the people, for the people."[91]

When Lincoln had trouble financing the Civil War, he turned to Congress to pass legislation to create the greenback, a direct issuance of $450 million in currency by the Treasury Department—something completely unheard of at the time, completely successful in financing the Northern war machine, and yet never to be followed again on such a grand scale.[92] Roosevelt's Treasury, lacking such authority, was expected to borrow from the so-called creditor class. So Roosevelt simply did what would be the unthinkable for the next generation of free-market fundamentalists: he forced the Federal Reserve to purchase government debt securities at whatever price necessary to keep interest rates pegged at near zero for Uncle Sam.[93] Finance capital had to bend to the needs of industrial capital; old wealth had to accommodate the needs of the present and the hopes for the future.

Janeway's description of Franklin Roosevelt as "the supreme artist of power" seems apt.[94] The Federal Reserve's independence was effectively suspended from 1941 to about 1951.[95] With the federal government demanding massive resources, and spending and borrowing on a far grander scale in relative terms than today,[96] the Federal Reserve was forced to channel credit away from consumer borrowing, homebuilding, and speculative uses such as stock market purchases.[97] Finally, with monetary policy neutralized, the administration found other ways to keep prices impressively stable, including wage and price controls to prevent price gouging and limit inflationary expectations, and bond sales to the public and high marginal tax rates on the top tax brackets to restrain private consumption.[98]

This "pegged period" of finance and the related system of price controls are often criticized for restricting people's economic freedoms and contributing to shortages and black markets in certain goods. But the system of controls provided the breathing space needed for the federal government to accomplish great objectives, from victory in World War Two to the Marshall Plan, which rebuilt war-torn Europe and Japan, and the G.I. Bill of Rights that provided education, housing, and employment opportunities for millions of returning U.S. veterans.[99]

Democracy, with all its faults and inefficiencies, was able to mobilize its resources—financial, industrial, technical, and human—more fully, more quickly, and more effectively than the fascist regimes in Germany and Japan during World War Two, demonstrating that there is no power on earth as strong as the mystical faith and energy of free people.[100]

Unfortunately, today's market fundamentalism rests on a kind of historical amnesia that ignores the financial practices (now considered heresies) that enabled the Union to prevail during the Civil War and that more than doubled the production of the U.S. economy during the four years of World War Two.[101] Lincoln's greenback and Roosevelt's control of Federal Reserve monetary policy both suggest that mystical faith, to be effective, requires political will and artistry to shape the course of human events. Even mystic ideals of liberty and justice must be supported in the here and now and at the level of the material and mundane. To unleash democracy's reservoir of mass faith and energy ultimately requires that financial resources be mobilized to enable willing citizens to participate in democracy's mystical calling.

The period spanning from the Great Depression and New Deal through World War Two, the Marshall Plan, and G.I. Bill was America's finest moment, the mystical moment gone global. The cause of freedom and equality swept up an entire generation.[102] The United States became the arsenal of democracy and a compelling model of social democracy at a time when democracy was most in peril.[103] Freedom was redefined to presuppose justice, justice to presuppose social security, and security rested on full employment of human potential, a job for every man and every woman to play a part in building the future.[104]

Generations since have become captives of fundamentalist thinking, with narrower definitions of liberty, and with far less faith in man.[105]

The Clashing Fundamentalisms

According to Erich Fromm, the monotheistic religions of the West drew strength from their claims to be the true faith,[106] claims that required respect for truth and rationalism, tolerance of others, and the flowering of belief into generally accepted normative values and ethical norms.[107] Fromm also recognized, however, that such claims of exclusivity could lead down the fundamentalist path of intolerance and contribute to the narrowing and freezing of religious doctrine by a clerical scholastic elite.[108]

It was the tolerant path—part of the mystical tradition—that permitted human progress by fostering the Enlightenment spirit of pride in reason and faith in man. If man is created in God's image, then it is rational to believe in man's unlimited potential and capacity for self-government. The amelioration of social injustices becomes enlightened self-interest; every step in the direction of a more inclusive, more perfect democracy requires its own contagion of enlightened and mystical belief in human potential and humanistic values.[109]

Critics of mysticism have claimed that it represents "a retreat from the realities of life into a purely subjective frame of mind which is declared to be more real than the plain evidence of our senses."[110] But others, including psychologists of faith and spiritual experience, say that mysticism is a step toward rationality and objectivity:

> [Mysticism] involves a far more acute awareness of the plain evidence of the senses than is usual, and that, so far from retreating into a subjective and private world of its own, its entire concern is to transcend subjectivity, so that man may "wake up" to the world which is concrete and actual, as distinct from that which is purely abstract and conceptual.[111]

Martin Lings, the great Sufi scholar, believed that the highest faculty in every human being is that of intellect, which includes a sense of transcendent realities.[112] Likewise, the early Gnostic Christians believed in the attainment of knowledge through innate and intuitive interpretation of images and experience,[113] a right-brain feminine approach that has been largely supplanted by the male linear thinking and orthodox fixation with written text and logic.[114]

Lings recognized that in modern times "intellect" has come to signify merely mental activity, "and since much of [that] activity is concerned with questioning the existence of the transcendent, many of the so called intellectuals are at the opposite pole from true intellectuality."[115] The modern skepticism with regard to spiritual knowledge has come at a high cost. There's more logic, but perhaps less wisdom and less practical intelligence. The idea of progress has been replaced by that of "realism," a word, said Fromm, that signifies "the utter lack of faith in man." Instead of believing in "Man" as a species with vast potentials, we now believe only in the ability of individual mortals to manipulate and flourish amidst the general decline of social morality.[116] This retreat to pessimism, Fromm warned, was propelled by the growing influence of the market.[117]

Market fundamentalism, like all fundamentalisms, stifles alternative views and agendas.[118] But its market ideology also reinforces a dangerous moral relativism that justifies commercial trade relations regardless of the levels of brutality and economic exploitation of any trading partners. It encourages the commodification of human relations and rewards the desecration of that which was once held sacred.[119] There are no values other than monetary values.

This moral relativism in market relations has arguably exacerbated the threat from Islamic fundamentalists who view American society as decadent and corrupt.[120] Market fundamentalism doesn't just clash with radical religious fundamentalism; it becomes a contributing factor. It dictates global financial and economic policies that are often associated with U.S. imperial aims, and also with deep and widespread economic hardship, fear, and social insecurity in much of the world.[121] It thereby creates vast social need and insecurity and a political and ideological vacuum that is often filled by religious fundamentalists.

Although concerns are often raised about the rise of Christian fundamentalism in U.S. politics,[122] the religious agenda has been relatively unsuccessful on a range of social and cultural issues where it might have contributed in a positive way to protecting human dignity from the commodification of market relations. For instance, with the globalization of new communication technologies, such as the Internet, cable and satellite television, the law of obscenity has been largely lost to an unregulated, global marketplace.[123] Instead of local community standards as the yard-stick, there has been a race to the bottom in public and private morals.[124] As audiences have gone global, the federal government has lost any meaningful role in defining obscenity standards.[125] Nation-states, weakened by the declining morals of the marketplace, seem powerless to harmonize minimum decency standards. Likewise, the breakup of the old Soviet Union and the collapse of currencies and job markets during the 1990s have undermined the security and wellbeing of women throughout Eastern Europe and East Asia, contributing to the trafficking of young women and girls for sexual exploitation. Market fundamentalism thereby encourages the commodification of sexual relations and an anything-goes morality in which the sacred is crowded out by the profane.[126]

The market fundamentalism of the West tolerates and even celebrates other obscenities. The cult of celebrity and the enormous riches bestowed upon entrenched elites suggest a society that has no sense of proportion or shame, no sense of shared responsibility or mystical balance.[127] Although today's vast inequities in wealth and power may not seem fundamentally Christian, they are not inconsistent with market fundamentalism.[128]

"Anything goes" is also the pattern in U.S. trade relations. How quickly we have forgotten the Greatest Generation's mystical, humane, and balanced approach, from prohibitions against trading with the enemy to sanctions against the Soviet Union and the divestment campaign against apartheid South Africa.[129] Instead, only a few years after the bloody 1999 crackdown at Tiananmen Square, the People's Republic of China was welcomed into the World Trade Organization. The U.S. trade deficit with China is already the largest bilateral deficit in history, and China is now one of our largest creditors.[130] It is unclear whether the point of the free trade agenda is to encourage real democratic change in repressive countries like China, or simply to undermine democracy in the West by squeezing unions and forcing back wages and pension benefits.[131]

Moral principles are now routinely sacrificed for commercial gain while the ideals of social justice and equality are marginalized by national governments and multilateral institutions. For instance, a major feature of the policy agenda of the International Monetary Fund (IMF) is that of central bank autonomy, a euphemism for agency capture, in this case by private bankers and financiers with an interest in keeping the public sector constrained and fiscal policy in check. While the autonomous structure of the Federal Reserve blatantly violates both the letter and spirit of the U.S. Constitution, the Supreme Court has repeatedly refused to rule on the merits, dismissing all challenges on narrow procedural grounds.[132] An autonomous central bank is the polar opposite of Roosevelt's de facto political control of the Federal Reserve that accommodated Treasury borrowing and wartime spending. It is not just undemocratic, but also anti-democratic by constraining the sovereign capabilities of the politically accountable branches of government.

A captured central bank, for all practical purposes, means an active monetary policy, that is, that short-term interest rates will be the sole weapon in maintaining price stability.[133] Other anti-inflation policies are surrendered, including voluntary guidelines and industry-labor accords at the national level, mandatory wage and price controls—or even just the threat of imposing wage and price controls—and antitrust enforcement in specific industries.[134] Moreover, an active monetary policy serves to neutralize fiscal policy. For instance, if fiscal policy is too expansive (i.e., too much government spending on physical and social infrastructure), then long-term interest rates will start rising on public and private debt alike. This prevents democracies from attempting any "mini–New Deals"[135] or any grand mobilizations as in World War Two, the Marshall Plan, and the G.I. Bill of Rights.

The IMF program, designed to keep inflation in check through an active monetary policy, exacerbates already weakened job markets and poverty conditions by privatizing state-owned assets and liberalizing trade in ways that are inherently unfair and destabilizing to Third World countries, but are often sweetheart deals for Western corporations. What's missing is any sense of equality, justice, or mystic balance. According to World Bank statistics, of the 4.7 billion people who live in the one hundred IMF and World Bank client states, about 2.8 billion people (or more than half the people living in developing countries) live on less than $2 a day; and about 1.2 billion people earn less than $1 a day. In addition, 1.5 billion people lack access to clean water supplies, and nearly 3 million children die each year from vaccine-preventable diseases. More than 113 million school-age children are not in school, with primary enrollment rates less than 50 percent in Sub-Saharan Africa. Life expectancy in developing countries is thirteen years lower than in developed countries; and there's been scant progress in infant, child, or maternity mortality rates.[136]

With such a record, one might expect some humility among financial and political elites concerning alternative policies. But unorthodox approaches are consciously ignored, even if they have proven successful in the past.[137] Among the market fundamentalists, there is the typical intolerance, the persistent belief that they have a monopoly on the truth and that no other perspective needs to be heard.[138] Historical references are dismissed as unscientific, inapplicable to modern conditions, or simply as "not realistic."[139]

The present global conflict pits a post-modern and soulless free-market fundamentalism against a pre-modern, Islamic fundamentalism.[140] There are some shades of gray to be sure, but these two fundamentalisms are the ideological powerhouses that suck the oxygen out of the air and close off alternative possibilities. The intellectual intolerance of each fundamentalism is matched by a cycle of dehumanization, from profound social neglect and the "collateral damage" of aerial bombardment to suicide bombings and macabre beheadings.[141]

The relationship between these two fundamentalisms is strangely symbiotic. The worst of each fundamentalism reinforces the backlash from the other.[142] For instance, the IMF's free-market dogma has resulted in severe economic and social conditions in such Muslim countries as Pakistan, Indonesia, and Turkey.[143] Quite predictably, these countries have cut back government spending on health programs, job training, and public education, and joblessness has risen sharply for young men in particular.[144] Meanwhile, the gas-guzzling SUV culture in the United States continues to buy enormous amounts of oil from a Saudi monarchy that has exported Islamic fundamentalism to countries like Pakistan and Indonesia by funding the madrassas and peasantrans that preach jihad against the West.[145] The austerity of market fundamentalism is met by the faith-based initiative of Islamic fundamentalists, and the mix has been explosive.[146]

This clash of fundamentalisms is not without its mystical possibilities. The most mystical moment of this generation was the morning of September 11th, 2001. As the magnitude of the horror unfolded on television, the whole world witnessed apparitions in the New York sky more disturbing than any seen by Juan Diego nearly five centuries earlier. Millions of people around the world felt shock and grief, and also mystical connections to each other. Others celebrated, and some Islamic and Christian fundamentalists saw the attacks as divine retribution for the sins of a decadent society.[147]

Public opinion polls recorded the mystical moment. According to a Gallup poll conducted ten days after the September 11th attacks, nearly

80 percent of Americans supported a military draft and military action against al-Qaeda.[148] The great reservoir of democracy's faith and energy was ready for mobilization. The richest and most powerful nation in history seemed suddenly awakened. In the painful mystical moment of September 11th, anything seemed possible.

Although the range of creative possibilities is limited by the faith and collective imagination of millions of people,[149] sometimes the more telling limits are those imposed by political elites and fundamentalist doctrines.[150] Sixty years ago after Pearl Harbor, the United States mobilized sixteen million Americans in uniform and many more tens of millions in civilian employment. In 2001, the United States had twice its World War Two population, untold potential and vast capabilities. Instead of a conventional army, perhaps the United States could have built a technologically advanced army, a massive force fluent in foreign languages such as Arabic, Urdu, Farsi, Turkish, and a wide range of other strategic languages. Not a bilingual nation, but "trilingual," willing to try anything lingual (perhaps Iraqi, Saudi, and other dialects of Arabic), and to do so on a grand scale, to better understand and engage the many cultural complexities raised by the confrontation of traditional societies with modernism and globalization.[151] Such a mobilization of the education and training of Americans would have altered consumption patterns, redirecting our spending from the consumption of imports to domestic production and the development of our declining infrastructure.

Instead of mobilizing the home front to mass produce tanks, warplanes, and aircraft carriers, imagine a home front mobilized for energy independence, high speed mass transit, border control, port security, detection of nuclear material, and the training of sufficient numbers of first responders. Instead of millions of Americans turning to drugs, languishing in prisons, or without any meaningful job prospects, imagine a role for every man and every woman willing to contribute to building a safer world.[152] Instead of a market fundamentalist model, imagine a full-employment model for many millions struggling around the world.[153]

At the critical September 11th moment, a moment of perceived maximum peril, the American public supported universal national service, but the political elites did not. Perhaps they were "realists" who did not believe in man or in democracy; certainly they did not believe there was much that could be done by a mobilized democracy. The message from President George W. Bush was clear: everyone's patriotic duty was to go back to business as usual, to take out their credit cards and continue shopping. Yesterday's mass consumption patterns and priorities would continue.

Such a complacent and self-satisfied approach could not have been more different from the mysticism of John Kennedy nearly forty years earlier: While campaigning for the presidency, Kennedy reminded Americans of their better angels:

> I want to be sure we haven't lost something important in this country, that we haven't gone soft, that we don't have so many cars and iceboxes and television sets that we just look to our own private interests and not to the welfare of the country. We who sit here today are the beneficiaries of millions of Americans who have fought and died and lived for this country to make it what it is.[154]

But in 2001 Americans were looking after their own private interests, and the man in the White House was the free market cheerleader-in-chief, without the pom-poms, but cheering on the bubble economy nonetheless. The housing bubble grew to more ominous heights,[155] the "shop till you drop" spending spree continued to be purchased on borrowed money (credit card debt and massive foreign purchases of U.S. government debt securities), and our largest creditors were now a corrupt communist China and a corrupt Saudi monarchy.[156] Our financial accounts, our monetary and spiritual values, and our karma all seemed increasingly out of balance.[157]

Only six months after September 11th, the Senate rejected proposals to raise automobile fuel efficiency standards. The Bush administration preferred to maintain loopholes that encouraged the sales of sport utility vehicles, Hummers, and other gas-guzzlers.[158] Not surprisingly, the average miles-per-gallon for cars sold in the United States actually fell in the years after September 11th.[159] Our dangerous dependence on foreign and Middle Eastern oil continues to this day.[160]

Two years after September 11th, a Gallup poll showed a complete reversal in public opinion: 80 percent of Americans now opposed national military service and only 17 percent were in support.[161] Certainly the quagmire in Iraq had greatly contributed to this reversal of public opinion. The opportunity to mobilize democracy was squandered, and not solely by Bush and the Republicans. In the closing days of the 2004 Presidential election, both parties overwhelmingly rejected a proposal in the House of

Representatives to mobilize the American people through universal service by a vote of 402 to 2.[162]

Without the active participation of the American people, little is possible. There would be no mass mobilization of human energies to better understand adversaries, monitor enemies, assist allies, and peacefully convert skeptical or hostile people to the cause of liberty. In early 2006, President Bush proposed spending $114 million on educational programs to expand the teaching of Arabic, Chinese, Farsi, and other foreign languages.[163] In a country with 300 million citizens, with a gross national product of more than $13 trillion a year, such a program could easily be ten times or a hundred times or even a thousand times larger.[164] With threats and fears of mass terrorism and suicide nuclear bombers, perhaps it should be.[165] With "an autonomous central bank" (i.e., an independent Federal Reserve), such a mass mobilization is simply not possible.

As with our paucity in foreign language training, so with countless other priorities related to national and homeland security that are ignored.[166] The War on Terror has become mostly spectator sport. Any call for sacrifice and action is considered unrealistic. And with the memory of images of September 11th collectively repressed,[167] perhaps feelings of meaninglessness have grown among Americans, already the most over-medicated people on earth and the largest consumer of prescription and illicit drugs.[168]

Viktor Frankl recognized the psychological dangers that nihilism posed to the individual and society when the existential search for meaning is frustrated. He saw the search for meaning as the primary motivation in people's lives, more important than the "mere gratification and satisfaction of drives and instincts."[169] When frustrated, the will to find meaning leads to an "existential vacuum," a widespread phenomenon that in modern society dooms many people to vacillate between extremes of distress and boredom, anger and depression.[170]

Miracle drugs—prescription and illegal drugs—have become the preferred American way of dealing with and escaping such spiritual and existential concerns. Too many in the generation introduced to drug use since September 11th have entered a new "ice age,"[171] blowing holes in their brains with crystal meth, otherwise known as "ice." With a weak job market[172]—though its weaknesses are systematically underreported in official unemployment statistics[173]—this generation is trapped in its own emotional great depression, a meaningless pursuit of material comfort in a society fixated with private consumption and the cult of celebrity.[174]

Frankl's theory of logotherapy suggests that people can find meaning through their labors, by giving of themselves to a larger cause.[175] The mobilization of democracy's latent energies is seen in this way as an imperative for the healthy society. The creation of work would fill the existential vacuum by helping each individual reach his or her fullest potential. Actualization for the individual, when aggregated under conditions of full employment, would enable society to actualize its fullest potentials.[176]

But instead of a future opening with possibilities, we are faced with a market fundamentalism that preaches the same old pessimistic "realism" that American democracy "can't":[177] we can't reform our trading relations, we can't rebuild our transportation infrastructure systems, we can't expect the American people to sacrifice for the greater good. We can't even do much better in Afghanistan or Iraq. Although prior to the war, Iraq was probably considered the weakest link in the Middle East in conventional military terms, the United States has failed to peacefully reconstruct the country as it did in Germany and Japan following World War Two. Prior to the Iraq War, General Eric Shinseki, then Army chief of staff, told Congress that the U.S.-led coalition would need "several hundred thousand" troops during any occupation of Iraq. A Rand Corporation study estimated that 500,000 American and coalition forces would be needed to secure Iraq.[178] Instead of the World War Two model of shared sacrifice— millions of Americans in uniform and hundreds of thousands fluent in the "host" country's language—there have been less than 150,000 American forces in Iraq, and very few who speak Arabic fluently, and fewer still with an Iraqi dialect.[179] Perhaps most disturbing is the realization that these were not just innocent mistakes by the Bush administration, but part of an ideological crusade to privatize the war, to reward their cronies with no-bid contracts, a confluence of self-interest and free-market fundamentalism that should have no place in foreign policy or the conduct of war.[180]

Less than a year after President Bush landed on the deck of the U.S.S. *Abraham Lincoln* aircraft carrier to declare "Mission Accomplished" and the end of major combat in Iraq, it was reported that the Sufi masters of Falluja had joined the Sunni resistance against U.S. occupation forces.[181] The loss of Sufi support demonstrated how violence and perceived injustices can lead significant populations of mystics into the hands of reactionaries and intolerant fundamentalists.[182]

The war in Iraq was justified in part by the Bush administration to make Iraq a model, a catalyst for democratic change throughout the

Middle East. But mystical rhetoric without the mobilization of democracy's latent energies is ineffective at best, as well as a sign of weakness and hypocrisy to friends and adversaries alike. As Gandhi said, "the means are the ends in the making." The means of present U.S. efforts have little to do with a mass participatory democracy or with tapping into democracy's great reservoirs of faith and energy. It is therefore not all that surprising that too many of those who were supposed to benefit by our efforts in Iraq and Afghanistan fail to believe that our end is to help them build a genuine democracy.

When the Sufis start joining an insurgency, that's a sobering indication that mysticism is waning and that fundamentalism is on the rise.[183] Conditions of hardship, social injustice, fear, and insecurity often contribute to fundamentalist authority and intolerance.[184] When squeezed between two opposing fundamentalisms, the Sufi mystics of Falluja threw their lot in with a coalition that included Islamic fundamentalists. This is a pattern that has differed from place to place, but sadly, only in degrees.

For instance, it was once widely hoped that Turkey would be the model of a Muslim country that was liberal and tolerant.[185] But "liberal" has come to mean little more than a liberalized economy and free-market fundamentalist dogma.[186] With its fiscal austerity, captured central bank, and liberalized and vulnerable currency, Turkey has no genuine possibility of mobilizing its masses of unemployed and underemployed men.[187] The land of the whirling dervishes, with its secular trend since the time of Atatürk,[188] has not provided a compelling mystical model of equality, social justice, and balance within the global Muslim community.[189]

The failure to mobilize American citizens has been a long-simmering problem that pre-dates September 11th and hampers American society at home as well. For instance, the lack of investment in the levies around New Orleans goes back many years and, along with the painfully slow federal response to Hurricane Katrina in September 2005, suggests a disturbing vulnerability to any natural or man-made disaster in the future. Ours is a society that has produced too few first responders, too few teachers and nurses and doctors, but plenty of lawyers, bankers, and real estate brokers.[190] Perhaps we have become an accident or catastrophe always waiting to happen.

A genuine mobilization of national energies would require the political commitment of inspired leaders to bend the financial system, as did Lincoln and Roosevelt, to accommodate the many and diverse needs of our time. But in 2001 there was no political leadership demanding any such accommodations by the Federal Reserve or sacrifice by the American taxpayer. It was common to hear that September 11th changed everything, and that nothing would ever be the same again. But a presidential election later, it seemed that nothing had changed.[191] The financial system continued to pump billions into speculative activity, and the housing bubble and foreign borrowing continued to mask our vulnerabilities. Finally, as the 2008 presidential election approached, the bubble economy reached a crisis with a meltdown in housing, credit, and currency markets.[192]

Although President Bush had invoked mystical rhetoric in calling for democratic change in the Middle East and the Islamic world,[193] there was no commitment of resources comparable to that of the Greatest Generation—no sense of shared sacrifice, no mobilization of human energies, no change in mass consumption patterns, no foreign assistance anywhere near the scale of the Marshall Plan, no program like the G.I. Bill of Rights to educate and integrate the nation's diverse and immigrant populations.[194] President Bush said repeatedly that he would do everything in his power to make sure another September 11th never comes.[195] But without harnessing the country's reservoir of mass faith and energy, the president's power was limited to ordering strategically ineffective military campaigns, detaining enemy combatants, and authorizing greater or lesser degrees of punishment and debatable standards for interrogation. The United States, once the beacon of individual freedom throughout the world and champion for the rights of the accused, was seen by many as the exporter of torture.

A year into his second term, in defending his National Security Agency's domestic eavesdropping program, President Bush said, "I was elected to protect the American people from harm."[196] How different from Lincoln or Roosevelt, both of whom became emblems of great mystic restorations because each knew that the American people have never needed a leader to protect them from harm, just one who would help empower them to defend themselves.[197] Each understood his role in the art of politics was to redirect national energies, to mobilize the nation's resources in support of a more dramatic mobilization of hearts and minds. In so doing, they refused to indulge Americans in private comforts and the pursuit of narrow interests and, instead, gave voice to the deeply mystical callings in each citizen to work together to build a better future and a newer world.[198]

1. According to Webster's English Dictionary, mysticism is "the belief that direct knowledge of God, spiritual truth, or ultimate reality can be attained through subjective experience (as intuition or insight)." Christian mystics often insist upon "the essential unity of God and man" and search for "the God within." See C. G. Jung, *Psychology and Religion* (New Haven: Yale University Press, 1938), 72–73 (concluding that such mystical ideas are natural tendencies of the unconscious mind).

2. It is also said that Juan Diego believed in the apparition even when others doubted and it was denied by the Bishop Juan de Zumárraga, the apostolic inquisitor of Mexico's Inquisition. John Ross, *The Annexation of Mexico From the Aztecs to the I.M.F.: One Reporter's Journey Through History* (Monroe: Common Courage Press, 1998), 16–17.

3. Ross, *The Annexation of Mexico*, 22 (within a few years of Juan Diego's reported Guadalupe sighting, an estimated five million Indians converted to the Cross—nearly one out of every two indigenous people in Mexico during a time of conquest, terror, and brutal genocide); Samuel Brunk, *Emiliano Zapata: Revolution and Betrayal in Mexico* (Albuquerque: University of New Mexico Press, 1995).

4. Martin Lings, *The Eleventh Hour: The Spiritual Crisis of the Modern World in the Light of Tradition and Prophecy* (Cambridge: Archetype, 2002), 103–106.

5. The search inward connects the mystic to "the higher reaches." See Daniel C. Matt, *The Essential Kabbalah: The Heart of Jewish Mysticism* (San Francisco: Harper, 1996). As suggested by Martin Lings, the inward path to heavenly truth is a central tenet of the Buddhist and Hindu traditions as well. See Lings, *The Eleventh Hour*, 8–9, fn.1 (equating the higher reaches with our inner reaches, "for there is a spiritual coincidence between height and inwardness or depth"). As for the individual, so for the polity. Mysticism may provide the deep inward roots for reaching higher stages of political and social development.

6. Erich Fromm considered mysticism as a natural consequence of monotheism. In mysticism, he argued, "the attempt is given up to know God by thought, and it is replaced by the experience of union with God in which there is no more room—and no need—for knowledge *about* God." See Erich Fromm, *The Art of Loving* (New York: Harper, 1956), 30.

7. Sheikh Ragip Robert Frager al Jerrahi, "Introduction," in *Essential Sufism*, ed. James Fadiman and Robert Frager (San Francisco: Harper, 1997), 2.

8. Another way of expressing this mystical view is that all men and women, regardless of present and past life karmic traumas, have the potential within this short lifetime of attaining liberation, full enlightenment, and Buddhahood. See Rajiv Mehrotra, ed., *The Essential Dalai Lama: His Important Teachings* (New York: Viking Press, 2005), 68–70, 223; Sogyal Rinpoche, *The Tibetan Book of Living and Dying*, ed. Patrick Gaffney and Andrew Harvey (New York: Harper Collins, 1994), 204–6, 227, 275.

9. R. A. Butler, *The Art of the Possible* (Boston: Gambit, 1971). The range of what's possible often narrows to the art of choosing lesser evils. According·to John Kenneth Galbraith, "politics is not the art of the possible. It consists in choosing between the disastrous and the unpalatable." See *Letters to Kennedy*,

ed. James Goodman (Cambridge: Harvard University Press, 1998). According to the economic historian Eliot Janeway, "Politics is the art of improvising third alternatives to dilemmas. And idealism embodies a dilemma, for by pointing men toward the unattainable, it destines them to frustration and threatens constantly to disintegrate into schizophrenia" (*The Struggle for Survival: A Chronicle of Economic Mobilization in World War II* [New Haven: Yale University Press, 1951], 2).

10. This is not a new or novel political critique. It is shared by process political theorists and public-choice economists. See, for example, Theodore J. Lowi, *The End of Liberalism: The Second Republic of the United States*, 2nd ed. (New York: Norton Publishers, 1979); James M. Buchanan, *Public Finance in Democratic Process: Fiscal Institutions and Individual Choice* (Chapel Hill: University of North Carolina Press, 1966).

11. Elites around the globe believe in free-market fundamentalism with a religious faith that is often inconsistent with any scientific methodology. See, for example, Joseph E. Stiglitz, *Globalization and Its Discontents* (New York: W. W. Norton, 2002), 35–36, 84–85, 134. Meanwhile, Islamic fundamentalism shapes the response of many others to the often confusing and sometimes threatening forces of postmodernism in the world today. See, for example, Tariq Ali, *The Clash of Fundamentalisms: Crusades, Jihads and Modernity* (London: Verso, 2002); Jim Dator, book review of *Islam, Postmodernism and Other Futures: A Ziauddin Sardar Reader*, ed. Sohail Inayatullah and Gail Boxwell (London: Pluto Press, 2003), in *Futures* 36 (2004): 115–29, available at www.futures.hawaii.edu/dator/reviews/ziau.html.

12. Carl Jung warned of the theocratic and fundamentalist tendency to suppress free thought and opinion, and thereby shield people from immediate experience or insight. See Jung, *Psychology and Religion*, 52–53, 58–59, 72–73.

13. According to the orthodox free-market consensus, the state is limited in its ability to mobilize or redistribute resources, thereby excluding such proposals as national health insurance, large-scale public works programs for unemployed teens, or federal subsidies for local school teachers' salaries. These alternative paths are defined from the start as unacceptable, regardless of whether they have been necessary in the past (i.e., public works during the Great Depression) or successful elsewhere in the world today (i.e., national health insurance in most developed countries).

14. As Harold Gilliam points out, although our present politics are superficial, "what is politically possible is determined by much deeper cultural and psychological currents of thought and feeling." See Harold Gilliam, "Poetry Can Get Outside the Box of Politics," *San Francisco Chronicle*, January 9, 2005, C1 (arguing that deeper insights into human political behavior are the province of poets, psychologists, philosophers, historians, novelists, religious leaders, and innovative thinkers in all of the humanities).

15. Lings, *The Eleventh Hour*, 9. The Gnostics were the mystics of early Christianity. They believed in the equality of all people, regardless of gender, wealth, education, or social strata. The Gnostic was often an oral tradition, and its written texts and gospels were largely burned and destroyed by the orthodox wing of the church under the Roman emperor Constantine. See Leonard Shlain, *The Alphabet Versus the Goddess: The Conflict Between Word and Image* (New York: Viking Press, 1998), 237–45, 250–51.

16. Lings, *The Eleventh Hour*, 15 ("The basic purpose of religion is to open up, for man, the way of return to his lost centrality."). According to Carl Jung, if religious experience means anything, "it means everything to those who have it. . . . One could even define religious experience as that kind of experience which is characterized by the highest appreciation, no matter what its contents are." See Jung, *Psychology and Religion*, 75.

17. Bernard Lewis, *The Crisis of Islam: Holy War and Unholy Terror* (New York: Modern Library, 2003). For an early exposition of this clash between major religions and cultures, see Samuel P. Huntington, *The Clash of Civilizations and the Remaking of World Order* (New York: Simon and Schuster, 1996).

18. Whereas mysticism seeks the experience of union with the Divine, fundamentalism seeks to understand God through strict and literal adherence to basic principles and dogmatic rituals. See C. Daniel Batson and W. Larry Ventis, *The Religious Experience: A Social-Psychological Perspective* (New York: Oxford University Press, 1982), 133.

19. Hindu and Buddhist traditions share this science and discipline of inward quest for spiritual truth. Martin Lings identifies such aspirations for union with divine perfection in the Hindu yoga and the nirvana of Buddhism. See Lings, *The Eleventh Hour*, 8–9. Also see Paramahansa Yogananda, *The Second Coming of Christ* (Los Angeles: Self-Realization Fellowship, 2004), exploring the mystic yogi Jesus and the similarities between his path of spiritual self-discovery and that preached by Krishna to his disciple Arjuna in the *Bhagavad Gita*. Jesus may have been influenced by Buddhist teachings in his early childhood in Egypt, or in travels to the Himalayas and Tibet between his ages of 13 and 29. Some Buddhists and some Christians believe that Jesus was actually the reincarnation of the Buddha. See Elizabeth Claire Prophet, *The Lost Years of Jesus* (Malibu: Summit University Press, 1984), reporting on the discoveries of Nicholas Notovitch, a late nineteenth-century Russian traveler, of Sanskrit documents demonstrating that Jesus had visited India and Tibet during his lost years. Also, see "The Lost Years of Jesus: The Life of Saint Issa," available at http://reluctant-messenger.com/issa.htm (providing translation of Notovitch's 1894 book, *The Unknown Life of Christ*) and "Gospel of Thomas: The Buddhist Jesus?" available at http://buddhistfaith. tripod.com/gospel. The Essene Gospel of Peace, which dates back at least to the 3rd century AD, written originally in Aramaic, and discovered in 1928 in the Vatican archives, presents a New Age Jesus, a healer espousing vegetarianism, fasting, raw foods, meditation, deep breathing, yoga, and colon hydrotherapy, along with a message of peace and love and compassion. See *The Essene Gospel of Peace*, ed. Edmond Bordeaux Székely (Cartago: The International Biogenic Society, 1981).

20. The influences of numerous religions and philosophies are apparent within mysticism. See Reza Aslan, *No god but God: The Origins, Evolution, and Future of Islam* (New York: Random House, 2005), 199 (discussing the Sufi "medley of divergent philosophical and religious trends"). The mystic perspective emphasizes "the importance and value of each and every gift, of each and every part of the body of this community." See Helene Tallon Russell, "We Are One But We Are Not the Same," Chapman University Baccalaureate Address, May 21, 2005. The title and theme of this address borrows from U2's "One": "We're one . . . /One life with each other: sisters, brothers/

One life, but we're not the same/We get to carry each other" (U2, "One," from *Achtung Baby* [1992]).

21. Mahatma Gandhi, *All Men Are Brothers: Life and Thoughts of Mahatma Gandhi Told in His Own Words* (New York: Columbia University Press, 1960).

22. Steven Emerson, *American Jihad* (New York: Free Press, 2002), 165.

23. Martin Lings, the great Sufi scholar, believed the Western world was no longer capable of "discerning the difference between a legally enforced restraint based on [transcendent] truths and a tyranny based on arbitrary human opinion" (Martin Lings, *The Eleventh Hour*, 48–49).

24. The mystic starts by purifying the inner self, then may seek to purify the outer society, and is by necessity more disciplined and balanced than the fundamentalist who seeks salvation simply by following the dogmas and dictates of religious authority. See Aslan, *No God but God*, 200–201, 204 ("Sufism is to Islam what the heart is to the human being: its vital center, the seat of its essence"). Likewise, a central concept in Hawaiian mysticism, seeking right action and balance, is that of *pono*, "in which all is right with the world and all aspects of life are working harmoniously together." See Charlotte Berney, *Fundamentals of Hawaiian Mysticism* (Freedom: Crossing Press, 2000), 25.

25. For instance, Reza Aslan points out that Sufism "spread like fire" in India as it synthesized "anti-caste Muslim values with traditional Indian practices such as controlled breathing, sitting postures, and meditation" (Reza Aslan, *No God but God*, 202).

26. The burning of Gnostic books was so complete that what "almost everything historians knew about the Gnostic movement had to be inferred from preserved anti-Gnostic-Orthodox polemics" until 1945, when Gnostic scrolls were discovered in a cave near Nag Hammadi in the upper Nile Valley. See Shlain, *The Alphabet Versus the Goddess*, 237–41, 251.

27. "In the Gnostic Gospel of Philip, Jesus intoned, 'To the universe belongs the dancer'" (Schlain, 239). In the tradition of the Gnostics are contemporary mystics who beckon us to dance in a place where "The jungle is your head/ Can't rule your heart . . . Your eyes are wide/And though your soul/It can't be bought/Your mind can wander" (U2, "Vertigo," from *How To Dismantle an Atomic Bomb* [2004]).

28. Rafi Zabor, "The Turn: Inside the Secret Dervish Orders of Istanbul," *Harper's Magazine*, June 1, 2004, 49; Shems Friedlander, *The Whirling Dervishes* (Albany: The State University of New York Press, 1992). Akin in purpose and impulse to the dance of the dervish are the rites and symbols of rhythmic repetition of breath and sound, termed *dhikr* in Sufism and *mantra* in Hinduism, rites of "remembrance," which are understood as "the power of the symbol to recall its archetype": "The repetition of these formulae is intended to bring about the harmonization of the different elements of the being and to cause vibrations which, by their repercussions throughout the whole hierarchy of states, are capable of opening up a communication with the higher states." See Lings, *The Eleventh Hour*, 73–74 (quoting René Guénon's *Fundamental Symbols, The Universal Language of Sacred Science* [1975]).

29. Maslow's hierarchy of needs places the peak experience at the top. His discussion of the religious aspects of peak experiences—the "characteristic disorientation in time and space, or even the lack of consciousness of time and space"—could well describe the whirling dervishes of Sufism.

See Abraham H. Maslow, *Religions, Values, and Peak-Experiences* (New York: Penguin Arkana, 1995 [1970]), 63.

30. John C. Eastman, "We are a Religious People, Whose Institutions Presuppose a Supreme Being," *Nexus* 5 (fall, 2000): 13, 17 (quoting Supreme Court Justice William O. Douglas in the Court's 1952 decision of *Zorach v. Clauson*). None of the first five U.S. presidents were conventional Christians. Rather, they were all influenced by Deism. See David A. Holmes, *The Faiths of the Founding Fathers* (New York: Oxford University Press, 2006); Brooke Allen, *Moral Minority: Our Skeptical Founding Fathers* (Chicago: Ivan R. Dee, 2006).

31. Lance Banning, *The Sacred Fire of Liberty: James Madison and the Founding of the Federal Republic* (Ithaca: Cornell University Press, 1995), 84–97.

32. Gordon S. Wood, *The Radicalism of the American Revolution* (New York: Alfred A. Knopf, 1992), 218–23. The great egalitarian ideals were sociability, love for one's neighbor, and cosmopolitanism. To be enlightened, said Washington, was to be "a citizen of the great republic of humanity at large." For the mystical aspects of freemasonry, see John Ferguson, *An Illustrated Encyclopedia of Mysticism and the Mystery Religions* (New York: Seabury Press, 1977).

33. William Hutchinson's *The Spirit of Masonry* was first published in England in 1775. George Washington, Benjamin Franklin, Samuel Adams, Richard Henry Lee, James Madison, and Alexander Hamilton were all members of the Freemasons. See Wood, *The Radicalism of the American Revolution*, 223. Others have pointed to the Illuminati influence (both the ancient Islamic Illuminati and the more recent Bavarian Order of the Illuminati) on the rise of cosmopolitanism and enlightenment ideals within the Masonic lodges of Western Europe, and on the course of the American Revolution and French Revolution. See, for example, Trevor W. McKeown, "A Bavarian Illuminati Primer," available at www.freemasonry.bcy.ca/texts/illuminati.html. By some accounts, Thomas Jefferson "strenuously defended the Illuminati," which was committed to enlightenment ideals of liberty and equality. After the French Revolution, monarchies and clerics throughout Europe suppressed the Illuminati, imprisoned its members, and published a flood tide of false propaganda that the order was an evil and wicked conspiracy of the elite against the interests of the many. See Richard Shand, "The Illuminati Exposed: Mysterious Beginnings," available at www.mystae.com/restricted/streams/masons/weishaupt.html.

34. Wood, *The Radicalism*, 223. Some of the alliances fostered by Freemasonry crossed national and geographic boundaries. For instance, LaFayette became a member of many Masonic and Grand Lodges in the United States and France (Thomas A. D. Canova, Master, LaFayette Lodge No. 64, Greetings to 200th Anniversary Banquet in Honor of General Marquis de LaFayette, Hotel Waldorf-Astoria, New York, Sept. 28, 1957).

35. Isaiah 1:18. The letterhead was my father's, Thomas A. D. Canova, when he founded and served as national director of the National Civic Association.

36. Mark A. Tabbert, *American Freemasons: Three Centuries of Building Communities* (New York: New York University Press, 2005), 39–42.

37. Wood, *The Radicalism*, 223. According to Wood: "There were twenty-one [Masonic] lodges in Massachusetts by 1779; in the next twenty years fifty new ones were created, reaching out to embrace even small isolated communities on the frontiers of the state. Everywhere the same expansion took place."

38. In concluding that the Founders' faith in action demanded "an intrinsic unity of divine and historical design," Erik Erikson saw Jefferson as anticipating Mahatma Gandhi's "unification of action and faith in a self-aware, all human identity." See Erik H. Erikson, *Dimensions of a New Identity* (New York: Norton Books, 1974), 44–47. Perhaps the mystical belief in natural law can also be traced to a view that all life is connected through nature, and nature is connected to the divine (Berney, *Fundamentals*, 31–32, 151, 153).

39. According to Paul Conkin, "Jefferson had clearly moved to a form of religious rationalism. He would accept only beliefs that he believed essential to religion, and thus beliefs common to all religions—or what some have called religious essentialism." See Paul K. Conkin, "The Religious Pilgrimage of Thomas Jefferson," in *Jeffersonian Legacies*, ed. Peter S. Onuf (Charlottesville: University Press of Virginia, 1993), 24.

40. "A brief history," *The Economist*, December 18, 2004, 36. Leonard Shlain traces mysticism to right-brain feminine wisdom that is eclectic and holistic in nature (*The Alphabet Versus the Goddess*, 303–4).

41. Stiglitz, *Globalization and Its Discontents*, 84–85, 134 (criticizing the excesses of today's secular free-market fundamentalism); Bernard Lewis, *What Went Wrong?: Western Impact and Middle Eastern Responses* (Oxford: Oxford University Press, 2002), 118–19, 174–75 (criticizing the intolerance of today's Islamic fundamentalism).

42. For its time, the American Revolution was radical in the cause of liberty and social justice, notwithstanding the terrible blight and horrors of slavery. See Thomas G. West, *Vindicating the Founders: Race, Sex, Class, and Justice in the Origins of America* (New York: Rowman & Littlefield, 1997). "The worst in us is intimately related to the best," writes Erikson. Even as we recognize the racism and brutality of our past, "it is more important to gain painful insights into our common evolutionary and developmental corruptibility than an easy moral superiority over our dead heroes" (Erikson, *Dimensions*, 32).

43. Wood, *The Radicalism*, 295 (quoting Benjamin Latrobe, a noted American architect and engineer of the early nineteenth century).

44. Histories of Jackson's presidency recognize that its populism was based on "sacred" egalitarian moral principles. See, for example, Leonard D. White, *The Jacksonians: A Study in Administrative History 1829–1861* (New York: Macmillan, 1954), 321, 344–45 (discussing the Jacksonian "fidelity to republican institutions" and the public trust); Arthur M. Schlesinger, Jr., *The Age of Jackson* (Boston: Little, Brown, 1945), 359–60 (discussing role of radical religious faith in releasing the energies of reform). The anti-Masonic period crested in the 1820s and 1830s. See "To Build and Sustain: Freemasons in American Community," National Heritage Museum, available at www.monh. org/Default.aspx?tabid=159. Anti-Mason literature and conspiracy theories continue to the present day. Perhaps the most widely repeated narrative is that Freemasons use the ideals of liberty and equality as cover to infiltrate government, industry, and finance, and to pursue elitist agendas. See Michael Howard, *The Occult Conspiracy: Secret Societies, Their Influence and Power in World History* (Rochester: Destiny Books, 1989).

45. Jackson's veto of the recharter of the Second Bank of the United States, at the time the most important presidential veto in U.S. history, was a bold egalitarian statement: "Every man is equally entitled to protection by law; but when the laws undertake to aid . . . artificial distinctions, to grant titles,

gratuities, and exclusive privileges, to make the rich richer and the potent more powerful, the humble members of society—the farmers, mechanics, and laborers—who have neither the time nor the means of securing like favors to themselves, have a right to complain of the injustice of their government" (message of President Andrew Jackson vetoing the Bank Bill, July 10, 1832). Jackson was easily reelected months after his veto of the bank recharter, which traced its heritage to the Jeffersonian opposition to the First Bank of the United States. See Charles A. Beard, *Economic Origins of Jeffersonian Democracy* (New York: Macmillan, 1915), 153–64.

46. Conkin, "The Religious Pilgrimage," 42 (characterizing transcendentalism as "that apotheosis of idealism or spiritualism"). One can hardly read Emerson without hearing the transcendental fervor and mystical commitment to social justice: "And we are now men, and must accept in the highest mind the same transcendent destiny; and not pinched in a corner, not cowards fleeing before a revolution, but reformers and benefactors, pious aspirants to be noble clay under the Almighty effort let us advance on Chaos and the Dark," in Emerson, "Self-Reliance," from *Emerson's Essays and Poems, Selected and Edited with an Introduction by Arthur Hobson Quinn* (New York: Scribner, 1926), 33.

47. Barrington Moore, Jr., *Social Origins of Dictatorship and Democracy* (Boston: Beacon Press, 1966), 111–55 (characterizing the American Civil War as the Last Capitalist Revolution).

48. Abraham Lincoln, Farewell Address, Springfield, Illinois, February 11, 1861, in Roy P. Basler, ed., *The Collected Works of Abraham Lincoln*, vol. 7 (New Brunswick: Rutgers University Press, 1953–55), 301–2.

49. As Lincoln said, "As I would not be a slave, so I would not be a master. This expresses my idea of democracy. Whatever differs from this, to the extent of the difference, is no democracy." Fragment, August 1, 1858, in Basler, *The Collected Works of Abraham Lincoln*, vol. II, 532. President Franklin Roosevelt would later quote these words of Lincoln in urging Americans to pledge their fidelity "to the faith which Lincoln held in the common man" (Franklin D. Roosevelt, Remarks on Visiting the Birthplace of Abraham Lincoln, June 24, 1936, The American Presidency Project, University of California at Santa Barbara, available at www.presidency.ucsb.edu/ws/index.php?pid=15306).

50. Contrary to John Kerry's assertions at the time of his defeat in the 2004 presidential election, wars are often not all that favorable for presidents seeking reelection. Harry Truman and Lyndon Johnson both decided against seeking reelection during the Korean War and Vietnam War, respectively, and George H. W. Bush lost his bid for reelection after winning the first Persian Gulf War.

51. Mysticism has its darker side when it becomes revolutionary and violent, rather than reformist, in the name of utopian ideals or fantasies of racial purity. See Norman Cohn, *The Pursuit of the Millennium: Revolutionary Millenarians and Mystical Anarchists of the Middle Ages* (Fairlawn: Essential Books, 1957); *Secrets of the Unknown: Mystic Hitler* (MPI Home Video, 2000); Wulf Schwartzwaller, *The Unknown Hitler* (New York: Berkley Books, 1990).

52. As in our present war, the sacrifices were unequal. Throughout the Civil War, financiers and industrialists profited from the war, while others did the fighting and dying. See Bruce Catton, *The Army of the Potomac: Glory Road* (Garden City: Doubleday, 1952), 13–14, 221, 235–40.

53. Janeway, *The Struggle*, 16.

54. Lincoln had said, "the world has never had a good definition of the word liberty, and the American people, just now, are much in want of one" (President Abraham Lincoln, address in Baltimore, Maryland, April 18, 1864, in Basler, *The Collected Works of Abraham Lincoln*, 301–2).

55. Janeway, *The Struggle*, 17.

56. Abraham Lincoln, First Inaugural Address, March 4, 1861, in *The Collected Works of Abraham Lincoln*. Among more recent leaders, Churchill was comparable to Lincoln in his appeal to people's mystic longings: "The destiny of mankind is not decided by material computation. When great causes are on the move in the world . . . we learn that we are spirits . . . and that something is going on in space and time, and beyond space and time, which, whether we like it or not, spells duty" (Winston Churchill, Radio Broadcast to America on receiving the Honorary Degree of Doctor of Law from the University of Rochester, New York, June 16, 1941). Compare this with Rumi, the great Sufi poet, who wrote that the Sufi is "not an entity of this world or the next" (Aslan, *No god but God*, 204).

57. Roosevelt spoke of the mysterious cycle in human events at the 1936 Democratic Convention when thundering against the economic royalists who opposed his New Deal: "To some generations much is given. Of other generations much is expected. This generation has a rendezvous with destiny." See Nathan Miller, *F.D.R.: An Intimate History* (New York: Doubleday, 1983), 384.

58. "A brief history," *The Economist*, December 18, 2004, 36 (quoting Norman Cohn's dismissal of egalitarian mysticism as fantasy and anarchy).

59. For the religious roots of free-market worship, see Max Weber, *The Protestant Ethic and the Spirit of Capitalism* (New York: Scribner, 1930).

60. Orthodox dogmas are enforced by conformed consensus where possible, and by brute force where necessary. See Fromm, *The Art of Loving* (1956), 12–13 (analyzing the deep-seated need to conform to the group, its customs, practices, and beliefs).

61. "Heroism," in *Emerson's Essays*, 186–87. "Times of heroism are generally times of terror," wrote Emerson, concluding that in an hour of maximum danger we should listen to "the higher voices." Martin Lings seems to agree: "The climate of the eleventh hour can also be favourable to spiritual fruition and fulfillment in the same incalculable and mysterious way." See Lings, *The Eleventh Hour*, 7–9, 10 (suggesting that the end of time, the eleventh hour, is "in the air" and "existentially sensed"). It is in such context that we may consider the works of modern mystics, such as U2's *How To Dismantle an Atomic Bomb* (2004) and Bob Dylan's *The Times They Are A-Changin'* (1964).

62. The belief that the end of time is approaching is a recurring one, perhaps intensified by the start of the new millennium and the horrendous spectacle of September 11th. "A Brief History of Time," *The Economist*, December 18, 2004, 34–36. The urgency of the mystic suggests an "eleventh hour" psychology: with the end approaching, every moment counts. See Huston Smith, "Foreword," in *Essential Sufism*, ix (referring to the Sufis as "the impatient ones [who] want God now—moment by moment").

63. According to historian Broadus Mitchell, the New Deal may have failed to bring about a fully functioning economy, but it "proclaimed, and went a distance to prove, that we need not be frustrated by inscrutable misfortune,

but could be masters of our future." See Broadus Mitchell, *Depression Decade: From New Era through New Deal, 1929–1941* (New York: Rinehart, 1947).

64. Lynn Dumenil, *Freemasonry and American Culture 1880–1930* (Princeton: Princeton University Press, 1984). Shriners, or members of the Ancient Arabic Order Nobles of the Mystic Shrine, are Master Masons. At its peak, in the 1940s to 1960s, there were a million Shriners in the United States, including Franklin Roosevelt. See Lisa Eisner and Glenn O'Brien, *Shriners* (Los Angeles: Greybull Publishers, 2004). See also, Robert D. Putnam, *Bowling Alone: The Collapse and Revival of American Community* (New York: Simon and Schuster, 2001), lamenting the decline in participation in civic groups.

65. "To Build and Sustain: Freemasons in American Community," National Heritage Museum, available at www.monh.org/Default.aspx?tabid=159.

66. Miller, *F.D.R.*, 307. Barack Obama's attempts to invest his 2008 presidential campaign with a message of moral and spiritual renewal were often met with criticism by the chattering classes of political pundits. According to Obama, what has been lost is "our sense of common purpose—our sense of higher purpose," the belief that I am "my brother's keeper; I am my sister's keeper," and that we have responsibilities to each other and to future generations (Barack Obama, Address to Democratic National Convention, August 28, 2008, available at http://elections.nytimes.com/2008/president/conventions/videos/20080828_OBAMA_SPEECH.html#. Of course, this is a message that has been articulated by great mystical leaders from Jesus and Ghandi to Lincoln and Roosevelt, Kennedys and King.

67. Max Freedman, ed., *Roosevelt and Frankfurter: Their Correspondence 1928–1945* (Boston: Little, Brown, 1968), 747–48 (from Frankfurter's remembrance of Roosevelt published in the Harvard Alumni Bulletin, April 28, 1945). According to Frankfurter, "This identification with his fellowmen was Roosevelt's profoundest characteristic and the ultimate key to his statesmanship. He was a democrat in feeling and not through abstract speculation about governments . . . The same qualities fitted him to serve as a symbol of hope for liberty-loving people everywhere, in resisting a seemingly invincible challenge to civilization."

68. The first time Roosevelt pledged a "new deal for the American people," he captured his audience with these words: "Let all of us here assembled constitute ourselves prophets of a new order of competence and of courage . . . in this crusade to restore America to its own greatness" (Miller, *F.D.R.*, 279).

69. Miller, *F.D.R.*, 262, 279. The lack of work and security—joblessness, hunger, poverty, fear—all of these undermine spiritual values and demoralize the individual. In *Gone With the Wind*, released in 1939, Scarlett O'Hara returns home to a ruined Tara and nothing to eat. She digs up a root from the barren ground, tries to eat it, and retches. She vows, "As God is my witness, I will never be hungry again." Rather than the mystical experience of union with God, we can see this dramatic moment as presupposing and preserving their separate existence. See Martin Buber, *I and Thou* (New York: Scribner, 1923) (from mysticism to dialogue). Hunger did not contribute to any lofty moral development. Scarlett vowed that she would "lie, steal, cheat, or kill" before she or any of her folk would ever go hungry again. Words like liberty can seem hollow when there is no freedom from want or hunger or fear.

70. Both Lincoln and Roosevelt recognized that the liberty of the privileged few must be restrained to nurture the freedom for all. "I am not for a return to

that definition of liberty under which for many years a free people were being gradually regimented into the service of the privileged few." See President Franklin D. Roosevelt, "On Moving Forward to Greater Freedom and Greater Security," Radio Address of the President, White House Fireside Chat, September 30, 1934, available at www.fdrlibrary.marist.edu/093034.html.

71. Miller, *F.D.R.*, 315, 366–69. The Works Project Administration (WPA) provided 8 million jobs during the Depression, including one for Ronald Reagan's father, Jack, the WPA boss in Dixon, Illinois. See Lewis Lord, "A Concrete Legacy of the Dole," *U.S. News & World Report*, October 6, 2003.

72. John M. Blum, Edmund S. Morgan, Willie Lee Rose, Arthur M. Schlesinger, Jr., Kenneth M. Stampp, and C. Vann Woodward, *The National Experience: A History of the United States since 1865*, 4th ed. (New York: Harcourt, Brace, and Jovanovich, 1977), 699.

73. The first Sufis were not just "whirling dervishes" but also eclectic, "wandering dervishes" (Aslan, *No god but God*, 199). Aslan asserts that "Sufism is characterized by a medley of divergent philosophical and religious trends" including principles of Christian monasticism and Hindu asceticism, Buddhist and Tantric thought, Islamic Gnosticism and Neoplatonism, and elements of Shi'ism, Manichaeism, and Central Asian shamanism. Freemasonry may also have borrowed from the esoteric tradition of Eleusinian, Dionysian, and Orphic cults (Shlain, *The Alphabet Versus the Goddess*, 240). For more on the religion of the Greeks, see Edith Hamilton, *The Greek Way* (New York: W. W. Norton, 1930).

74. *The General Theory of Employment, Interest and Money*, written by John Maynard Keynes (London: Macmillan, 1936), provided the theoretical justification for the hyperactivist fiscal state, federal deficit spending, and the neutralization of private financial interests.

75. The wide variety of New Deal approaches included the corporatism of industry trade councils and price supports, the social contractualism of promoting union organizing and collective bargaining, the communitarianism of Social Security, and the Keynesianism of hyperactive fiscal policy, massive public works projects, and wartime mobilization (Mitchell, *Depression Decade*).

76. Roosevelt said: "The country needs and unless I mistake its temper, the country demands bold, persistent experimentation. It is common sense to take a method and try it. If it fails, admit it frankly and try another. But above all, try something. The millions who are in want will not stand by silently forever while the things to satisfy their needs are within easy reach" (Miller, *F.D.R.*, 263). One is reminded of Emerson's calls for eclectic experimentation: a "foolish consistency is the hobgoblin of little minds" and "new actions are the only apologies and explanations of old ones" (*Emerson's Essays*, "Self-Reliance," 42, and "Character," 334).

77. Perhaps the mystical commitment to social justice can be made compatible with classical liberal philosophy: instead of the individual pursuing his narrow short-term self-interest, there is a greater appreciation for one's long-term or enlightened self-interest and a greater willingness to restrain one's activities and sacrifice for the common good.

78. John Donne, *Devotions upon Emergent Occasions* (1623), edited by Anthony Raspa (New York: Oxford University Press, 1987), 87.

79. Janeway, *The Struggle*, 13.

80. Alfred Lord Tennyson, "Ulysseus" (1842), in *Poems*, edited by Leslie L. Lewis (New York: Macmillan, 1975), 518. *To Seek a Newer World* was also the title and epigraph of the last book written by Robert F. Kennedy in the final months of his life. See Arthur M. Schlesinger, Jr., *Robert Kennedy and His Times* (Boston: Houghton Mifflin, 1978), 735, 879.

81. Miller, *F.D.R.*, 289. In 2008, Barack Obama struck a similar note of humility: "I realize that I am not the likeliest candidate for this office . . . But I stand before you tonight because all across America something is stirring. . . . You have shown what history teaches us—that at defining moments like this one, the change we need doesn't come *from* Washington. Change comes *to* Washington. Change happens because the American people demand it—because they rise up and insist on new ideas and new leadership, a new politics for a new time." Acceptance Speech of Barack Obama at Democratic National Convention, August 28, 2009, at www.nytimes.com/2008/08/28/us/politics/28text-obama.html?pagewanted=all.

82. Janeway, *The Struggle*, 16.

83. Ibid., 13.

84. William L. O'Neill, *The Oxford Essential Guide to World War II* (New York: Berkley Books, 2002), 162–66.

85. In 1944, the last full year of the war, the reported U.S. unemployment rate fell to 1.2 percent. See Lynn Turgeon, *Bastard Keynesianism: The Evolution of Economic Thinking and Policymaking since World War II* (Westport: Greenwood Press, 1996), 5.

86. Lynn Turgeon, *The Advanced Capitalist System: A Revisionist View* (White Plains: M. E. Sharpe, 1980), 47. According to Eliot Janeway, Roosevelt was convinced "that America's decisive contribution [to the war] would have to be made on the home front . . . All that Roosevelt thought important about the home front was its size . . . the participation of the people would push it forward faster than any leaders could lead it, and the spontaneous dramatics of democracy would organize it. So long as the home front was big at the base, Roosevelt was willing to bet that he could afford to let it be confused at the top" (Janeway, *The Struggle*, 12–13).

87. A stable peace is a just peace, one that's founded on security and social justice. See Kenneth E. Boulding, *Stable Peace* (Austin: University of Texas Press, 1978).

88. William O'Neill, *The Oxford Essential Guide to World War II; U.S. Army Center of Military History*. Also see www.army.mil/cmh-pg/books/Lineage/mi/ch5.htm.

89. Major Allied victories—from Midway to D-Day—were aided by the intelligence derived from massive armies of cryptographers that monitored German, Japanese, and Italian communications (William L. O'Neill, *The Oxford Essential Guide to World War II*, 168–71). Particularly crucial, says O'Neill, was the MAGIC program that broke the Japanese diplomatic and, eventually, military codes, leading to the shooting down of the Commander-in-Chief of Japanese forces, Admiral Isoroku Yamamoto; and ULTRA, the program that cracked the German ENIGMA code "played an important part in the Battle of the Atlantic, enabling the Allies to divert convoys from areas to which U-boats had been ordered."

90. Daniel Bergner, "Where the Enemy Is Everywhere and Nowhere," *New York Times Magazine*, July 20, 2003, 38–44 (reporting U.S. soldiers' lack of trust in their Afghan translators); Barry R. Posen, "Fighting Blind in Iraq," *New York Times*, June 7, 2005, A23; Awadh al-Taee and Steve Negus, "Shoot First, Pay Later Culture Pervades Iraq," *Financial Times*, March 19–20, 2005, 5 (reporting that western private security forces and contractors, heavily armed, but with limited intelligence and language capabilities, take no chances on the streets of Baghdad).

91. These words from Lincoln's Gettysburg Address speak of the responsibility of citizens to one another, a theme repeated in countless works of art and literature. "Always remember that the purpose of freedom is to create it for others." See Bernard Malamud, *The Fixer* (New York: Farrar, Straus, and Giroux, 1966), 317.

92. William F. Hixson, *Triumph of the Bankers: Money and Banking in the Eighteenth and Nineteenth Centuries* (Westport: Praeger, 1993), 131. According to Gretchen Ritter, the Legal Tender Act of 1862 and two similar subsequent acts were passed "to save the national economy and provide financing for the war" by creating a new government-issued currency known as the "greenback." See Gretchen Ritter, *Goldbugs and Greenbacks: The Antimonopoly Tradition and the Politics of Finance in America* (New York: Cambridge University Press, 1997), 29–30. Many Lincoln scholars and admirers miss the significance of the greenback. For instance, Mario Cuomo hails Lincoln for calling upon Congress to spend $400 million to raise and supply the Army of the Potomac, but he is completely silent as to the unorthodox means by which Congress obtained the funds, that is, by having the Treasury Department issue currency and spend it into circulation, rather than raising all war funding exclusively by borrowing and taxation. See Mario M. Cuomo, *Why Lincoln Matters: Today More Than Ever* (Orlando: Harcourt, 2004), 69.

93. The yield on short-term bills was pegged at 0.375 percent and on long-term bonds at 2.5 percent. See Milton Friedman and Anna Jacobson Schwartz, *A Monetary History of the United States, 1867–1960* (Princeton: Princeton University Press, 1963), 562–63; Lester V. Chandler, *The Economics of Money and Banking*, 5th ed. (New York: Harper & Row, 1969), 482–93. With the Treasury borrowing at near zero percent, it paid for the federal government to borrow, and therefore spend, on a massive scale, thereby helping to bring World War Two to an end in less than four years.

94. Janeway, *The Struggle*, 11.

95. The period of neutralized monetary policy lasted from World War Two and postwar reconstruction through the Korean War and critical alliance-building stages of the Cold War (Turgeon, *Bastard Keynesianism*, 55, 72, 83).

96. During World War Two, the federal budget deficit peaked at 31.1 percent of Gross Domestic Product (GDP) and the federal debt at 127.5 percent of GDP. For much of the past three decades, the deficit has been far less than 5 percent of GDP and the federal debt perhaps 60 to 75 percent of GDP, while real interest rates (i.e., inflation-adjusted) and market interest rates were far higher today than during World War Two. See Timothy A. Canova, "The Transformation of U.S. Banking and Finance: From Regulated Competition to Free-Market Receivership," *Brooklyn Law Review* 60, no. 4 (1995): 1295–1354, see particularly page 1301, n. 17.

97. Allan H. Meltzer, *A History of the Federal Reserve, Vol. I, 1913–1951* (Chicago: University of Chicago Press, 2003), 602–5 (recounting the Federal Reserve's use of selective credit controls); Arthur Smithies, "Uses of Selective Credit Controls," in *United States Monetary Policy*, ed. Neil H. Jacoby (New York: Praeger, 1964), 94–105 (lamenting the surrender of selective credit controls).

98. William J. Barber, *Designs Within Disorder: Franklin D. Roosevelt, the Economists, and the Shaping of American Economic Policy, 1933–1945* (New York: Cambridge University Press, 1996), 142–51; Janeway, *The Struggle for Survival.*

99. Peter Drucker concluded that the G.I. Bill of Rights and the mass participation of U.S. veterans "signaled the shift to the knowledge society," and that future historians would "consider it the most important event of the 20th century." See Peter F. Drucker, *Post-Capitalist Society* (New York: Harper Business, 1993), 3. Also see Michael J. Bennett, *When Dreams Came True: The G.I. Bill and the Making of Modern America* (Washington, DC: Brassey's, 1999); Suzanne Mettler, *Soldiers to Citizens: The G.I. Bill and the Making of the Greatest Generation* (New York: Oxford University Press, 2005).

100. For instance, neither Germany nor Japan was able to reduce the interest rate for government wartime borrowing to the low U.S. levels. Both fascist regimes had to contend with private financial interests that were unrestrained by the countervailing demands of any free public opinion. Germany had "moderate, but not really low, interest rates" that were far above U.S. and British levels. "The lowest average [interest] rates for Japan reached during World War Two were not very low" and never reached the low U.S. levels. See Sidney Homer, *A History of Interest Rates* (New Brunswick: Rutgers University Press, 1963), 469, 476–77, 535; Michael Schaller, *The American Occupation of Japan* (New York: Oxford University Press, 1985), 5 (recounting how Japan's traditional conservatives resented wartime economic controls as threatening the old order).

101. This was the most explosive economic expansion in U.S. history, with real economic growth rates approaching 20 percent a year. See *Economic Report of the President and Annual Report of the Council of Economic Advisers* (Washington, DC: U.S. Government Printing Office, 1984), 220, table B-1 (showing the increase in U.S. gross national product from $100 billion in 1940 to $210 billion in 1944), and 223, table B-2 (showing annual inflation-adjusted growth rates in the same period of 7.6, 16.3, 15.3, 15.1, and 7.1 percent).

102. Tom Brokaw, *The Greatest Generation* (New York: Random House, 1999). These were the years—"the hardest years, the wildest years, the desperate and divided years"—remembered in song by Midnight Oil, the Australian rock band (Midnight Oil, "Forgotten Years," on the album *Blue Sky Mining*, 1987).

103. Whether or not the world was ultimately saved *for* democracy, it was certainly saved *by* democracy or, more precisely, by the mobilization of American social democracy.

104. During the Battle of Britain, Churchill summoned every man and woman to their posts: "We shall . . . draw from the heart of suffering itself the means of inspiration and survival, and of a victory won not only for ourselves but for all . . . Long, dark months of trials and tribulations lie before us . . . We must be united; we must be undaunted; we must be inflexible. Our qualities and deeds must burn and glow through the gloom of Europe until they become

the veritable beacon of its salvation." See James C. Humes, *Winston Churchill* (New York: D. K. Publishers, 2003), 90–91.

105. The words and programs of John Kennedy, Robert Kennedy, and Martin Luther King, Jr., revealed strong mystical overtones, but each was assassinated young. Ronald Reagan's mysticism was mostly personal and rhetorical. His definition of liberty was closer to pre–New Deal freedom-of-contract than to New Deal freedom-from-want conceptions of liberty.

106. Albert Camus also recognized the West's mystical and enlightened legacy when he quoted approvingly that the Allies "were fighting a lie in the name of a half-truth." That half-truth, Camus claimed, was the idea of liberty: "And liberty is the way, and the only way, of perfectibility. Without liberty heavy industry can be perfected, but not justice or truth." See Albert Camus, *Resistance, Rebellion, and Death* (New York: Alfred A. Knopf, 1960), 248.

107. Erich Fromm, *Man For Himself: An Inquiry Into the Psychology of Ethics* (New York: Rinehart, 1947), ix, 5. "Dare to know" was the motto of the Enlightenment that provided the greatest incentive for all of the great efforts and achievements of modern man. According to Fromm, "dare to conform" would be a more apt description of fundamentalist psychology (Fromm, *The Art of Loving*, 12–13).

108. Among the monotheistic religions, Islam has been particularly frozen by this narrowing of doctrine. According to Ziauddin Sardar, as qualifications to become an Islamic religious scholar (an ulema) became stricter, "Muslim thought ossified and became totally obscurantist," the "Muslim community was transformed from an open to a closed society," and "Muslim culture lost its dynamism and degenerated." See Ziauddin Sardar, *Islam, Postmodernism and Other Futures: A Ziauddin Sardar Reader*, ed. Sohail Inayatullah and Gail Boxwell (London: Pluto Press, 2003), 99–100.

109. The belief in man is enlightened because such ethical norms are "formed by man's reason and by it alone" and it is mystical because only through faith in himself can man fully exercise his reason (Fromm, *Man for Himself*, 6–7).

110. Alan W. Watts, *Myth and Ritual in Christianity* (Boston: Beacon Press, 1968), 15.

111. Ibid. According to Leonard Shlain, mysticism is primarily associated with right-brain processes, and typified by such values as empathy, generosity toward strangers, tolerance of dissent, love of nature, nurturing of children, laughter, playfulness, forgiveness of enemies, and nonviolence. Left-brain attributes are more masculine, and fixate on work, power, money, argument, cruelty, violence, disregard for nature, and lack of concern for the lame (Shlain, *The Alphabet Versus the Goddess*, 338).

112. Lings, *The Eleventh Hour*, 1–2. The faculty of intellect, said Lings, includes a residue of "heart knowledge," at the center of man's soul, which places man as mediator between heaven and earth.

113. Carl Jung considered intuition as "a superior analysis or insight or knowledge which consciousness has not been able to produce" (Jung, *Psychology and Religion*, 49). Fromm considered the source and basis of virtue and vice to be "the character structure of the mature and integrated personality, the productive character" (Fromm, *Man for Himself*, 6–7). According to Lings, esoteric knowledge is the height of intellectual awareness, for it informs reason. See Lings, *The Eleventh Hour*, 1–3 ("The reason must become conscious of its need for the guidance of a higher authority"). Perhaps Jefferson's

rationalism was also informed by what Lings calls heart knowledge: Jefferson came to believe "that a creator god had implanted in all normal people a moral sense . . . [and] that the type of self-discipline, and at times the courage, to do right, to follow the dictates of conscience, was the pressing practical moral problem for himself and for others" (Conkin, *The Religious Pilgrimage*, 24).

114. Shlain, *The Alphabet Versus the Goddess*, 240–41.

115. Lings, *The Eleventh Hour*, 2.

116. For the view that John Kennedy will be remembered for his "prophetic conception of a new Society of Mankind," see James Hepburn, *Farewell America: The Plot to Kill J.F.K.* (Roseville: Penmarin Books, 2002), 358.

117. According to Fromm, people no longer define themselves by their thoughts and beliefs, but by what they can purchase or sell of themselves in the market. Identity formation shifted from "I am what I think" to "I am what I have, what I possess," which in a market economy becomes "I am as you desire me" (Fromm, *Man for Himself*, 135–37). This is the pessimistic shift from "dare to know" to "wear to conform."

118. The free-market orthodoxy, known as the Washington Consensus, is fundamentalist in its claim to exclusivity and its literal adherence to dogmatic texts and doctrines, namely the neoclassical paradigm and sado-monetarist economic models. Stiglitz, *Globalization and Its Discontents*; Michael Hardt and Antonio Negri, *Multitude: War and Democracy in the Age of Empire* (New York: Penguin Press, 2004), 155; Ali, *The Clash of Fundamentalisms*.

119. Postmodernism preaches that all value judgments and ethical norms are matters of taste and arbitrary preference and that there are no objectively valid norms (Fromm, *Man for Himself*, 5). Jim Dator considers the alternative to privileging certain views: "should we accept the 'truth' that there is no 'truth' but that learning peacefully yet powerfully to negotiate meanings and beliefs among people with highly diverse views is the challenge—the ethical challenge—of humanity from now on?" See Dator, Review of *Islam*, 115–29, at 124.

120. Karen Greenberg, ed., *Al Qaeda Now: Understanding Today's Terrorists* (New York: Cambridge University Press, 2005).

121. Stiglitz, *Globalization and Its Discontents*. Numerous empirical studies suggest that the market fundamentalist agenda of trade liberalization has resulted in slower global economic output and widening inequalities in income. See Elizabeth Becker, "U.N. Study Finds Global Trade Benefits Are Uneven," *New York Times*, February 24, 2004, C5.

122. Esther Kaplan, *With God on Their Side: George W. Bush and the Christian Right* (New York: W. W. Norton, 2005); Dan Cohn-Sherbok, *The Politics of Apocalypse: The History and Influence of Christian Zionism* (Oxford: One World Books, 2006).

123. Carol Platt Liebau, "Separation of Sex and State," *Los Angeles Times*, December 11, 2005, M3 (criticizing the pollution of the public commons with images of sex and pornography that are offensive to traditional religious sensibilities).

124. A recent volume of one opinion journal was aptly entitled, "Is Anything Obscene Anymore?" See, *Nexus: A Journal of Opinion* 10 (2005).

125. The Supreme Court has been closely divided on whether Congress has the constitutional authority under the First Amendment to apply local community standards in regulating obscene material on the Internet. See *Ashcroft v. American Civil Liberties Union*, 535 U.S. 564 (2002) (upholding the Child Online Protection Act). See also, *Ashcroft v. The Free Speech Coalition*, 535 U.S. 234 (2002) (striking down, on First Amendment grounds, the Child Pornography Act of 1996, which prohibited sexually explicit images that appear to depict minors, but were in fact produced without the use of real children, such as by use of adult actors or computer imaging). The Supreme Court has also struck down provisions of the Telecommunications Act of 1996 that had required cable channels dedicated to sexually oriented programming to scramble, block, or limit the times of their transmissions. See *United States v. Playboy Entertainment Group, Inc.*, 529 U.S. 803 (2000) (holding that audience must assume the burden of avoiding offensive speech by requiring objecting parents to request cable operators to block unwanted channels).

126. Ronald Weitzer, *Sex for Sale: Prostitution, Pornography, and the Sex Industry* (New York: Routledge, 1999). Martin Lings considered modern civilization as "nothing other than an organized system of subversion and degeneration. Instead of trying to resist the natural downward tendencies of man . . . it welcomes and encourages them in the name of progress and evolution" (Lings, *The Eleventh Hour*, 48).

127. One indication of this degeneration in values is the shift in the programming of the TV documentary series *Biography*. A generation ago, the original series featured the lives of world leaders and influential thinkers in the arts and sciences. Today, the lives of actors and actresses seem to be the norm on *Biography*, which is now aired on the Arts & Entertainment cable channel.

128. Peter G. Gosselin, "How Bedrock Promises of Security Have Fractured Across America," *Los Angeles Times*, December 30, 2005, A1 (reporting on the new raw deal of U.S. corporations discarding their workers' pensions).

129. It was Ronald Reagan's hard line against Soviet communism in the name of liberty and justice that lays claim to a mystic heritage. See David Gelernter, "What Ronald Reagan Understood," *Weekly Standard* 9, no. 39 (June 21, 2004). Proponents of liberalized trade with the People's Republic of China (PRC) are often found among professionals and corporate executives who are themselves protected from foreign competition. See Dean Baker, "The Conservative Nanny State," Center for Economic and Policy Research, May 2006, available at www.conservativenannystate.org/cnswebbook.pdf. In addition, these free-traders are likely to play down the PRC's atrocious human rights violations while praising the regime's largely cosmetic steps toward legal and economic reform. For instance, the Center for Strategic and International Studies and the Institute for International Economics, two establishment think tanks, jointly published a positive assessment of China that would have been considered appeasement of communism during the Cold War. See C. Fred Bergsten, Bates Gill, Nicholas R. Lardy, and Derek Mitchell, *China: The Balance Sheet* (New York: Public Affairs, 2006), 8 (justifying liberalized trade with the PRC, ignoring its atrocious human rights record, and praising its token steps at legal and regulatory reform, even while understating the PRC as a single-party system, far from a liberal democracy and not a rule-of-law country).

130. Richard McGregor and Mure Dickie, "China's Reserves Hit \$819 bn," *Financial Times*, January 16, 2006, 1; Niall Ferguson, *Colossus: The Rise and Fall of the American Empire* (New York: Penguin Press, 2004), 281–85.

131. David Barboza, "China Drafts Law to Empower Unions and End Labor Abuse," *New York Times*, October 13, 2006, A1 (reporting opposition by U.S. Chamber of Commerce, Goodyear Tire and Rubber Co, and other big U.S. business interests to a proposed crackdown on sweatshops and any improvement in the protection of workers' rights in China). Also see Mary Williams Walsh, "Many Companies Ending Promises for Retirement," *New York Times*, January 9, 2006, A1.

132. Timothy A. Canova, "Financial Liberalization, International Monetary Disorder, and the Neoliberal State," *American University International Law Review* 15 (2000): 1295–96, n. 67–68 (discussing the several constitutional challenges to the Federal Reserve System based on the private nondelegation doctrine and appointments clause, and the unconvincing dismissals by the U.S. Court of Appeals for the D.C. Circuit on procedural grounds of standing and equitable discretion).

133. Ben Stein, "Master of the Art of Taming Inflation," *New York Times*, January 1, 2006, Business Section, 4. Praising the art of Alan Greenspan seems rather one sided and finally anachronistic as well by absolving Greenspan of any responsibility for constraining fiscal policy, deregulating the financial sector, and enabling the development of a bubble economy.

134. In the past, the threat of imposing wage and price controls may have served as an effective restraining influence on price determinations in oligopolistic industries. Every president from Franklin Roosevelt to Gerald Ford has had emergency wage and price control authority; some imposed controls, others simply threatened to do so. Soon after his election to the presidency in 1976, Jimmy Carter rejected the offer of a Democratic-controlled Congress to reauthorize such emergency wage and price controls. Carter claimed the free market would take care of any inflationary problems. In 1979, when the consumer price index rose to double-digits, Carter lacked the legal authority to impose wage and price controls and, therefore, his rhetorical opposition to the inflationary spiral lacked any real credibility. See Alexander Cockburn, *The Golden Age Is In Us* (London: Verso, 1995), 264.

135. Timothy A. Canova, "Mismanaging Integration in a Monetary Straight-Jacket: A Prescription for Social Disintegration, Insecurity and Political Fragmentation," in *Integration in the Americas* (Albuquerque: University of New Mexico Latin American & Iberian Institute, 2002), 10.

136. "About Us: What is the World Bank," at The World Bank Group (2005), available at http://web.worldbank.org/WBSITE/EXTERNAL/EXTABOUTUS /0,,contentMDK:20040558~menuPK:34559~pagePK:34542~piPK:36600,00. html. See also Elizabeth Becker, "Number of Hungry Rising, U.N. Says," *New York Times*, December 8, 2004, A5 (the United Nations Food and Agriculture Organization estimated that the number of chronically hungry people in the world rose to nearly 852 million, an increase of 18 million since 2000).

137. Stiglitz, *Globalization and Its Discontents*, 185, 222; Canova, "Financial Liberalization," 1279, 1300.

138. Despite evidence that its program has failed to correct major global inequities, the IMF continues to push its orthodox line. See Bob Davis, "IMF Wants Further Economic Liberalization in Latin America," *Wall Street*

Journal, February 9, 2005, A9; Mehran Kamrava, *The Modern Middle East* (Berkeley: University of California Press, 2005), 216. Again, the similarities between fundamentalisms. Neither Islamic fundamentalists nor market fundamentalists listen very effectively to dissenting opinions. They are more likely to enforce conformity or resort to violence.

139. Canova, "Financial Liberalization," 1288–90; Timothy A. Canova, "Global Finance and the International Monetary Fund's Neoliberal Agenda: The Threat to the Employment, Ethnic Identity, and Cultural Pluralism of Latina/o Communities," *University of California-Davis Law Review* 33 (2000): 1547, 1556.

140. Ali, *The Clash of Fundamentalisms*.

141. This cycle is reminiscent of the dehumanization of the enemy that existed between the U.S. and Japan during World War II. Few prisoners were taken on either side, beheadings and summary execution of prisoners were not uncommon, until the cycle ended with two atomic mushroom clouds. See O'Neill, *The Oxford Essential Guide*, 191–98, 299–300.

142. Islamic fundamentalism has been explained as a confrontation with modern social change and urbanization, along with the failure of economic reform in much of the Muslim world. Edward Luce, "Divine Inspiration," *Financial Times*, April 24/25, 2004, W4.

143. For instance, in 2005 Pakistan announced its first sharp rise in development spending in more than a decade; but tellingly, it was also Pakistan's first budget in a decade without many of the constraints routinely imposed by an IMF program. See Farhan Bokhari, "Pakistan's Spending on Development to Rise 35%," *Financial Times*, June 7, 2005, 5.

144. Global Employment Trends, International Labour Office (Jan. 2003), 40, 50, 64, 99 (reporting official unemployment rates of 9.2 percent in Turkey, 7.8 percent in Pakistan, 8.1 percent in Indonesia, 9.2 percent in Egypt, 15 percent in Saudi Arabia, 14.1 percent in the West Bank and Gaza, and 28.7 percent in Algeria), available at www.oit.org/public/english/employment/strat/download/trndeno3.pdf.

145. Bernard-Henri Lévy, *Who Killed Daniel Pearl?* (Hoboken: Melville House, 2003); Loretta Napoleoni, *Terror Incorporated: Tracing the Dollars Behind the Terror Networks* (New York: Seven Stories Press, 2005).

146. Likewise in the occupied territories of the West Bank and Gaza, where the failure of the Palestinian Authority to deliver social services has created a vacuum filled by Hamas, "which provides impoverished people there with welfare, health services, schools and kindergartens." See Steven Erlanger, "Israel Cuts Back Military Actions to Answer Abbas," *New York Times*, January 29, 2005, A1, A5 (reporting Hamas gains in local elections in Gaza).

147. Gustav Niebuhr, "U.S. 'Secular' Groups Set Tone for Terror Attacks, Falwell Says," *New York Times*, September 14, 2001, A18 (quoting Rev. Jerry Falwell that God had permitted the September 11th attacks because America had turned away from God).

148. Jeffrey M. Jones, "Support Remains High Even if Military Action is Prolonged, Involves Casualties," *Gallup Poll News Service*, Oct. 4, 2001 (reporting results of Gallup poll conducted September 21–22, 2001).

149. *9/11 Commission Report* (2004), 339–48. According to Thomas J. Kean, the chairman of the 9/11 Commission, the September 11th attacks represented

"a failure of policy, management, capability and, above all, a failure of imagination." See "Failure on a Number of Fronts," *Los Angeles Times*, July 23, 2004, A13.

150. Benjamin R. Barber, "A Failure of Democracy, Not Capitalism," *New York Times*, July 29, 2002, A19 (warning that private interests weaken American public life).

151. Thomas X. Hammes, "Lost in Translation," *New York Times*, August 25, 2005, A23; Lynnley Browning, "Do You Speak Uzbek? Translators Are in Demand," *New York Times*, October 21, 2001.

152. Mass unemployment and mass incarceration are epidemic and global. See Michael Wines, "Wasting Away, A Million Wait In African Jails," *New York Times*, November 6, 2005, A1 (reporting that many people in overcrowded prisons in African countries were never tried for any crime).

153. The International Labour Organization's 2001 World Employment Report warned that "a passive policy stance that leaves to markets alone" would not solve the global employment crisis and would only reinforce global inequities in access to education and technology. See Christopher S. Wren, "World Needs to Add 500 Million Jobs in 10 Years, Report Says," *New York Times*, January 25, 2001, A13.

154. *John F. Kennedy: A Self-Portrait* (Harper/Caedmon Audio, September 1988), Side 1.

155. Robert J. Shiller, *Irrational Exuberance*, 2nd ed. (Princeton: Princeton University Press, 2005).

156. For instance, see Mure Dickie, "Don't Mention Democracy, Microsoft Tells China Web Users," *Financial Times*, June 11–12, 2005, 4 (reporting that "Microsoft's new Chinese Internet portal has banned the words 'democracy' and 'freedom' from parts of its website in an apparent effort to avoid offending Beijing's political censors").

157. President Kennedy articulated an approach to U.S. trade and currency relations with other free nations that recognized a concern for balancing of objectives: "We can assist the developing nations to throw off the yoke of poverty. We can balance our worldwide trade and payments at the highest possible level of growth" (James Hepburn, *Farewell America*, 120).

158. David E. Rosenbaum, "Senate Deletes Higher Mileage Standard in Energy Bill," *New York Times*, March 14, 2002, A28 (reporting that sport utility vehicles have become more popular and average gas mileage of vehicles sold in the U.S. has fallen accordingly).

159. Dan Mitchell, "Rules to Warm Detroit's Heart," *New York Times*, August 27, 2005, C5 (reporting on loopholes in the National Highway Traffic Safety Administration's proposed fuel efficiency standards to assist gas-guzzlers such as sport utility vehicles).

160. Michael T. Klare, *Resource Wars: The New Landscape of Global Conflict* (New York: Henry Holt, 2002). Some 600,000 Americans lost their lives in the Civil War; 400,000 Americans were killed in World War II far from home and to bring freedom to others. Yet, our generation cannot even raise fuel efficiency standards.

161. Darren K. Carlson, "Public Support for Military Draft Low," *Gallup Poll News Service*, November 18, 2003, available at: www.gallup.com/poll/9727/Public-Support-Military-Draft-Low.aspx.

162. Carl Hulse, "Bill to Restore the Draft is Defeated in the House," *New York Times*, October 6, 2004, A5.

163. Michael Janofsky, "Bush Proposes Broader Language Training," *New York Times*, January 6, 2006, A15.

164. The deficiencies in U.S. foreign language capabilities are jarring. See Eric Lichtblau, "F.B.I. Said to Lag on Translations of Terror Tapes," *New York Times*, September 28, 2004, A1 (reporting that more than 120,000 hours of potentially terrorism-related surveillance recordings had not yet been translated by FBI linguists); Richard B. Schmitt, "Translation Capacity Still Spotty After 9/11," *Los Angeles Times*, May 1, 2005, A24; Douglas Jehl, "C.I.A. Reviews Security Policy for Translators," *New York Times*, June 8, 2005, A1; Eric Lichtblau, "At F.B.I., Translation Lags, as Does the System Upgrade," *New York Times*, July 28, 2005, A20.

165. President George W. Bush has repeatedly invoked the image of the nuclear mushroom cloud. See David E. Sanger, "A Doctrine Under Pressure: Pre-Emption is Redefined," *New York Times*, October 11, 2004, A10 (quoting President Bush as warning that "we cannot wait for the final proof, the smoking gun that could come in the form of a mushroom cloud"). As Lings recognized, "the herald of the end" must assume a grave responsibility for mankind (Lings, *The Eleventh Hour*, 11).

166. Damien Cave, "Vital Military Jobs Go Unfilled, Study Says," *New York Times*, November 18, 2005, A16; James Risen, "C.I.A. Unit on bin Laden Is Understaffed, a Senior Official Tells Lawmakers," *New York Times*, September 15, 2004, A18; Rachel L. Swarns, "Officers Lack Skills to Vet Saudis Seeking U.S. Visas, Report Says," *New York Times*, September 10, 2004, A20.

167. Even Michael Moore's *Fahrenheit 9/11* did not show the collapsing Twin Towers, an image that has been airbrushed from network television in the United States but is more common on videos available in the markets of Islamic fundamentalist states.

168. Christopher Lasch, *The Culture of Narcissism* (New York: Norton Books, 1979).

169. Viktor E. Frankl, *Man's Search for Meaning* (New York: Washington Square Press, 1959), 103–15. Frankl defined his methodology as Logotherapy, derived from the Greek "logos," which denotes "meaning." He argued that mental health requires a certain degree of tension between "what one is and what one should become."

170. Frankl pointed to surveys showing that American students were twice as likely to be in the existential vacuum. Some seek vicarious relief through the pursuit of money or power; others through prescription medication or illegal drug use (Frankl, *Man's Search*, 111–12).

171. Robert Frost's poem, "Fire and Ice," reflected on the destructive forces of hatred and desire: "Some say the world will end in fire, some say in ice. From what I've tasted of desire, I hold with those who favor fire. But if it had to end twice, I think I've seen enough of hate, to say that for destruction, ice is also good, and would suffice." As prophesy, perhaps the fire that Frost referred to could be the loose nuke or global warming or a pandemic's funeral pyres. Who would have guessed that ice could be the addiction of crystal meth blowing holes in the brains of a generation left behind.

172. Turgeon, *Bastard Keynesianism*, 57 (citing studies by Harvard economist, James Medoff, showing the decline in the quality of jobs).

173. Official U.S. unemployment rates do not count those who want and are available to work, had looked for a job sometime during the past year, but "did not actively search for work in the four weeks preceding the [Labor Department's] survey," often because of "family responsibilities" (the so-called discouraged workers). Nor do the official statistics count those who are seriously underemployed, such as those working part-time (i.e., working for free or as little as an hour a week) who would like full-time work. When the nearly 10 million discouraged and underemployed workers are added, the jobless rate more than doubles. See "Hidden Unemployment," National Jobs for All Coalition, available at www.njfac.org/jobnews.html. Finally, the official unemployment rate does not count the nearly two million U.S. citizens who are confined in the nation's jails and prisons. See "The Employment Situation: December 2005," News, The Bureau of Labor Statistics, U.S. Department of Labor, available at www.bls.gov/news.release/pdf/empsit. pdf. In January 1994, the Bureau of Labor Statistics discontinued its calculation of U-7 that measured discouraged and part-time workers, which was about 1.5 times larger than the official unemployment rate (Turgeon, *Bastard Keynesianism*, 57).

174. For instance, see Paul Krugman, "The Joyless Economy," *New York Times*, December 5, 2005, A23 (reporting on public opinion surveys showing widespread economic insecurity in the United States and declining real household income for fifth consecutive year).

175. Frankl, *Man's Search*, 115 (concluding that "self-actualization is possible only as a side effect of self-transcendence").

176. Abraham H. Maslow, *Toward a Psychology of Being* (Princeton: Van Nostrand, 1968), 25 (defining self-actualization, the pinnacle of the hierarchy of needs, "as ongoing actualization of potentials, capacities and talents . . . as an unceasing trend toward unity, integration or synergy within the person").

177. Canova, "Financial Liberalization," 1289 (equating "neoliberal cant" with "neoliberal can't"). "Our contemporary education, then, indoctrinates us in the glorification of doubt, has created in fact what could almost be called a religion or theology of doubt, in which to be seen to be intelligent we have to be seen to doubt everything, to always point out what's wrong and rarely to ask what's right or good, cynically to denigrate all inherited spiritual ideals and philosophies, or anything that is done in simple goodwill or with an innocent heart" (Rinpoche, *The Tibetan Book*, 127–28).

178. Albert R. Hunt, "What Might Have Been," *Wall Street Journal*, December 4, 2003, A17. Fred Kaplan, "The Army, Faced With Its Limits," *New York Times*, January 1, 2006, Week in Review, 4.

179. Communication between American soldiers and Iraqi civilians has often consisted of little more than confusing hand signals. As a result, accidental "friendly fire" roadside shootings added to Iraqi hostility early in the U.S. occupation. See Thomas L. Friedman, "Worried Optimism on Iraq," *New York Times*, September 21, 2003, W11 (arguing that "non-Arabic-speaking Americans cannot fight an urban war in Iraq").

180. Naomi Klein, *The Shock Doctrine: The Rise of Disaster Capitalism* (New York: Picador, 2007).

181. "Who wins this theological battle for the Sufi lodges will largely determine the U.S.'s future in Iraq" (Nicolas Pelham, "Siege of Falluja Ignites Wrath of Iraq's Mystical Sufi Masters," *Financial Times*, April 21, 2004, 6). There are an estimated 2–3 million Sufi adherents in Iraq. See Ashraf Khalil, "Iraq's Sufi Community Shaken by Deadly Attack," *Los Angeles Times*, June 5, 2005, A8 (reporting deadly terrorist attack on Sufi lodge in Mazaari that killed ten worshipers and injured twelve).

182. Likewise, a United Nations Development Program survey of more than 18,000 Latin Americans in eighteen nations found that a majority said they would support the replacement of democratic government with an "authoritarian" government if it would produce economic development. Democracy itself was blamed for failing to deliver social equality or justice. See Warren Hoge, "Latin America Losing Hope In Democracy, Report Says," *New York Times*, April 22, 2004, A3.

183. C. J. Chivers, "A Whirling Sufi Revival With Unclear Implications," *New York Times*, May 24, 2006, A4 (reporting the resistance to Wahhabi influence and democratic yearnings of Sufi brotherhoods in post-Soviet Chechnya, Russia).

184. Malise Ruthven, *Fundamentalism: The Search for Meaning* (New York: Oxford University Press, 2004); Michael Slackman, "Under Duress, Egypt's Islamist Party Still Surges at Polls," *New York Times*, November 28, 2005.

185. Michael R. Hickok, "U.S. Should Bolster Ties to Turkey," *Newsday*, July 29, 2002, A21; Vincent Boland, "Azerbaijan Looks to Turkey as Model for Cult of Dead Leader," *Financial Times*, June 4/5, 2005, 3.

186. Joseph Kahn, "U.S. Backs Aid to Turkey Tied to Economic Overhaul," *New York Times*, April 27, 2001, A8 (reporting that in exchange for $10 billion in emergency U.S. aid, Turkey agreed to a list of fifteen major changes, including central bank autonomy, currency convertibility, fiscal austerity, and privatization, "typical of [IMF] programs during the Clinton administration").

187. Vincent Boland, "Turkey Moves to Formal Inflation Targeting in Final Phase of Reforms," *Financial Times*, December 6, 2005, 2; Brian Lavery, "Turkey: Economic Measure Passes," *New York Times*, April 26, 2001, W1 (reporting passage of law granting autonomy to the Central Bank in context of Turkey seeking international support for recovery program).

188. Patrick Kinross, *Atatürk: The Rebirth of a Nation* (London: Widenfeld and Nicolson, 1964).

189. The Justice and Development Party, a conservative party that draws on elements of Islam, was elected to power during Turkey's financial crisis in 2002. Under Prime Minister Recep Tayyip Erdogan, the government at times resisted U.S. demands for IMF surveillance, while also accepting major conditions of the IMF program. See "The End of the Dance," *The Economist*, March 1, 2003, 25.

190. Just weeks after Hurricane Katrina, thousands of Houston residents attempting to flee another category five hurricane, Hurricane Rita, sat in their cars for hours, stuck in gas-guzzling cages in a massive traffic jam to nowhere. See Ralph Blumenthal, "Miles of Traffic As Texans Heed Order to Leave," *New York Times*, September 23, 2005, A1. Also Pink Floyd, "Wish You Were Here," on the album *Wish You Were Here* (1975) ("And did you exchange a walk-on part in the war for a lead role in a cage?").

191. Stephen Flynn, *America the Vulnerable* (New York: Harper Collins, 2004); Edward Alden, "Commission Hits at 'Shocking' Post-9/11 Failures," *Financial Times*, December 6, 2005 (reporting the September 11th Commission's follow-up report giving the U.S. failing grades on homeland security and intelligence reform).

192. Timothy A. Canova, "Legacy of the Clinton Bubble," *Dissent* (summer 2008): 41–50.

193. David E. Sanger, "Bush Asks Lands in Mideast to Try Democratic Ways," *New York Times*, November 7, 2003, A1.

194. The Marshall Plan pumped $13 billion into war-torn countries, mostly in Western Europe, between 1947 and 1951. Marshall Plan spending made up about 13 percent of the U.S. budget in 1948. That would be comparable to more than $325 billion in the present U.S. budget, whereas total U.S. foreign assistance spending is actually less than a tenth of that figure. Curt Tarnoff, "The Marshall Plan: Design, Accomplishments, and Relevance to the Present," in *The Marshall Plan: From Those Who Made It Succeed*, ed. Constantine Menges (Lanham: Program on Transitions to Democracy/ University Press of America, 1999), 349, 379. Instead, the annual U.S. foreign aid budget is about $20 billion, or 0.17 percent of U.S. GDP, far below the target of 0.7 percent set by the United Nations. See Aid at a Glance Chart for the United States, Organisation of Economic Cooperation and Development, available at www.oecd.org/dataoecd/42/30/41732048.jpg; Sanjay Suri, "More Aid Still Short of Goal," *Inter Press Service*, April 11, 2005, posted at Global Policy Forum, available at www.globalpolicy.org/socecon/develop/oda/2005/0411moreaid.htm.

195. President George W. Bush, State of the Union Address, January 28, 2003, available at http://frwebgate.access.gpo.gov/cgi-bin/getdoc.cgi?dbname=2003_presidential_documents&docid=pd03fe03_txt-6.

196. Eric Lichtblau, "Bush Defends Spy Program and Denies Misleading Public," *New York Times*, January 2, 2006, A11.

197. Janeway, *The Struggle*, 16. As Lincoln said, "The people will save the government if the government itself will allow them." See Abraham Lincoln, Americans Who Tell the Truth: A Collection of Portraits and Quotes, available at www.americanswhotellthetruth.org/pgs/portraits/Abraham_Linclon.html.

198. For Lincoln and Roosevelt, the art of political leadership meant inspiring the American people to imagine and believe in a wider range of possibilities for the future—"a place that has to be believed to be seen" (U2, "Walk On," from *All That You Can't Leave Behind* [2000]). Likewise, Barack Obama has sought to raise our sights to an American promise "that binds us together in spite of our differences, that makes us fix our eye not on what is seen, but what is unseen, that better place around the bend." Barack Obama, Acceptance Speech, Democratic National Convention, August 28, 2008, available at www.nytimes.com/2008/08/28/us/politics/28text-obama.html?pagewanted=6.

The Contributors

GREGORY CAJETE is a Native American educator whose work is dedicated to honoring the foundations of indigenous knowledge in education. Dr. Cajete is a Tewa Indian from Santa Clara Pueblo, New Mexico. He has served as a New Mexico humanities scholar in ethnobotany of northern New Mexico and as a member of the New Mexico Arts Commission. In addition, he has lectured at colleges and universities in the United States, Canada, Mexico, New Zealand, Italy, Japan, and Russia. Currently, he is director of Native American Studies and an associate professor in the Language, Literacy, and Sociocultural Studies department of the College of Education at the University of New Mexico. Dr. Cajete has received several fellowships and academic distinctions, including an American Indian Graduate Center fellowship from the U.S.-DOE Office of Indian Education; the D'arcy McNickle fellowship in American Indian History from the Newberry Library; and the Katrin Lamon fellowship in American Indian Art and Education from the School of Advanced Research. Dr. Cajete is a practicing ceramic, pastel and metal artist and is the author of five books, including *Ignite the Sparkle: An Indigenous Science Education Curriculum Model*, *Native Science: Natural Laws of Interdependence*, and *Spirit of the Game: Indigenous Wellsprings*.

TIMOTHY A. CANOVA is the Betty Hutton Williams Professor of International Economic Law and associate dean for academic affairs at the Chapman University School of Law in Orange, California. Previously he was a professor of law at the University of New Mexico School of Law. He practiced law in New York City and served as a legislative assistant to the late U.S. Senator Paul Tsongas in Washington, DC. His research has been prophetic, anticipating the deflation of the housing bubble, the collapse of banking institutions, and the crisis in the U.S. economy and global financial markets. He has presented his work at leading universities and forums throughout the Americas, Europe, and the Middle East.

MARTINUS CAWLEY, born in Western Australia, became fascinated with Guadalupe upon entering her monastery in New Mexico at age seventeen, fifty-eight years ago. He has studied her literature ever since. Trained in biblical and patristic literature in Rome and Jerusalem, he is currently writing biographies of the evangelists of Guadalupe for the University of New Mexico Press. Guadalupe Abbey is now located near Lafayette, Oregon.

FRANCISCO J. CRESPO is a doctoral candidate in the department of ethnomusicology at the University of California, Los Angeles. A native of Mexico City, his interest in music was sparked by his grandfather (a corrido performer during the 1910–1920 Mexican Revolution) and his family's summer vacations, which exposed him to music from nearly every corner of Mexico. His general research focus is music of Mexico and Cuba; cultural exchange between Cuba and Mexico, with special focus on music; and music and mass media of Latinos/as in the United States. He has taught college courses and lectured on Latin American music. His publications include contributions to *Musical Cultures of Latin America: Global Effects, Past and Present* and *Women and Music in America Since 1900: An Encyclopedia*. Presently he is writing a dissertation on Spanish-language radio music programming in Los Angeles.

AKIN EUBA studied at UCLA (B.A., M.A.) and at the University of Ghana, Legon (Ph.D.). He is the author of four books, including *Yoruba Drumming: The Dundun Tradition*. He is active both as a composer and musicologist and is currently the Andrew Mellon professor of music at the University of Pittsburgh.

JUAN GÓMEZ-QUIÑÓNES is a professor of history at the University of California, Los Angeles, where he has taught for over thirty years. He is one of the seminal scholars in the field of Chicano Studies and has written numerous books and essays on issues related to Chicano and Mexican history and culture, including *Chicano Politics: Reality and Promise, 1940–1990* and *Sembradores, Ricardo Flores Magón y el Partido Liberal Mexicano: A Eulogy and Critique*. He was a founding member of the Latino Museum of History, Art and Culture in Los Angeles and served as director for the UCLA Chicano Studies Research Center in its formative period during the 1970s and 1980s.

LINDA B. HALL is distinguished professor of history at the University of New Mexico. Her most recent book is *Mary, Mother and Warrior: The Virgin in Spain and the Americas*, and she is currently completing a biography of Dolores del Río, film star in Hollywood and Mexico.

CLARENCE BERNARD HENRY is an independent scholar. He completed a doctorate in ethnomusicology at UCLA in 2000. His primary areas of research include Afro-Brazilian, Africa American, and African musical and religious traditions. Henry has taught at the Indiana State University and University of Kansas. He has recently published a book titled *Let's Make Some Noise: Axé and the African Roots of Brazilian Popular Music*.

RAY HERNÁNDEZ-DURÁN is assistant professor of early modern Ibero-American colonial arts and architecture in the department of art and art history at the University of New Mexico. He received his Ph.D. in art history at the University of Chicago in 2005. Dr. Hernández-Durán has been the recipient of various awards, including two Fulbright-Hays fellowships, a MacArthur fellowship, and a National Endowment for the Humanities grant. His primary research interests include late colonial visual culture, early modernity, performance, and urbanism. He has delivered conference papers and published articles on eighteenth-century painting, the nineteenth-century art academy in Mexico City, and contemporary Latino art, and is currently developing two book manuscripts, one on the Academy of San Carlos and colonial art history, and the second on late-eighteenth-century painting in Mexico City.

STEVEN LOZA is professor of ethnomusicology at the University of California, Los Angeles, and adjunct professor of music at the University of New Mexico, where he served as director of the Arts of the Americas Institute from 2002–2005. Among his numerous publications are *Barrio Rhythm: Mexican American Music in Los Angeles* and *Tito Puente and the Making of Latin Music*, as well as editing the anthologies *Musical Cultures in Latin America: Global Effects, Past and Present* and *Hacia una musicología global: Clásicos y nuevos pensamientos sobre la etnomusicología*.

He presently serves as president of the Board of Trustees for the Latino Museum of History, Art and Culture in Los Angeles and, for ten years, directed the UCLA Mexican Arts Series and was co-director of the Festival of World Music in Mexico City. He has recorded two jazz CDs and composed the multimedia tone poem *America Tropical*, based on the mural by David Alfaro Siqueiros and premiered by the Mexico City Philharmonic Orchestra in 2008 at Disney Hall in Los Angeles.

TERESA MARRERO, a scholar, salsa and tango dancer, and creative writer, is associate professor of Spanish at the University of North Texas. She was born in Havana and raised in Southern California. Marrero is the author of the collection of short stories *Entre la Argentina y Cuba: Cuentos nómadas de viajes y tangos* and the co-editor of the anthology of plays *Out of the Fringe: Contemporary Latina/Latino Theatre and Performance*. Marrero has also published articles on the visual and performative aspects of contemporary social movements such as the Zapatistas in the Mexican state of Chiapas, contemporary Mexican indigenous women in armed struggle, and, more recently, on prostitution and tourism in Cuba.

ORLANDO RICARDO MENES is the recipient of an NEA Literature Fellowship in Poetry for 2009 and an associate professor in the creative writing program at the University of Notre Dame. His recent books include *Furia* and the edited anthology *Renaming Ecstasy: Latino Writings on the Sacred*, and new poems have appeared in *Shenandoah*, *Indiana Review*, and *Third Coast*.

FRANCISCO GODÍNEZ MIRANDA is a professor at the Colegio de Michoacán in Zamora, Mexico, and is currently conducting research on the foundational devotional beliefs of Guadalupe and Los Remedios, the history of Michoacán and the establishment of its cities and provinces, and the life and work of Vasco de Quiroga. He has also initiated a new line of research related to the work of the secular or diocesan priest in the development of the Mexican community since the sixteenth century to the present.

MARGARET MONTOYA is a professor of law at the University of New Mexico School of Law. During spring 2009 she held the Haywood Burns chair in Civil Rights at CUNY Law School. She also has an appointment in the Department of Community and Family Medicine in the University of New

Mexico School of Medicine. She writes in the areas of critical race theory and Latina/o critical legal theory. Her interests focus on access to higher education, law and culture, critical race pedagogy, and cross-cultural legal narratives.

CHARLES E. MOORE earned his doctorate in ethnomusicology at the University of California, Los Angeles. He has served as visiting professor at Loyola University; University of California, San Diego; University of California, Los Angeles; and California State University, Long Beach. He currently works as a scholar, producer, performing artist, and composer. He resides and works in both Los Angeles and Paris.

LORENA DÍAZ NÚÑEZ completed her graduate work in history at the Universidad Nacional Autónoma de México (UNAM) and is a musicologist based at the Centro Nacional de Investigación, Documentación e Información Musical "Carlos Chávez" (CENIDIM), an organ of the Centro Nacional de Artes and Instituto Nacional de Bellas Artes (INBA) in Mexico City and for which she previously served as director. She has conducted extensive research on sacred music in Mexico during the first half of the twentieth century as well as music of the Renaissance and of the Viceroyality period in Mexico. Her work on composer Miguel Bernal Jiménez includes the biography *Miguel Bernal Jiménez: Catálogo y otras fuentes documentales*. A musician, she was a founding member of the chamber groups Cuarteto Tempore and Grupo Euterpe.

LUIS ANTONIO PAYAN is an associate professor of political science at the University of Texas at El Paso and professor-researcher at the Universidad Autónoma de Ciudad Juárez. He obtained his B.A. in Philosophy and Classical Languages and his M.B.A., Graduate School of Management, from the University of Dallas, and his Ph.D. in International Relations from Georgetown University. He is the author of various articles and several books, including *Cops, Soldiers, and Diplomats: Explaining Agency Behavior in the War on Drugs* and *The Three U.S.-Mexico Border Wars: Drugs, Immigration, and Homeland Security*.

STAFFORD POOLE is a Roman Catholic priest and belongs to the congregation of the Mission of Saint Vincent de Paul (Vincentian Community). Now retired, he is a full-time research historian, specializing in sixteenth-century

Mexico and Náhuatl studies. He is the author of *Our Lady of Guadalupe: The Origins and Sources of a Mexican National Symbol, Juan de Ovando: Governing the Spanish Empire in the Reign of Philip II, The Guadalupan Controversies in Mexico,* and co-editor with Susan Schroeder of *Religion in New Spain.*

ALI JIHAD RACY is a professor of ethnomusicology at the University of California, Los Angeles. A specialist in Middle Eastern music, he teaches a variety of music-related courses, often covering such topics as trance, ecstatic experiences, and mysticism. He is well known as a performer and composer and is also recognized for his numerous publications, including his award-winning book *Making Music in the Arab World: The Culture and Artistry of Tarab.*

JOE SANDO is an elder leader of the Jemez Pueblo in New Mexico. He has been an important link in preserving the history and tradition of the Jemez culture and has contributed an enormous amount of knowledge and wisdom to Native Americans and to the world.

JANICE SCHUETZ is a professor of communications at the University of New Mexico. She has written nine books and numerous articles in political and legal communication. She is the former editor of the *Journal of Communication and Religion.*

SYLVIA TAN received her master's degree in ethnomusicology from the University of California, Los Angeles. She is currently working as a public health professional at a not-for-profit organization in Washington, DC.

MARIA WILLIAMS is associate professor of music and Native American studies at the University of New Mexico and has served as associate director of the Arts of the Americas Institute there. Williams's research incorporates an interdisciplinary approach to understanding and learning about music cultures. She is Tlingit, of the Decitaan clan, and enrolled in the Carcross/Tagish First Nations and Tlingit/Haida, a federally recognized tribe. Her main area of research is Alaska Native indigenous cultural practices. She recently produced a documentary, *Nilgaq: 5th Annual Kinigikmiut Dance Festival June 25–27, 2004,* working in partnership with the Native village of Wales and Alaska's National Park Service. She has completed a major project with the King Island, Alaska, Inupiat community documenting their entire music/dance repertoire via audio/video recordings to establish a tribally controlled archive. Williams's publications include "Alaska Native Music and Dance: The Spirit of Tradition," in *Native American Dance: Ceremonies and Social Traditions* and "Heritage Preservation in the 21st Century: Two Alaska Native Music and Dance Projects," in *Alaska Park Science.*